Indian
Block Printing

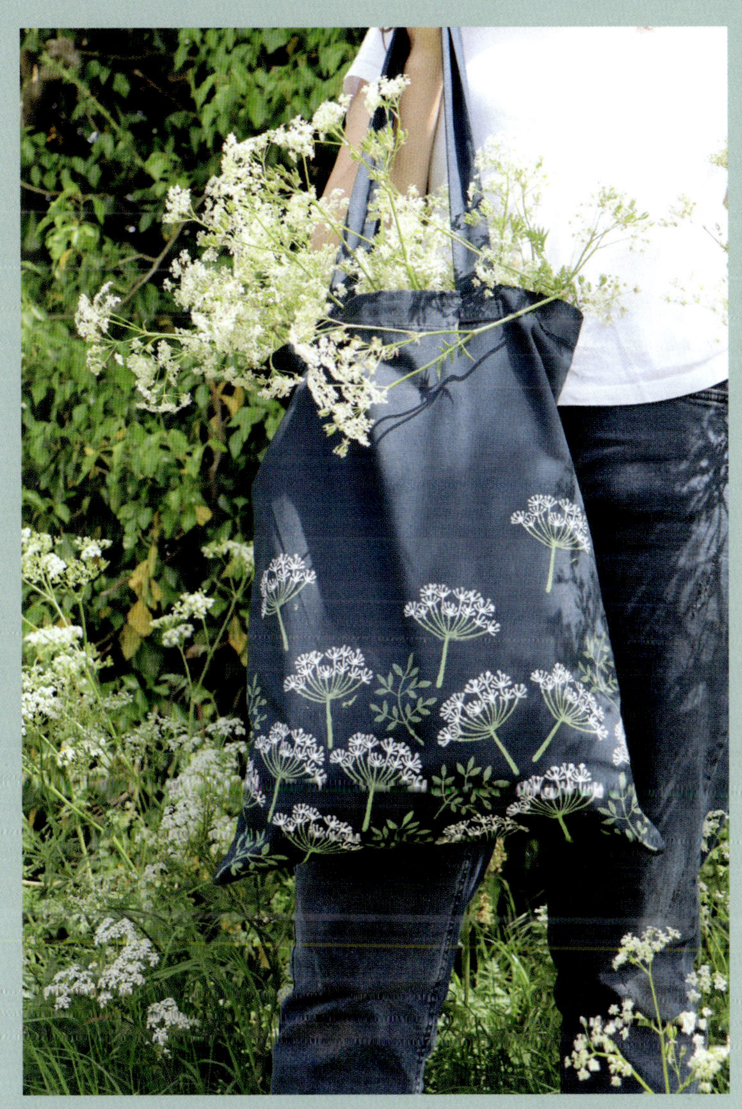

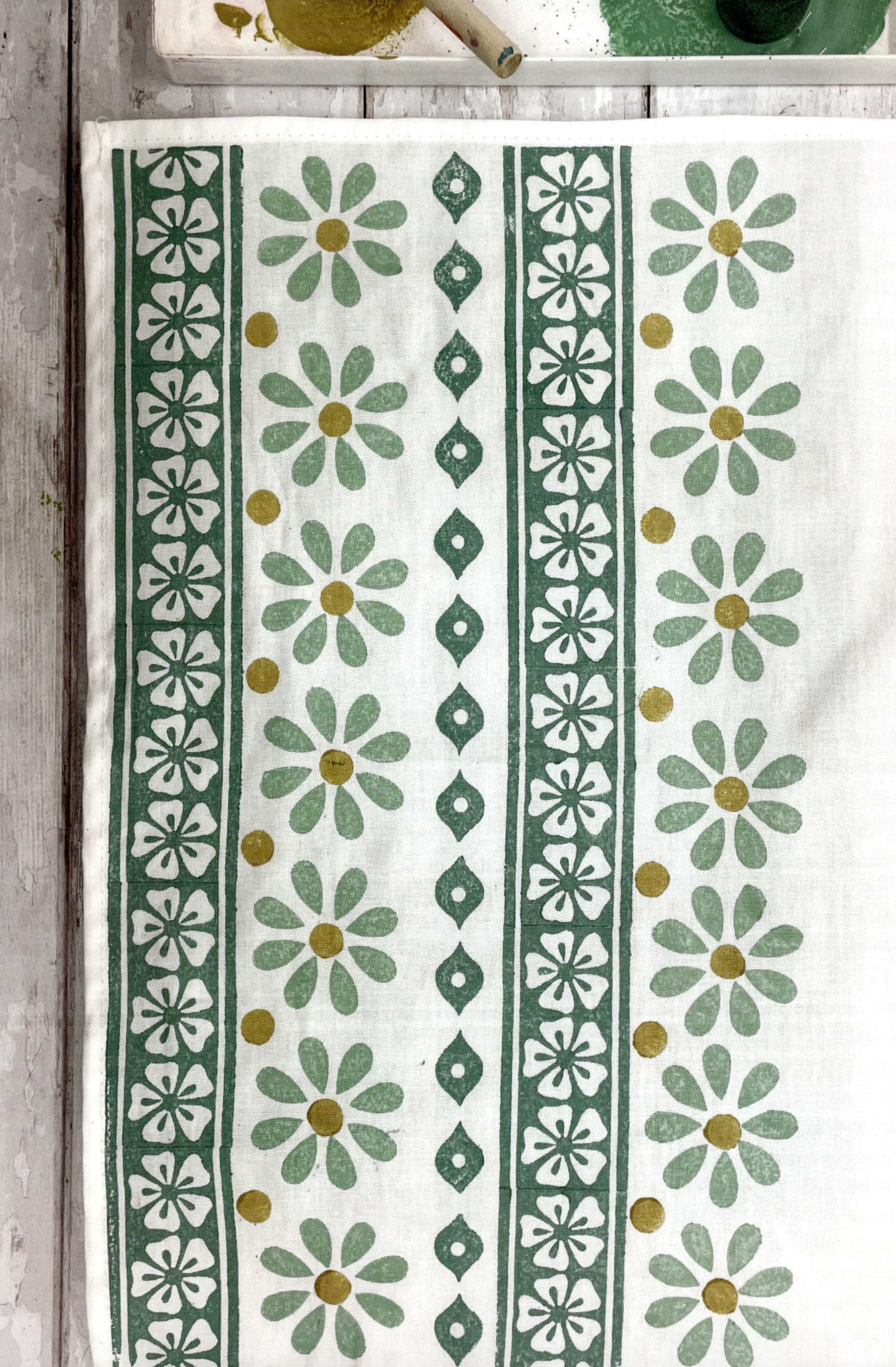

Tess Grace & Holly Jones

Indian Block Printing

An Inspirational Project Book

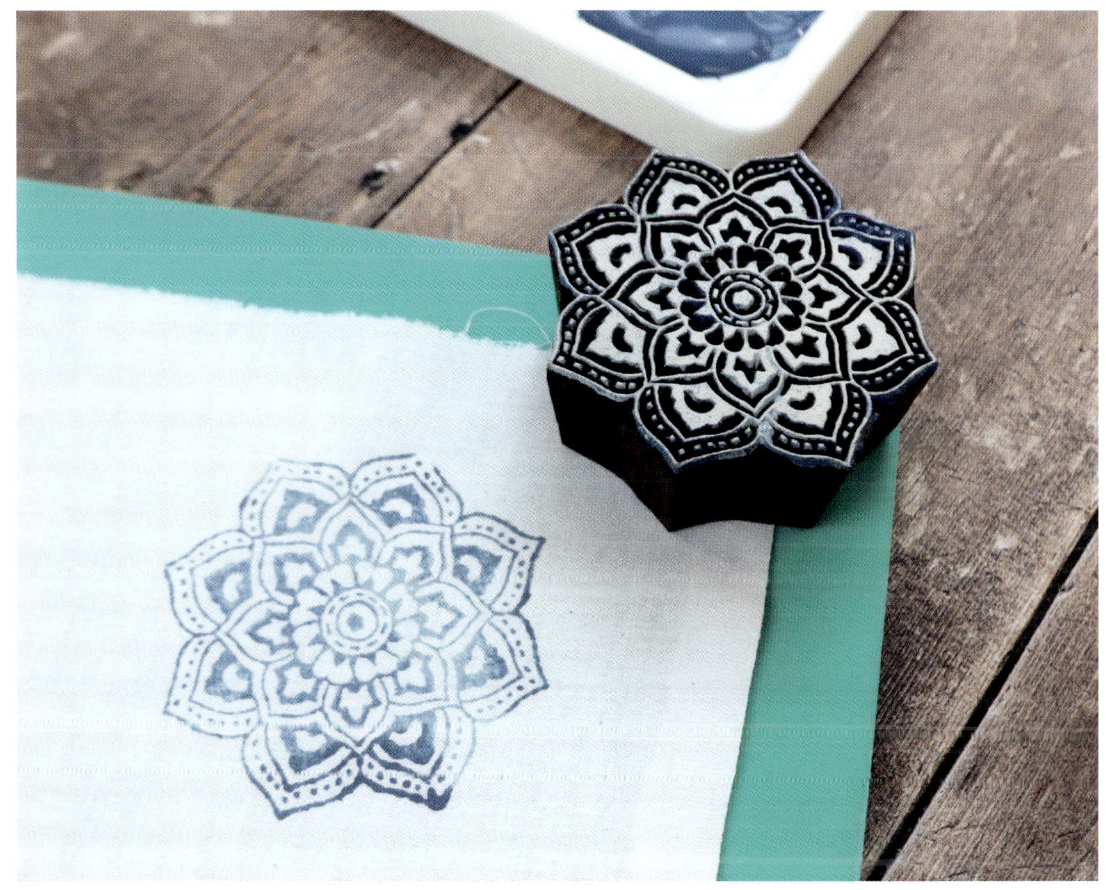

HERBERT PRESS

LONDON · OXFORD · NEW YORK · NEW DELHI · SYDNEY

HERBERT PRESS
Bloomsbury Publishing Plc
50 Bedford Square, London, WC1B 3DP, UK
Bloomsbury Publishing Ireland Limited,
29 Earlsfort Terrace, Dublin 2, D02 AY28, Ireland

BLOOMSBURY, HERBERT PRESS and the Herbert Press logo
are trademarks of Bloomsbury Publishing Plc

First published in Great Britain 2025

A catalogue record for this book is available from the British Library

Library of Congress Cataloguing-in-Publication data has been
applied for

ISBN: 978-1-7899-4341-2; eBook: 978-1-7899-4340-5

2 4 6 8 10 9 7 5 3 1

Page layout design by Jerry Goldie Graphic Design
Printed and bound in China by RR Donnelley Asia Printing Solutions
Limited

To find out more about our authors and books visit
www.bloomsbury.com and sign up for our newsletters
For product safety related questions contact
productsafety@bloomsbury.com

For Maggie

*Your creativity radiates, even though you claim you have none.
Thank you for sharing your knowledge, imagination and kindness
with us, we will be forever grateful to have you as a teacher.*

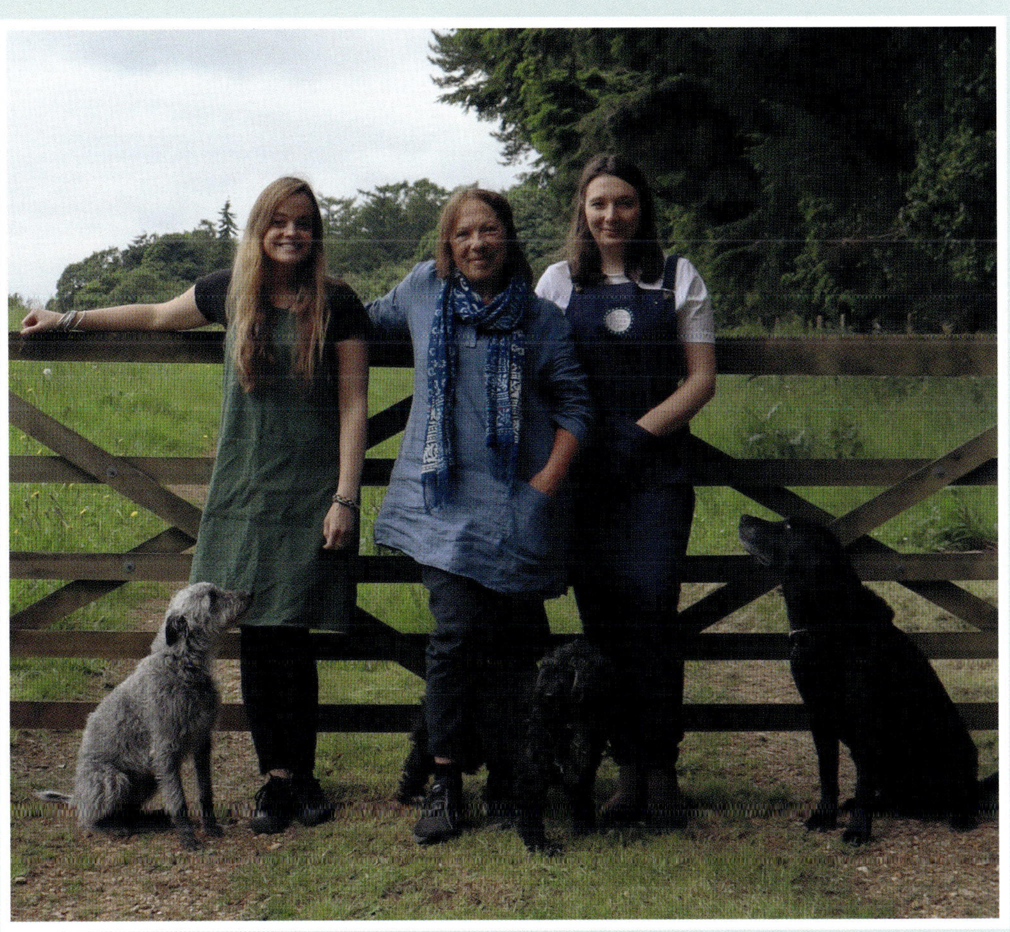

Holly and Tess with Maggie, founder of the Indian Block Print Co.

CONTENTS

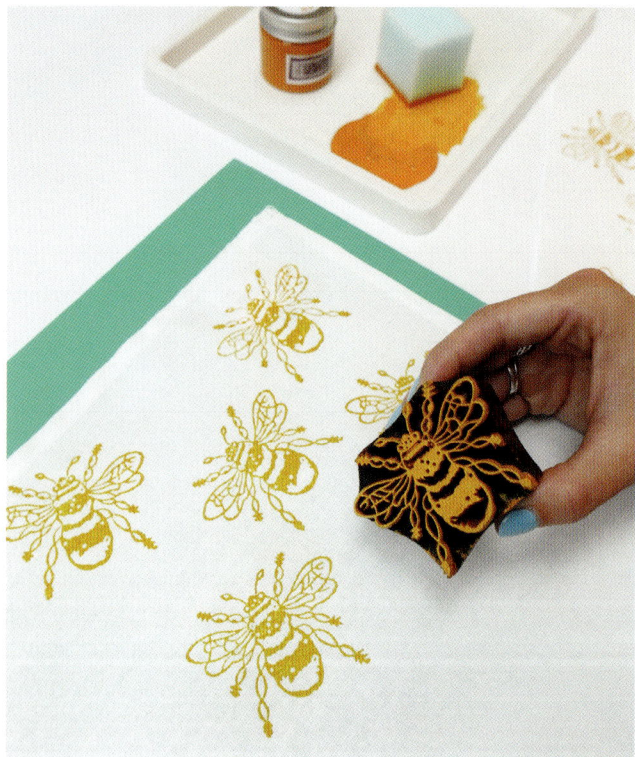

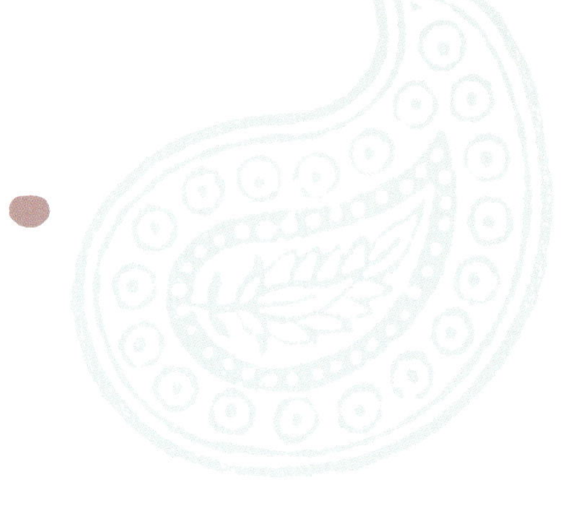

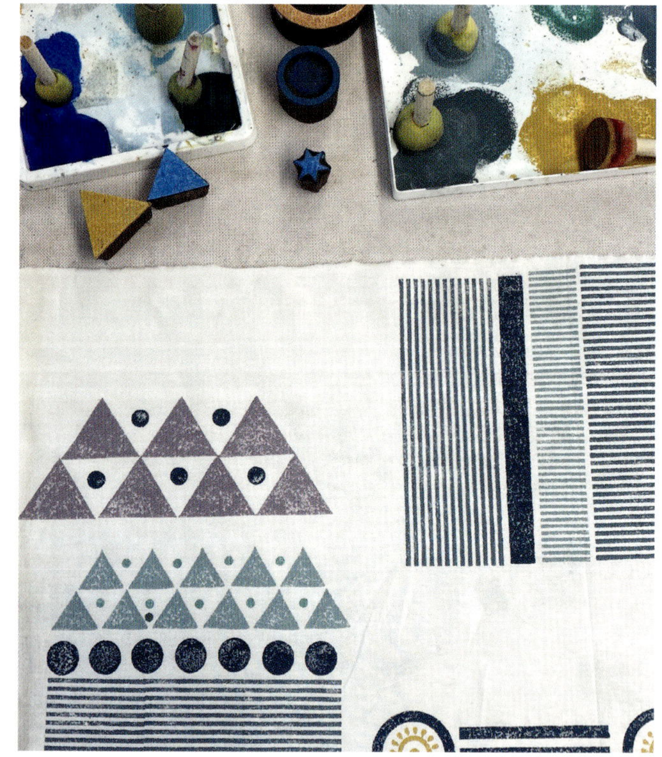

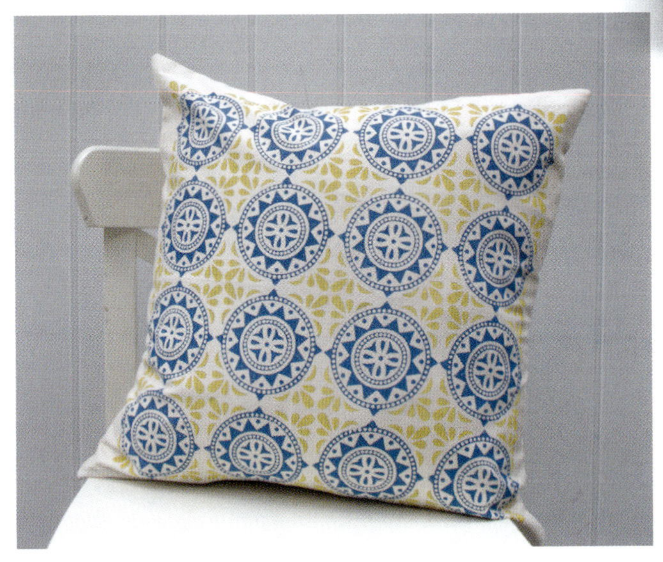

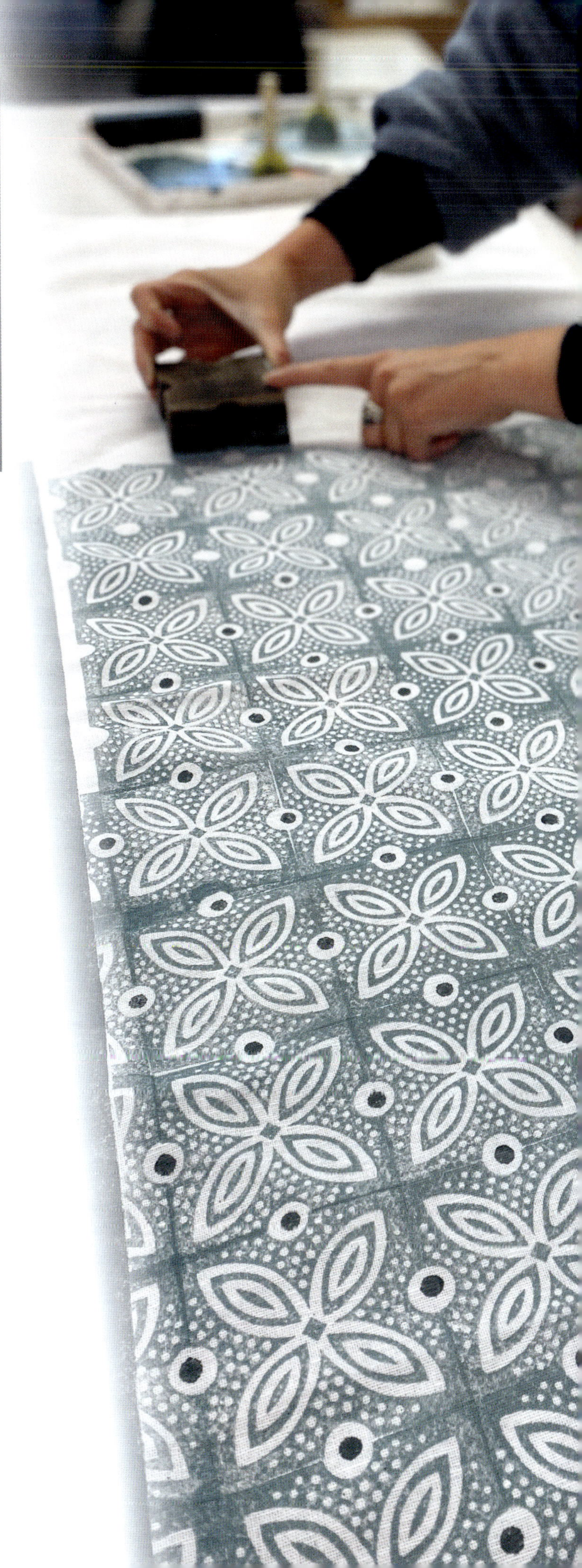

Introduction

Many of us struggle to find the time to be creative in our everyday routines. Often, when speaking to guests in our workshops or customers we meet at craft fairs, we hear, 'Oh, I haven't printed since I was at school,' or 'I wish I had time to be more creative.' Creativity is a passion that the demands of day-to-day life make many of us feel we don't have time to pursue.

This book is here to show how anyone can reconnect with their creative side and find lasting joy and confidence through the ingenuity and craftsmanship of Indian block printing. Whether you have 20 minutes or 10 hours to spare, you'll learn to create instantly beautiful designs and to cultivate calm, confidence and joy in the process.

It's important for anyone reading this book to know that you don't have to be artistic to enjoy the art of block printing; creativity is within all of us, though it may be found in different forms. Some will like creating their own designs, totally freestyle; others will enjoy the process of following a project from start to finish and will need that initial inspiration to start off their creative journey.

You also don't need a craft room to enjoy block printing; you only need a kitchen table and the desire to create. Embrace the learning process, including any mistakes, which we call 'happy accidents'. Our mantra is: 'It's not meant to be perfect, it's handmade.' And that's where its charm comes from – if you wanted perfection, you would have bought the item instead.

From simple motifs to intricate designs, this book is a comprehensive guide for both beginners and experienced crafters looking to expand their skills. We will guide you step by step through a range of stunning projects that will bring this ancient craft from the printing studios of Jaipur to your kitchen table. Each project will teach a new technique, sharing tried-and-tested tips from years of practice. Not only will you learn how to print beautiful creations but, we hope, you'll also feel the mindful benefits that block printing can provide.

We want to give you the chance to experience the joys of Indian block printing and see how it has adapted to suit the modern crafter. Looking deeper, inspirational sections peppered throughout this book will guide you through the streets of Jaipur

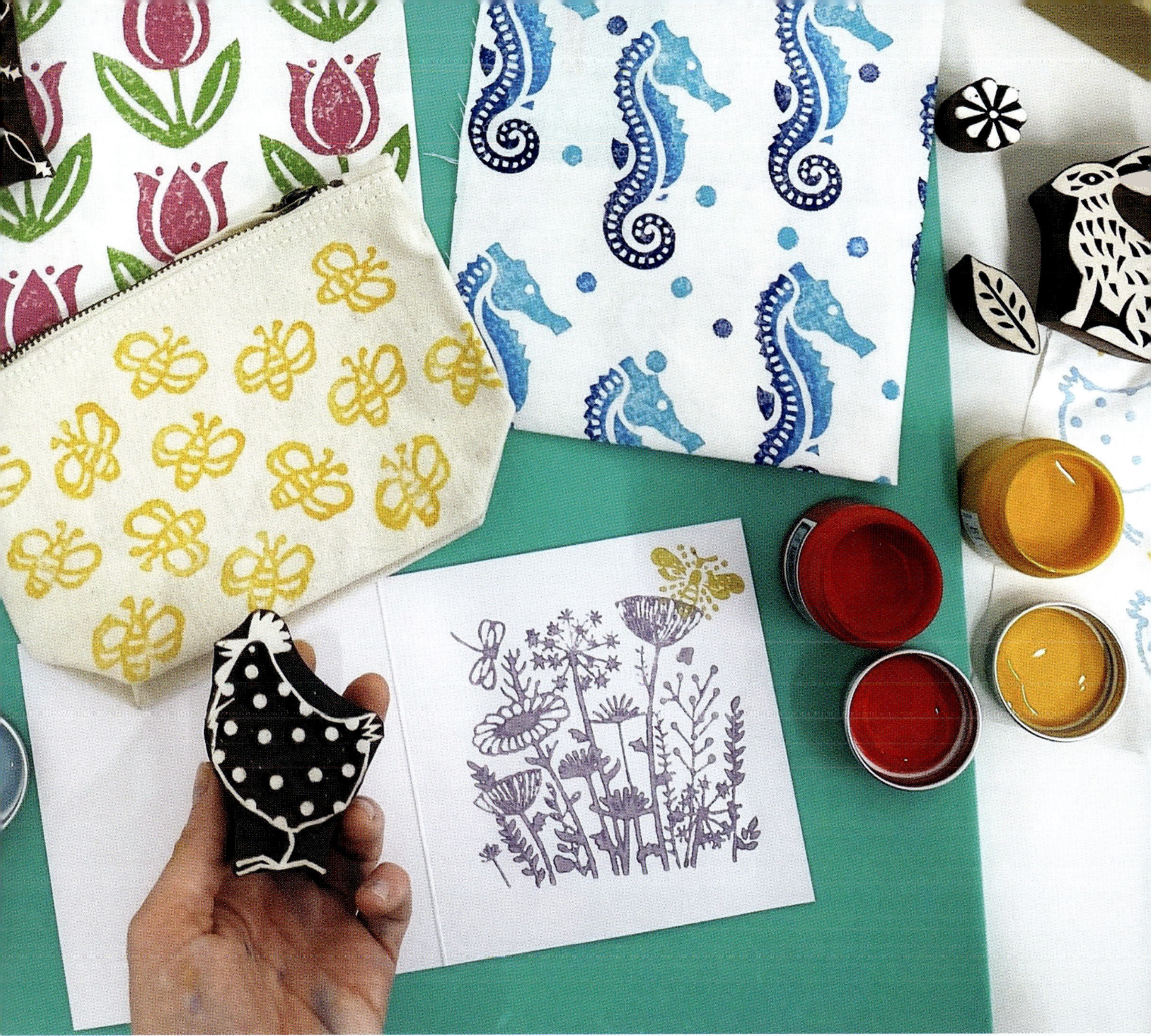

to teach you more about this ancient craft and where it originated, and to meet some of the many skilled artisans that are involved in block carving and the printing process.

Learn how we have adapted traditional methods of printing and brought back knowledge of techniques from India to teach in our Cotswold studio. At the centre of it all is our passion for teaching, sharing and fostering creativity, knowing that people benefit from it. We demonstrate how block printing is more than just art – it's a conscious and creative way of living.

Our Journey Into Block Printing

Tess Grace

From a young age, I grew up surrounded by creativity. My mum, Maggie, has owned a pottery café since 2001, and I spent a lot of time there growing up and helping out on the weekends. The shop is still running now in Witney and is one of the longest standing shops on the high street. It was there I found a passion for helping others develop and explore their own creative abilities.

The business grew and developed into other creative areas, and in 2010 a sister company was founded, the Indian Block Print Co. (formerly known as the Arty Crafty Place), which saw the introduction of wooden printing blocks from India. After finishing school and travelling, I joined the business full-time in 2011 after realising university wasn't a path I wanted to go down. We quickly became a strong working team, and over the years the business developed into a team of nine individuals. I'm very lucky to have a job that is also a passion; it feels like a hobby that I get to do every day.

The wonderful thing about teaching a class is that you can give everyone the same materials, colours and designs and each person will come up with something totally different. Each creation is unique – it's very inspiring.

Holly Jones

I started my journey into arts and crafts at school. After struggling with dyslexia, I knew that the academic route wasn't the right fit for me and that my skills lay more in practical and creative practices. I studied for a national diploma in Art & Design for two years, followed by a three-year degree in Creative Art and Design Practice. As part of my degree I specialised in textile design, which is where I developed a love of screen-printing and working with textiles. During my degree I started a placement at the Annie Sloan shop in Oxford; this developed into a full time position after my graduation where I worked alongside Annie Sloan for 2 years as a studio assistant specialising in furniture upcycling.

In 2015 I met Tess at the Handmade Festival with Kirstie Allsopp, a craft fair hosted at Hampton Court. Both of us were running workshops at the event for hundreds of crafters at a time, and we enjoyed chatting about our mutual love for printing and design. A couple of weeks after we met, I applied for a position at the Indian Block Print Co. and joined their growing team.

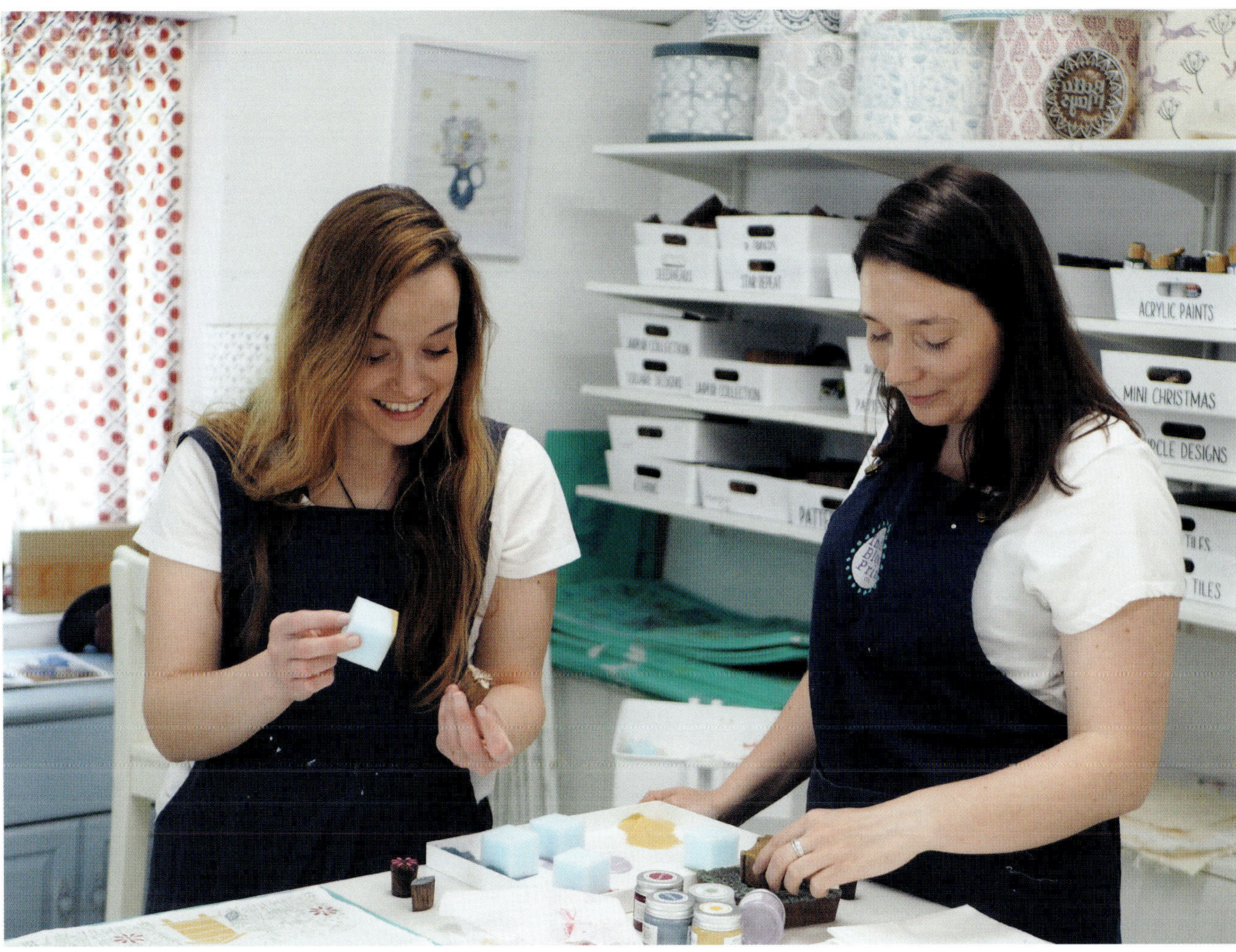

Above: Holly and Tess in the Indian Block Print Co. Oxfordshire studio.

When I print, whether it's at home or in a studio environment, I feel a sense of escapism, which comes from the action of focusing on one thing. It becomes a mindful, positive escape from what I might have going on around me in my day-to-day life and pressures. It's a form of therapy for me, and I know others have the same release, which is one of the reasons I enjoy teaching block printing so much.

Working Together

Later that year after meeting, we opened a workshop studio at the Indian Block Print Co., and in the past seven years we have taught and inspired hundreds of individuals to block print. As well as running workshops, we also develop new project ideas, always striving to increase our knowledge of block printing and improve our teaching. We both harbour a real passion for helping others find their creativity through the art of Indian block printing, at the same time sharing with guests the mindful and therapeutic benefits of crafting.

For both of us it's more than just a job; the love of what we do is part of our everyday living and a passion that follows us through every aspect of our lives.

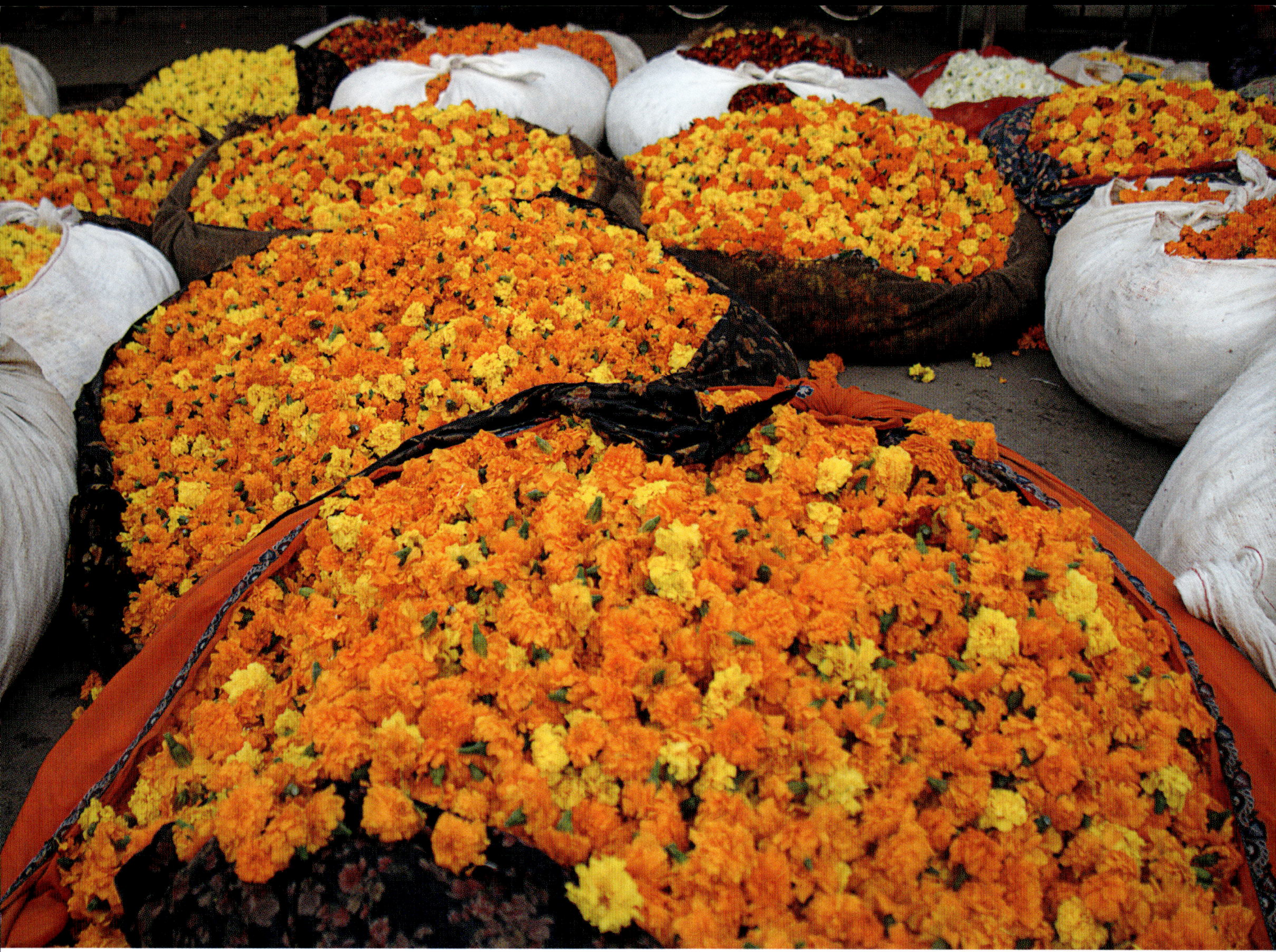

Inspired by India

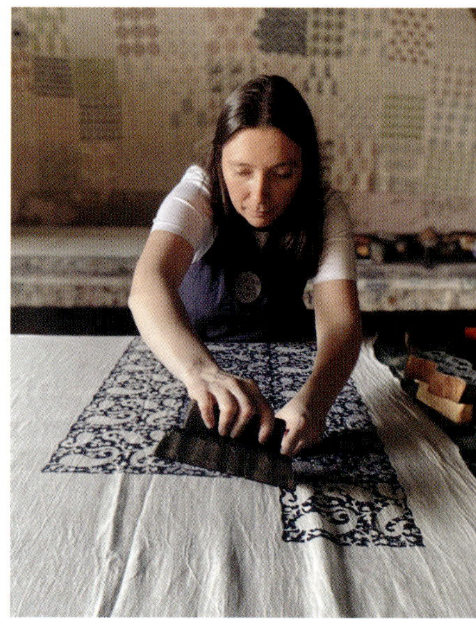

Above: Tess block printing in Bagru, India.

Top: Freshly picked marigolds found at the flower market in Jaipur.

Block printing is a centuries-old technique, using carved wooden blocks with intricate patterns to hand-print fabric and paper. India became a hub for block-printed fabrics in the twelfth century and it remains globally renowned, with unmatched craftsmanship in hand-carving detailed wooden blocks and the labour-intensive printing process that continues to thrive.

Hand-printed fabrics have become increasingly popular in recent years as the printing process has become much more widely recognised. The use of hand-printed fabrics by designers and fashion houses helps to promote the tradition and heritage of this ancient art form. In the UK brands such as East have long used traditional wood-block and heritage-inspired prints in their collections.

Visiting India

Having block printed here in the UK, we were well-versed in the hand-printing process and knew some of its history. However, nothing compares to experiencing block printing in India, at the very heart of this ancient craft. Immersed in the vibrant culture and surrounded by master artisans, we were able to gain a deeper appreciation for the skill, tradition and precise effort that goes into each piece. Witnessing the craft in its birthplace brought the history to life in ways we could never have imagined.

Our first visit to India was an experience we'll never forget, and it remains a significantly influential trip that has shaped our entire journey with block printing. A trip to Rajasthan is now an annual fixture for us and still gives us the same sense of elation as our first visit. These trips keep us connected to a place where we feel completely at home and we can recharge with inspiration for the year ahead. Being there allows us to get together with many of the artisans we collaborate with.

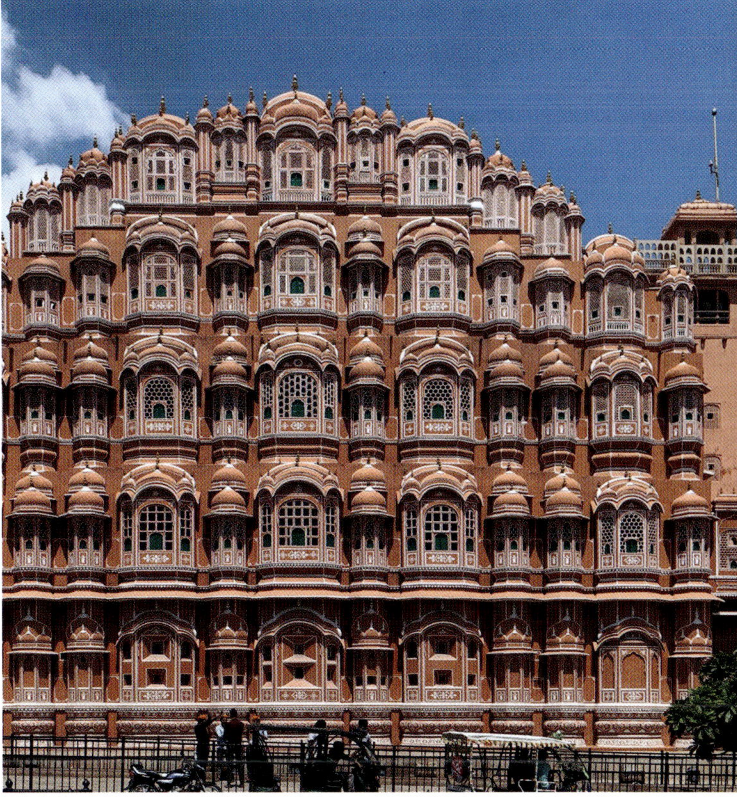

Above: East façade of Hawa Mahal, also known as Palace of Winds, located in City Palace, Jaipur.

Below: Annabel, Tess, Maggie and Anna with master block printer Vijendra in his studio, Bagru Textiles in Bagru, India.

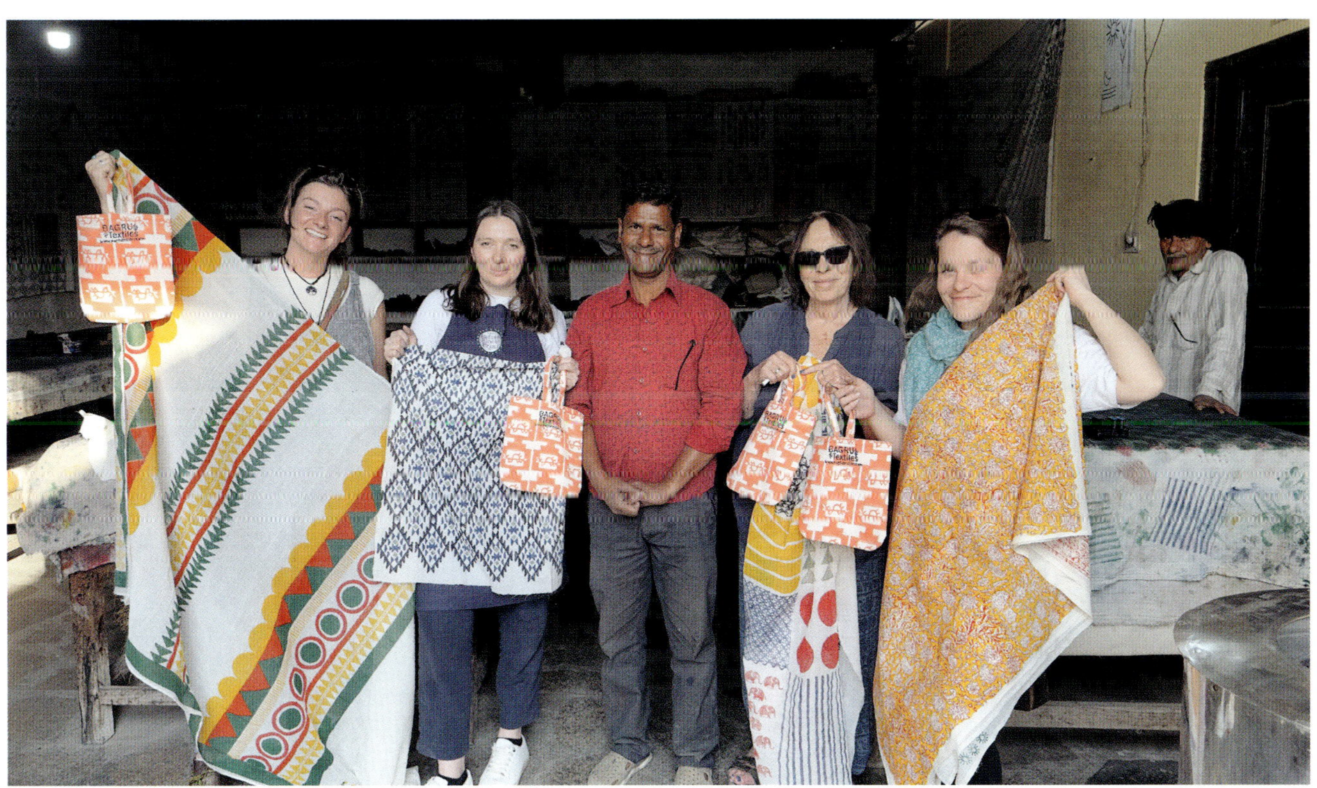

During our trips, we spend as much time as we can in the printing studios, where there is a captivating array of designs, colours and possibilities of what can be created with the tools in front of us. We could happily spend our entire trip immersed in printing, experimenting with every colour, design and block combination, and then returning the next day to do it all over again.

It's not just the printing aspect of India that is to be admired; the country itself is deeply inspiring. With its vibrant atmosphere, rich cultural heritage, wonderful people and abundance of colour and intricate patterns, there's inspiration at every turn. There's so much to explore, which is why we return year after year.

Tess says: 'The feeling that I get when printing in India can only be described as a sense of belonging, and of being "home", and that's something that I love more than anything to share with others. To offer them a chance to explore colour and pattern, and

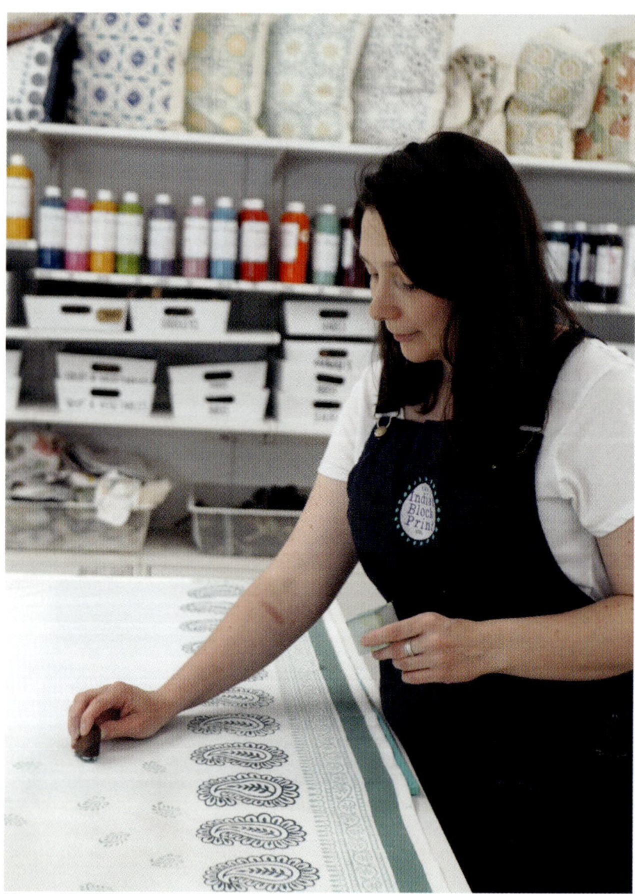

Above: Tess block printing in the studio.

that wonderful feeling of creating. I understand we are incredibly lucky to have experienced Indian block printing first hand.'

Bringing It Home

On our return from India, we have a revived energy to recreate – through our own teaching – the joy we experience while printing there. 'Designed in the UK, inspired by India' perfectly captures the relationship between us and India.

As Tess says: 'I believe my passion for printing originates from a love of pattern. I'm immensely drawn to it, especially block-printed fabrics. It's hard for me to walk past something block printed and not pick it up. The mix of colour and pattern – traditional and contemporary – I can appreciate it all. Block printing, and the wooden blocks themselves, enable us to be part of that world of printing, pattern and colour.'

The block printing carried out in India – with its multi-layered designs and complex patterns – is an advanced art form that takes years of practice for master artisans to perfect. Replicating that exact process can be challenging, requiring more technical instruction due to the complex nature of the craft. When developing our own printing workshops and projects, we aim to ensure that guests are able to create something they feel proud of. That's why our series of workshops start at the beginner level, using smaller printing blocks accessible to anyone new to the craft. From there, people can progress to more advanced, traditional Indian-style block printing as their skills grow.

Holly says: 'What I love about teaching in a workshop environment is that it's a safe, comfortable place. When you're surrounded by like-minded people, all focusing on the printing in front of you, it is amazing how people feel comfortable enough to open up and have conversations that might not have happened in a different context. I've developed very personal relationships with guests who I've taught over the years, over shared experiences, creativity and an exchange of ideas.'

Working With the Artisans

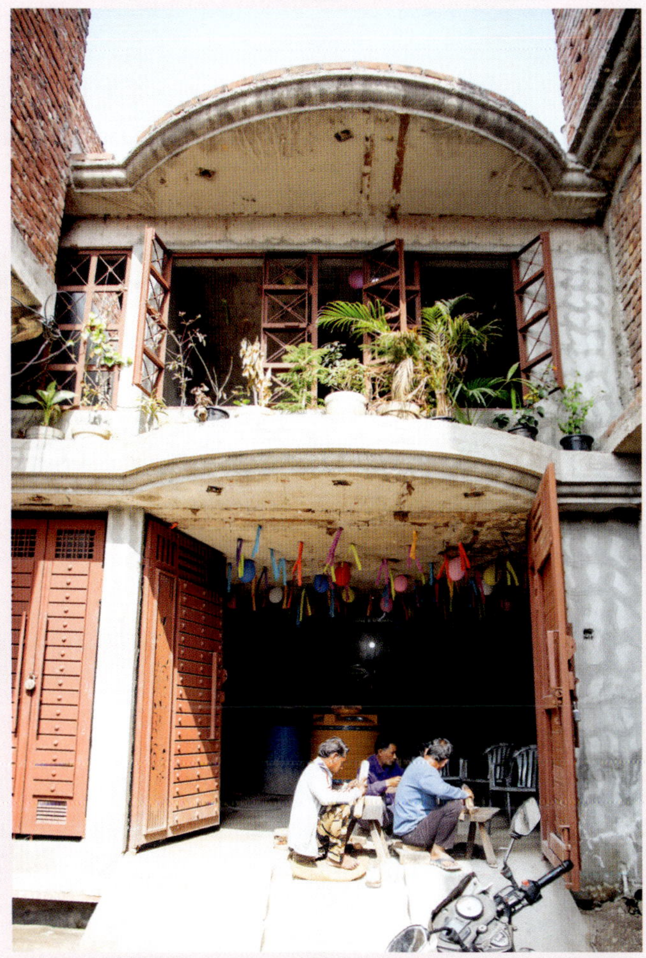

Above: Malik's workshop in Uttar Pradesh.

Below: Visiting block carvers in India.

Since 2010, we've been collaborating directly with block carvers from rural villages outside Jaipur to bring our designs to life. Today, we work with around 40 skilled artisans who hand-carve our designs into wooden printing blocks, with deliveries arriving from India each month. Being able to design our own printing blocks in our chosen patterns gives us a lot more creative freedom. We can stay up to date with current trends and seasons, as well as stocking a broad range of designs so every guest finds something that appeals to them.

Even with modern technology, communication can still be challenging. During each visit, we discuss areas for improvement and brainstorm new design ideas. Our skilled carvers play a key role in simplifying intricate, traditional Indian patterns into more accessible designs that can be used by amateur block printers in the UK, while still achieving incredible results.

Over the years, we've seen the positive impact of our ongoing connection with the artisans and their families. During our 2024 trip, we visited Malik, one of the carvers we began working with many years ago. Since we started working together, he has built his own workshop in his town and now employs several other carvers who help create our designs.

For the artisans, these relationships are important because steady work can be hard to find in India. They truly value the opportunities we provide and, in turn, we value their skills and knowledge to continue our block printing and teaching.

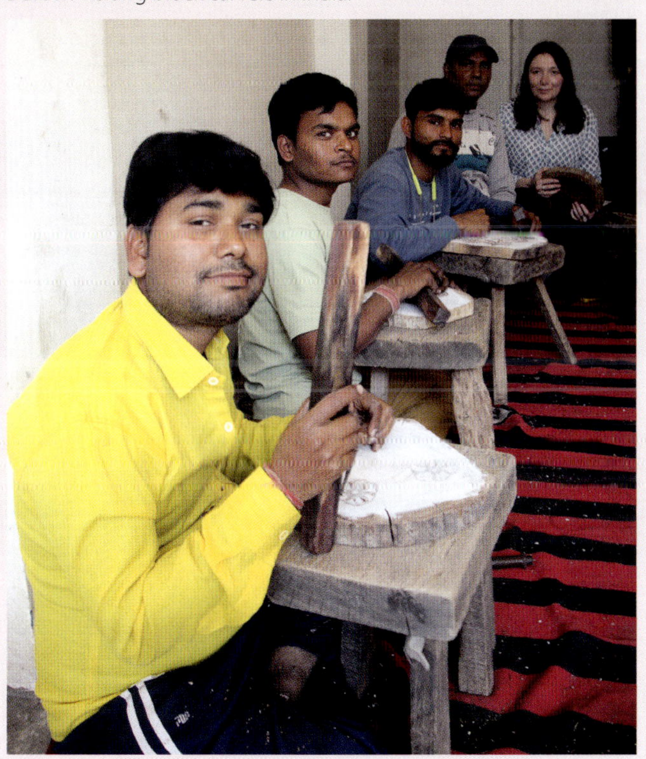

PART 1

The Basics of Printing

This section covers the basics you'll need to get started with block printing and is one of the most important parts of the book.

Having the right equipment and learning the basic techniques can make a big difference in whether your prints are successful or not. It's common to feel discouraged and lack confidence if things don't go to plan, so we always recommend that our customers and workshop guests take their time with the basics before moving on to the next step.

Making mistakes is part of learning how to do it right, which is why practice is so important. It can also help to understand why a print didn't turn out as expected. We've included a section on understanding your results (see page 27) to help you see how your prints should or shouldn't look.

The printing equipment you'll need is basic; you should be able to find all the required materials at home or from your local art and craft store.

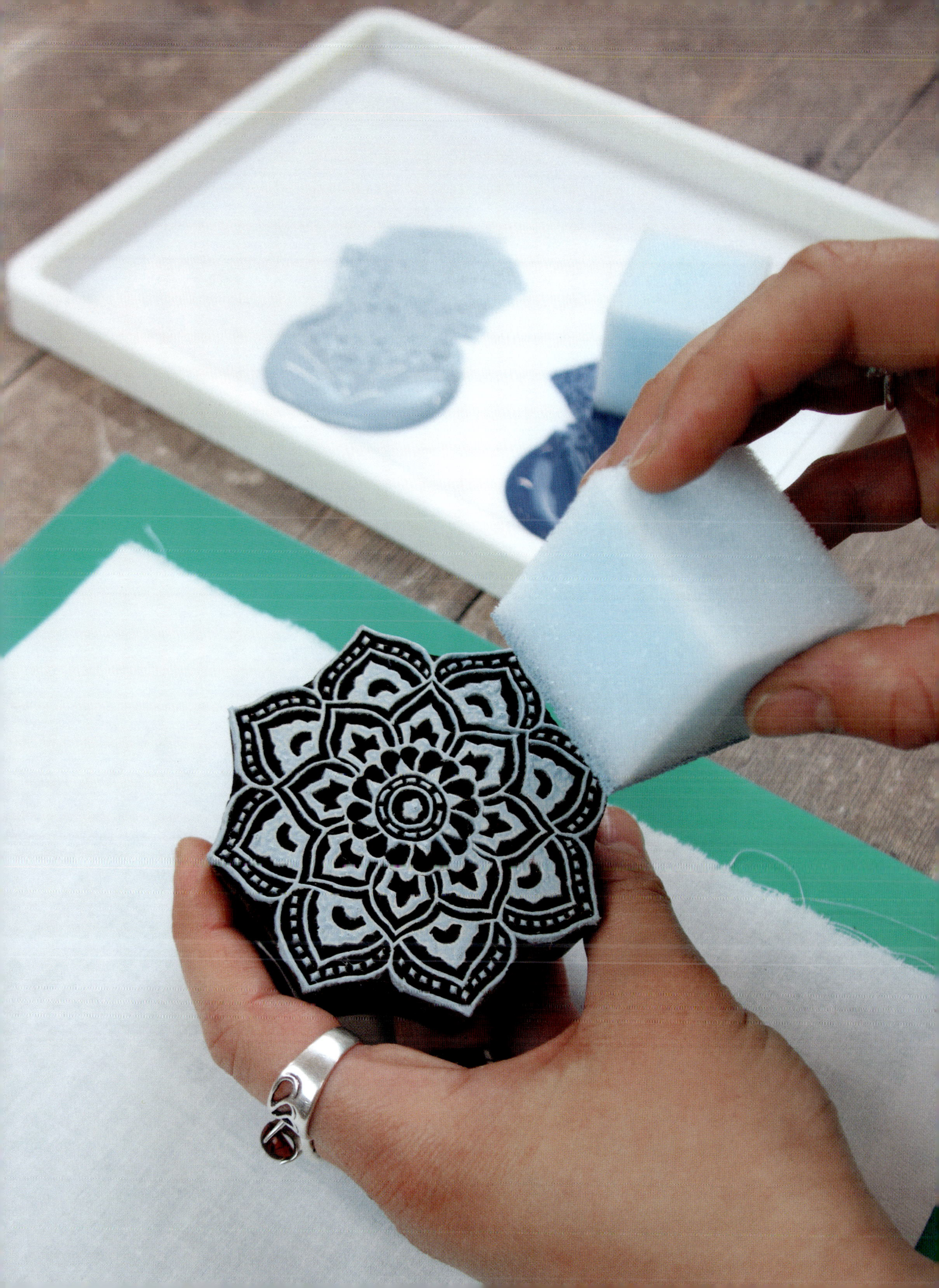

Basic Printing Equipment

Block printing doesn't require fancy or expensive equipment. Aside from the blocks themselves and the blanks you print onto, you should be able to source everything you need from around your home or your current craft supplies.

Each printing project will require most, if not all, of the equipment items featured below. The paints and printing blocks used will vary depending on the project being completed. All the materials we use throughout this book have been provided by the Indian Block Print Co. and the exact colours and designs used for the projects can be found on their website. You can also source printing equipment and materials from other craft suppliers.

For each project we will list the equipment that is needed. To save repeating ourselves, when we refer to 'basic printing equipment', this includes all the items below and is the basic toolkit needed for a block-printing project.

Foam printing mat

Apart from the printing block itself, a foam mat is the most important piece of equipment you will need when printing with a wooden block. A wooden block has no give, so if you print on a hard surface, it is difficult to get the paint to transfer across evenly. It's essential to print on a soft surface to ensure you get a good print. In India the master block printers have padded tables, but we replicate this using a foam mat. A camping or yoga mat also works well. This is a crucial piece of equipment, which is often missed but can greatly affect the quality of prints you make with your block.

Paint tray

We recommend using a flat paint tray to dispense your paint onto. It's important to allow each shade enough space on the tray so you can dab the excess paint off your sponge without the different colours blending. We like to use washable plastic trays, meaning we can reuse them each time, but old Tupperware also works well.

Paint

We've done a lot of research into different paints and inks over the years. In our experience, we recommend using water-based, non-toxic paints, as these are easy to work with and to wash off equipment (see page 33). We swap between fabric paint and acrylic paint, depending on the project we're working on. It's important to remember that fabric paint works on both fabric and paper, whereas acrylic paint is only suitable for using on paper or card. Most fabric/textile paints will require heat setting with an iron to fix and make permanent and washable (see page 32). It is possible to add a fabric medium to acrylic paint which makes it permanent and washable when used on fabric.

Sponges and dabbers

These are used to apply paint to the printing block, using a dabbing action. We recommend sourcing a mixture of sponges to keep in your printing kit. We tend to use square sponges for one-colour printing, and sponge dabbers (sponges on sticks) in multiple sizes for more detailed precision printing. Rollers don't work well with wooden printing blocks – we've tried

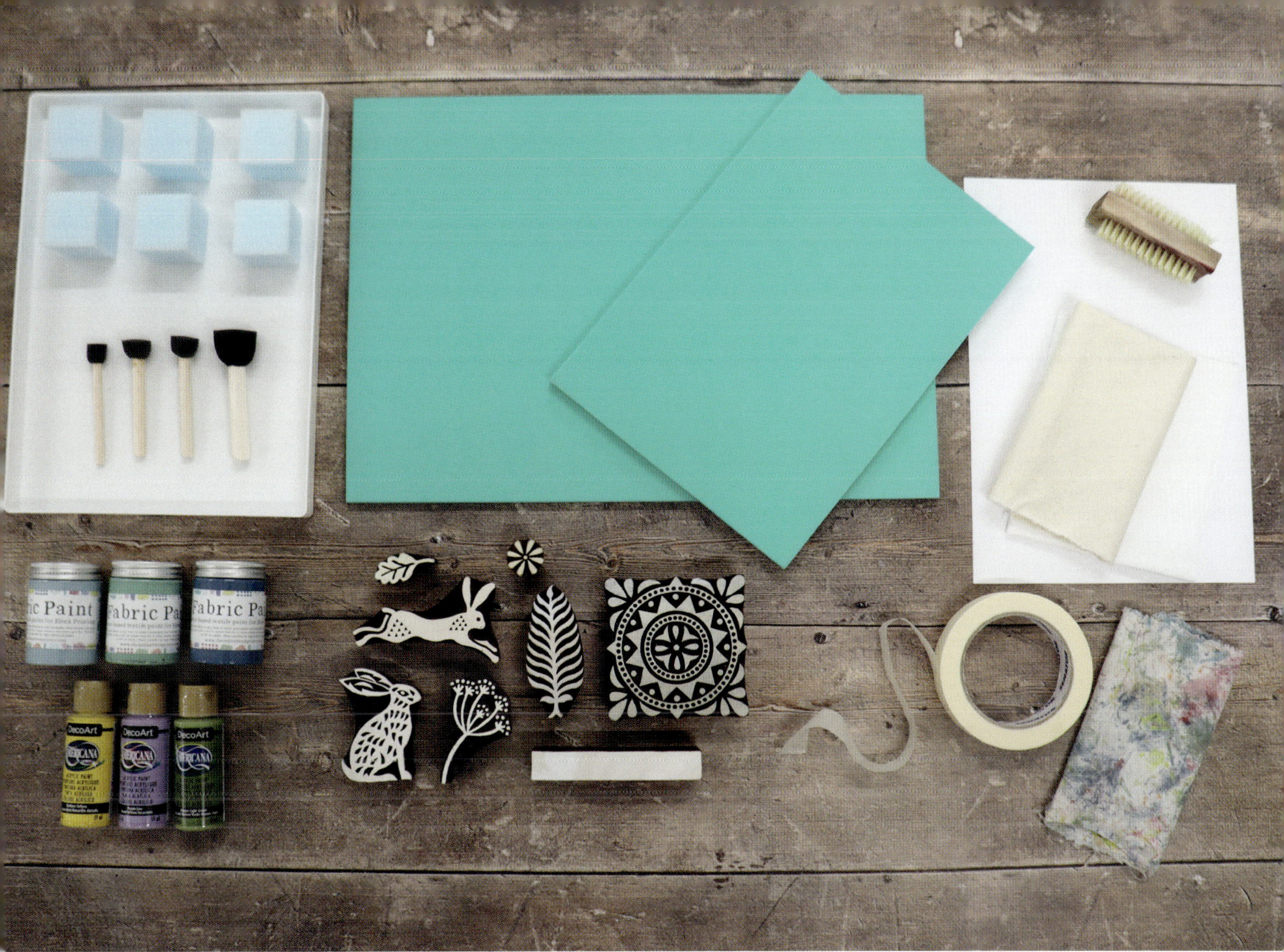

and tested many methods and always go back to using sponges. These can be washed and reused after each printing session.

Rags or cleaning cloths

It isn't necessary to wash your printing blocks with water between each paint shade. We use a piece of scrap fabric or rag to wipe off the previous colour before applying the next one, and only wash the blocks between printing sessions. An old piece of dry cloth will be handy to keep in your equipment box for this.

Printing blocks

There are various forms of printing blocks available, from rubber stamps to linocut to potato prints, but here we are specifically using wooden blocks. When buying a wooden block, it's important to look for a high-quality wood such as sheesham. Softer woods like mango wood won't withstand much use and will wear away quickly.

You can usually tell a good-quality block from its colour and surface quality. The block should have a dark wood stain with edges that are smooth to touch, showing that it has been sanded and treated for lifelong use. Softer wood blocks often look lighter and are flaky or rough to touch.

Nail brush

A useful piece of equipment we like to have on hand when printing is a nail brush. Printing blocks can become clogged with paint over time, especially when printing repeatedly with the same design, but you can use a nail brush to clean paint out of the details. They are also helpful for washing your printing blocks after use (see page 33).

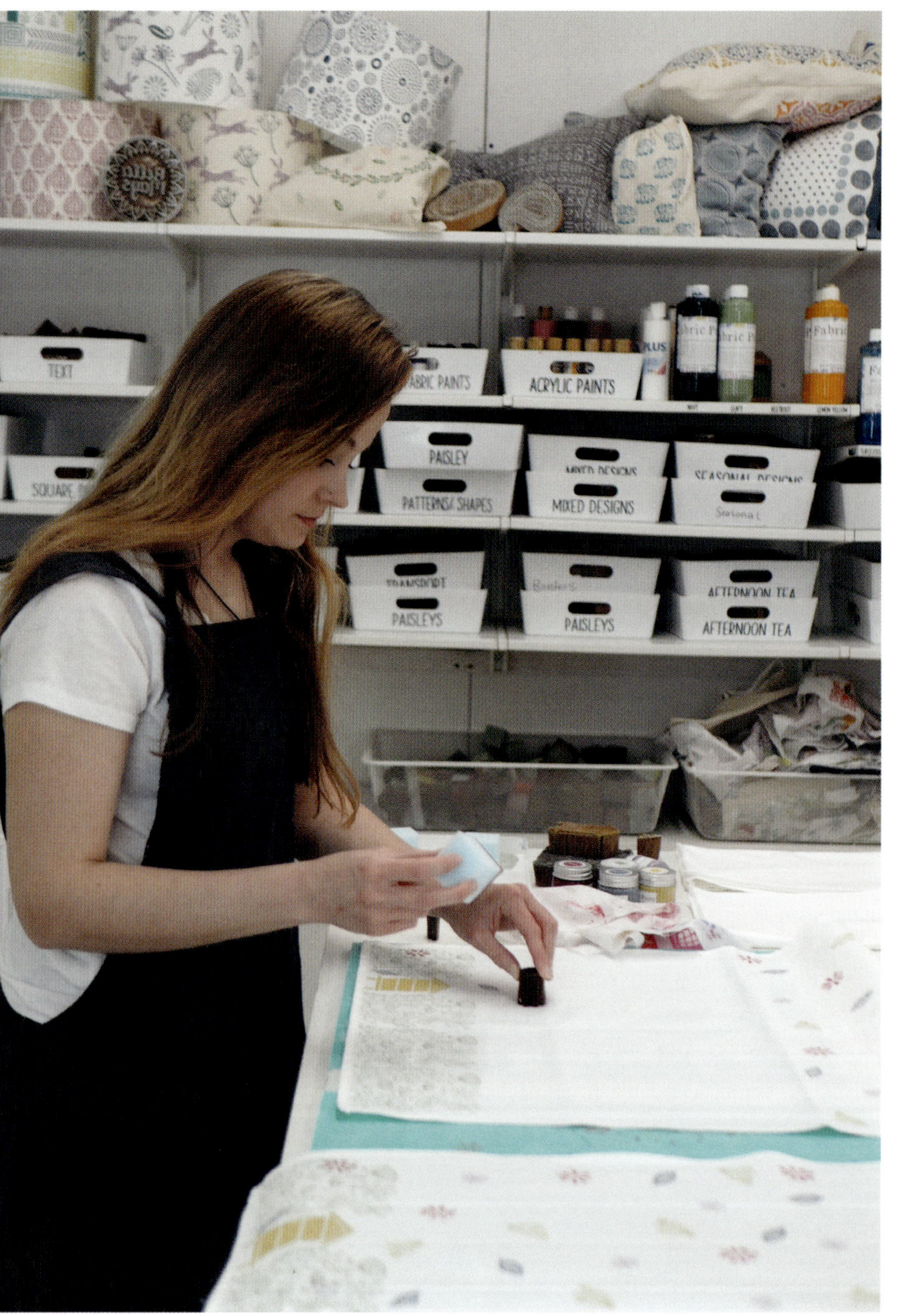

Above: Holly printing in the Oxfordshire studio.

Masking tape

Masking tape can be used to create a straight line to follow when printing, or to hold your fabric down to avoid it moving or smudging.

Scrap fabric or paper

We suggest collecting a stash of scrap fabric, card or paper to use before starting a new printing project, or when testing designs and colours. We source plain, light-coloured cotton such as old bedding to use for practice as it is low cost and it doesn't matter if you make a mistake. You could even rip up old pillowcases – we use calico or white cotton.

Iron

An iron is required for heat setting your fabric paint. You can use your normal household iron as the paint will not come off onto your iron. We'll talk you through how to do this later (see page 32). We also use an iron to prepare fabric items before printing to remove any wrinkles or to add crease lines to act as a guide.

One-Colour Printing

Before you are ready to start printing, there are a couple of key things you need to do. Wash any new printing blocks with warm, soapy water and dry them before use (see page 33). This will remove any dirt from the surface of the blocks, which might affect the paint sticking to them.

You will notice that new printing blocks often come with a covering of white paint on the surface of your design. The paint will start to come off or become stained once you start printing, but we suggest scrubbing the block and removing some of this white paint before you begin.

Fabric is easier to print onto than paper. We suggest you practise printing onto fabric at first and then move on to paper once you are confident with the basics.

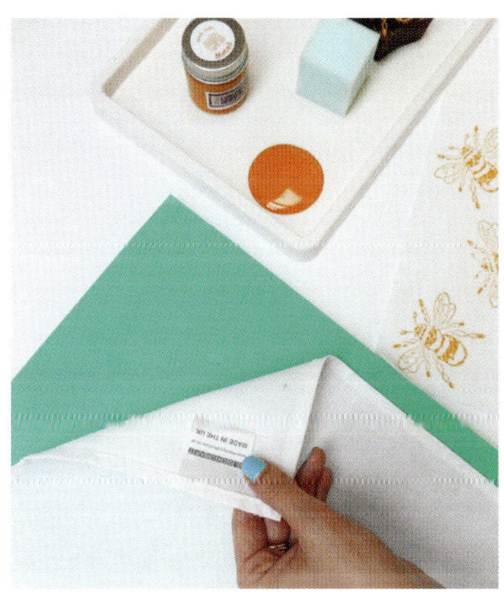

1 Don't forget you need to print onto a soft surface. Use something like a foam mat under your paper or fabric.

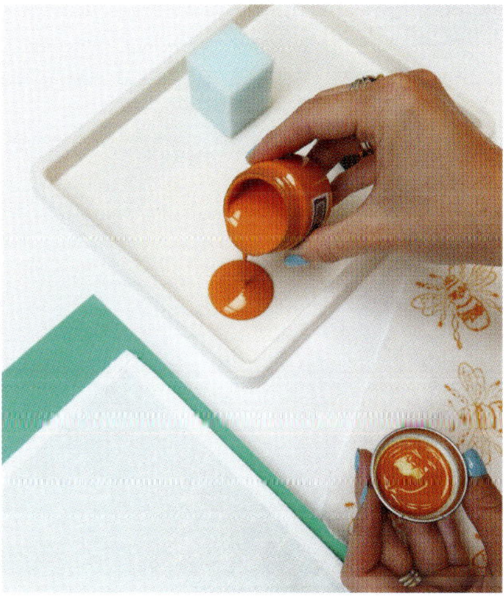

2 Pour a small blob of paint onto your paint tray. We suggest a ketchup-sized amount, but you can always add more when needed.

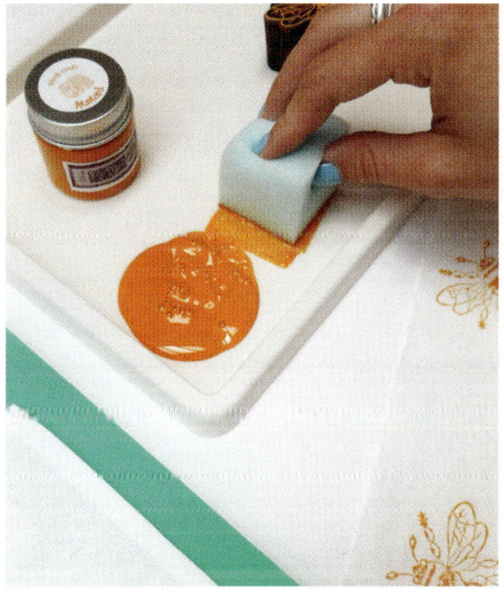

3 Dip the sponge into the paint. Tap your sponge onto the paint tray several times to remove any excess and help the sponge absorb some of the paint. Ensure the entire side of the sponge has paint on it, not just the corner. If you can't see the texture of the sponge, tap it onto the tray again.

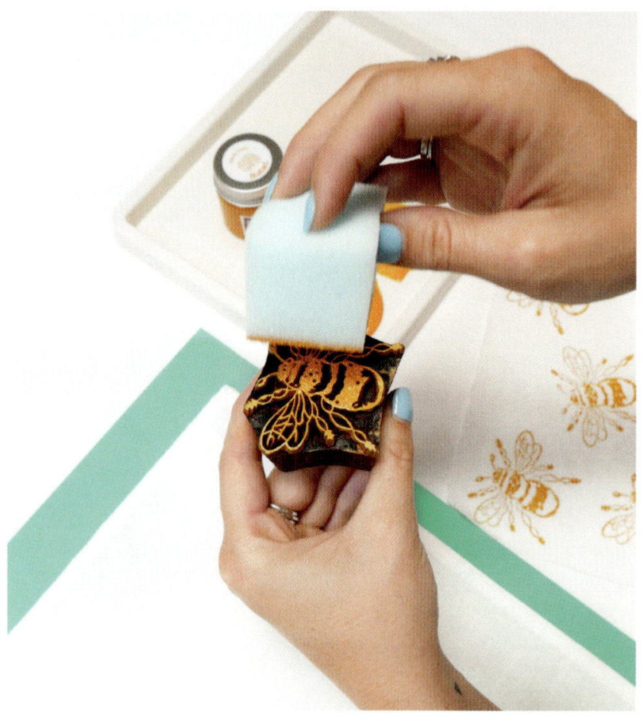

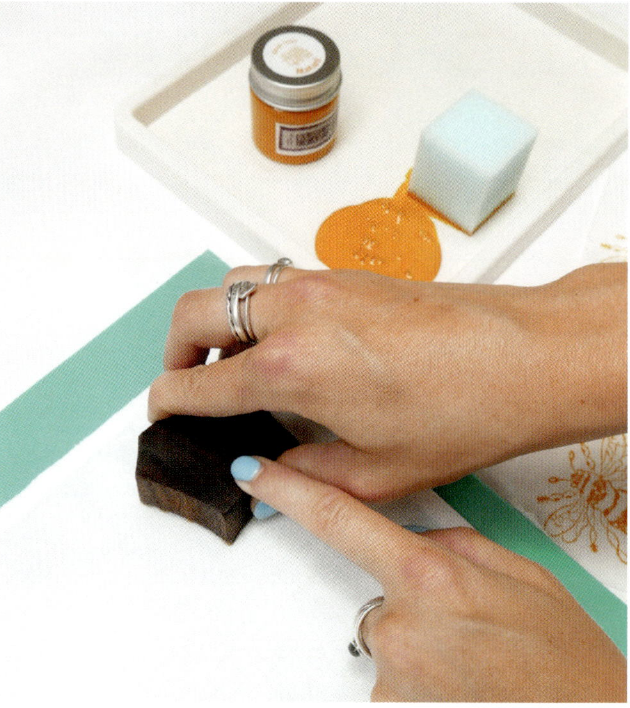

4 Use the sponge to tap lightly several times over the printing block to get a nice even coverage of paint. Be careful not to squeeze or wipe the paint onto the printing block as this can fill up the detail – you just want a light layer. Always use your sponge flat; using just the corner or the edge can result in poor paint application.

5 Turn your printing block upside down and place it onto your material. Apply a gentle pressure all over the block (the bigger the design, the more pressure you will need to apply). Give the printing block a slight wiggle so all the edges get pushed down. You don't want to push so hard that your block indents into the mat; just use even pressure all over.

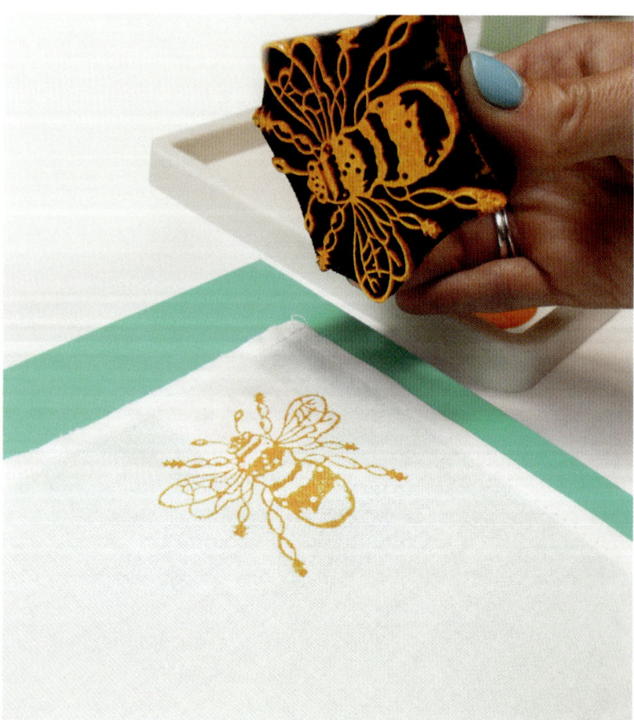

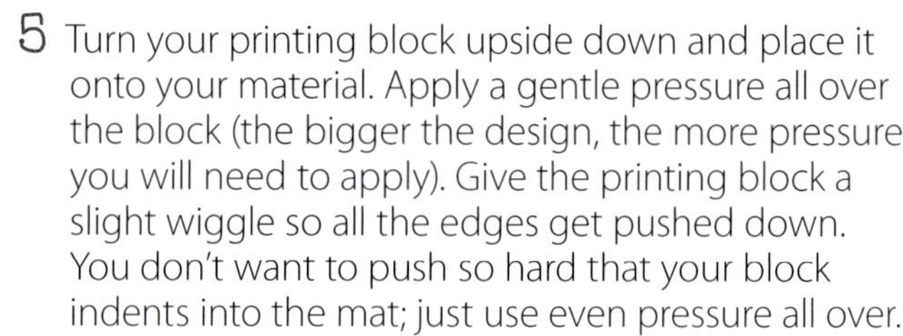

6 Pull the printing block straight up and off the material to reveal your print. Peeling it off can cause the edge that's touching the fabric to smudge. Hold the material you're printing onto with your free hand to stop it lifting with your printing block.

7 You need to apply a fresh coat of paint each time you print. Dip your sponge back in the paint, tap off the excess and reapply a fresh coat of paint (see Step 3).

Printing Tip

If you'd like to change colour, use a dry rag to wipe or rub any remaining paint off the printing block. Once the paint has been removed, you can apply your next colour. You don't need to wash the printing block in-between colours.

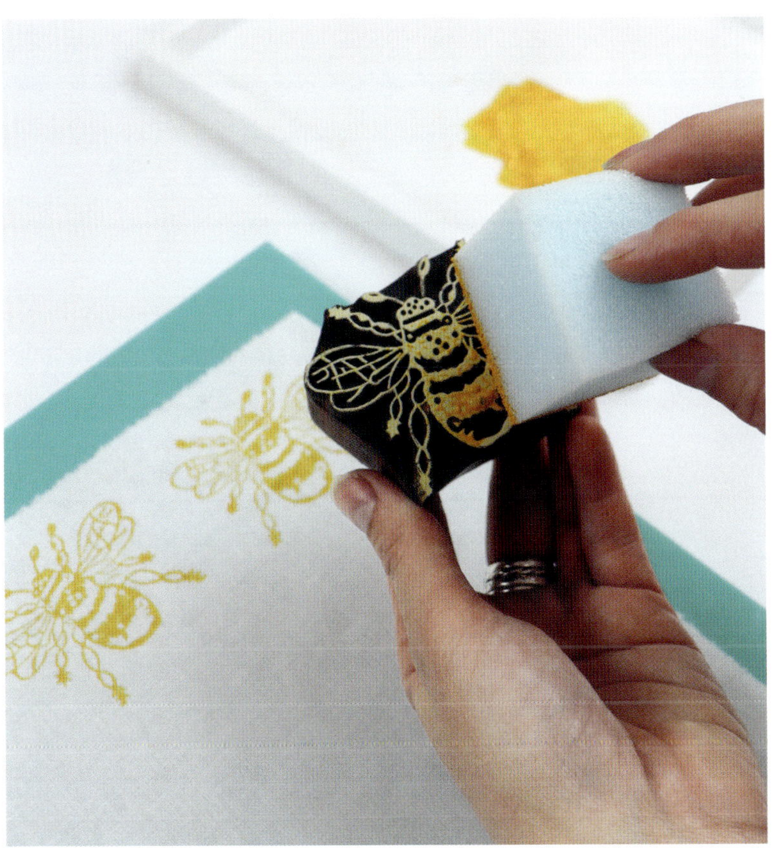

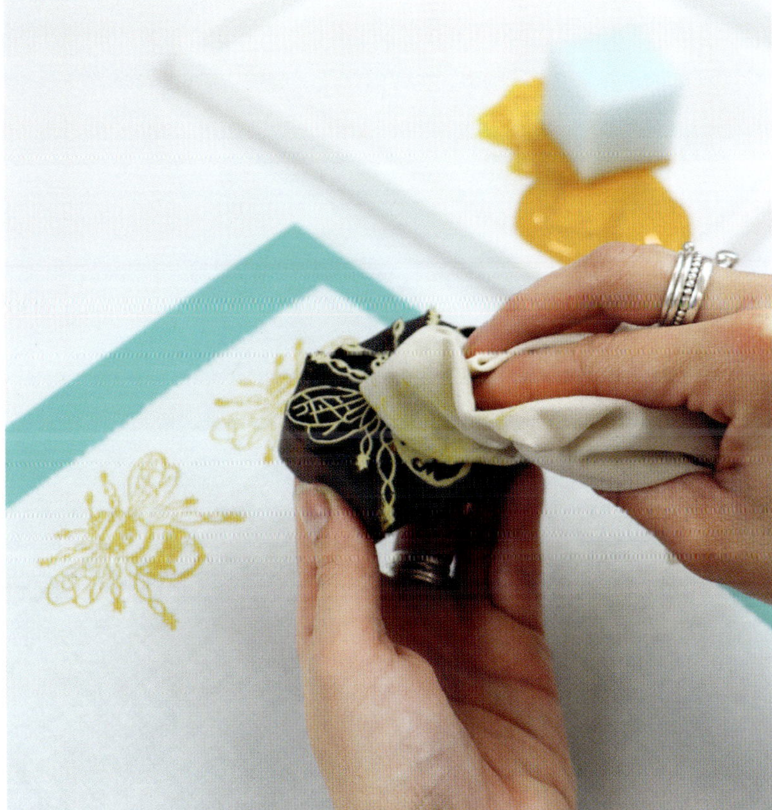

8 Once you have finished with the printing block, wipe all the excess paint off with your rag and put it aside to use again later or ready for washing up once you have finished printing. You don't want the paint to dry on the printing block as over time this can clog the design up.

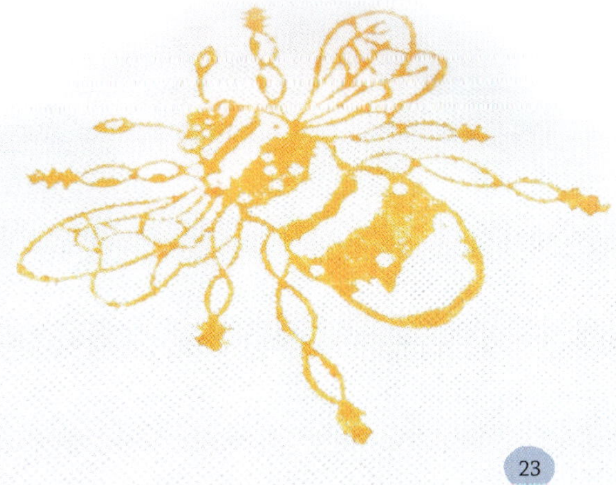

Two-Colour Printing

Once you have mastered printing with one colour, you can advance to printing with multiple colours on the printing block. Applying more than one colour to a design can bring the print to life and emphasise the detail of the prints you can create.

There are two ways of applying multiple colours: precise two-colour printing and random two-colour printing.

Precise Two-Colour Printing

This style of precise printing works well on floral and botanical designs, which have stems that you can print in a different colour. When precisely applying two colours, we use sponge dabbers. You can find these in a variety of sizes.

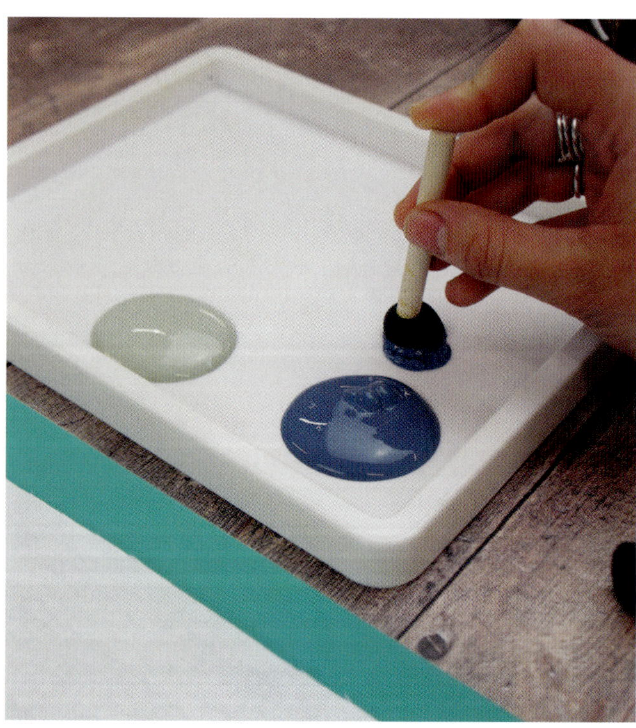

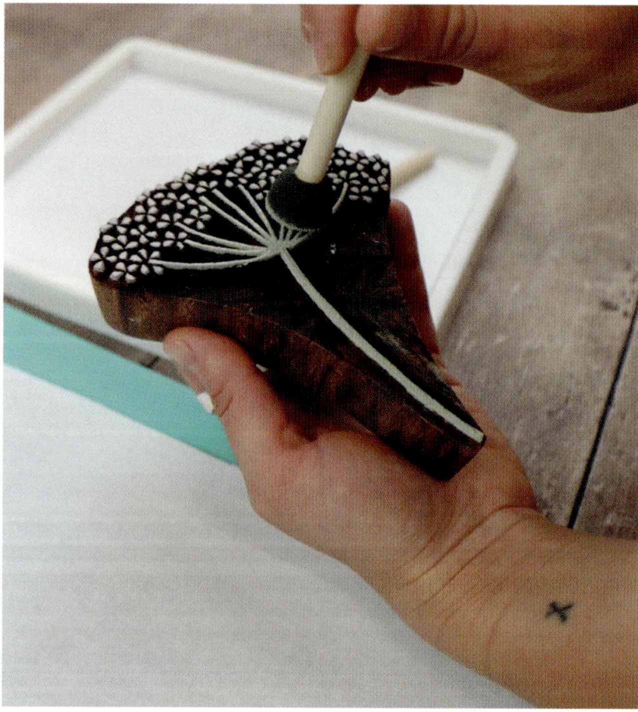

1 Use the sponge dabber in the same way as a square sponge. Tap the dabber in the paint and then tap off the excess. Make sure the entire bottom of the dabber is wet with paint, but avoid having any blobs on it.

2 Apply the first colour to the printing block, starting with the lightest colour. Ensure your sponge dabber is flat when applying the paint; don't turn it to the side and wipe or brush the paint onto the block.

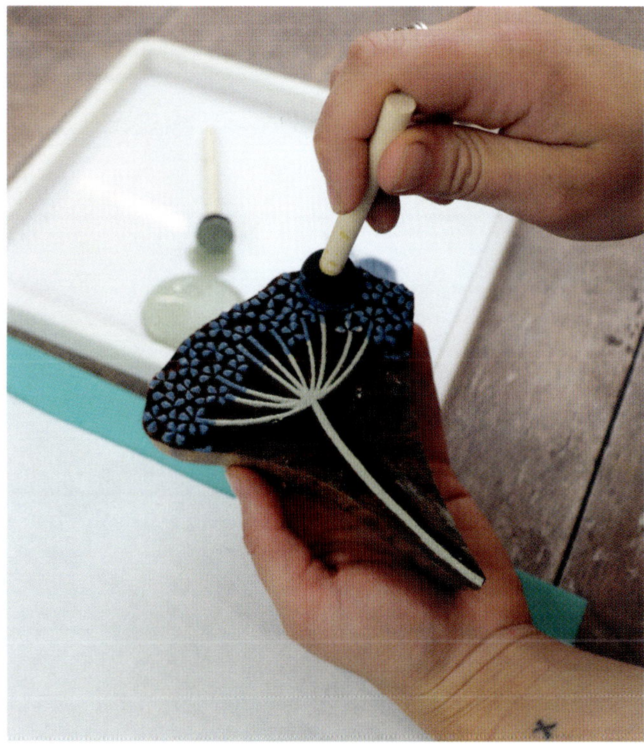

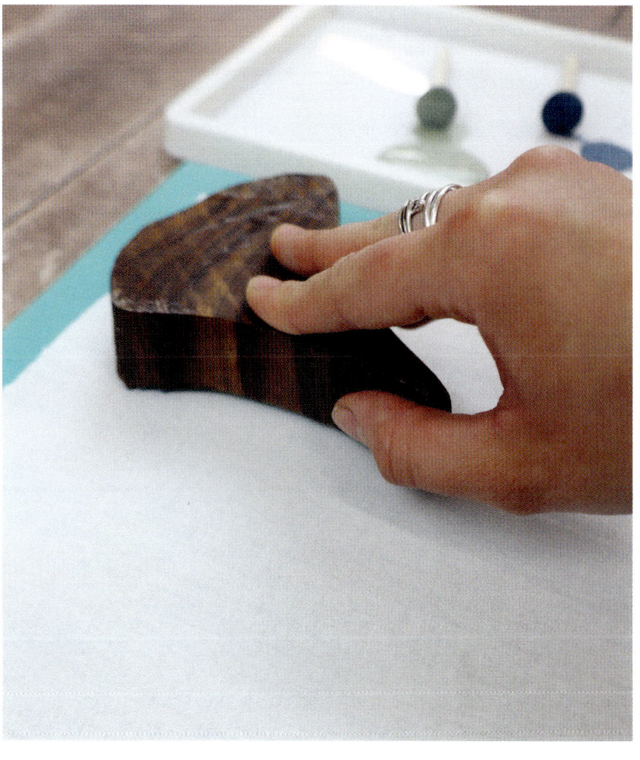

3 Once you have applied the first colour, you can apply the second. Again, don't wipe or brush – always tap the paint onto the block, holding the sponge dabber straight and flat. Ensure there is a small overlap or blend between the two colours, otherwise you may have a blank gap in between them when printed.

4 Turn the printing block upside down and print.

5 Pull the design straight up from your material to reveal your decorative two-colour print.

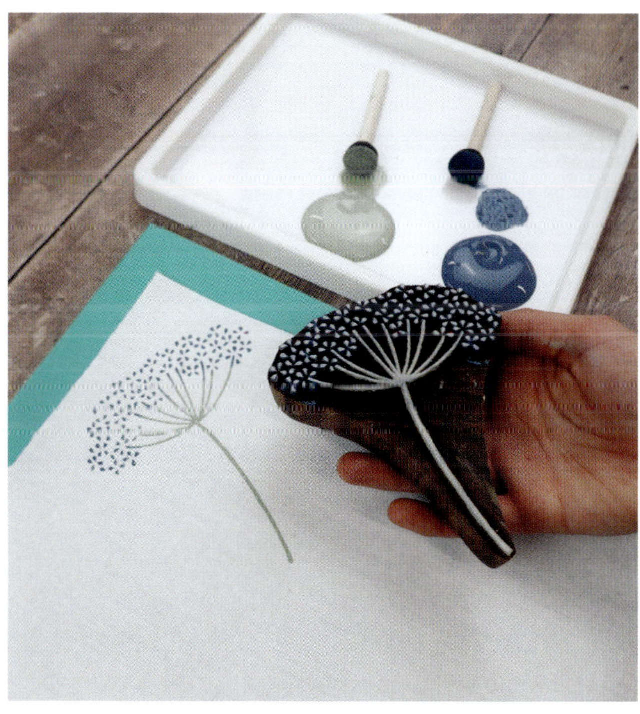

Printing Tip

Don't apply so many colours that the paint dries on the printing block before you print it. Practise on scrap fabric or paper to test how many colours you can apply and still get a successful print. We would recommend no more than three colours on a design, if you are precisely adding them.

Random Two-Colour Printing

Another way in which you can add more than one colour to your printing block is to randomly sponge colours onto the design, which will result in a mottled, multi-toned effect. Random two-colour printing works well on designs such as paisleys or leaves.

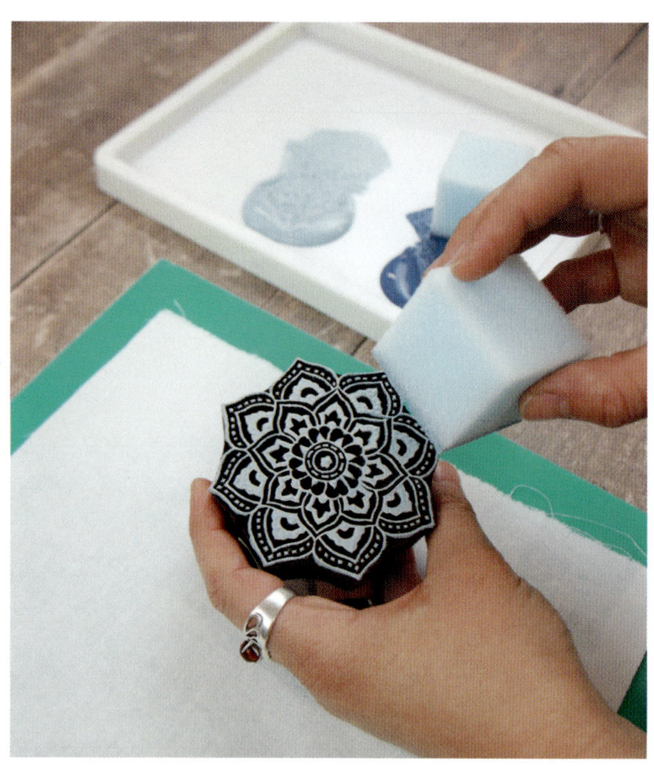

1 Use a sponge to tap your lightest coloured paint all over the printing block.

2 Randomly tap your next darkest colour over the printing block, adding more or less paint depending on how strong you want the second colour to appear.

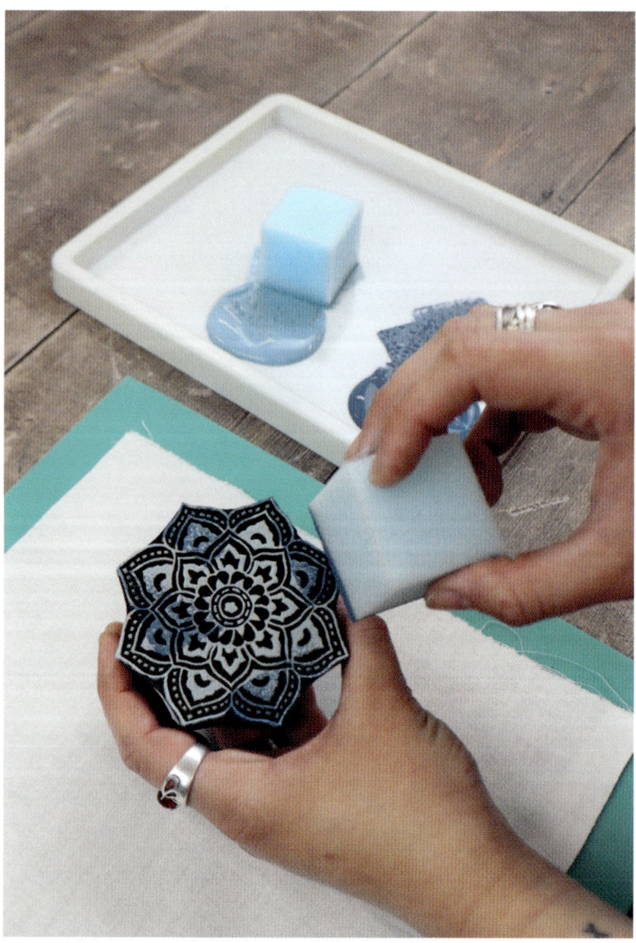

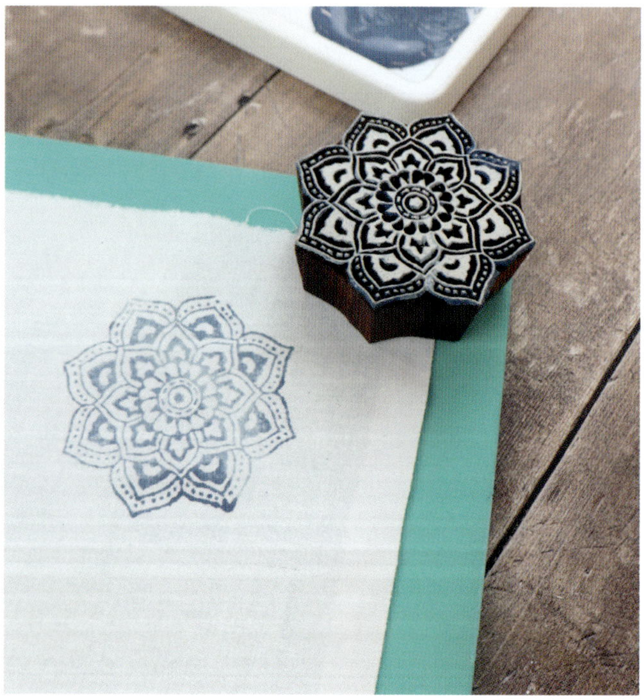

3 Turn the printing block upside down and print, then lift to reveal your mottled two-tone design.

Understanding Your Results

Starting your journey into Indian block printing can be a learning curve. Remember, making mistakes is a natural part of learning and helps you figure out how to fix them. Don't worry about these slip-ups; they're all part of the fun and creativity along the way!

We have pointed out below a few common mistakes, as you might find it useful to know what causes them and how to avoid them.

The perfect print (a)

The edges of the print are sharp and crisp, and there is a lovely even colour all over the design. Compare your results with this picture to understand where any mistakes might be being made and how to fix them.

Too much pressure (b)

Too much pressure has been applied to this print. The edges are smudged and the print doesn't have that clean, crisp feel.

Too much paint (c)

Too much paint has been applied to this design, making the print blobby.

Not enough pressure or paint (d)

Not enough pressure or too little paint has been applied when printing this design, making the print light, unclear, faint and patchy.

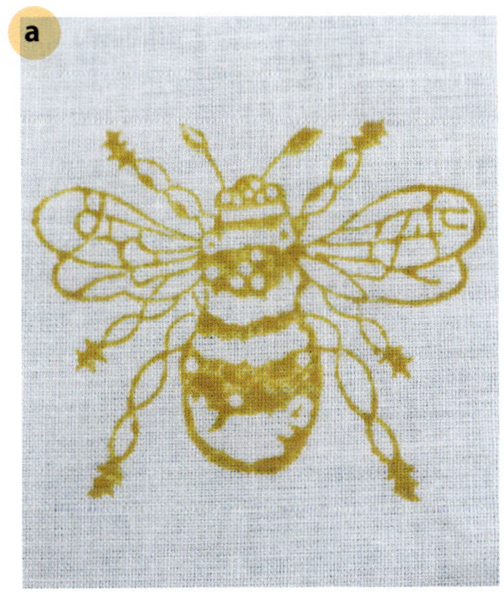

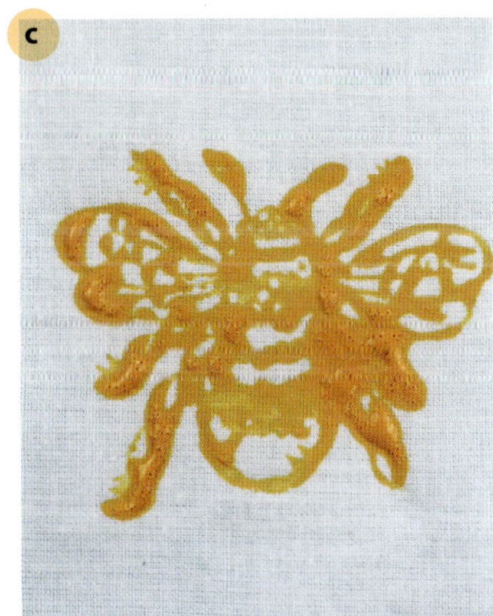

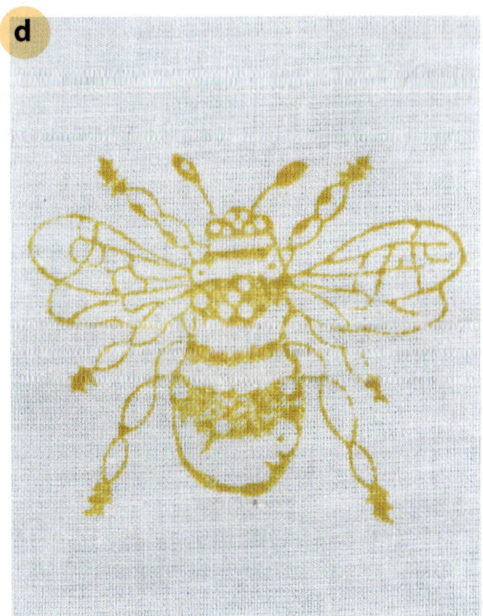

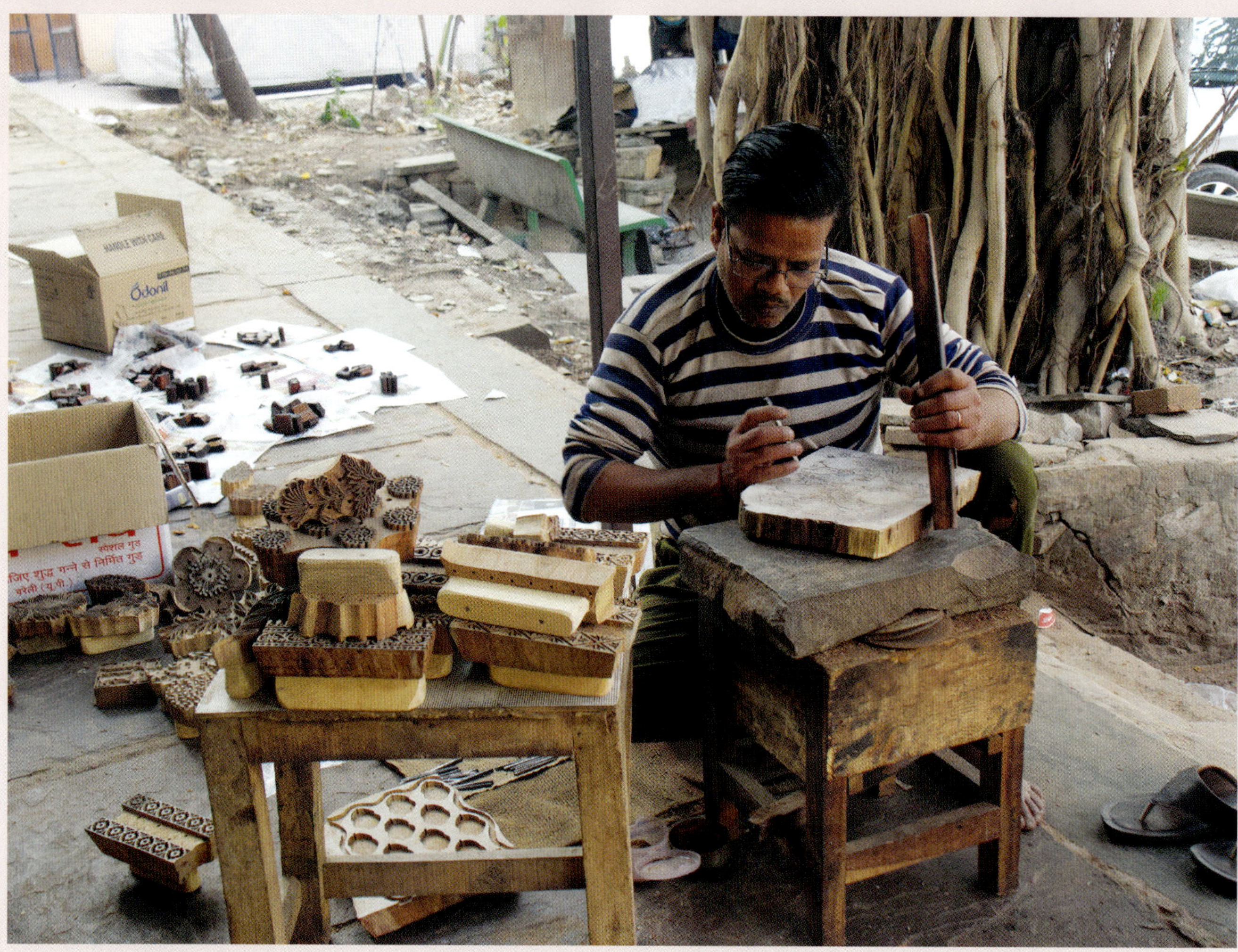

Above: Sanjeev, an artisan block carver in Sanganer.

Block Carving in Sanganer

To understand where the ancient art form of block printing originated from, let us travel to Jaipur, the home of hand-printed textiles.

Two small villages outside of Jaipur – Sanganer and Bagru – are the main hubs for both wood carving and printing. The textile industry is widely spread across India and you'll find wood-block carving and printing in many other regions, but these two villages specialise particularly in the printing industry.

Sanganer sits just to the south of the pink city walls of Jaipur. Here you'll find various textile-printing factories as well as a large focus on paper printing, both screen and block printed. In recent years, screen-printing has become much more widely introduced, with many printing houses swapping from hand-block printing to screen-printing due to the efficiency and lower costs involved, but still offering wood-block printing as a more premium technique.

Sanganer is commonly known as the home of wood carving. Walking down the streets, you'll be sure to come across block carvers, piles of wood stacked up in small lock-ups, boxes of hand-carved blocks and carvers hard at work. These artisans will be carving designs from the printing houses, with the finished design most likely heading further up the road to Bagru (see page 44). Carvers will be commissioned by the printing houses to produce intricate, multi-layered designs that will be used to print hundreds of metres of fabric.

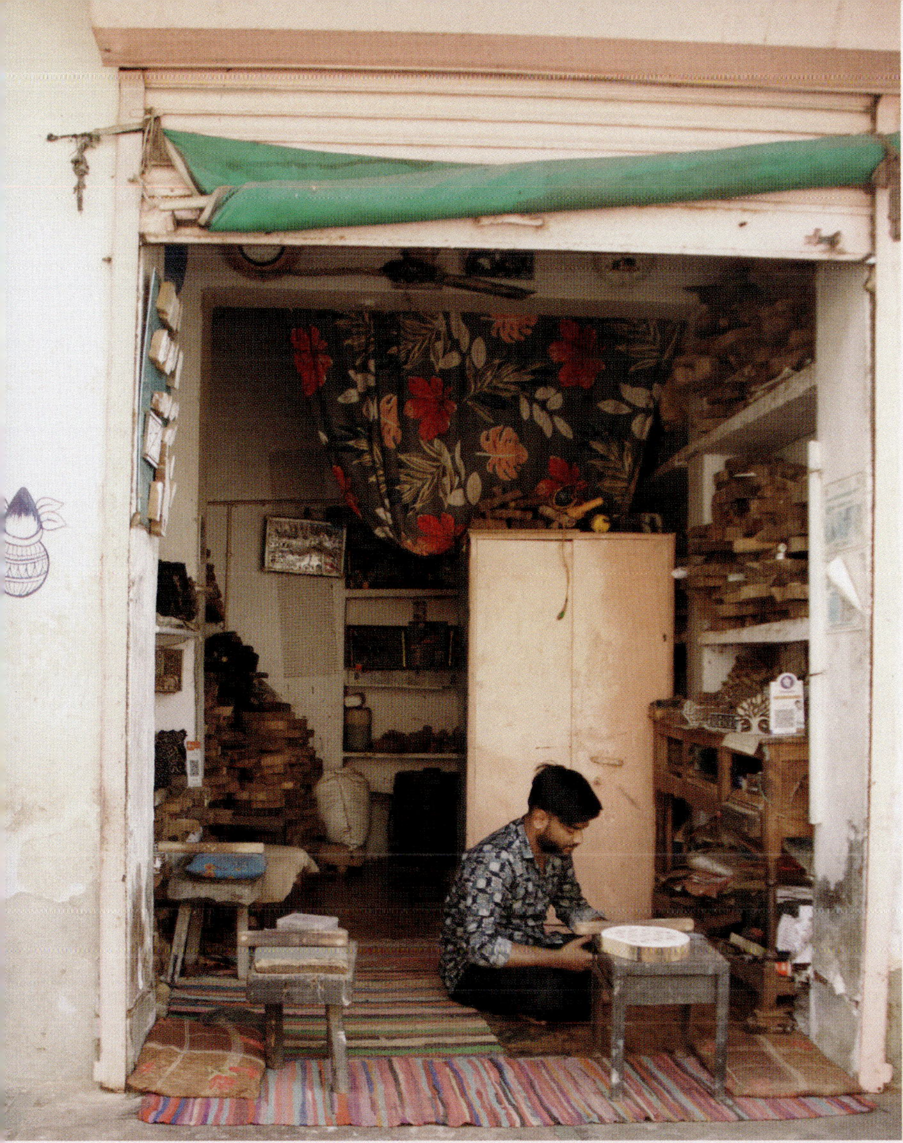

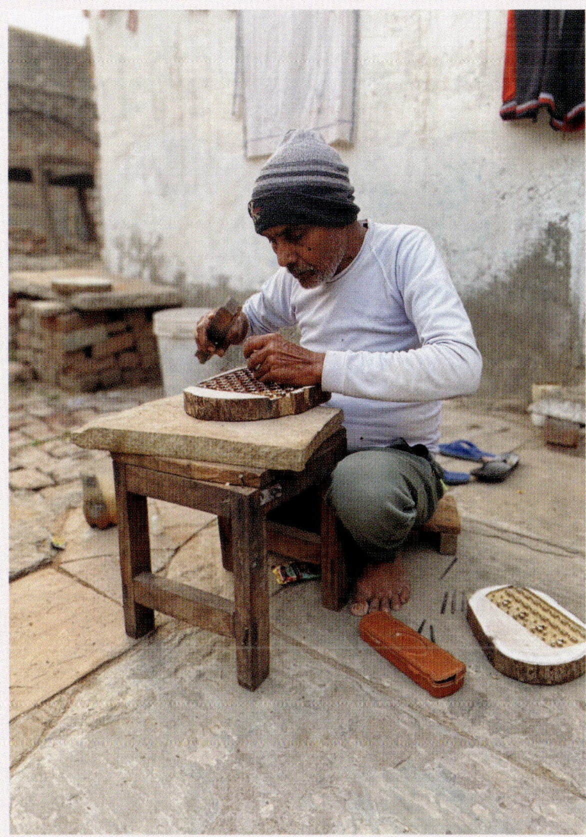

Above and below: Block carvers and wood-carving workshops in Sanganer.

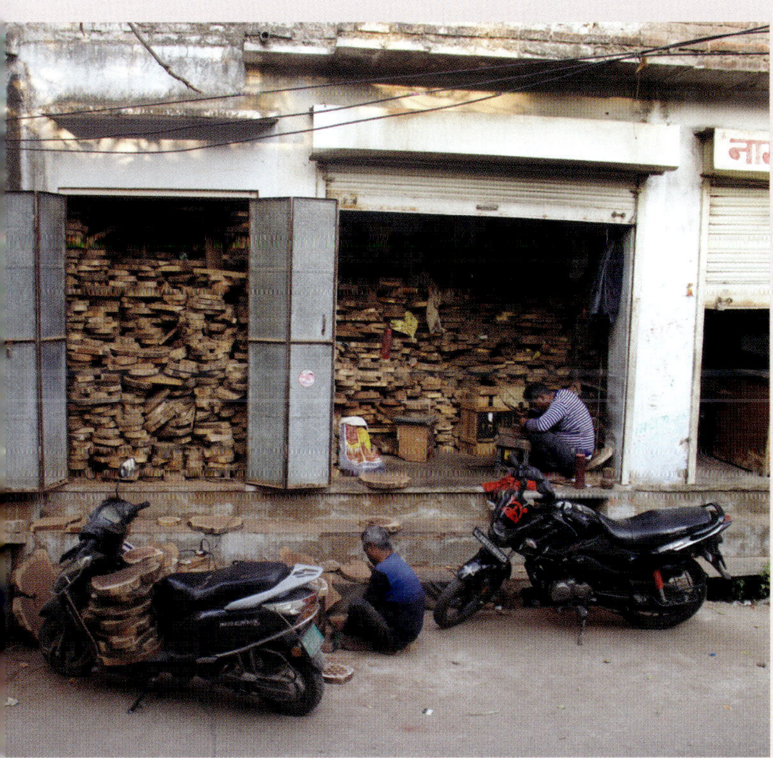

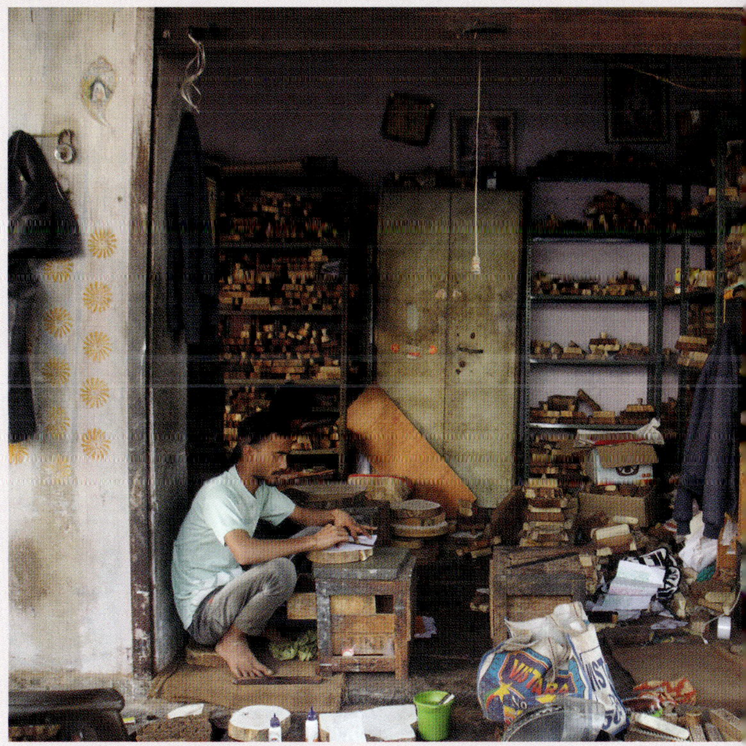

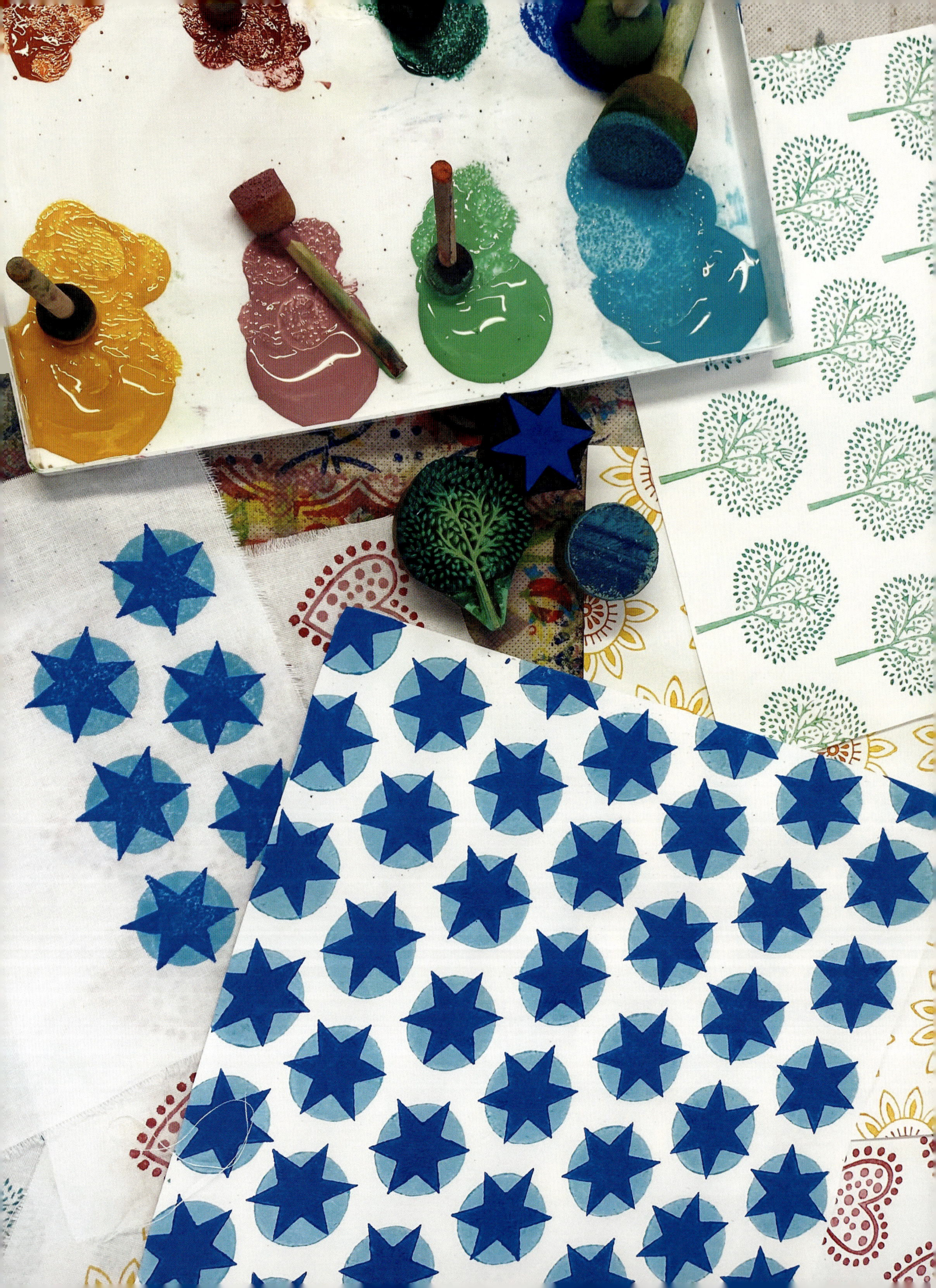

Things You Need to Know

Fabric and blank items to print on

A wonderful aspect of block printing is that you can print on nearly any fabric you can find. We often pick up items to print onto from shops such as Dunelm, H&M and IKEA, which all offer good-quality blank fabrics such as napkins, tablecloths and cushion covers. You can also look at upcycling old fabrics, which you might have at home or find in charity stores.

We would suggest pre-washing any fabric or blank items that you purchase before printing. Some materials are treated with a stiffener, which can affect the way the paint is absorbed by the fabric. By pre-washing your fabric you can be assured it is safe for printing, and any shrinkage that might occur will happen before printing.

Practise, practise, practise

When printing with a new design or before starting any project, it's important to practise. Every block prints differently and will require a unique amount of pressure or attention when printing. You need to know how each print works before using it properly, and the only way you can do this is by practising. We often say, 'You have to get it wrong, before you get it right.' This can be the case with most printing blocks: the first couple of times you print with it you might not get the perfect print, but as you get to know and understand the design, your prints will get better and better.

Once you start moving on to the projects in this book, we would suggest reading through each project and then practising the design and spacing with your printing blocks onto scrap fabric before moving on to the actual item you are going to print. This will save making any unnecessary mistakes.

If it fails, try again

Something we often notice with guests in our workshops is that if a block doesn't print correctly, or prints in a way they hadn't envisaged, they put it aside. We would always suggest persevering with it; it can knock your confidence if you make a mistake and then don't try again to improve next time. You can spend as much time as you need practising with a design until you get your desired result.

Printing blocks get better with time

As they start to get used, printing blocks will soften to the paint and will print better and better over time. If at first your prints are a little light, you will find that by having a couple more goes, the prints will improve each time.

Heat Setting

Most fabric or textile paints require heat setting to fix the paint onto the material, making it permanent and washable. Ensure you correctly follow the instructions on the paint label as each brand of paint can vary.

If a fabric paint requires heat setting, ensure the fabric is fully dry before ironing – this stage will reduce any fading of the paint during washing. It's an important step so please take your time to ensure it's done properly.

Lay your dry, printed fabric on the ironing board with the print side facing up. You can iron directly on top of the paint (unless instructions state otherwise). The water-based fabric paint we use, for example, does not come off on the iron or smudge when completely dry.

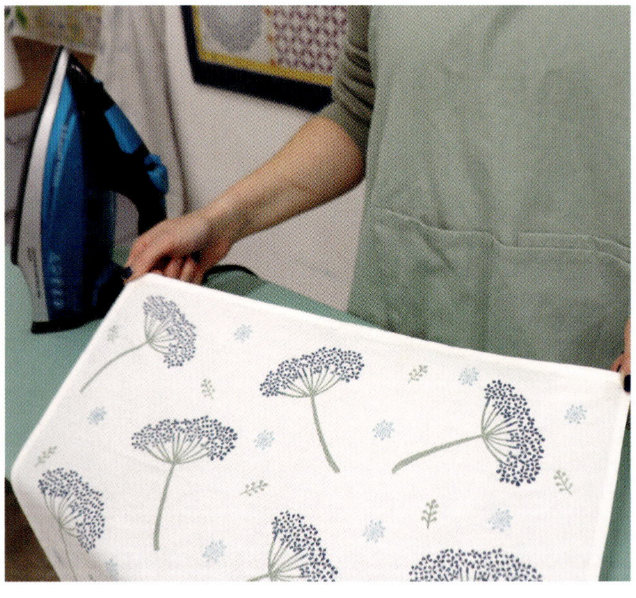

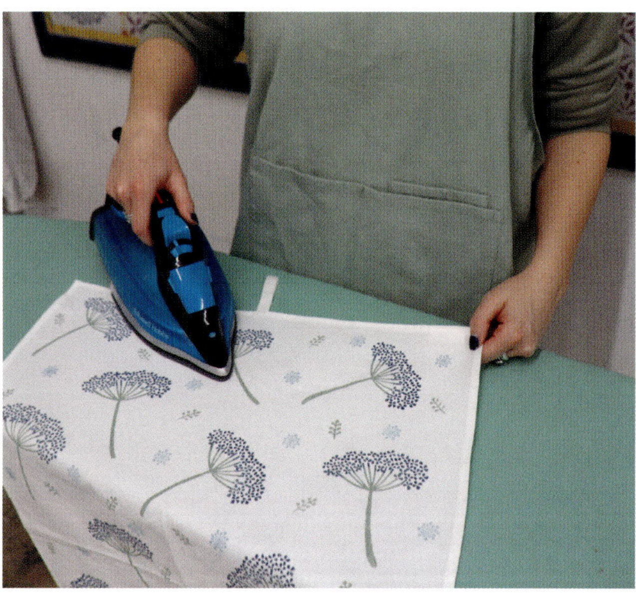

1 Using a dry or steam iron – we prefer steam as it penetrates the fabric better – gently move the iron across the entire piece of fabric, ensuring each print gets almost too hot to touch. Do not leave the iron in one place for too long as the fabric will burn. Iron the fabric for a generous period of time to ensure it is thoroughly heat set.

2 After heat setting, your material will be protected from fading when washed.

Washing Your Printing Blocks

After each printing session it's very important to throughly wash both your printing blocks and equipment to keep your supplies in the best condition. If paint, especially acrylic paint, is left on the printing block to dry for too long it will obstruct the detail of the design over time. Note that not all printing blocks are suitable for washing, so please check any instructions provided by the manufacturer.

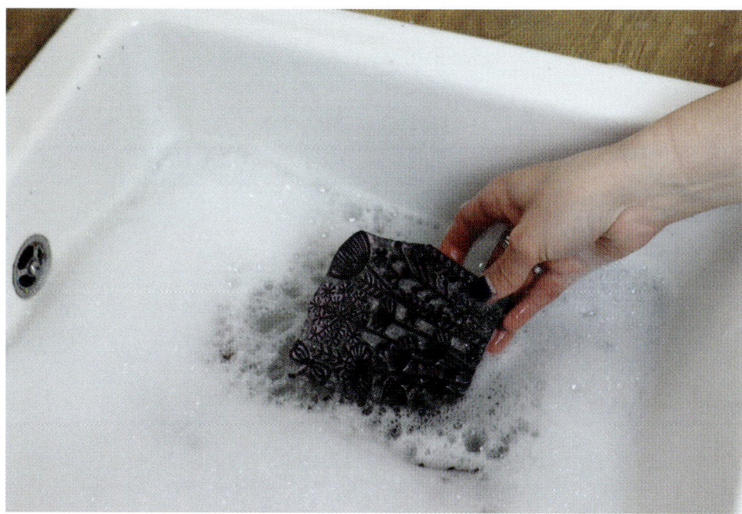

1 Run a bowl of hot, soapy water and leave your printing blocks submerged to soak for no longer than 5 minutes.

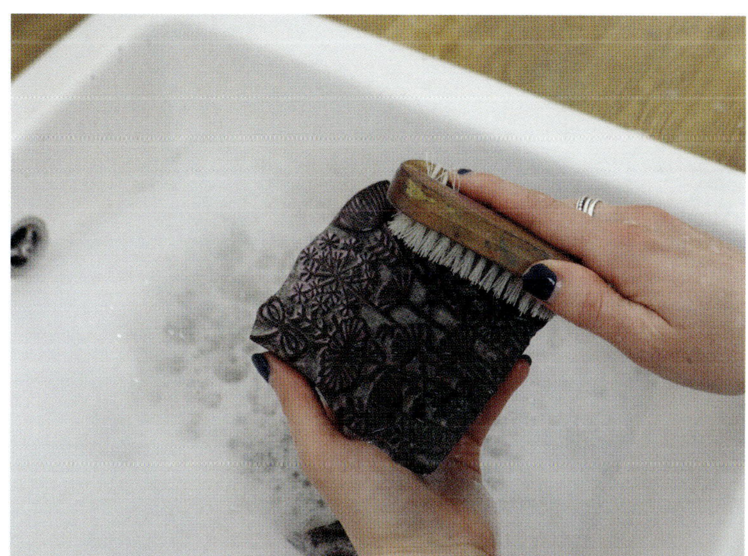

2 Using a medium stiffness nail brush and soap, scrub the surface and the edges of the design, to remove any paint from the details.

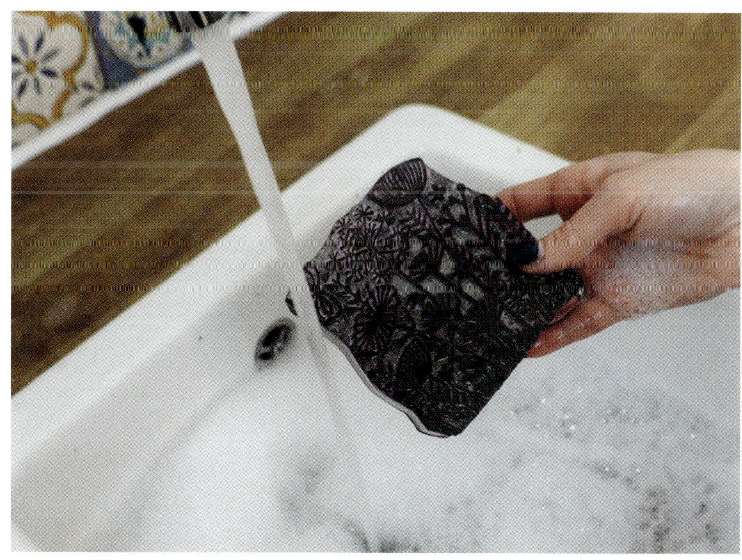

3 Rinse under clean water to remove soap and paint residue. Leave to dry fully before packing away.

PART 2

Advanced Printing Techniques

Once you've mastered the basics, this section will help you expand your printing skills. Using our simple practices, tips and tricks, you'll deepen your technical knowledge and improve your ability to create high-quality prints and designs.

Some of these advanced techniques might be challenging at first, so we recommend practising on scrap fabric to ease the pressure of making mistakes. Remember, there's no need to master these techniques immediately. As you work through the projects in this book and develop your own printing style, your confidence and skills will naturally grow, making these techniques feel easier with practice.

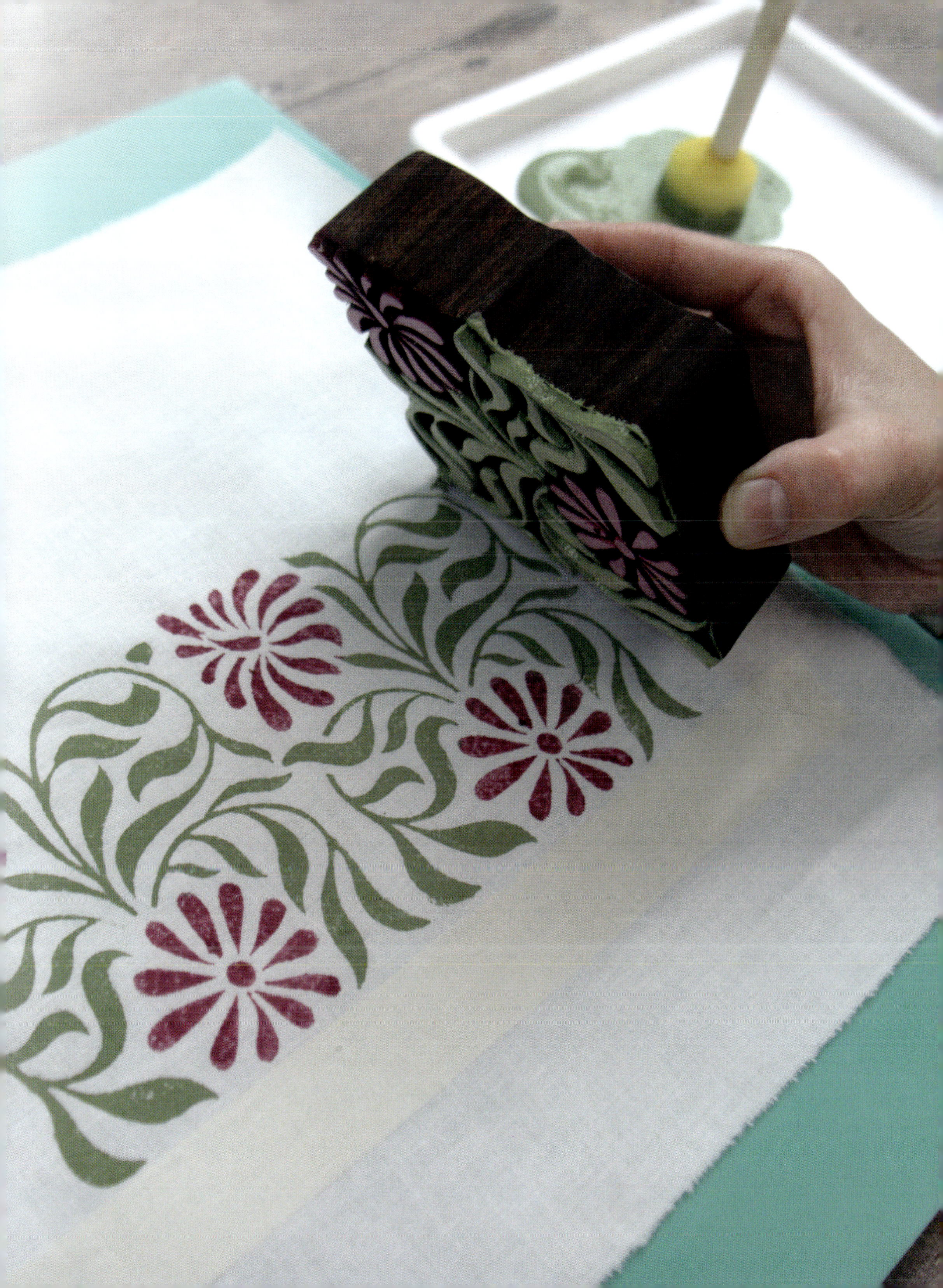

The Fold and Iron Technique

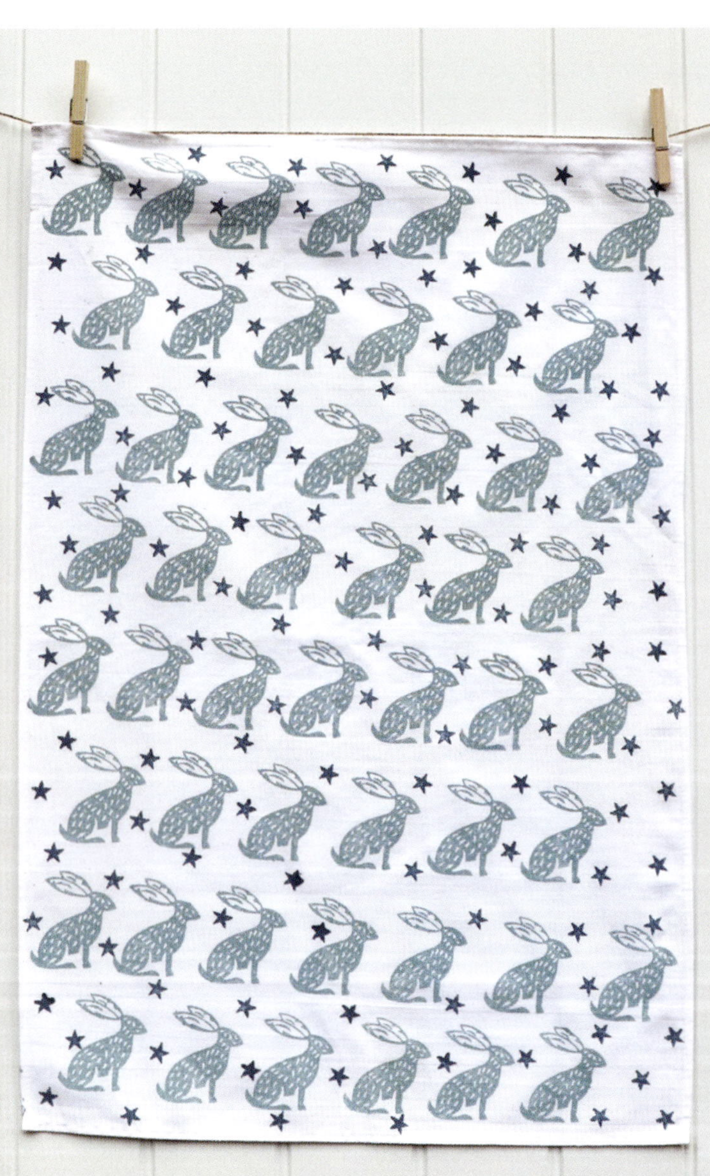

Understanding spacing and knowing how to work it out before starting a project is an important factor for every printer to understand. Without this knowledge, you may lack the confidence to start certain projects, or never be happy with the finished results. Each project talks you through the spacing that you will need to follow during the steps, but once you start printing your own creations, you'll need to know how to do this yourself. Spacing can be difficult to work out by eye, which is why we have a couple of handy tips to help you get started.

If you are planning to print a design all over a piece of fabric in straight lines (we refer to this as a straight line repeat), you need to know how many prints you can fit across the width and height of your fabric. In the activity shown, we worked out that we could fit four prints down the height and width of our square of fabric. This method works with all shapes of fabric; take the time to work out your spacing and fold the fabric.

To replicate this pattern on paper, use a ruler and pencil to measure the page into equal segments and faintly mark each box. After printing, you can rub out the pencil marks.

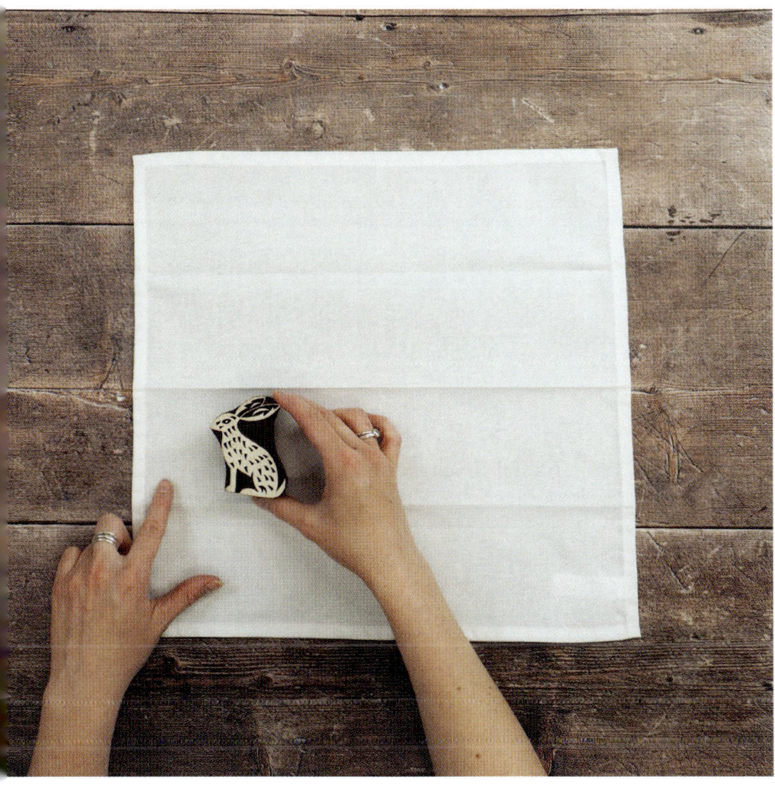

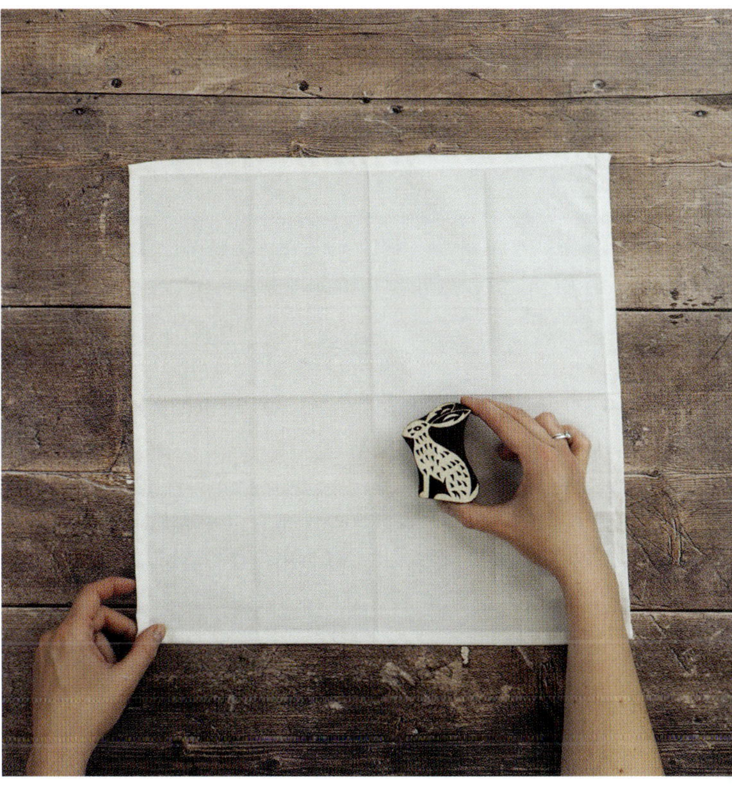

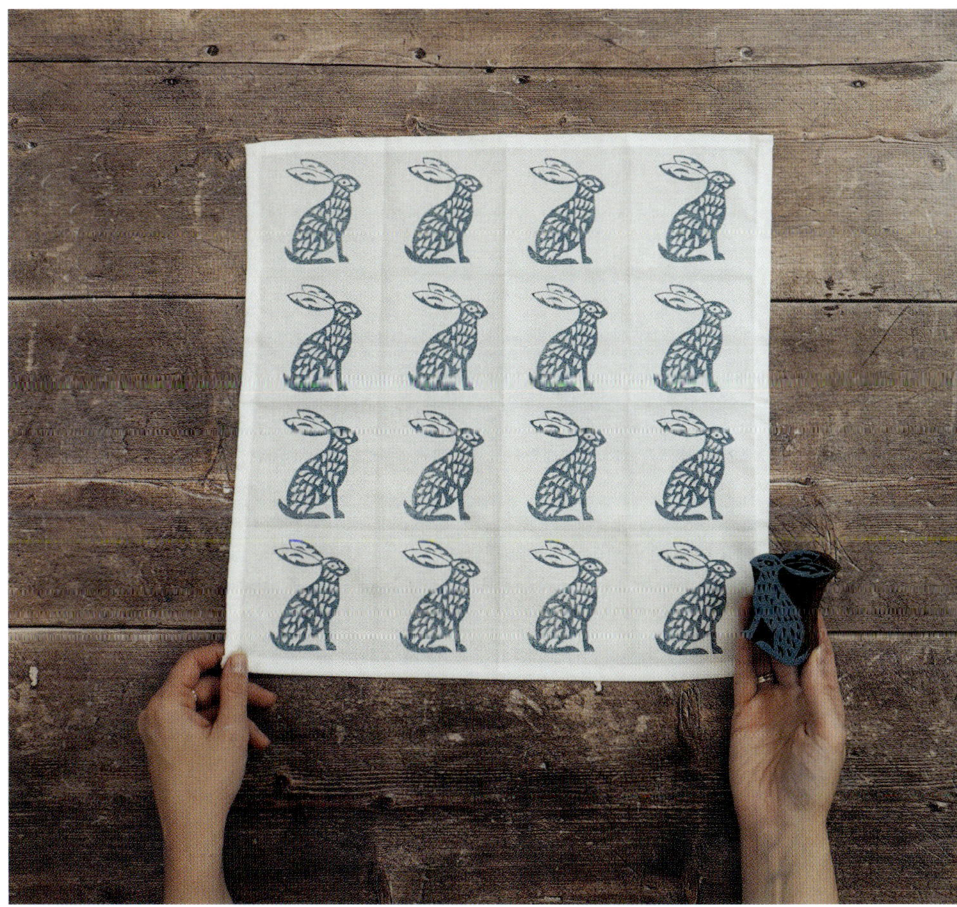

1 Hold the printing block onto the fabric to measure how wide you will need each row to be, then fold the fabric to form the number of rows you require. Iron the fold lines and then unfold the fabric to reveal the crease marks, which will perfectly outline where your four rows of prints should go.

2 You can use the same fold and iron technique to work out how many prints you can fit across the width of your fabric. When you unfold your fabric, you'll be left with a grid system showing you exactly where to print within

3 Print your design centrally in each square (see one-colour printing, page 21), and you'll be left with a perfectly spaced piece of printed fabric.

The Block Carving Process

In Sanganer we get the chance to visit our own block carvers and take a closer look at how the printing block is carved from the piece of wood. A variety of wood types is used to make printing blocks. You'll find soft, low-cost wood such as mango wood in the markets being sold to tourists, whereas printing houses will have their designs carved onto a higher quality wood, such as teak or sheesham, which is a hard, sustainably forested wood, robust enough to withstand the demands of daily printing. The sheesham is cut and purchased from managed forests in rural India, and then brought back to the carvers' workshop to dry.

Wood-block carving in India is a skill passed down through the generations of a family. The master carvers are often the grandparents who then train younger family members to be able to carry on the work. Wood-block carving has typically been considered a prosperous job, since carvers are able to remain at home to complete their work and don't have to travel into the city. With the modernisation of India, we have seen a decrease over the years in the number of younger carvers learning the skill. However, as long as the demand for hand-block printing remains high, we hope the wood-carving industry will continue for many years to come.

The first step in the process is to whiten the wood with a chalky paint mixture, after which the exact scale of the design is traced onto the wood using pencil.

The carvers use a mixture of tools to carve the design. The metal carving tools are a *kalam* – a chisel-like tool which comes in a mixture of shapes and sizes – and a wooden hammer. The hammer is used to tap the *kalam*, which in turn chips away at the wood. The outline and the detail of the design are carved away first, known as the 'negative' part of the design. The remaining raised area is known as the 'positive'.

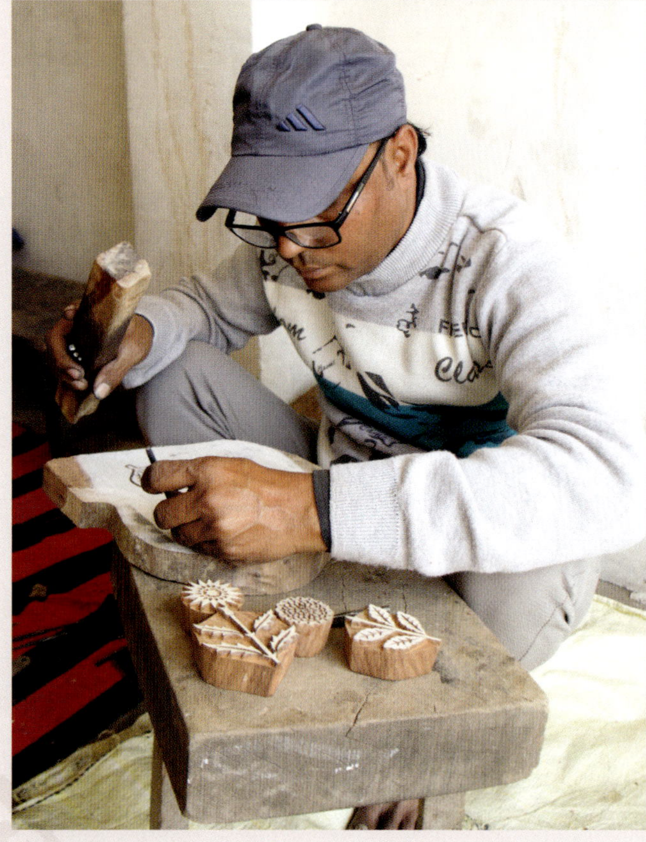

Above: Bhanu, a master block carver in Sanganer, carving into sheesham wood.

The carving process leaves as little waste as possible. Carvers fit as many designs onto a piece of wood as they can. Any remaining wood is then used for miniature designs, and anything left is used for firewood.

Once the carving is complete, a machine cuts precisely around the design and a sanding machine is used to smooth the edges. The printing blocks are then soaked in mustard seed oil, a process that strengthens the wood and stops the printing block absorbing any paint or water, increasing its longevity.

The finished printing blocks are works of art themselves, with hours of working and a unique carving 'signature' going into every block.

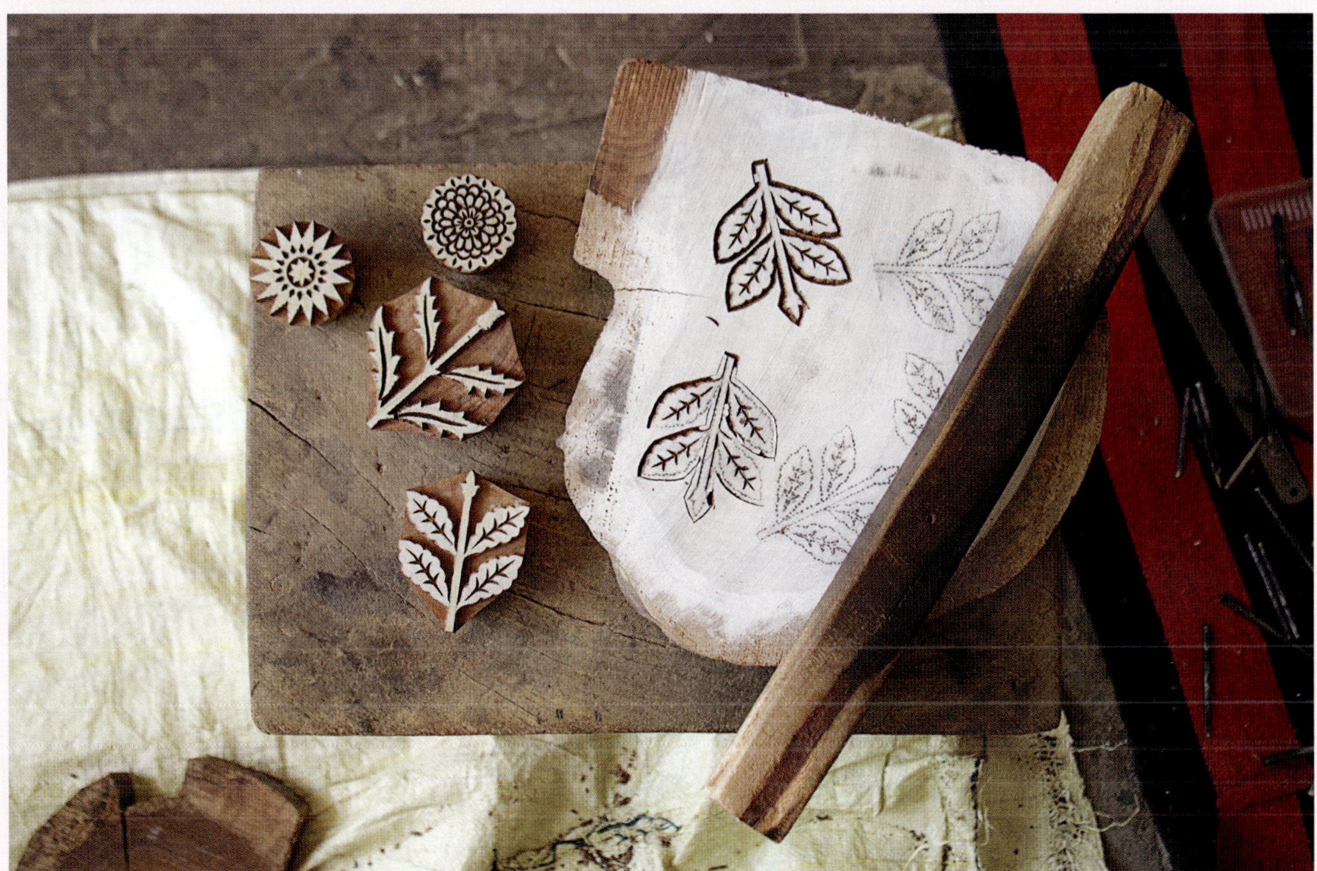

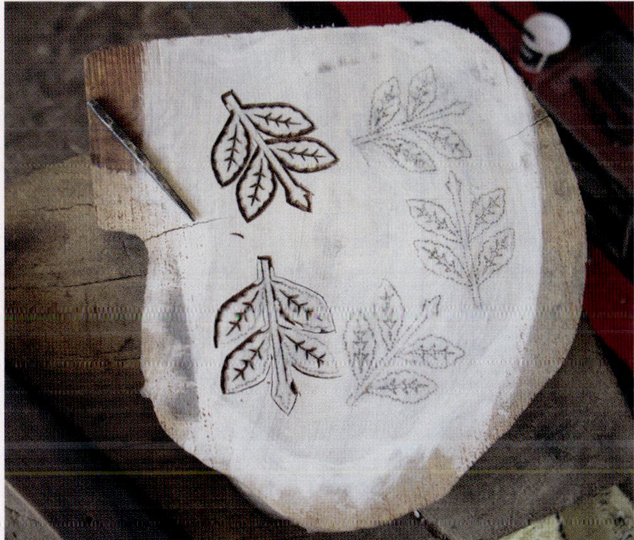

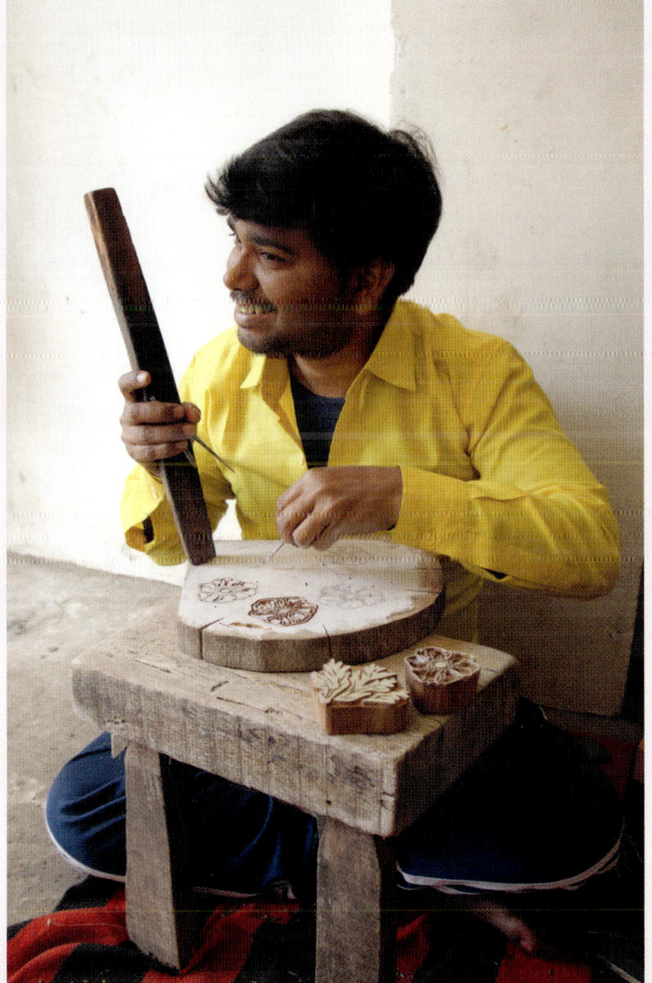

Top: Carved printing blocks alongside designs in process.

Above: Partially carved designs into sheesham wood.

Left: Sanjay carving our designs onto sheesham wood in Sanganer.

Random Printing

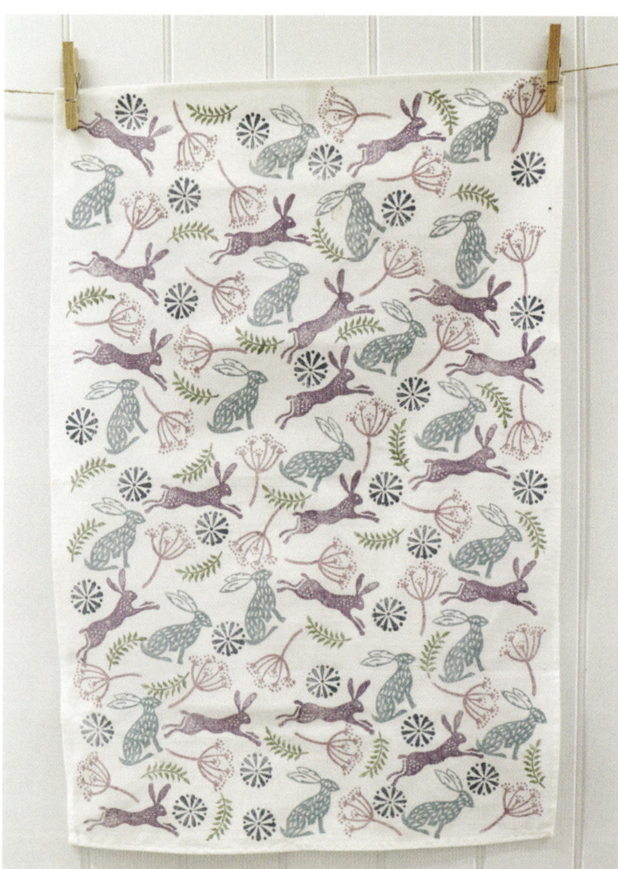

Random printing is a technique that block printers can struggle with. The process can often be overthought and feel difficult, and it's easy to lose sight of how the pattern should look. The following printing tips should put a method to the madness!

We have developed a technique that you can use when printing a random, 'all over' pattern that involves printing each design in order, one at a time. This method takes the randomness out of the process: by thinking about the placement of each design you gradually build up a 'random' printed effect in a manageable way, which is easy to replicate.

In this pattern we are printing with five designs and using five colours that tonally all work together. The order in which we printed our designs was: Sitting Hare, Country Seedhead, Leaping Hare, Twisted Leaf Stem, then Circle Flower.

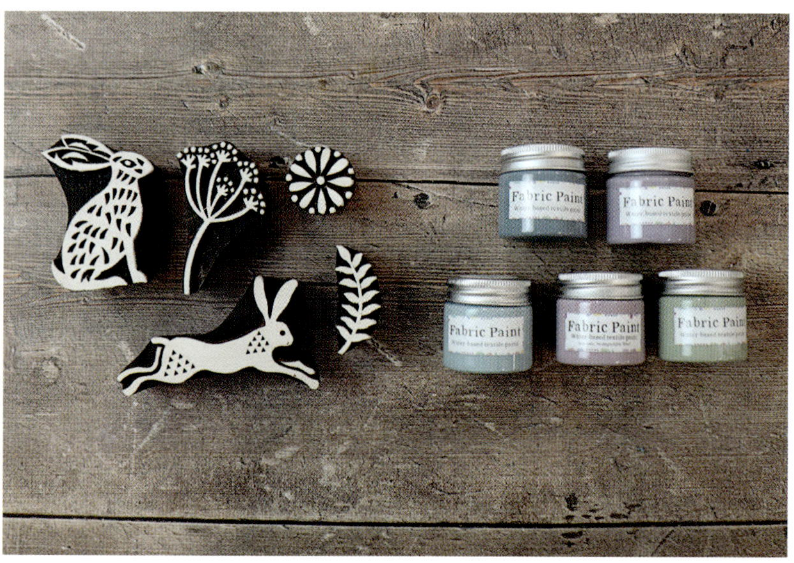

1 When printing in a 'random' pattern, it's important to start with the right colours and printing blocks. Use a set of printing blocks whose designs all work together and print with the same amount of colours as you have printing blocks. Use around five designs in a variety of sizes, with the biggest designs being the main focal point. Smaller prints will be used as 'fillers'; these help fill in the white space and bring the design together. It's good to use designs that have a natural twist in them; you don't want anything too rigid.

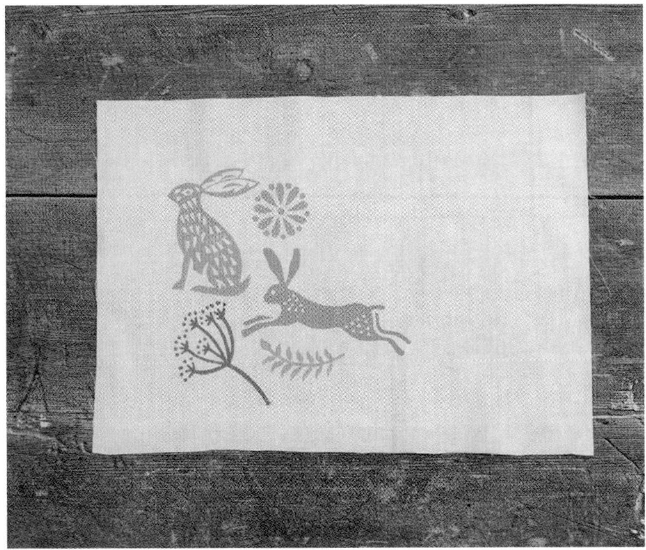

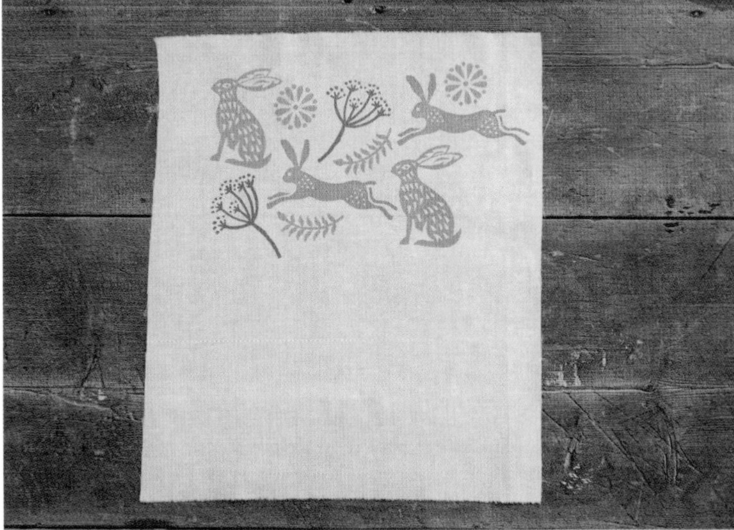

2 Pick an order in which you will print each design and line them up on the table in front of you. Start with your biggest design and work your way down in size. Choose a colour for each design, and stick with this colour for the entirety of your printed pattern. Print each design in order (see one-colour printing, page 21), working through blocks one to five.

3 Print each design in the same order, one after another, to create a cluster. Ensure you are printing close to the other designs to reduce the amount of white space between each print, but don't leave too big a gap or overlap them. Carefully position each print, changing the direction and angle to help the design fit into the space. You may need to swap designs around so you don't have two of the same next to each other.

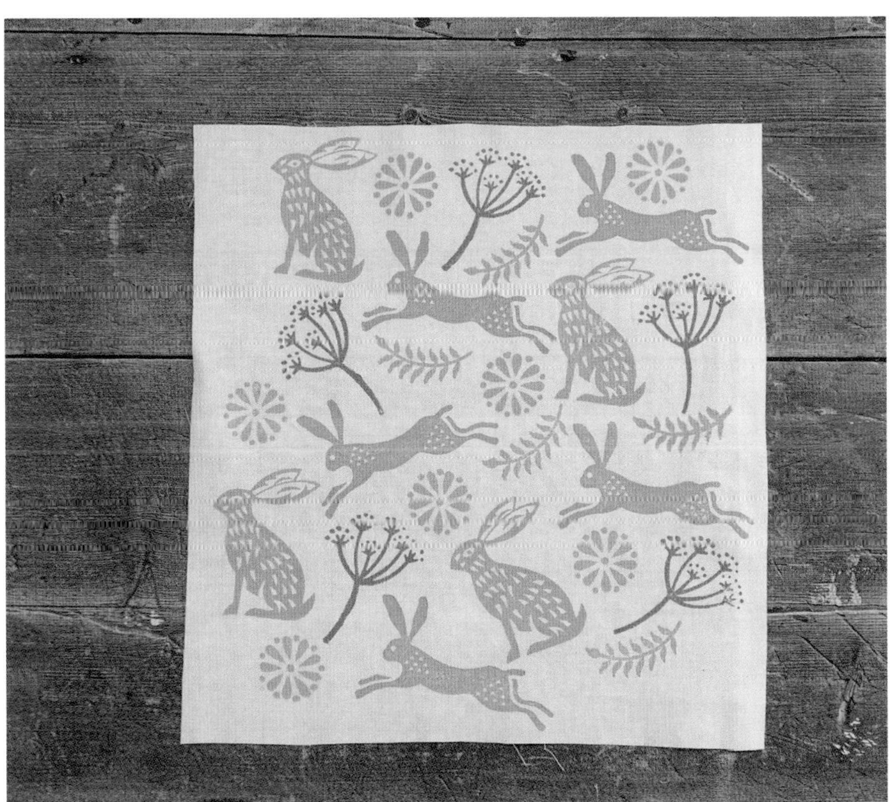

4 It's important to slightly change the direction of each print to help the design to feel free-flowing and random. For example, if you printed the Leaping Hare straight, make sure you print it facing down the next time. Continue with this method until your entire piece of fabric is covered. If you have any gaps, use smaller designs to fill them in or introduce a new mini design in a new colour.

Pattern Repeats

As well as straight line and random printing, there are other layout options for you to try. Knowing the different forms of repeats and how they work will help you progress with your printing, allowing you access to a range of pattern options to choose from when starting a printed creation and widening your knowledge and capability. We talk about certain types of pattern repeats during the projects; you can refer to this section to understand the printing placement.

The easiest way to experiment with different repeating patterns and placements at home is to create a line guide (examples can be found on our website, see page 143). We create ours using an A3 piece of paper, and using a pencil and ruler draw lines that show the spacing for various pattern types.

Straight line repeat

In block printing a straight or block repeat pattern refers to a design where the printed designs are aligned both horizontally and vertically in a grid-like formation. Each block is placed directly next to its neighbours, creating a consistent and uniform pattern. The motifs in this type of repeat align perfectly in rows and columns, resulting in a structured and orderly appearance.

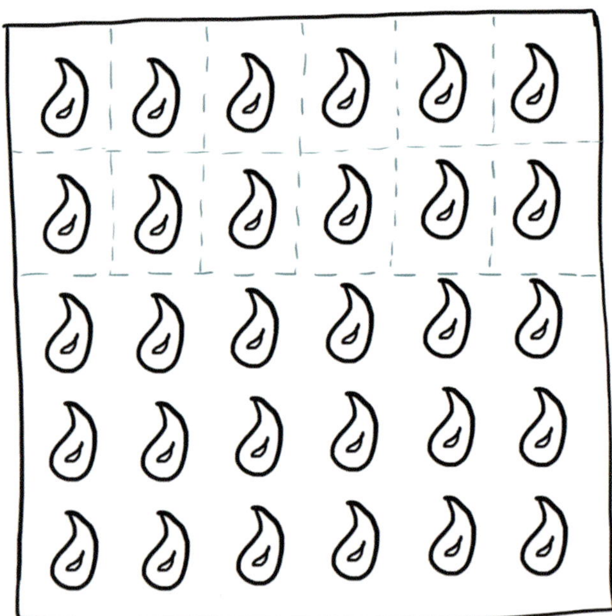

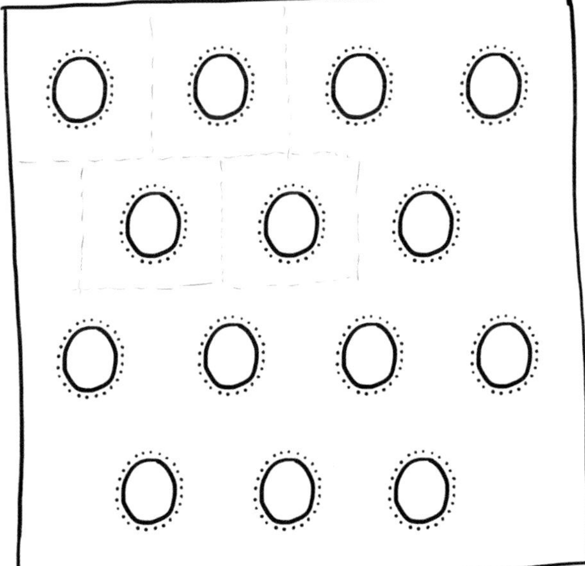

Brick repeat

A brick repeat is a pattern layout where the blocks are aligned in a staggered manner, as bricks are laid in a wall. Each row of blocks is offset by half the width of the block from the rows above and below it. This creates a repetitive yet visually dynamic pattern, where the motifs do not align vertically but are instead shifted to create a sense of movement and continuity.

Half-drop repeat

A half-drop repeat pattern is a design where each row of blocks is offset by half the height of the block from the row above and below it, normally when working on the vertical. This creates a staggered, diagonal effect, as each block in a new row is positioned halfway down the block in the previous row. This type of repeat helps to break up the uniformity and can add a sense of movement and flow to the printed fabric or surface.

Half-drop diamond repeat

A half-drop diamond repeat pattern is a design in which each block is offset diagonally, forming a diamond shape. This pattern involves aligning blocks so that the motifs create a diamond configuration, with each subsequent row of blocks shifted halfway both horizontally and vertically. This results in a visually appealing and intricate pattern where the motifs appear in a diamond-like arrangement, providing a sense of complexity to the printed fabric. It is a common pattern repeat found on Indian printed fabrics but only works with certain designs.

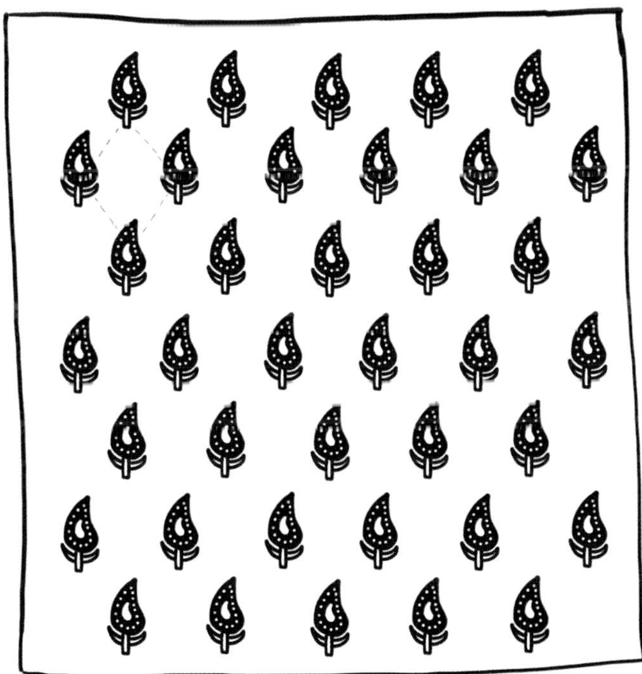

Block Printing in Bagru

If you want to try your hand at block printing, you'll be able to find workshops across India, but if you are looking to experience the home of block printing, then Bagru – situated to the west of Jaipur – is the place to visit. Every house and business within the village play some part in the journey of a piece of printed fabric.

Walking through Bagru, you'll see colourful fabric hanging from buildings and dyed fabric covering the ground, drying in the Indian sun in a space known as the 'drying fields', an area of land shared by the residents. The ground here remains permanently dyed in colourful shades.

Whether it's preparing the fabric, block printing, washing, dyeing, ironing or packaging, in Bagru the work is shared by the residents. Artisans work together in the production of printed and dyed textiles. Every building and workshop is involved in some part of the journey; it's not often you'll find one factory that does it all. The work is sent out to the relevant departments (if you're putting it in modern terms), and hand-block printing is just one part along the chain of processes that are carried out to create a piece of hand-printed fabric.

Wandering through the narrow lanes, if you pop your head into a building, it's likely you'll find someone block printing. Many forms of printing are carried out in Bagru, from Dabu (printing with mud) to pigment printing and natural dye printing (which is commonly known as 'Bagru print').

The block printers work on long, padded tables, enabling them to print metres of fabric at once. Typically, these printers will be producing a design that involves a multi-layered print. The design will be

Below: Bagru's drying fields.

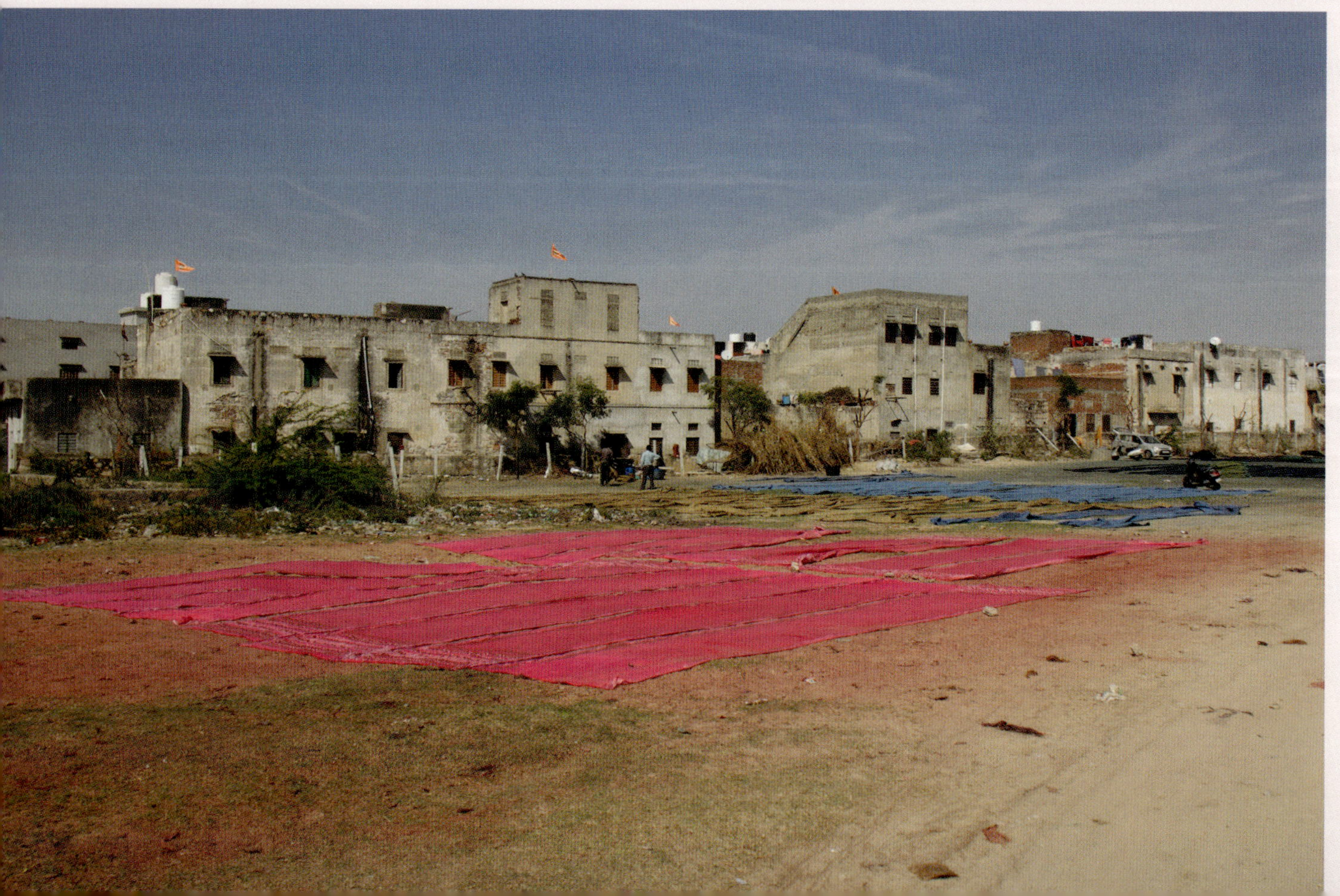

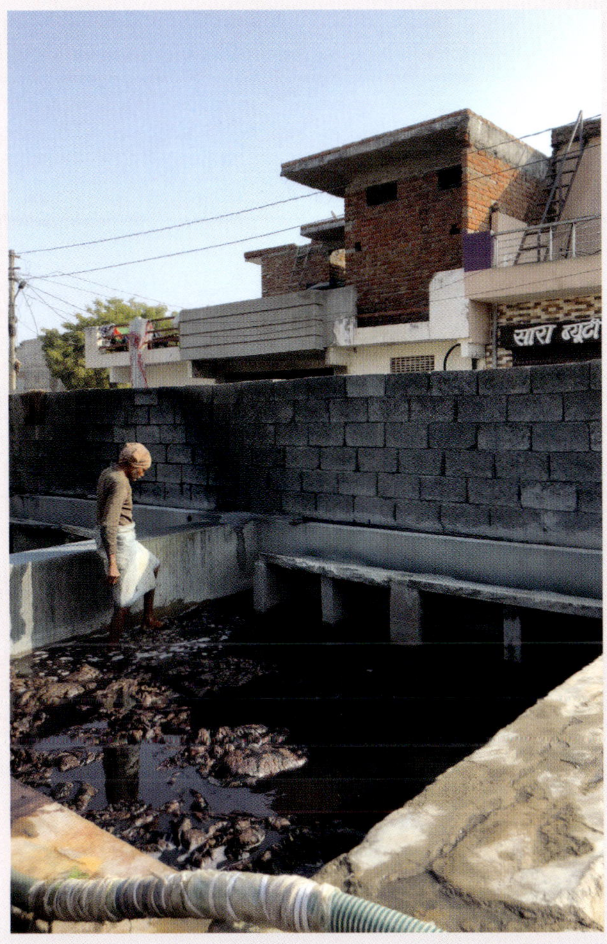

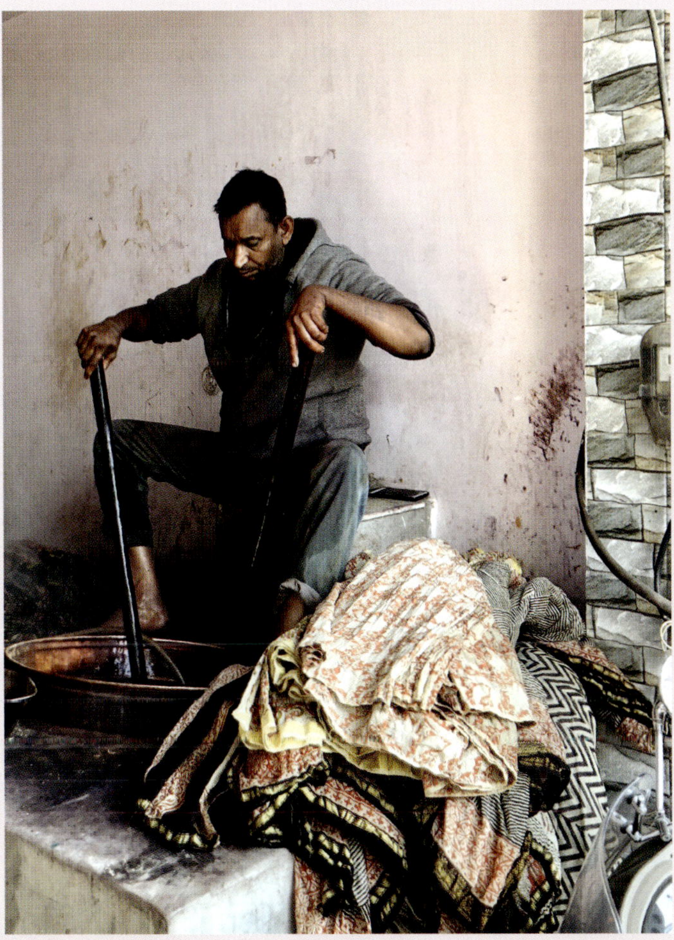

Above left: Hand-printed fabric going through a washing process.

Above: Naturally dyed fabric going through a boiling process.

Left: Colourful fabrics drying in Bagru.

Below: Master block printer in Bagru.

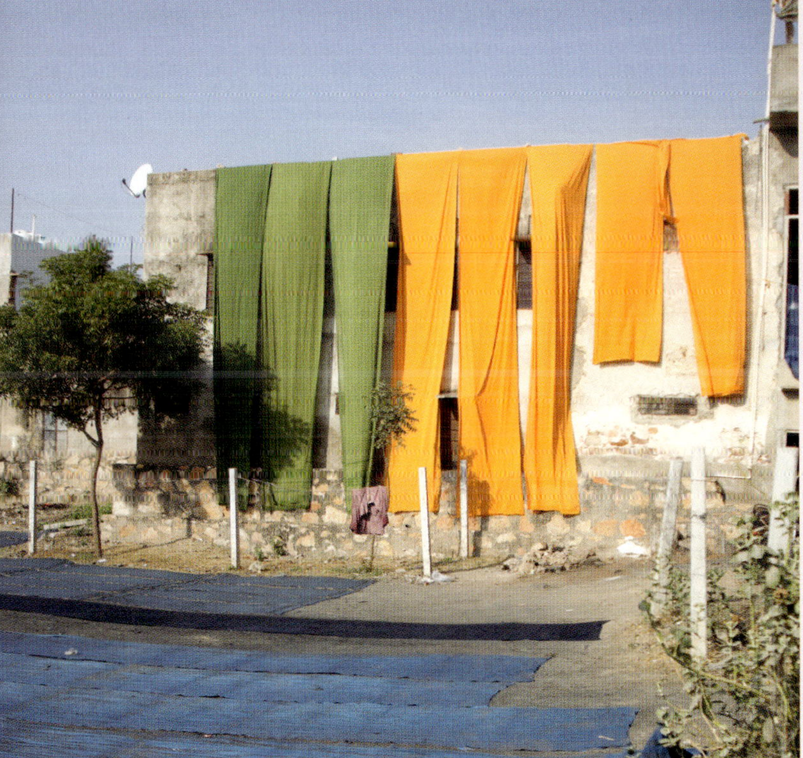

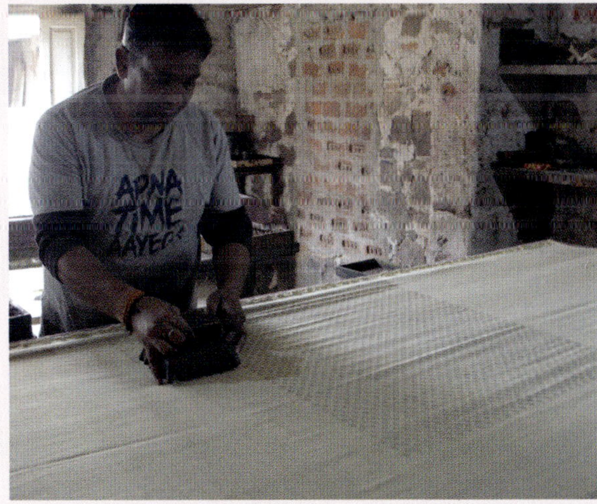

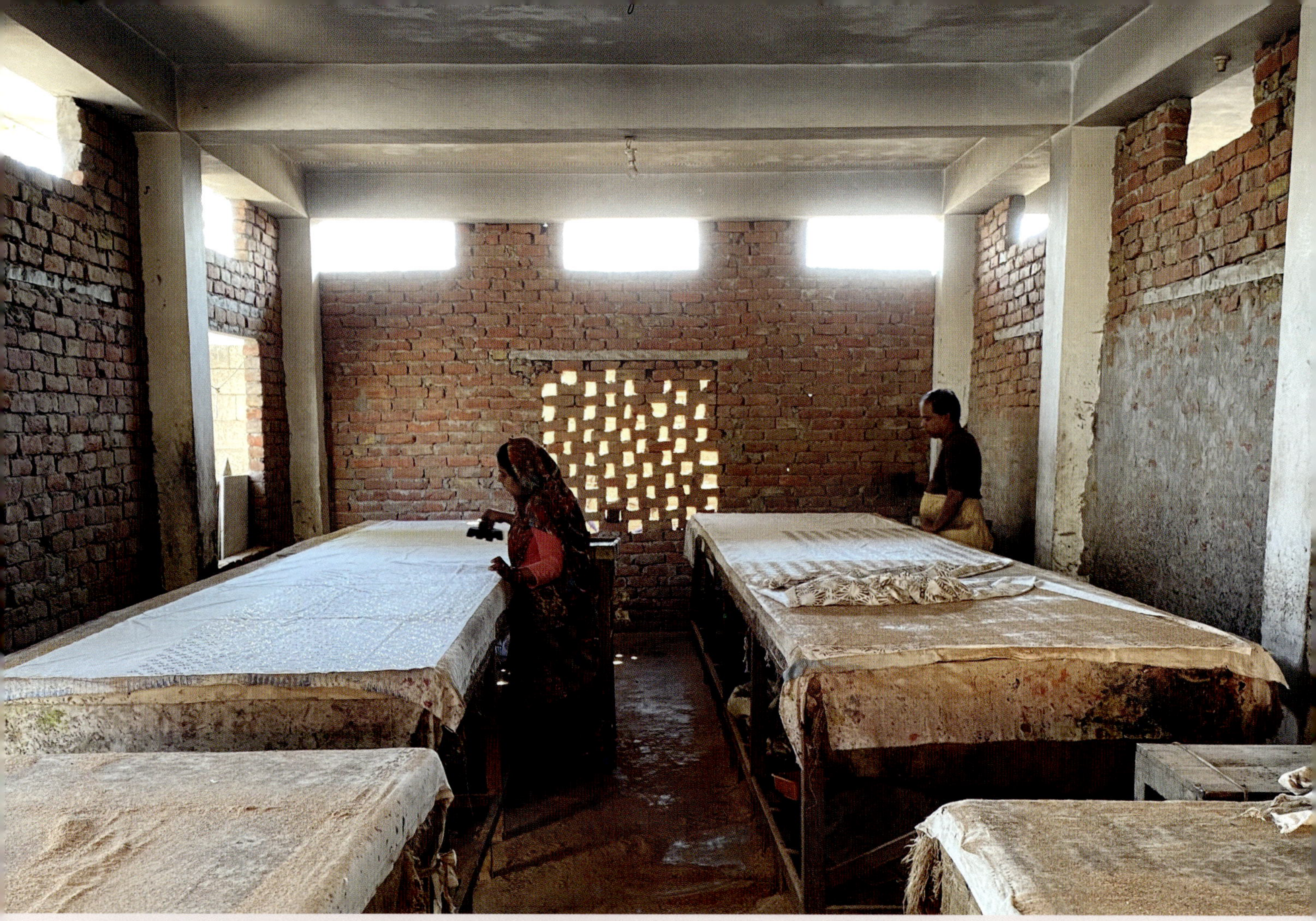

The photo at the top shows a Dabu printing studio in Bagru.

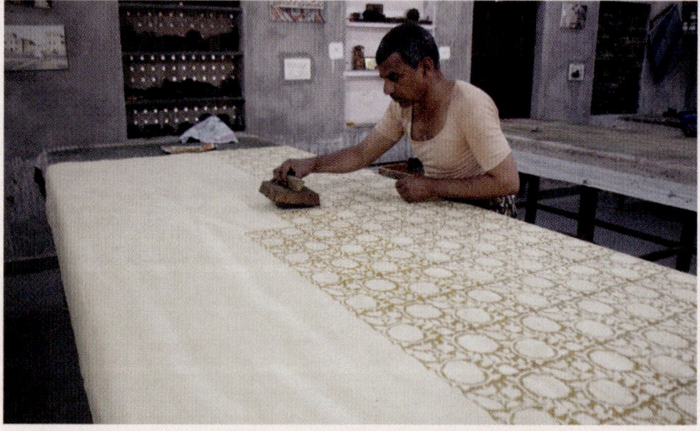

Above: Dabu printing studio in Bagru.

Left: Printing in a studio in Bagru.

There's something truly special about Bagru. Visiting the village is always a highlight of our trips to India, full of learning and inspiration. Away from the loud noises of Jaipur, the village seems serene, even with all the residents hard at work. Cows happily wander the streets and children play cricket on the drying fields in any space available that isn't taken up with drying fabric.

Bagru feels resourceful – the residents use the space and materials available to them. For example, we heat set our fabric using an iron to make the paint or dye permanent, whereas they use the sun. We use pigment paint, whereas they can use natural dyes from the materials they have around them. We highly recommend anyone who visits India or Jaipur to go to Bagru, both to take a tour around the village to learn more about how the artisans of India work and to book on to a printing workshop.

made up of three, four or sometimes five individual block prints. They are printed one at a time, each in a different colour, building up the overall design until the pattern is completed. Often, the master block printers are older and more experienced, since it's a technique that requires much skill and precision and can take years to learn. Block-printed fabric is often not quite perfect. Due to the handmade factor, small defects in the printed fabric can occur, but this is all part of the charm.

Printing With Borders

Our favourite printing style involves using border designs to outline a printed creation. Most hand-block printed fabric from India features a border design around the edges. We first encountered this technique of printing detailed straight-line border designs in Bagru, working alongside master block printers.

You can find a wide variety of border designs, from intricate patterns to solid straight lines. They all require the same printing technique to ensure they print straight and match up on either end to create a continuous print.

Practise this on scrap fabric, as it can take multiple attempts to get it right. Some borders are harder to print than others; we suggest starting with a less detailed design and working towards more intricate patterns as your confidence builds. The following steps will help you to develop your border-printing skills further.

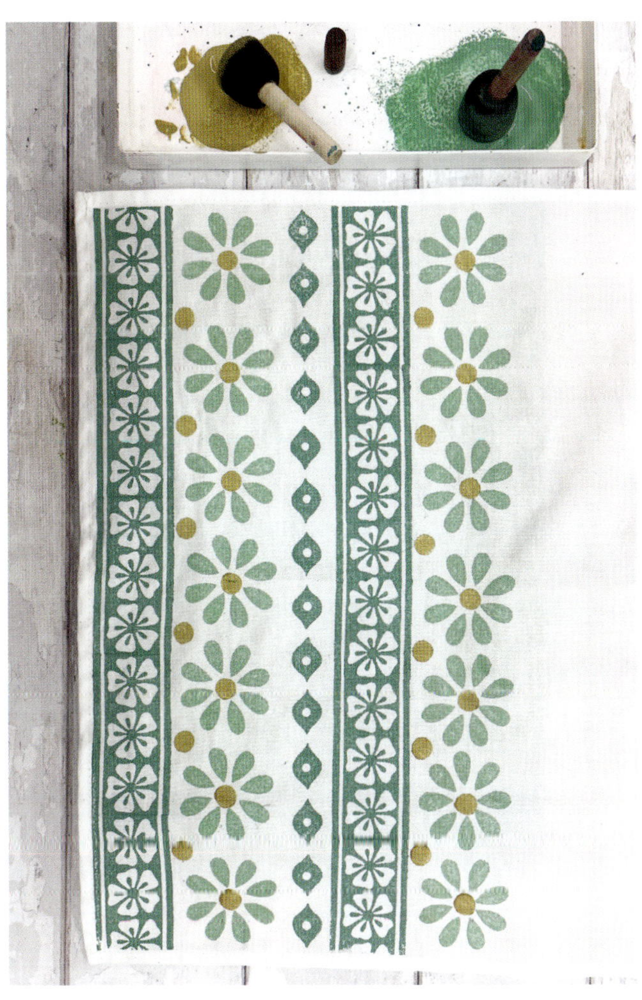

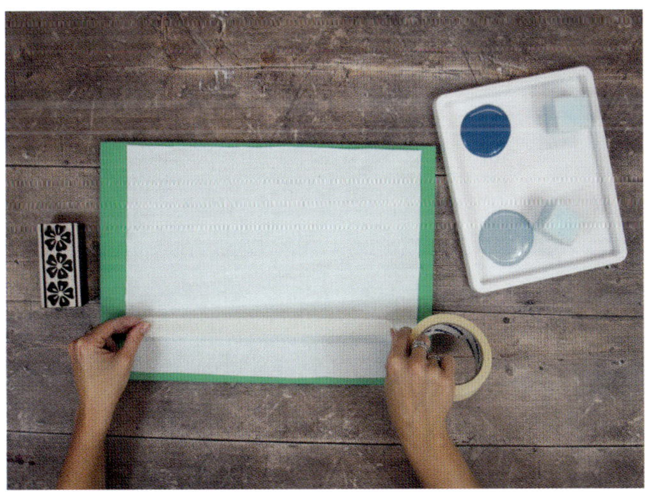

1   When printing in a straight line, it's important you have one to follow. The fabric you are printing may have a straight line; if it doesn't, you can fold and iron a crease mark into it. Alternatively, put a strip of masking tape down onto the item you are printing, then print alongside (not on) the tape to keep the design as straight as possible.

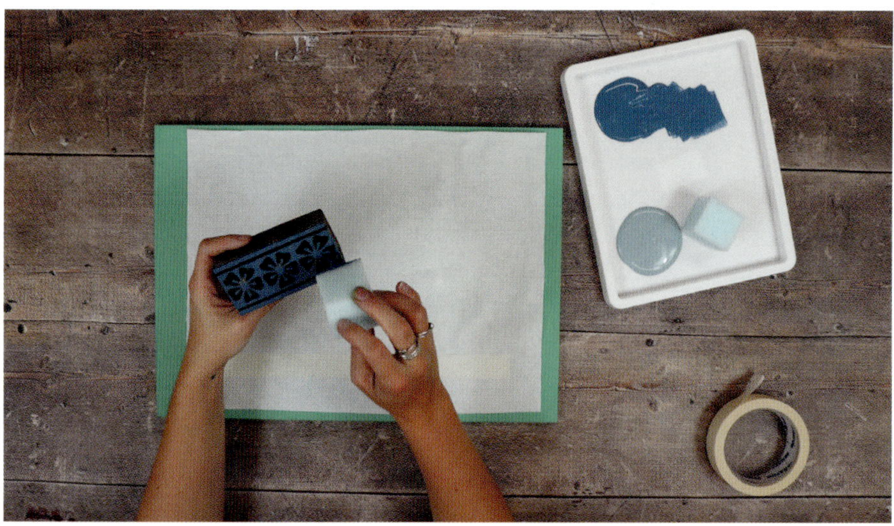

2 Apply the paint to your border design printing block (see one-colour printing, page 21).

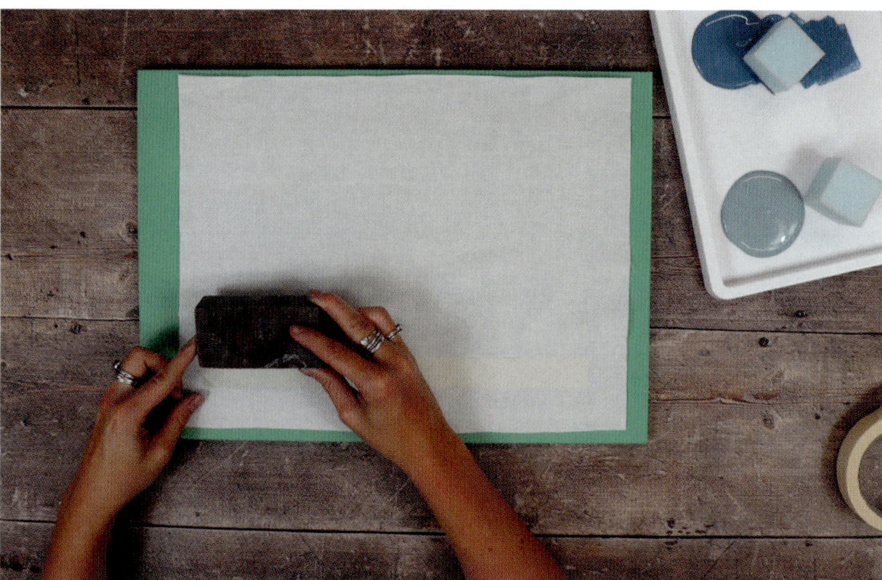

3 Starting with the bottom-left corner of the printing block, touch the bottom edge to your material, just above the masking tape. Touching just one corner down first gives you full control over the printing block and how it is positioned on your material.

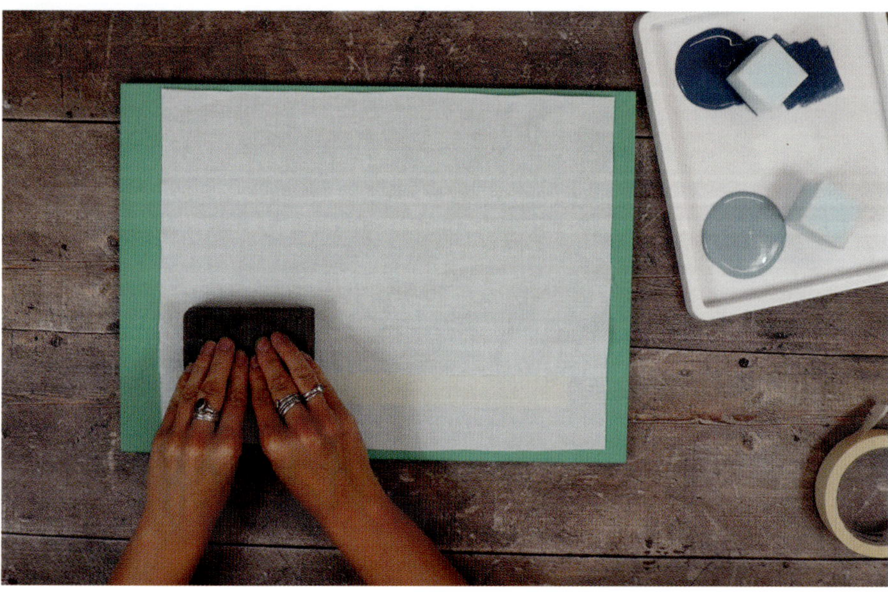

4 Once you have correctly positioned the bottom corner, use it as a pivot point and twist the printing block up or down. Allow the rest of the printing block to slowly lower down onto your material, ensuring it lines up alongside your tape. Apply pressure all over the design.

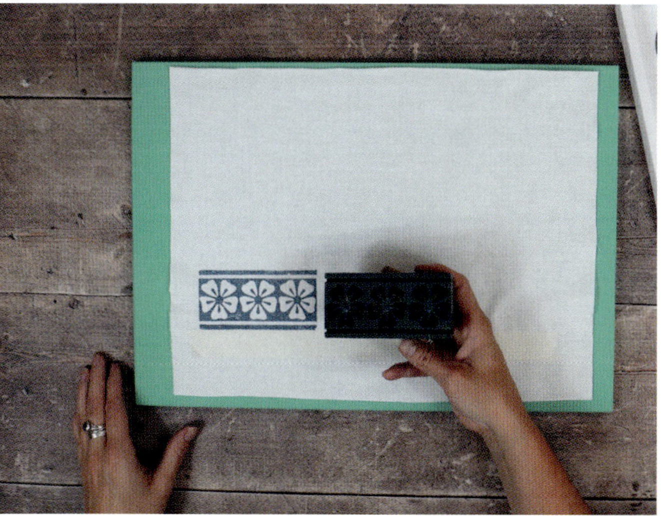

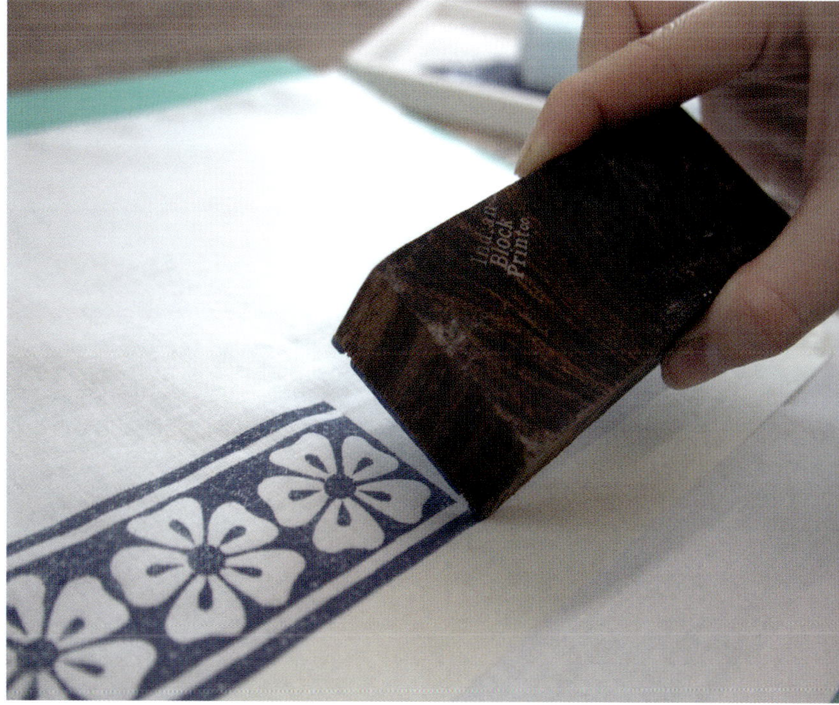

5 Lift the printing block up to reveal your print. The design should sit straight alongside your masking tape on the material. Your next print should be positioned exactly next to the previous print – they shouldn't overlap but they should touch to create a continuous pattern.

6 Print in the same way as in Step 3, touching only the bottom-left corner to the material to ensure the printing block is positioned correctly. When you are happy, allow the rest of the block to come down towards the material, using that pivot point to twist the design up or down to ensure it lines up alongside your tape.

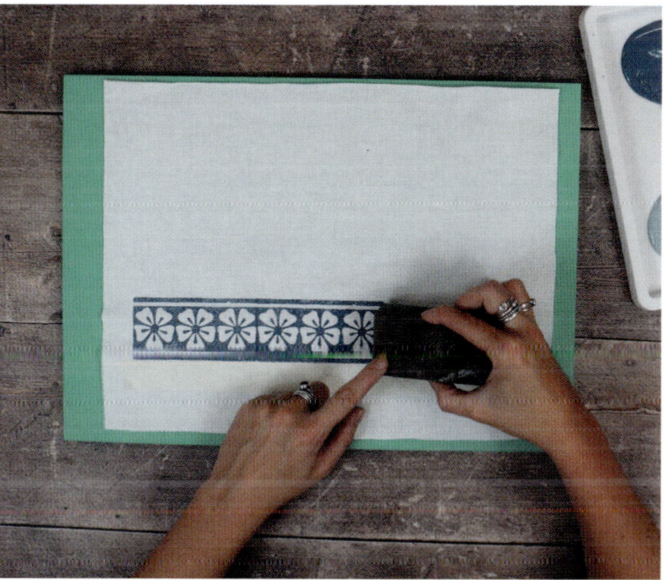

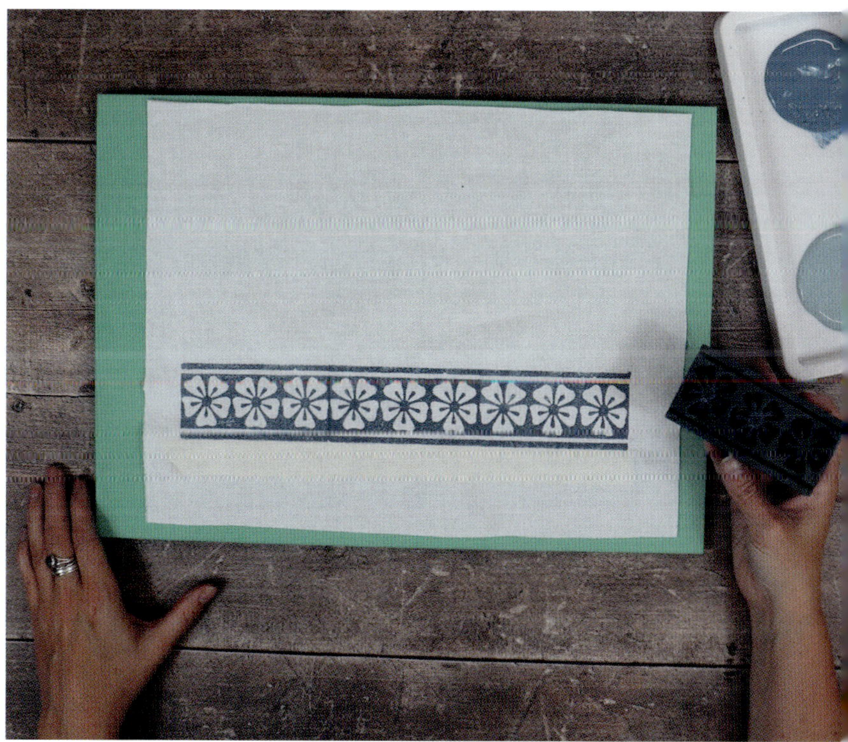

7 Repeat the process alongside your tape, adding or shifting the tape to continue your straight line.

Using Colour

Choosing the right colours for a printing project is an essential part of the creative process and can impact the final result. When a colour combination isn't quite right, it can throw the entire design off balance. For example, during one of our introductory workshops, a customer wasn't enjoying what she was printing. After chatting, we discovered she was using colours she didn't personally like because she was making something for a friend.

When you're new to printing, it's important to choose a colour palette that truly resonates with you. As you gain confidence, you'll feel more comfortable experimenting with colours outside of your comfort zone.

Throughout the printing projects (see page 56), you'll find examples of colour combinations that we believe work well together. When starting your block printing journey, it can be helpful to purchase a 'set' of paint colours that are designed to complement each other.

The Itten colour circle

Below, we've shared a couple of starter palettes that provide a versatile range of colours to work with.

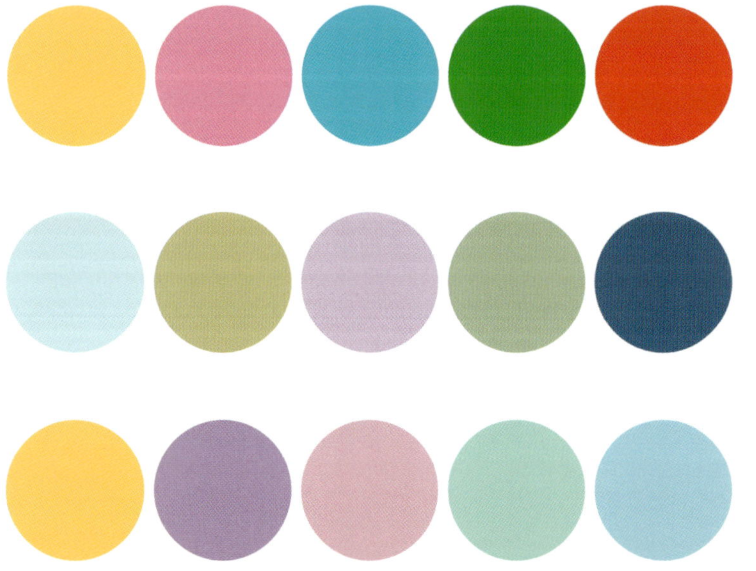

Bright
Great for using with children, fun and colourful.

Dusky
Muted more subtle tones, preferred by adults.

Pastel
Perfect for spring themed printing.

We love using tonal palettes that work well together. They're perfect for creating gifts in someone's favourite colour or matching a design to their home or kitchen. We especially enjoy printing in shades of blue, though it can be hard to step away from favourite colours. Having a variety of colour palettes on hand can inspire new creations with different colours.

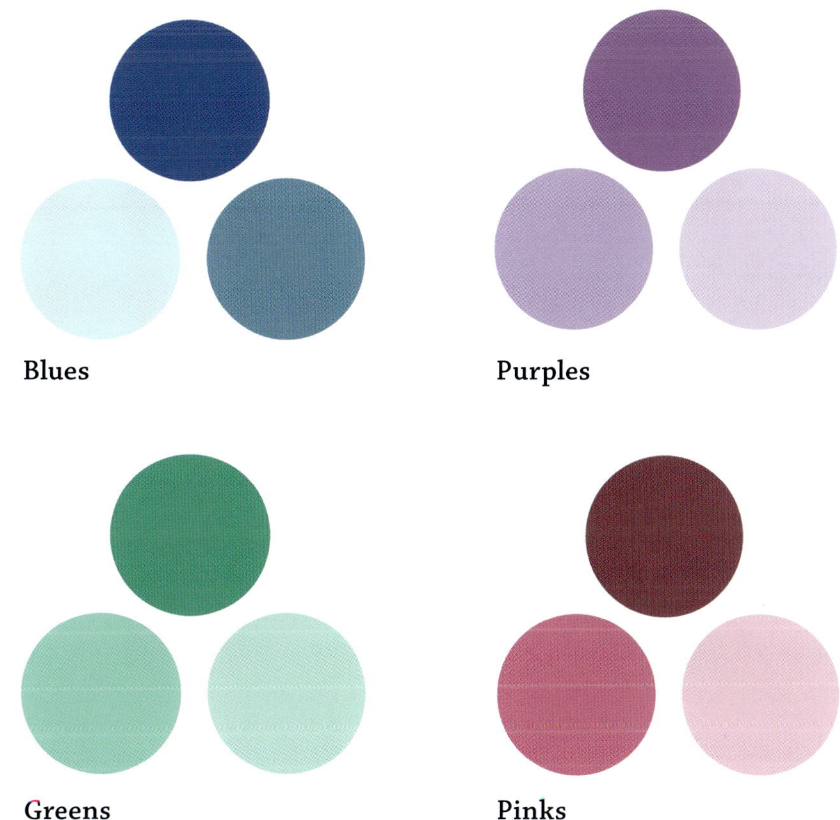

Blues

Purples

Greens

Pinks

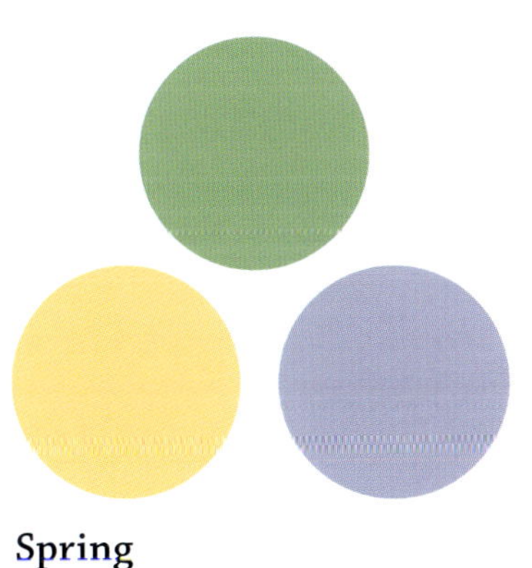

Spring

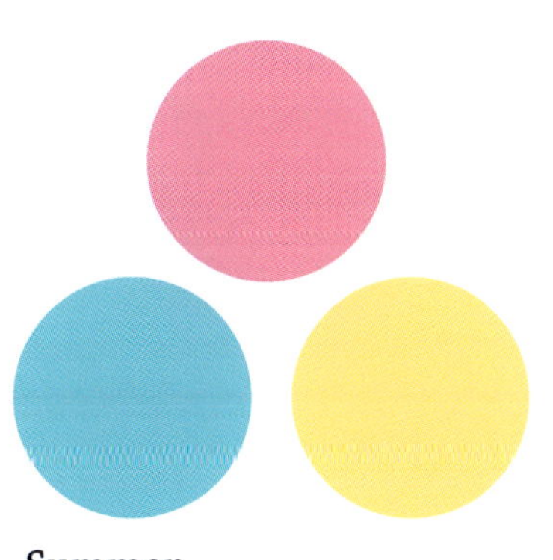

Summer

Another way to think about colours is to consider seasonal themes. We often use the seasons as inspiration for our printing – spring cards, summer beach bags, autumn scarves, or winter stationery. This approach can be a great way to choose a colour palette that works.

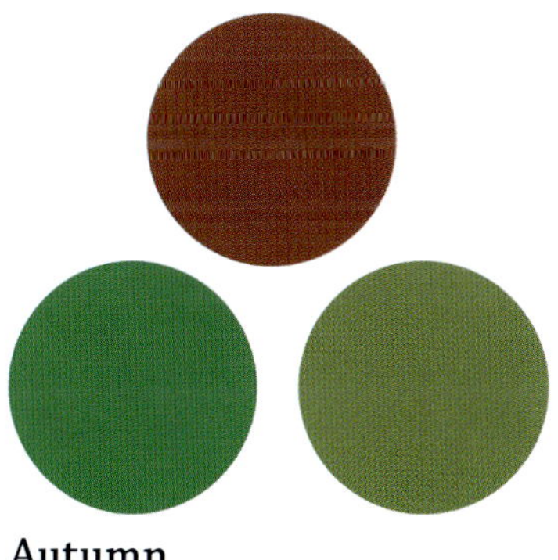

Autumn

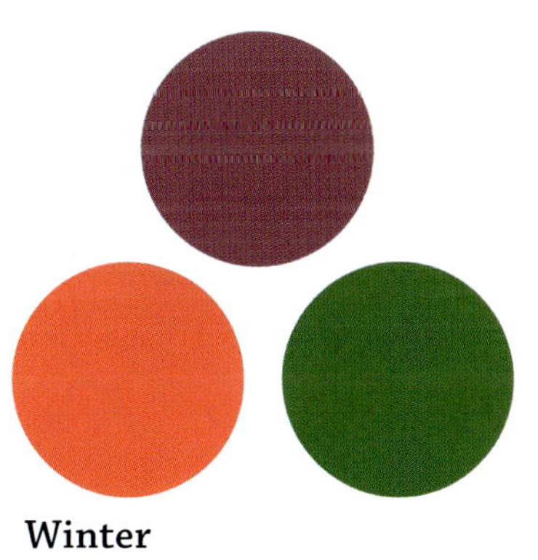

Winter

A great way to keep track of colour combination ideas is to save the ones you love. When you print with a selection of colours you like or want to use again, try printing them on a piece of scrap fabric or in a notebook. This makes it easy to revisit them for inspiration next time.

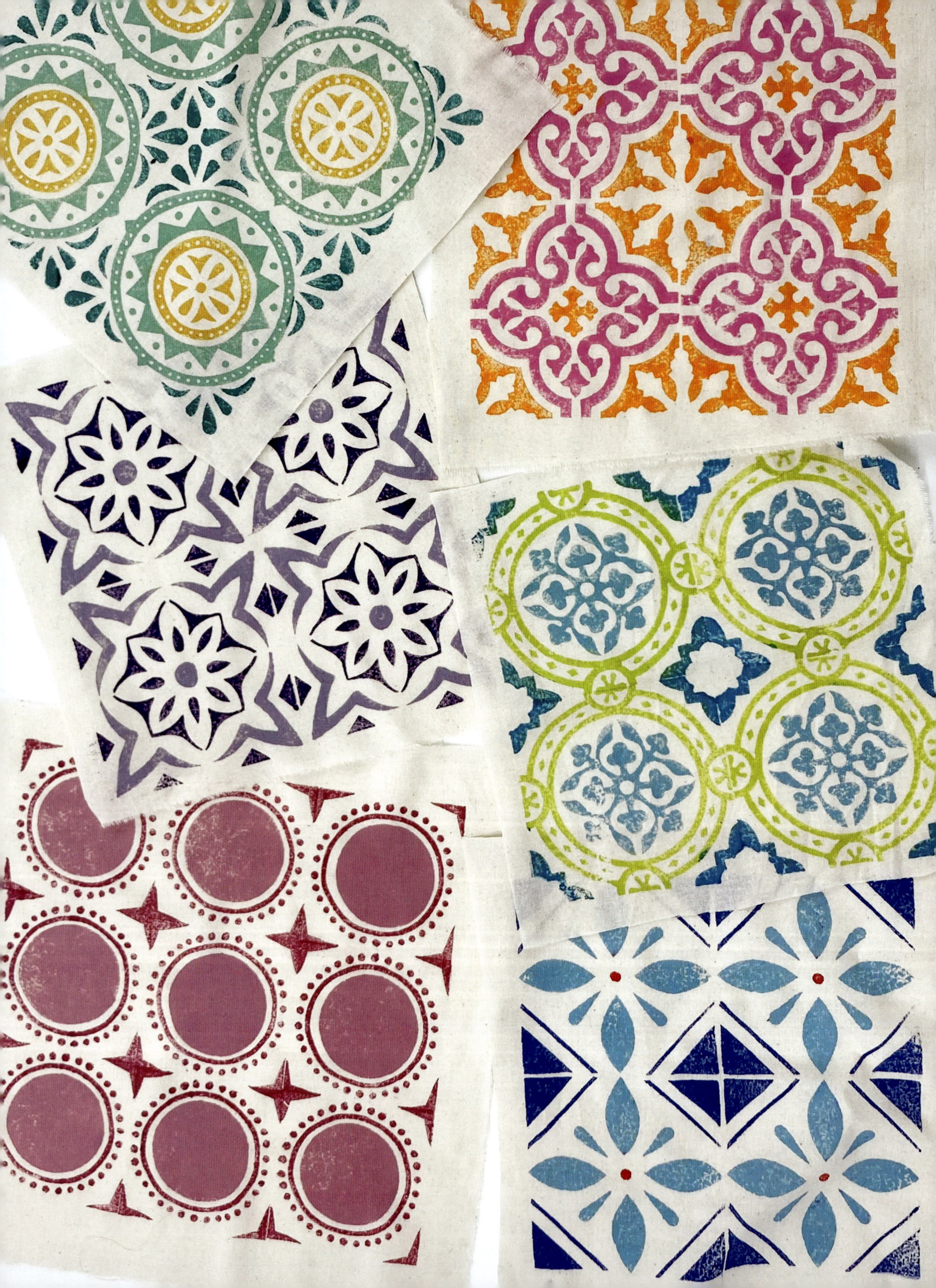

Repeating Patterned Tiles

Patterned tile printing blocks are a popular choice, offering beautiful designs that can stand alone or be used for repetitive prints with full coverage of colour. These blocks are commonly used in our advanced workshops, as they require careful alignment, making them more challenging for beginners. Tile designs vary – some can be printed side by side while others must connect for a continuous pattern (the latter being more difficult). We recommend starting with a simple tile design that only requires printing next to the previous one when you are starting out.

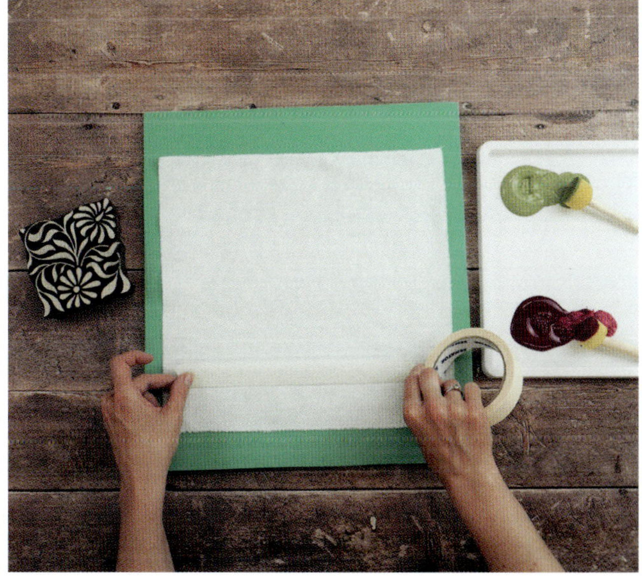

1   When printing with a tile printing block that will create an overall pattern on your material, it's important to ensure your first row of prints is as straight as possible. This gives you the best starting point to continue printing from. We suggest using the fold and iron technique (see page 36) to create a straight crease line. Alternatively, use a piece of masking tape – don't go over it but print alongside it, staying as straight as possible.

2   It's common when using a tile printing block to use multiple colours on the design to emphasise the intricate details or pattern (see precise two-colour printing, page 24). It can take time to precisely add multiple colours, so if you are printing the tile design over a large area, we suggest only using two or three colours.

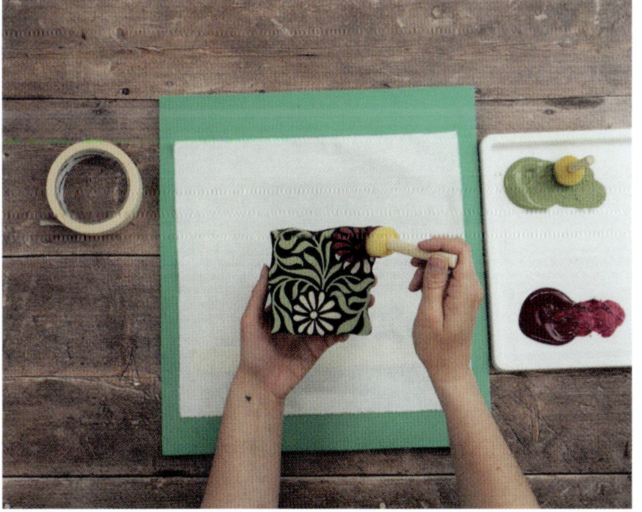

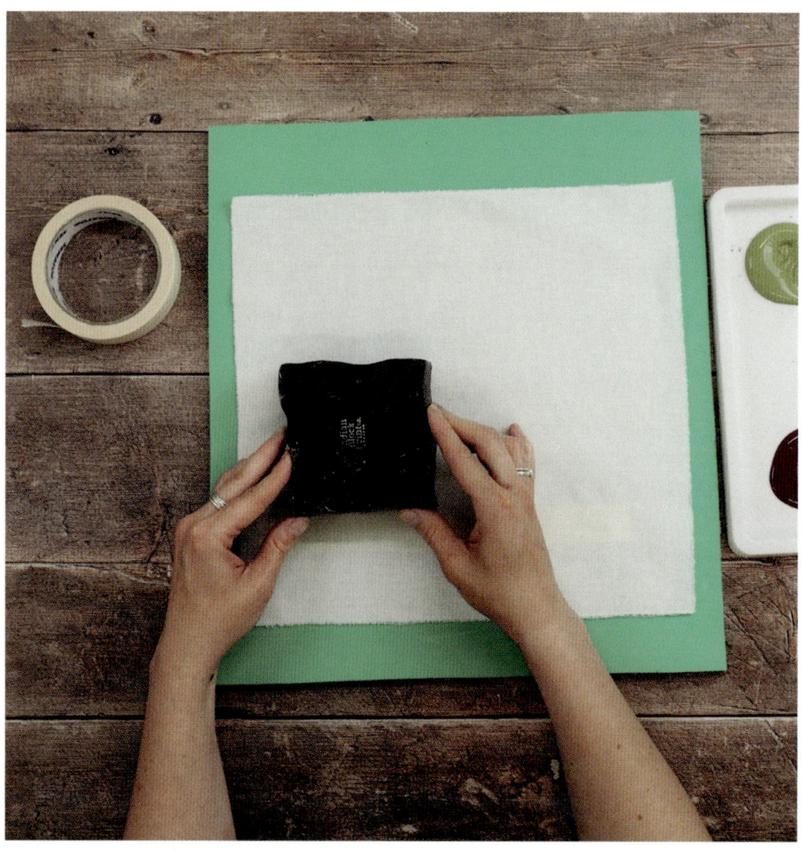

3 Holding the printing block, slowly lower the bottom-left corner down onto your material, positioning it just above the masking tape or crease line. Using this corner as a pivot point to control the positioning, twist the block up or down as you lower the rest of the design onto your material, lining it up straight alongside the masking tape or crease line.

4 Lift the printing block straight up off the material to avoid smudging, and reapply the paint. With the same printing technique, touch down the bottom-left corner next to your previous print, just above the masking tape or crease line, using the same pivoting action to bring the rest of the printing block down.

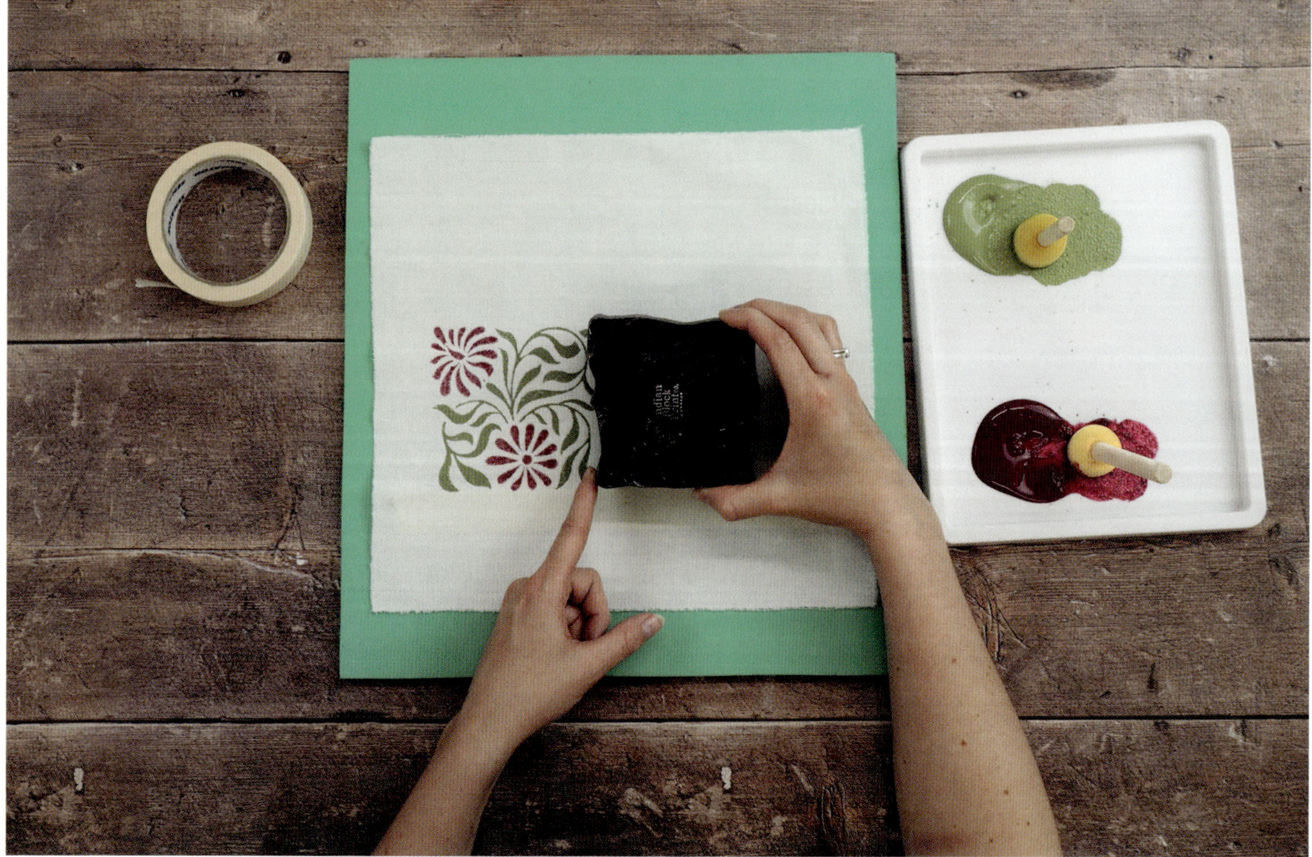

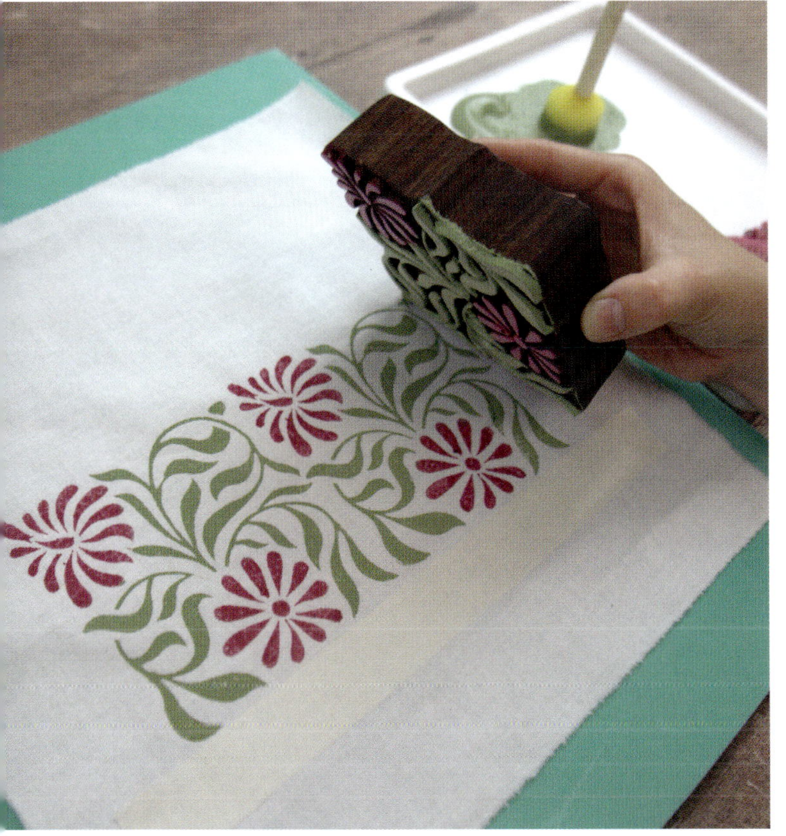

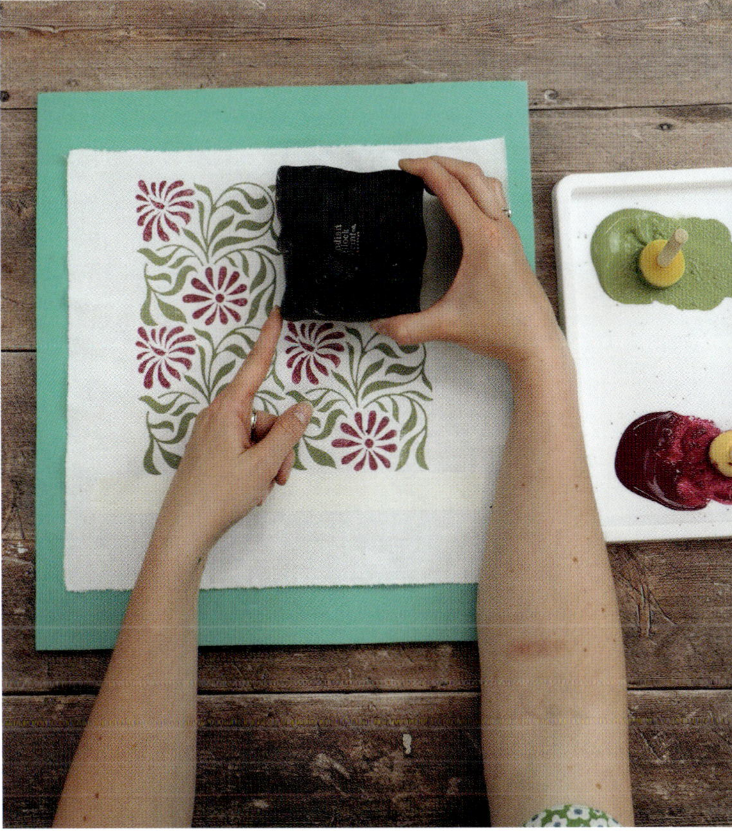

5 Work horizontally along your straight line, before moving up to the next row.

6 For your next row, either lay a new piece of masking tape once the paint has dried or position the printing blocks by eye. Use the same method of touching the bottom-left corner of the printing block down first as you continue.

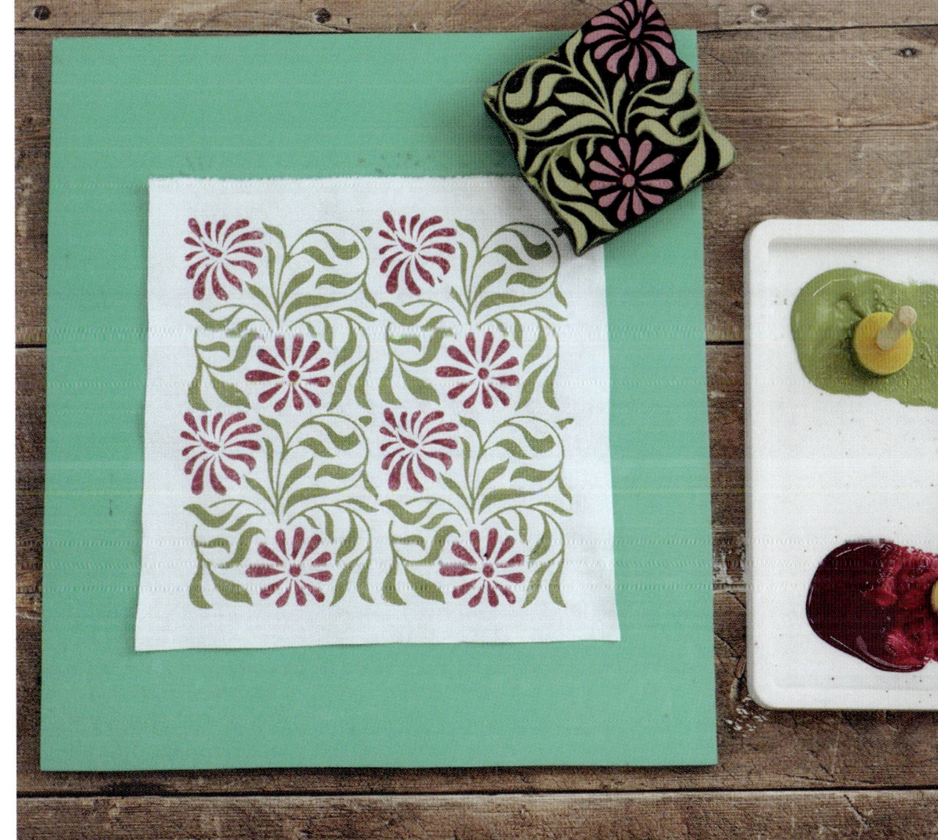

7 This printing method requires slow and careful positioning, but once you get the technique correct, you can achieve impressive results.

PART 3

Printing Projects

During the project section of the book, we will take what you have learnt in the previous chapters and put your printing skills and new techniques into practice. You don't need to know everything before getting started as you will continue to develop your printing techniques while you work through the projects.

Each project can be adapted to suit your own style, giving you the ability to input your design and colour preferences. Our aim for each project is to inspire your own creations at home, whether you use them as a starting point or follow the entire project step by step. From our years of experience printing and teaching others, we have selected our very best creations, which have been tried and tested by new and experienced printers.

We look forward to sharing our love of block printing with you. We hope that as you progress through the projects and experience more of the world of block printing, you will find much joy and gain mindful benefits from being creative.

Remember to embrace the learning process, including any happy accidents! It's not meant to be perfect, it's handmade.

Happy printing,

Tess Grace   Holly Jones

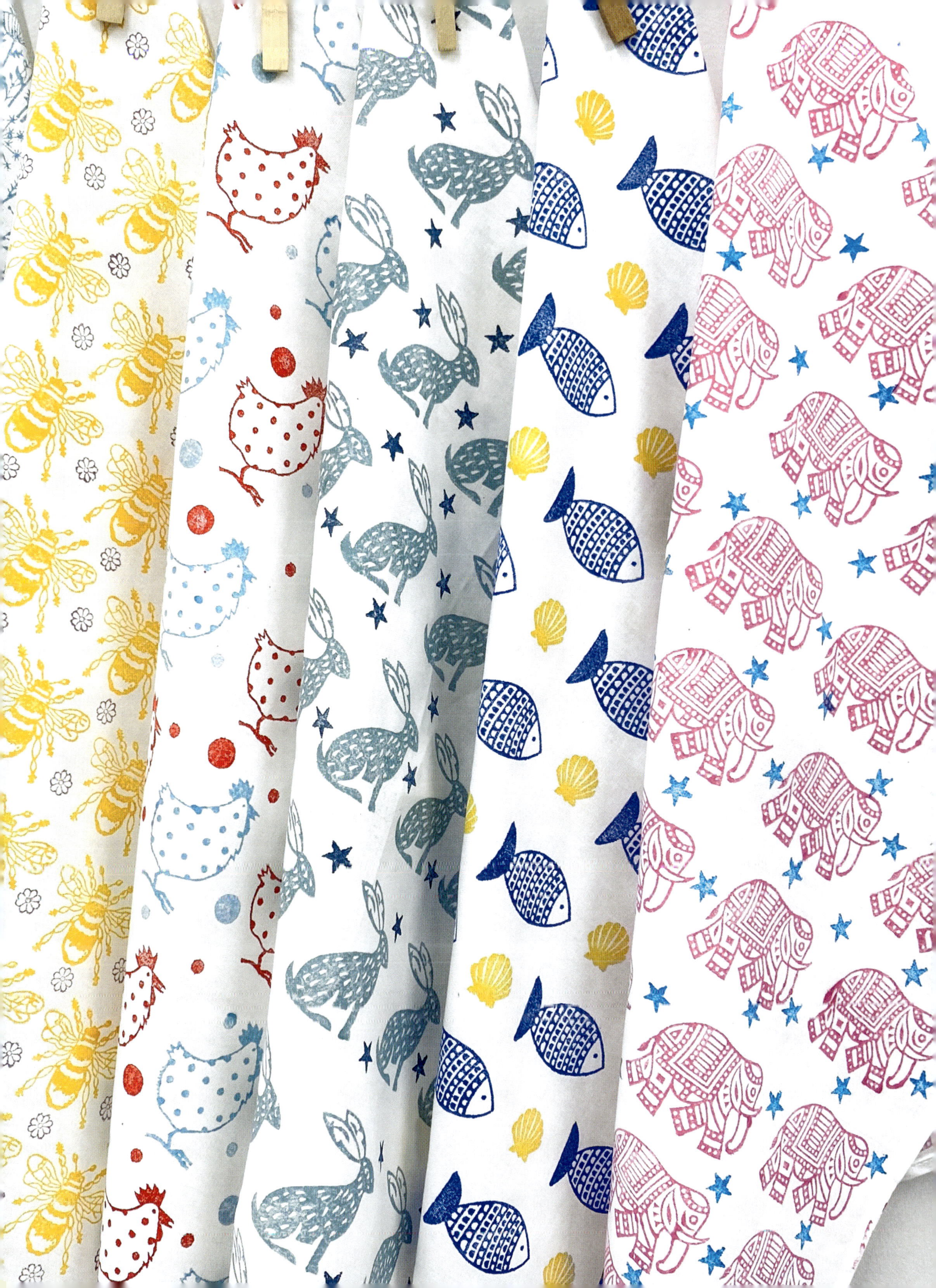

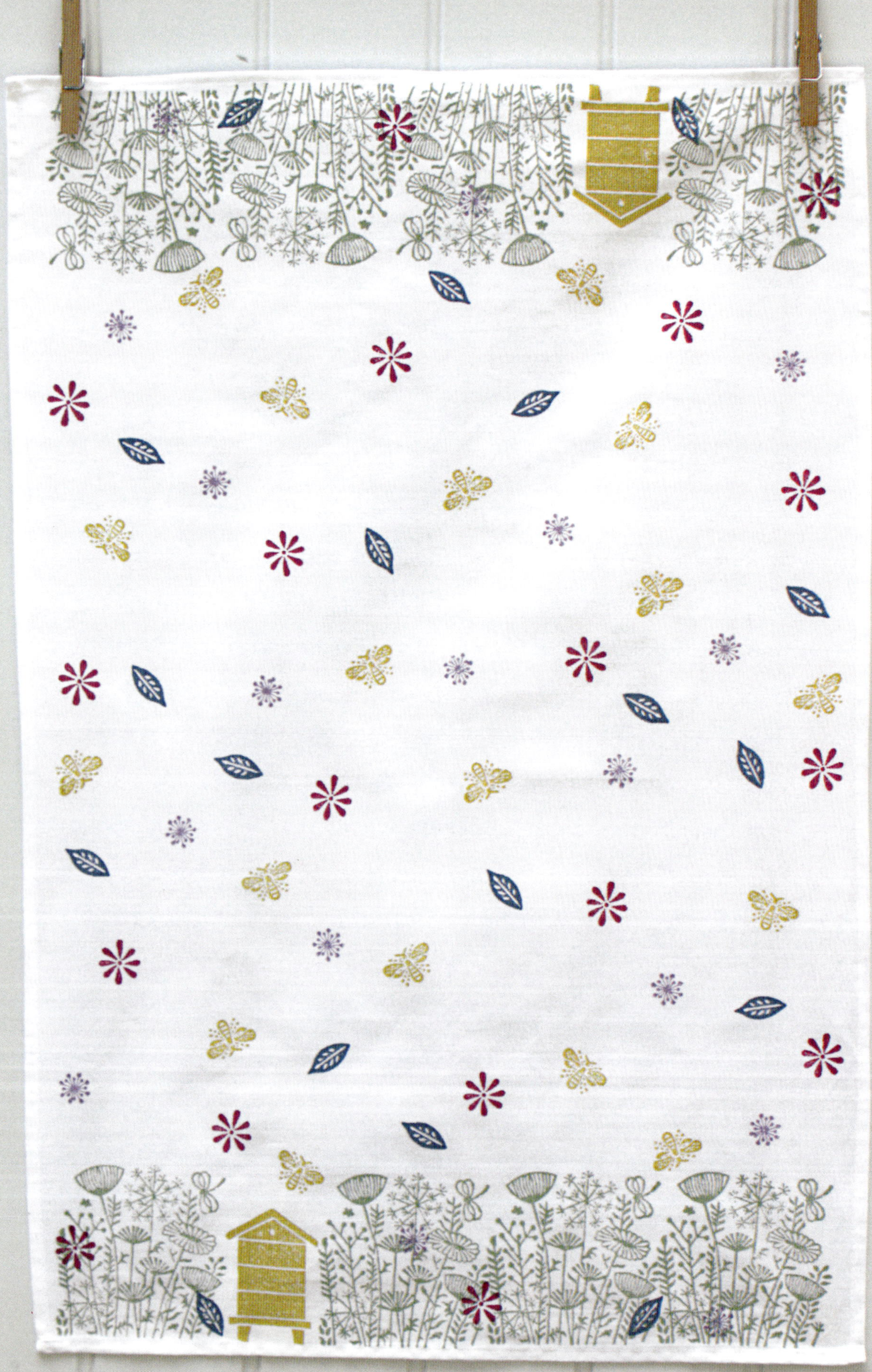

Meadow Tea Towel

Inspired by a customer's own creation, this pretty project quickly became a firm favourite. The intricacy of the design gives the initial impression that it will require advanced printing skills, when in fact it's simple and achievable to create, even for a novice block printer.

The finished pattern tells the story of a wildflower garden, in which you'd find a variety of blooms and bees. There's growing interest and popularity in wildflower gardens, as they offer natural beauty and attract diverse wildlife, which is possibly why this project is so popular. It works in a variety of colour combinations.

- White cotton tea towel
- Printing blocks – we used a set of printing blocks called Meadow Scene
- Fabric paints – we used Khaki, Indian Yellow, Raspberry, Indigo and Violet
- Basic printing equipment (see page 18)

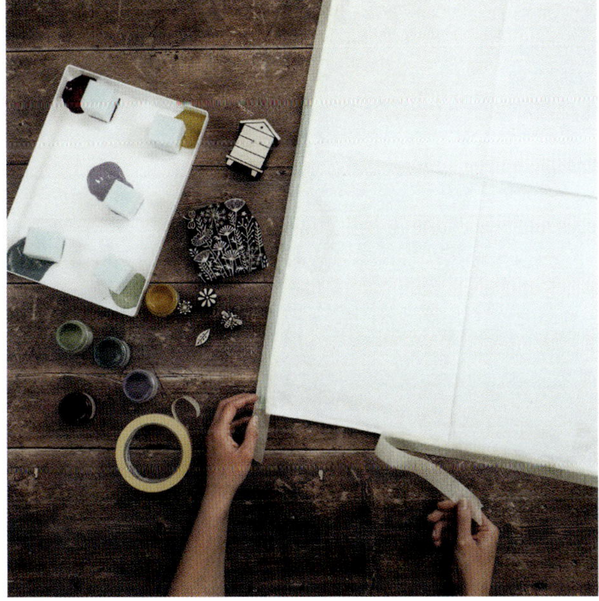

1 Fold your tea towel in half and then in half again. Iron the fold lines to create creases, showing you the centre. Start with one end of the tea towel on your printing mat, applying masking tape to the bottom of the fabric and the two sides, taping over the hemmed edge.

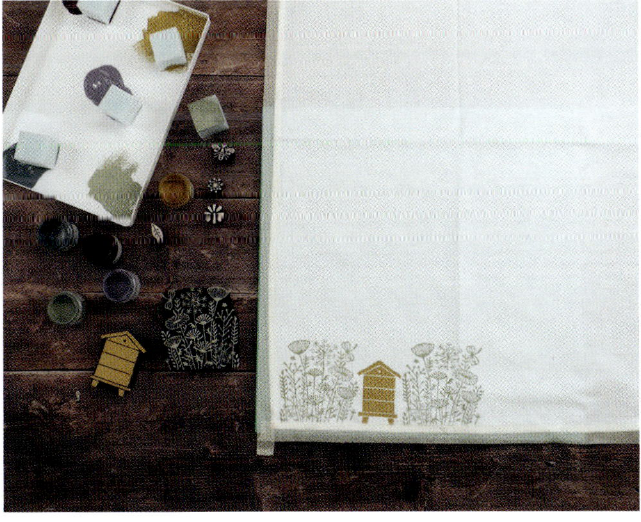

2 Before getting started, you will need to practise the spacing to give you an idea of how many prints you can fit along the bottom of your tea towel (see page 42). Start the design in the bottom-left corner and work your way across the width of the tea towel. First, print the Meadow block in Khaki in the bottom-left corner, then print one Bee Hive in Indian Yellow, and another Meadow. Use the masking tape as a guide to help you print in a straight line.

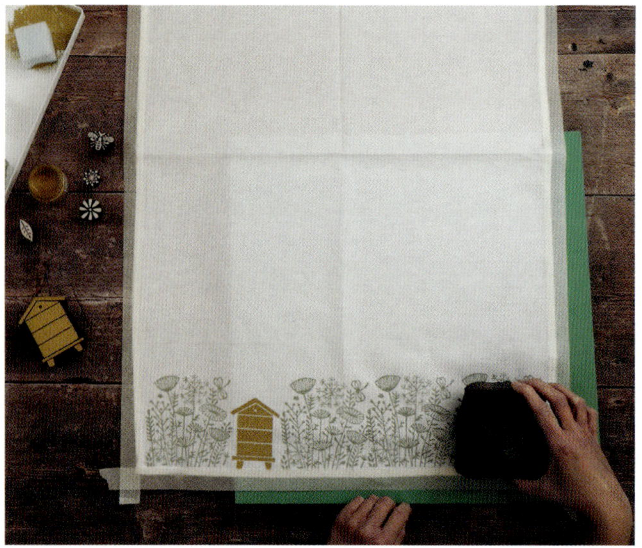

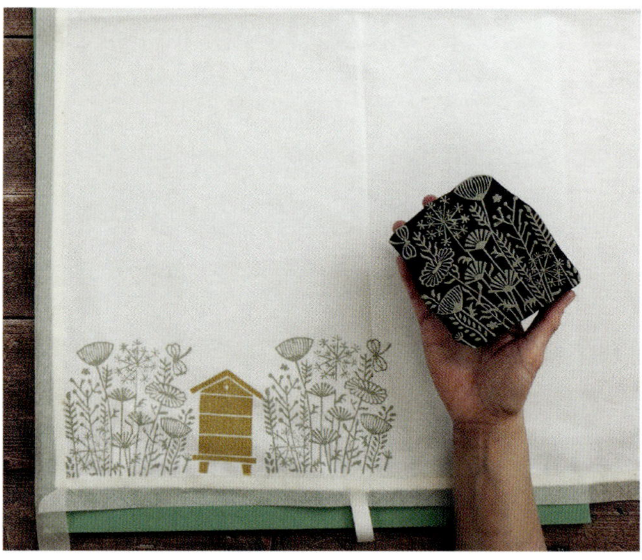

3 Continue printing the Meadow block until you have a line of three. Print each design as close together as you can, but avoid overlapping. You want the design to appear continuous with no gaps in between each print.

4 Flip the tea towel and repeat Steps 1–3 on the opposite end.

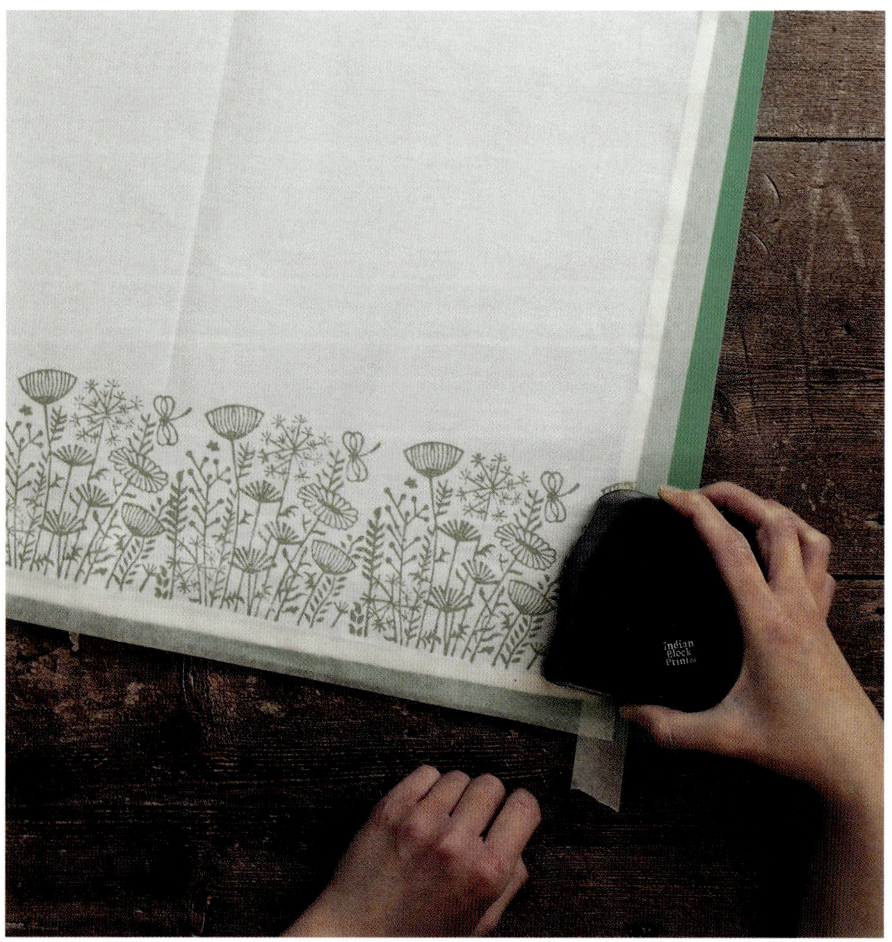

5 Depending on the width of your fabric, you may need to add a half or quarter Meadow print when you reach the end of the row. To do this, ensure the masking tape is covering the hemmed edge of the fabric, then print your meadow going off the edge of your tea towel.

Printing Tip

Cut a piece of scrap fabric the same width as your tea towel and practise Steps 1–3. This will give you an understanding of how the spacing will work before you move on to the project.

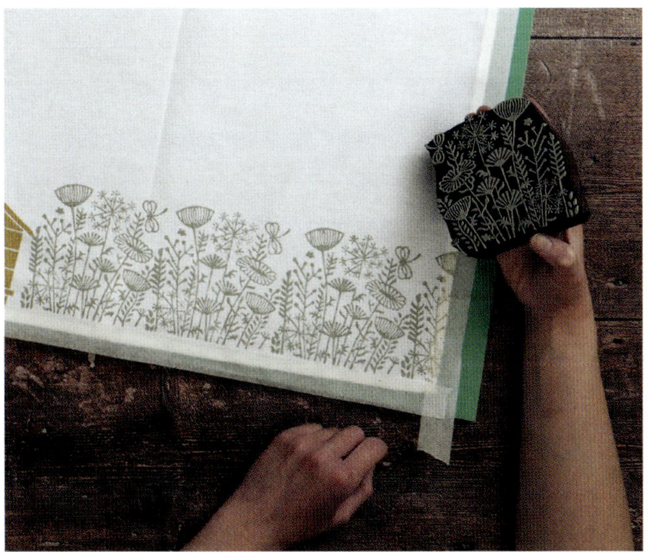

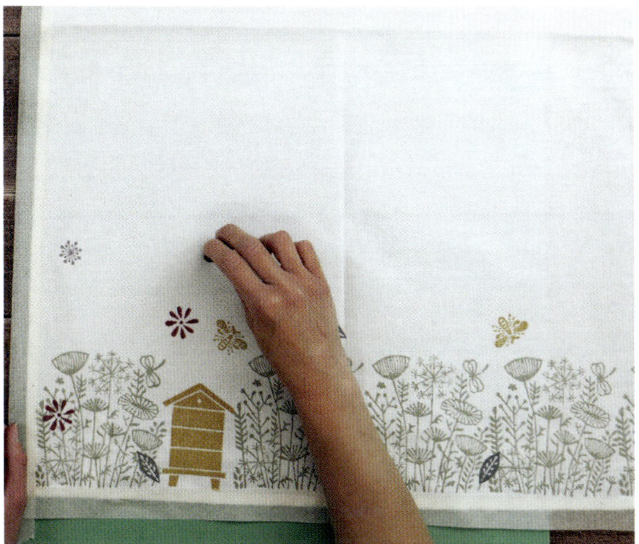

6 When you remove the tape, you'll be left with a clean hemmed edge and a half print, which looks professional.

7 Once you have printed your Meadow and Bee Hive designs on each end, you can start to bring the design together with smaller prints (using Mini Funky Flower, Mini Seedhead Starburst, Single Leaf and Detailed Bee). Start to introduce brighter colours – Raspberry, Indigo and Violet – which will help the prints pop. Print these randomly, but relatively evenly spaced, over half the tea towel. You can also layer prints over your Meadow print border to give depth to the design.

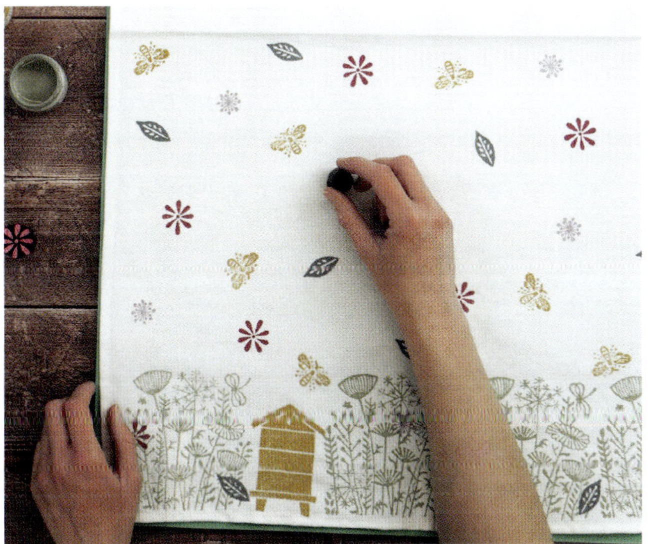

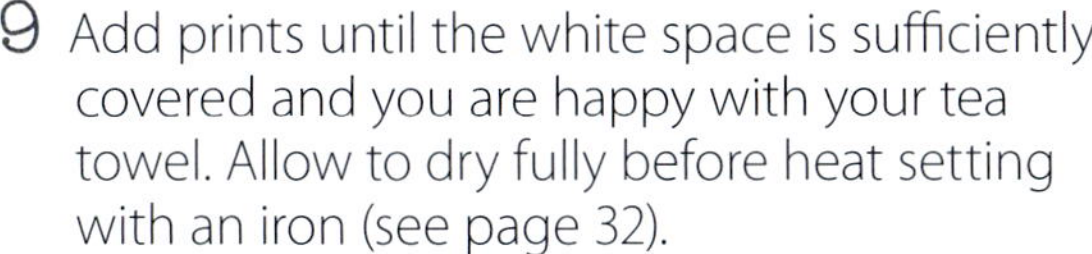

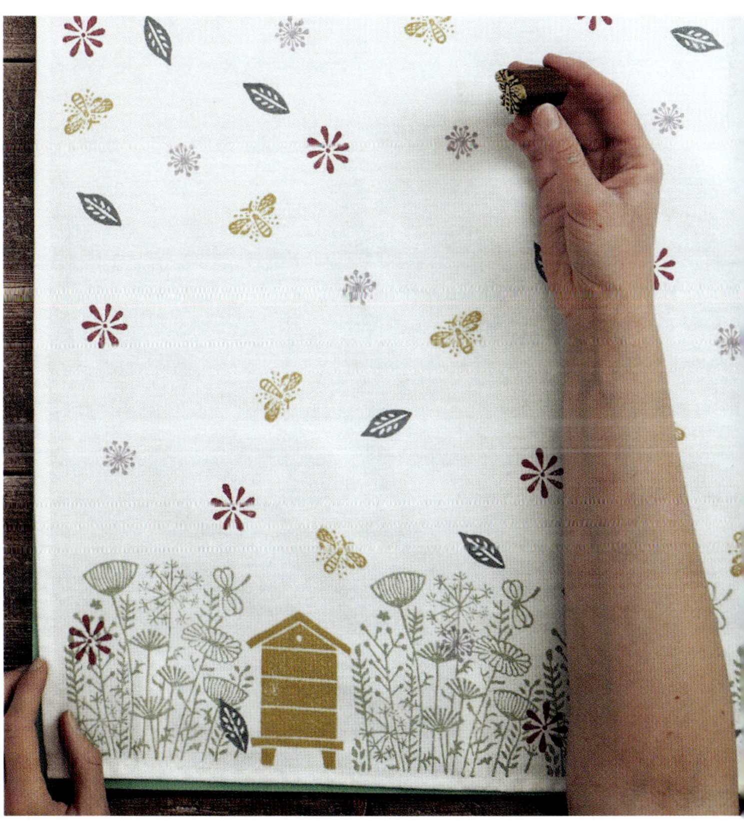

8 Once half the tea towel is covered, flip it and repeat Step 7 on the opposite side.

9 Add prints until the white space is sufficiently covered and you are happy with your tea towel. Allow to dry fully before heat setting with an iron (see page 32).

Initial Tote Bag

Our simple but effective letter tote bag makes the perfect personalised gift, which is sure to impress. Thanks to the simple printing techniques required, this project can be carried out by all abilities of block printers and is great for adults and children alike.

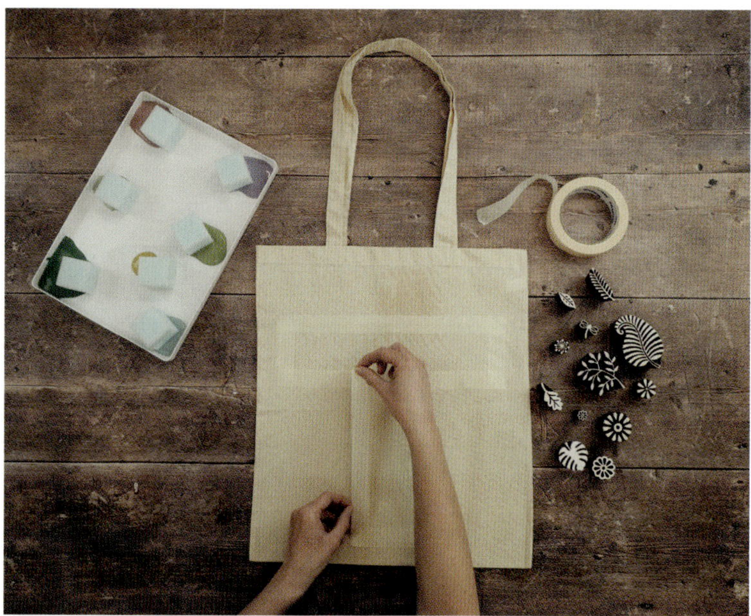

YOU WILL NEED

- Natural cotton tote bag
- Letter stencil or card
- Printing blocks – we used Leaf Bunch, Small Curly Leaf, Simple Monstera Leaf, Mini Seedhead Starburst, Simple Dragonfly, Small Outline Flower, Mini Daisy, Straight Petal Daisy, Mini Flower, Single Leaf, Small Acorn Leaf and Small Detailed Leaves
- Fabric paints – we used Khaki, Violet, Indian Aqua, Leafy Green, Indian Yellow, Aquamarine and Coral
- Basic printing equipment (see page 18)

1 Start by marking up your initial. If the shape of the letter is simple, you can do this with masking tape. To find the centre of your bag to correctly position and space the letter, fold and iron the item to create a crease line. The masking tape will act as a guide, which you will print within.

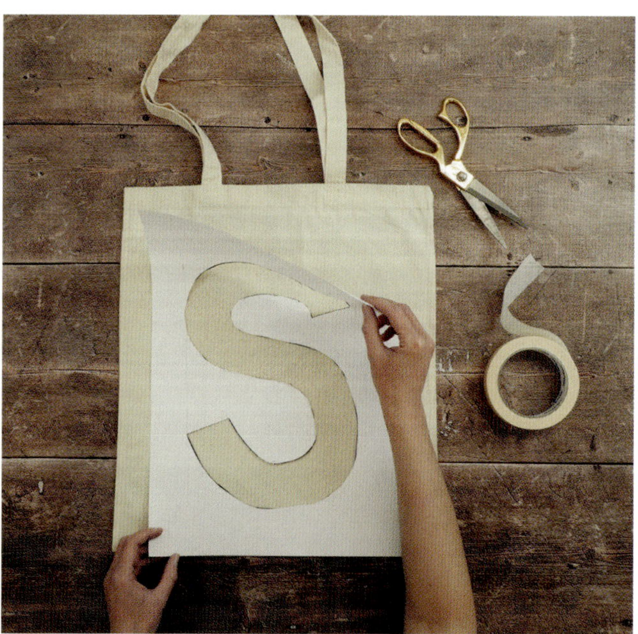

2 For more complicated letters that you can't mark with masking tape, you can use a letter stencil or make your own. We created an 'S' stencil using A3 paper. To do this, draw your letter in bubble writing, cut the inside of the letter out and fix the stencil in place on your bag with masking tape.

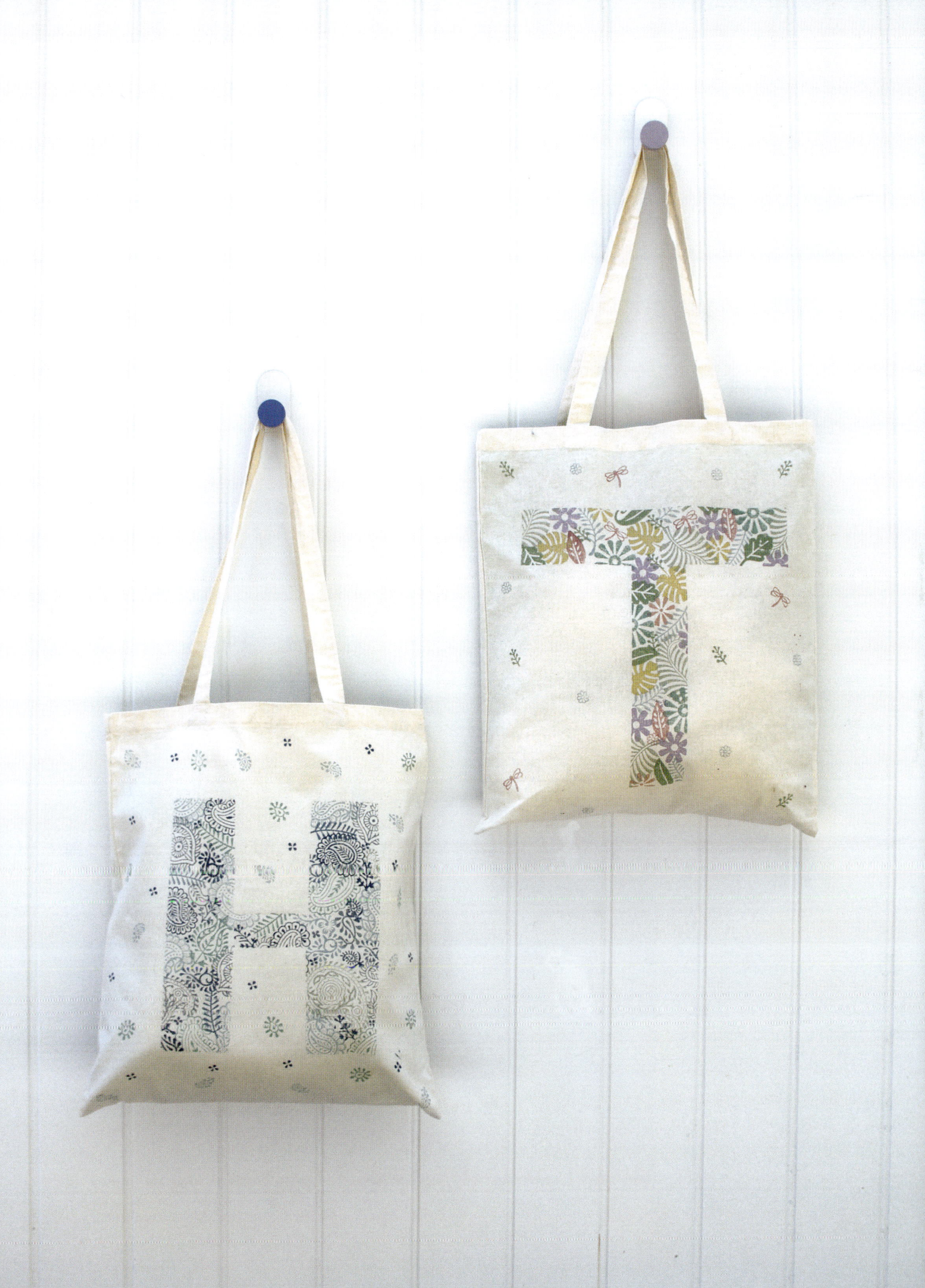

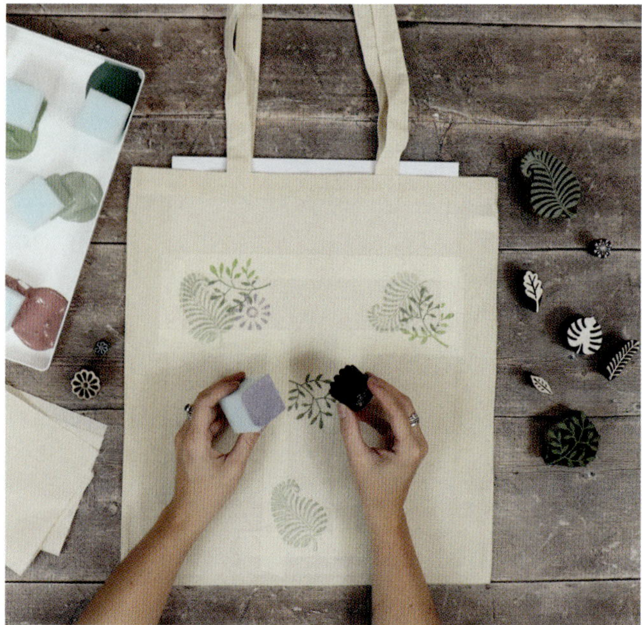

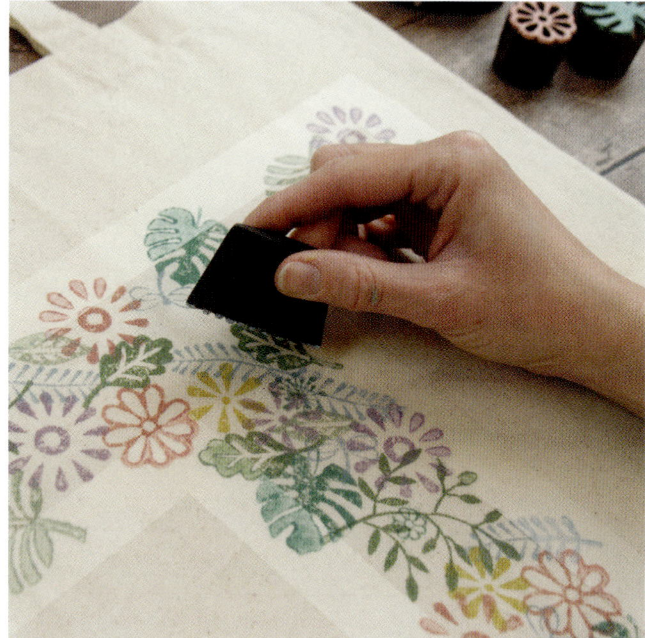

3 Start the design by using your biggest printing blocks – these will take up the most space so it's harder to squeeze them in at the end. Print each design several times within the masking tape. It works best if you overlap your prints onto the masking tape, as this will help create the edges of your printed letter.
We suggest sticking to the same colour on each printing block, so you don't confuse the design.

4 Each time you print with a new design, the amount of blank space will reduce. Continue printing within the masking tape, with each design close together or partially overlapping – this will bring the whole design together.

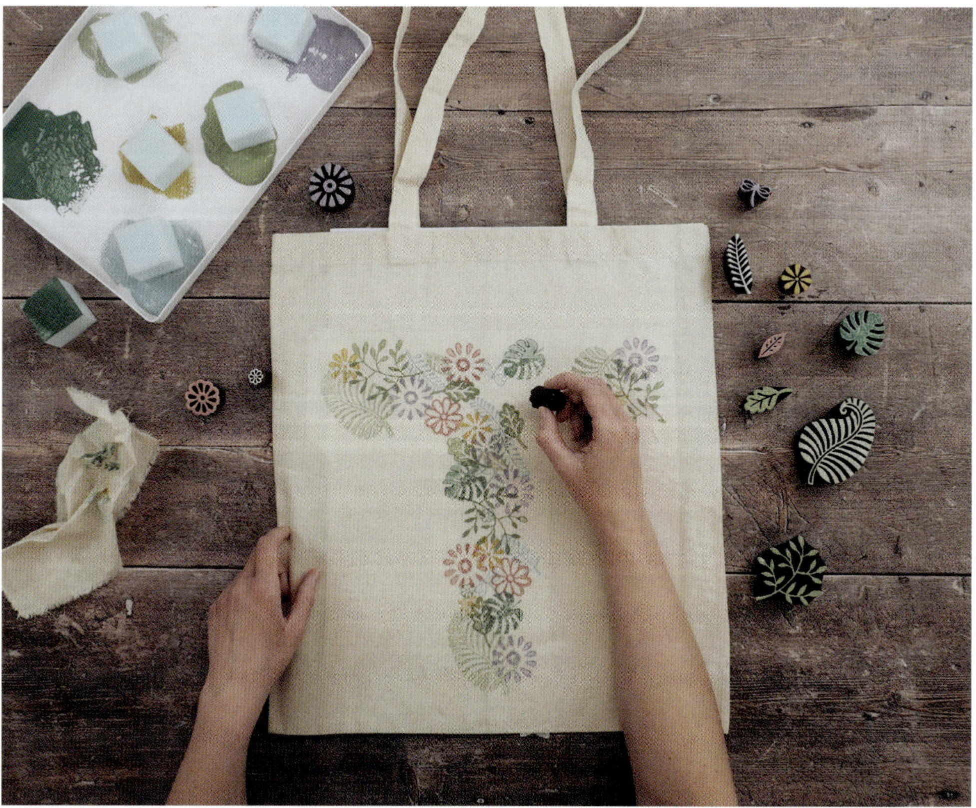

5 Using the smaller designs, fill in any gaps until the entire inside of the letter is printed.

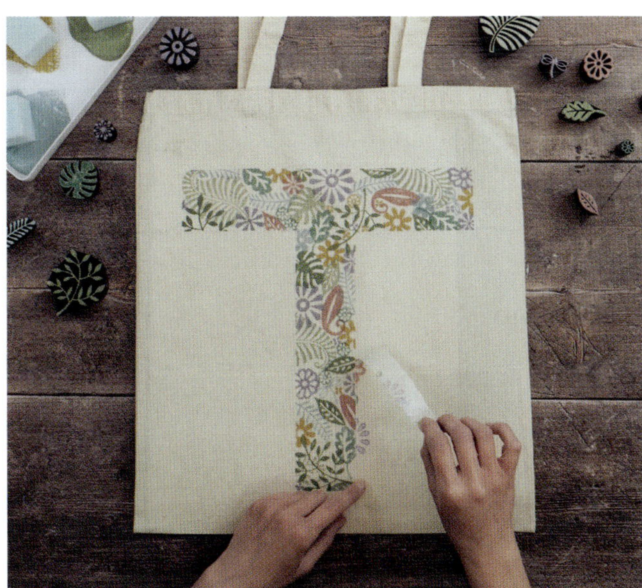

6 Once you've finished your printed letter and all the gaps have been filled in, allow it to dry. You can then peel away the masking tape to reveal your printed initial.

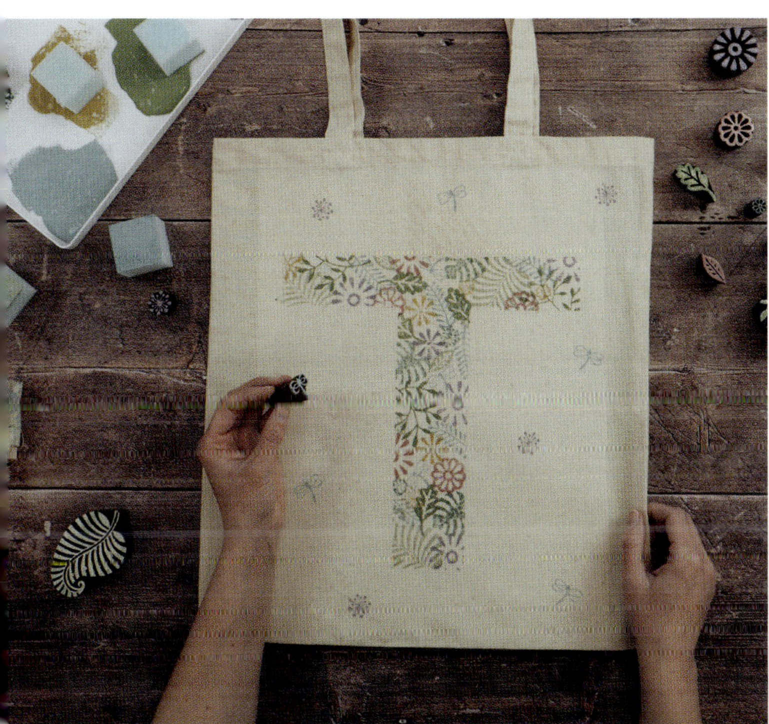

7 To finish, use a couple of the smallest designs in your collection to add detail to the blank space around the printed letter. Keep it simple by using subtle designs in two or three colours, not detracting from the letter itself.

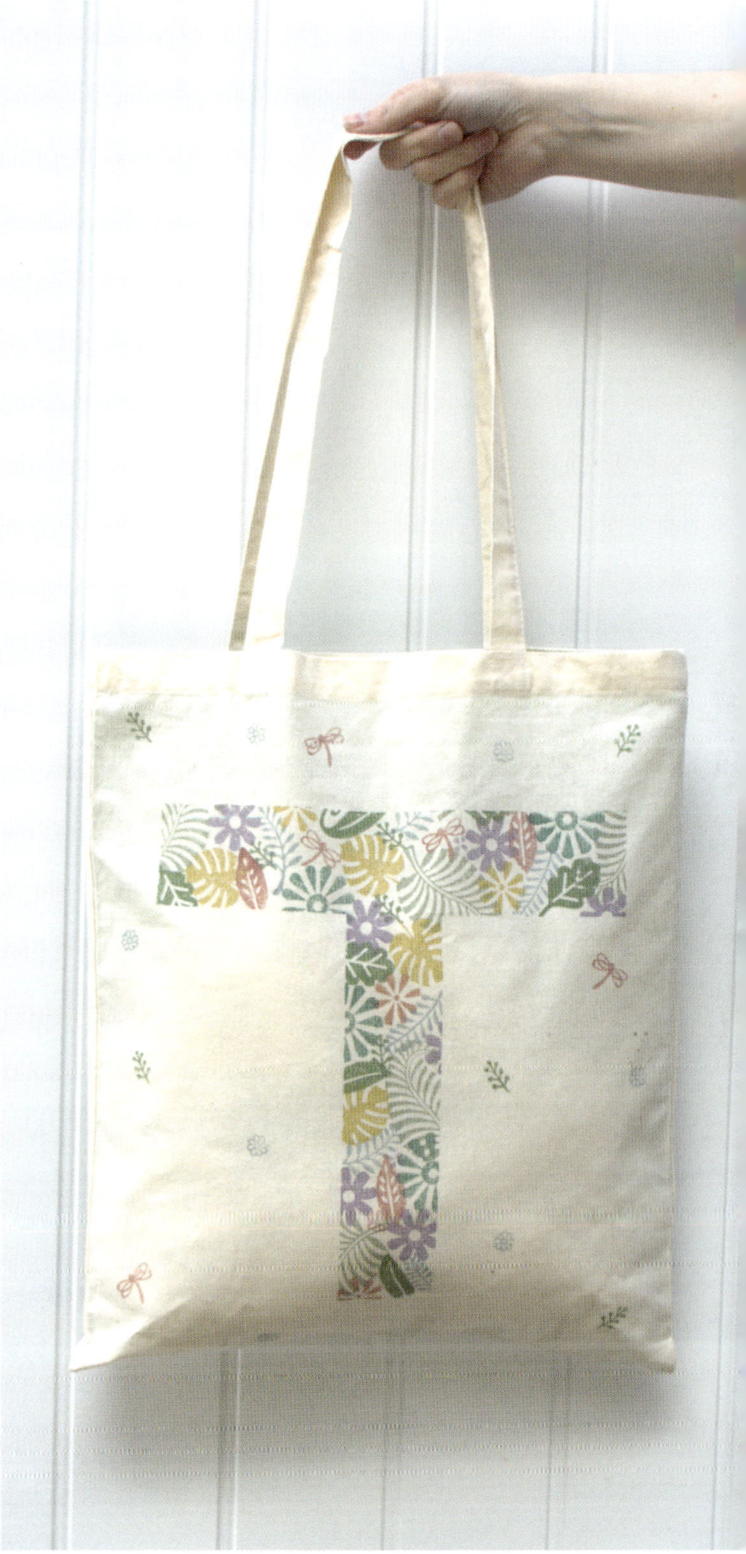

8 Once you have printed your bag, turn it over and repeat on the other side. Leave to dry before removing from the mat and heat setting (see page 32).

Printing in India – Dabu

One of our favourite types of printing in Bagru is Dabu printing – the process of resist printing with mud. As we do not have access to the materials used for this method of printing, we haven't been able to replicate this printing process in the UK, so we're always eager to try it when visiting India.

Dabu printing involves printing a mud and clay mixture onto fabric. This paste is made from locally sourced clay and mud, combined with lime and gum (often derived from trees), which strengthen the mixture to ensure it adheres to the fabric during the printing, drying and dyeing process.

The mud mixture is poured into printing trays with a wire mesh on top, and you tap the printing block onto the wire to load the paste onto the design you are printing with. You'll find with Dabu printing that less intricate designs are used as the mud paste is a thicker consistency than paint – the details of intricate designs are often lost, so more successful prints are achieved by using solid shapes and thicker patterns. Before the paste dries, sawdust from the studio floor is sprinkled over the printed fabric. The material is then left to dry in the sun, and the combination of mud and sawdust creates a hardened resist for the dyeing process.

The next step in the Dabu printing process is to dye the fabric blue. For this, traditional indigo dye is used. In Bagru, walking around the village, you'll see many underground indigo vats – large holes lined with concrete, dug into the ground and filled with an indigo dye. Some printing houses will use a natural

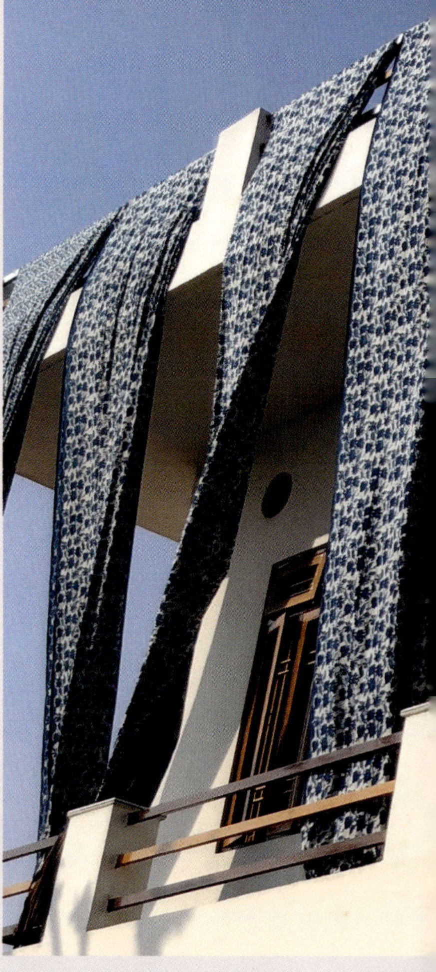

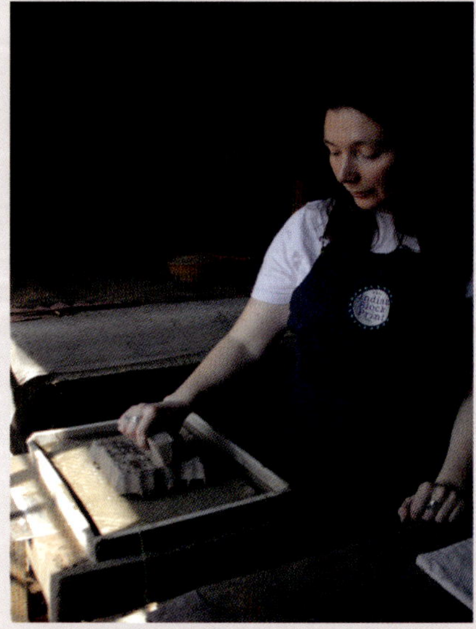

Dipping the wood block into the mud paste.

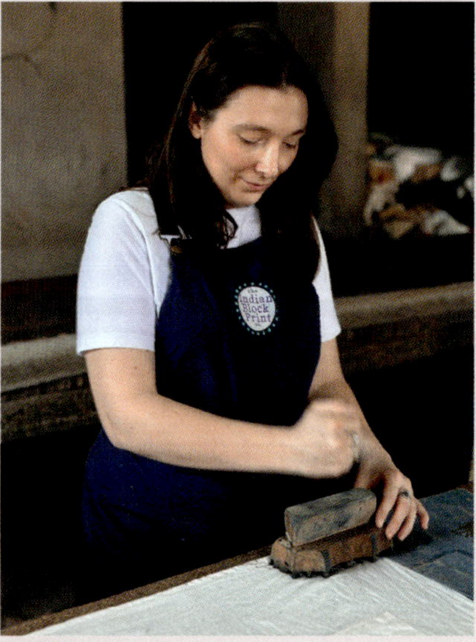

Printing onto fabric.

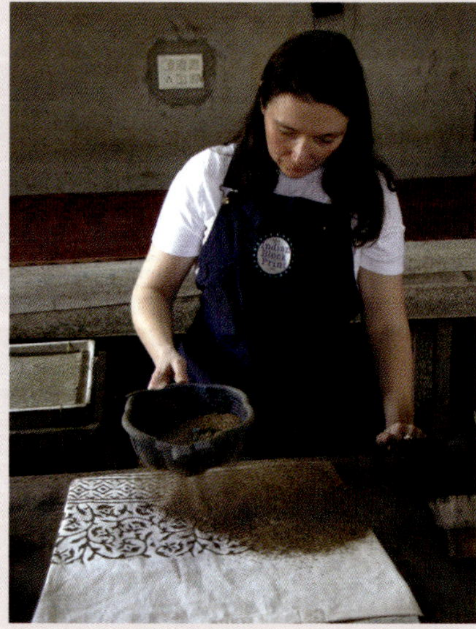

Sprinkling sawdust over mud block prints.

Right: The finished Dabu (mud) printed fabric before being indigo dyed.

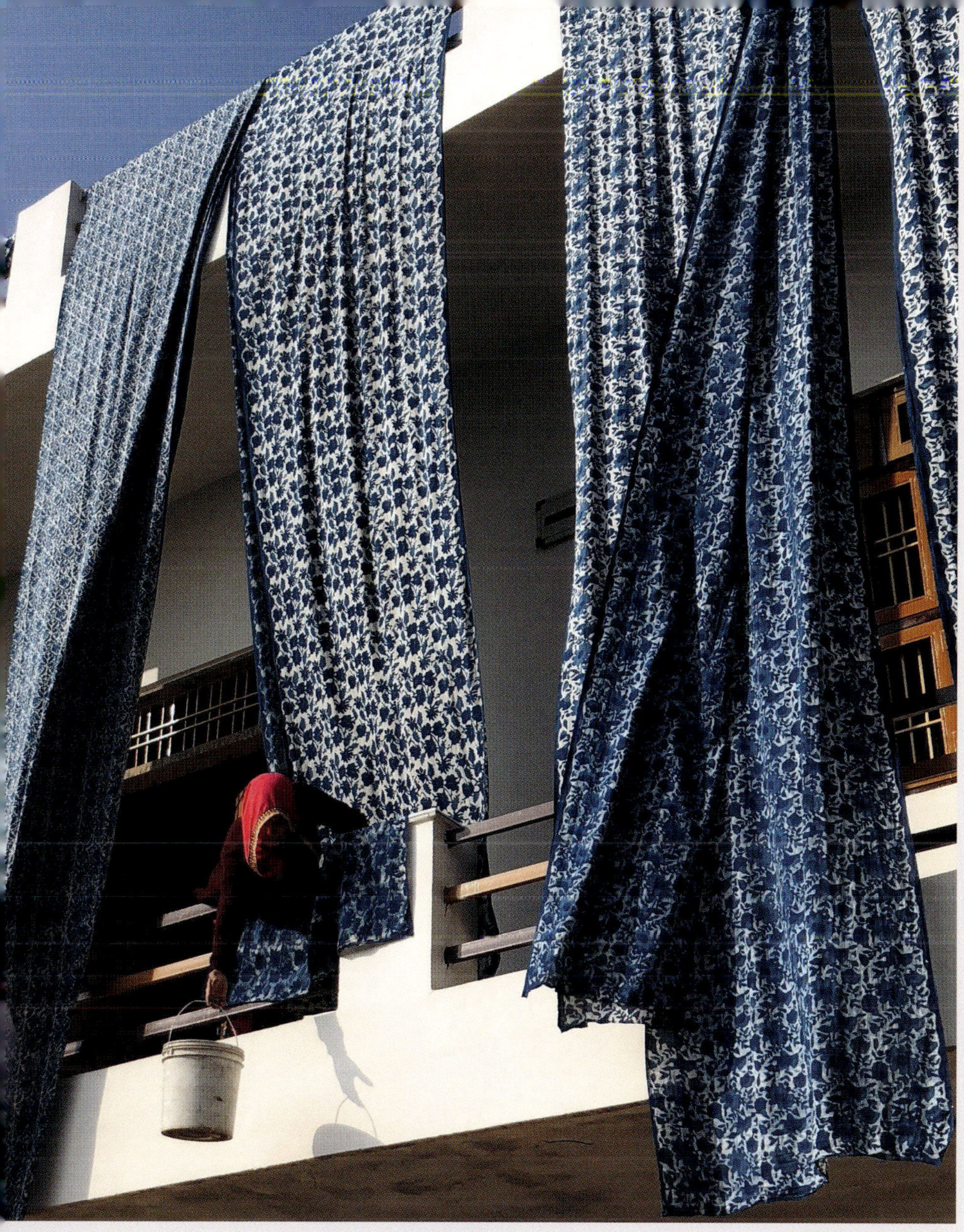

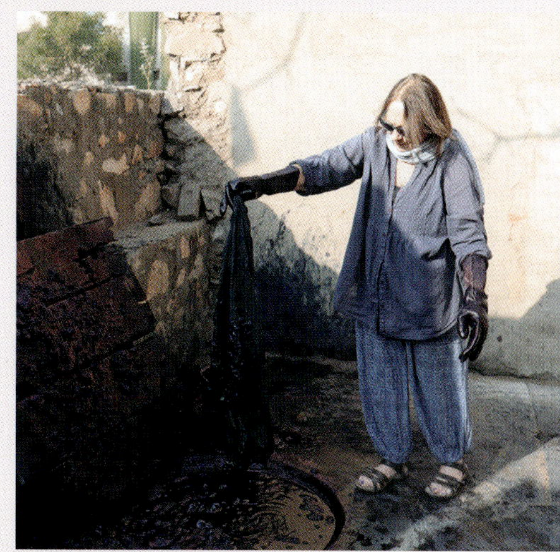

Above: Concrete chamber in the ground that holds an indigo dyeing vat.

Below: Tess dipping her Dabu-printed fabric into the indigo vat.

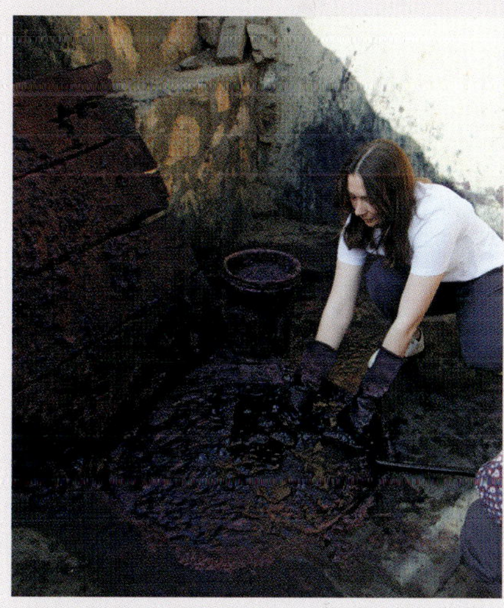

Above: Dabu printed fabric drying in the sun after dyeing.

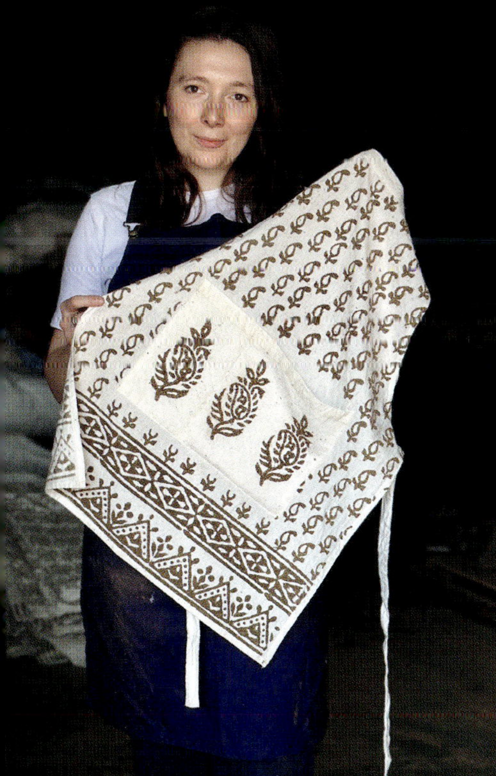

indigo, but many will use a synthetic indigo dye, which is favoured due to the consistency of colour and lower costs. A natural indigo vat would require much more maintenance and often does not reach the same deep blue colour that a synthetic indigo dye can.

The mud-printed fabric gets dipped and fully submerged into the indigo vat. It will be dipped several times to increase the depth of colour, and, after its final dip, it is left to dry in the sun. The mud and sawdust mixture acts as a resist and is not removed during the dyeing process, meaning the fabric underneath the mud will remain the original colour before printing.

The fabric dries for an hour in the sun, and is then washed to remove the mud paste to reveal the contrasting colours: the white of the printed design and the blue of the remaining dyed fabric.

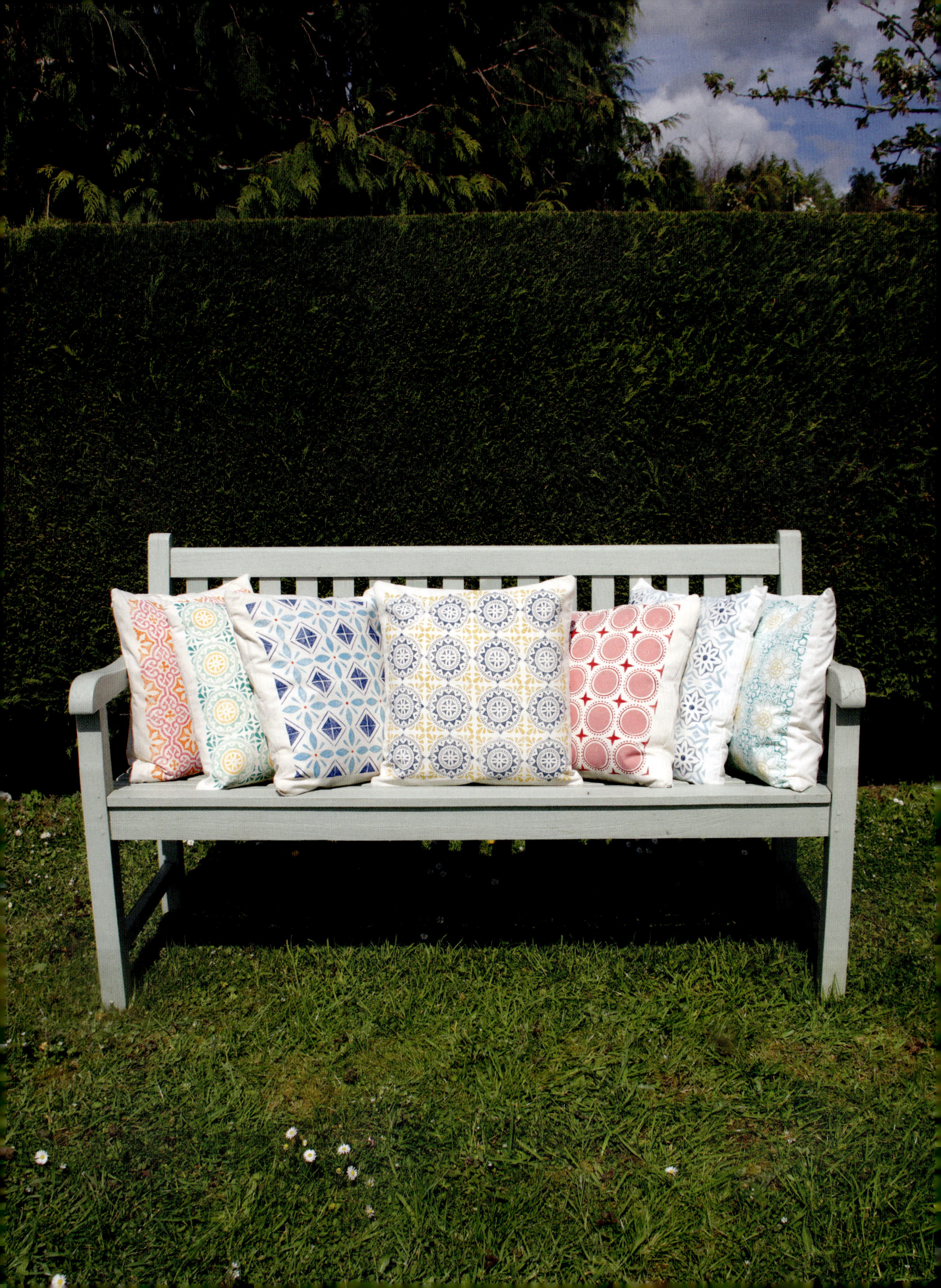

Striking Cushion Covers

A vibrant project to spark your creativity and brighten your garden! Printing your own patterned cushion covers is easy and impactful. We've printed a whole set of cushions in various patterns and colours, and have chosen our favourite for this project which is a Moroccan tile design. These tile printing blocks provide excellent coverage and look impressive when repeated across the fabric.

- Natural cotton cushion cover (ours measures 45 × 45 cm)
- Printing block – we used Moroccan Tile
- A3 card or paper
- Two fabric paint shades – we used Midnight Blue and Indian Yellow
- Basic printing equipment (see page 18)

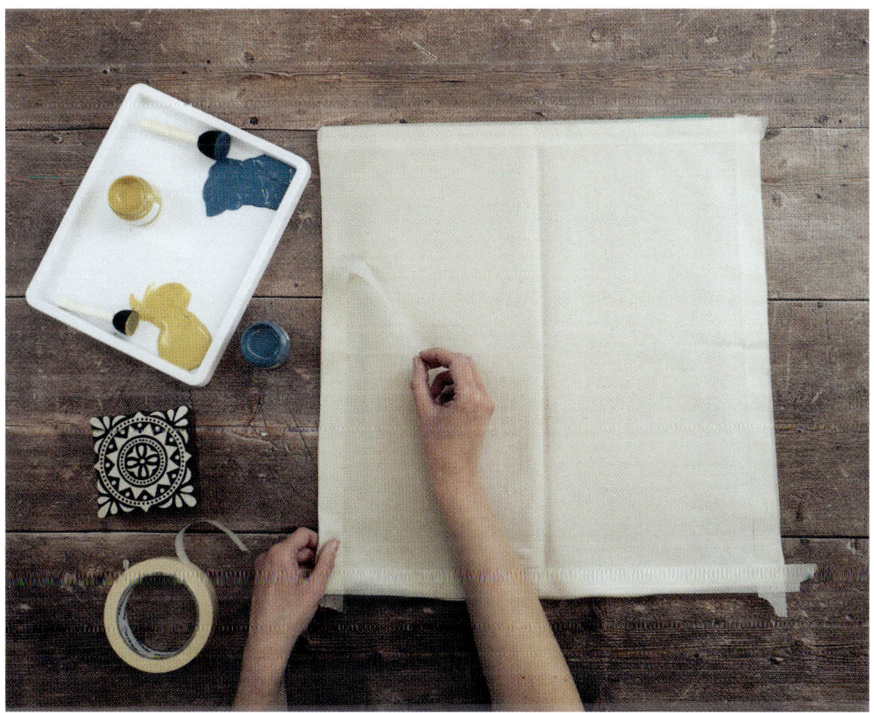

Printing Tip

Always practise on a piece of square fabric when printing with a repeating design. It's important to learn how the printing block repeats before moving on to your final fabric piece (see pattern repeats, page 42).

1 When printing a cushion in a patterned tile design, always start from the centre point and work your way outwards. To find the centre point of the cushion cover, which helps to evenly space the design, fold the fabric in half and then in half again and iron the fold lines to create crease lines. Add masking tape to all four edges of the cushion.

2   Before you start printing, work out how many full prints you can fit across the width and height of your cushion. Avoid half prints over the edge of the fabric as these can smudge. You have two starting point options: either place your first print in the centre of the cushion (Diagram A) or print around the centre point (Diagram B). Try both and pick the one that gives you the most amount of full prints. Option B works best for the printing block we are using, and allows us to print four tiles across the width and height of our cushion.

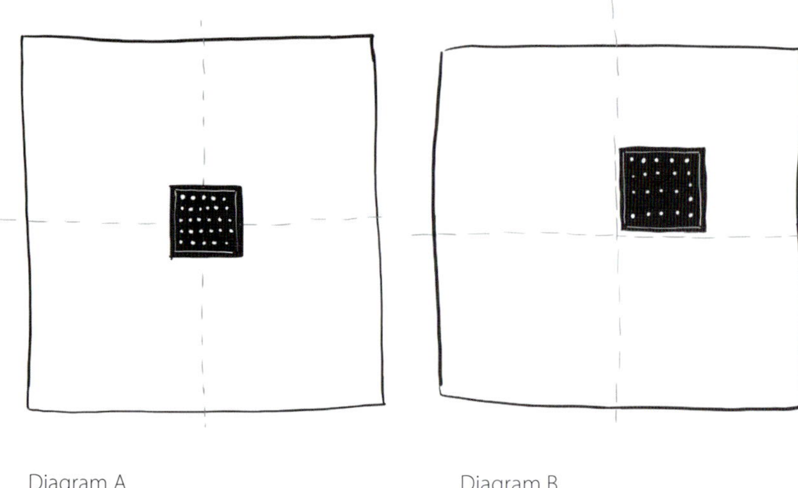

Diagram A   Diagram B

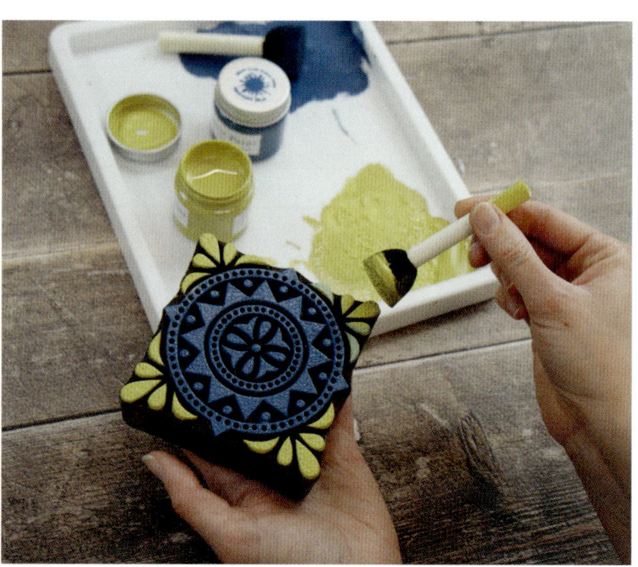

3   Place the card or paper inside your cushion cover to stop any paint going through the fabric onto the reverse side. Apply Midnight Blue and Indian Yellow paint onto your Moroccan Tile block using sponge dabbers (see precise two-colour printing, page 24). Do this quickly but carefully; if you apply too many colours to the printing block, the paint can dry by the time you are ready to print.

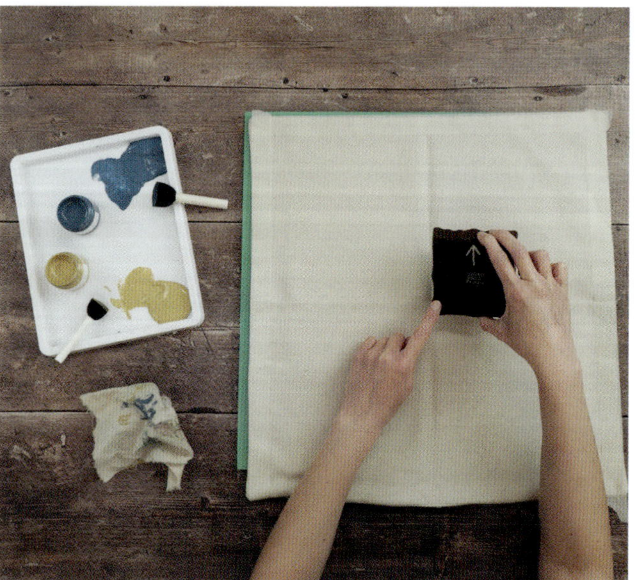

4   When putting your first print down, touch the bottom-left corner of the block onto the centre point – you can then use this as a pivot point. Adjust the block by turning it left or right so the rest of the design lines up with your centre lines before putting it down onto your fabric.

Printing Tip

For consistency in your design, mark the top on the reverse side of your printing block, then always print the block with the mark facing the same way.

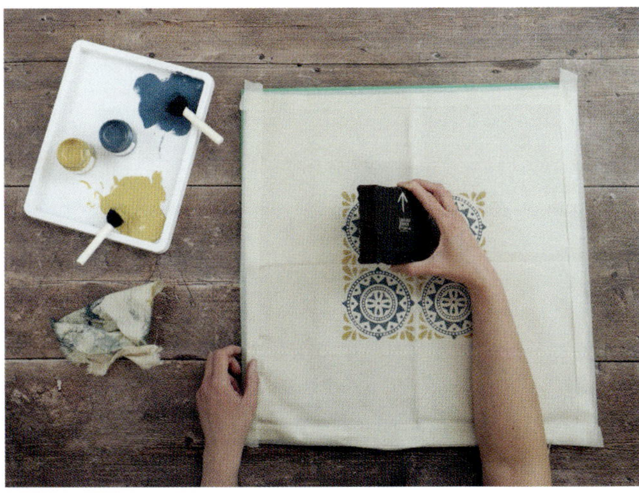

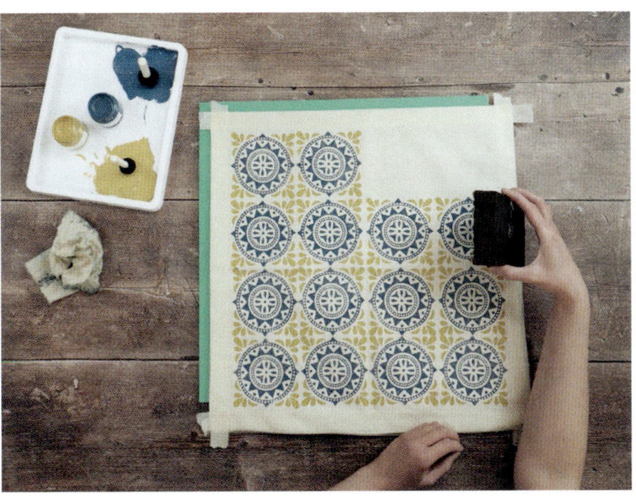

5 After printing your first tile in the correct position, you can then print your next three, so you have four prints surrounding the centre point of the cushion cover. With the tile design we are using, we don't want the prints to touch; leave a gap of approximately 2 mm between each print. Some patterned tiles need to connect to each other to create a continuous design – it depends on the design you are using.

6 After printing the four central tiles, you can work your way outwards. By starting from the middle, you will be left with an evenly spaced border on all four sides. When printing with the same design repeatedly, you may find the block becomes clogged with paint. If this starts to happen, wipe the block clean and reapply a fresh coat of paint before printing again.

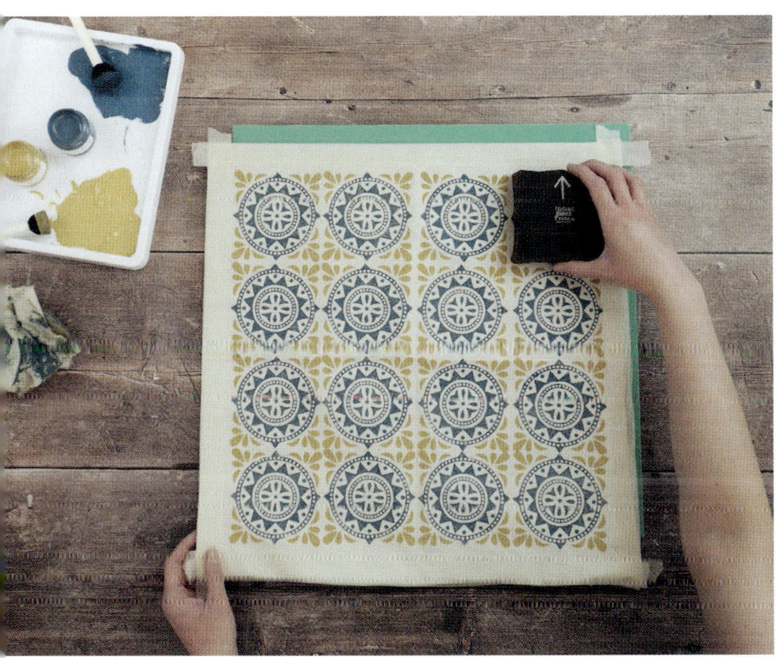

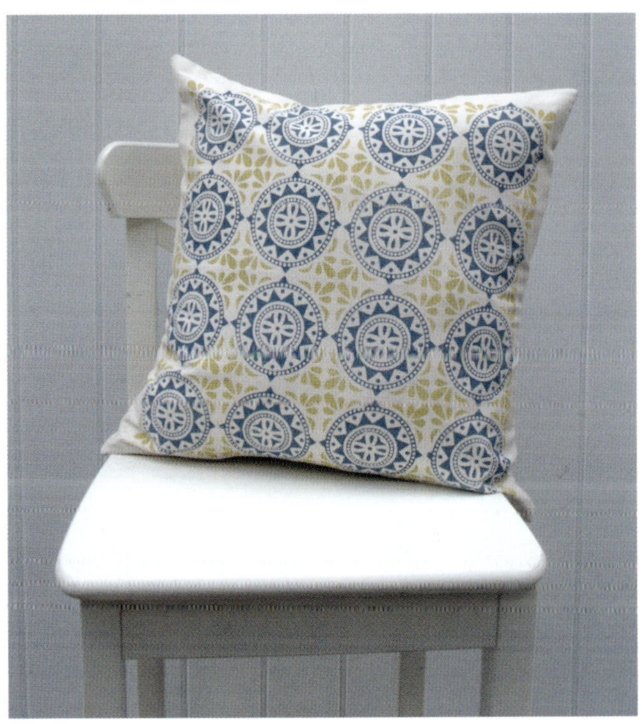

7 Once you have added your final print, allow time for the cushion to dry before removing the masking tape. You can then turn it over and print on the opposite side, repeating the same steps as above. Why not try swapping the colours on the opposite side to create an alternative colour variation?

8 Once both sides are dry, heat set your cushion cover thoroughly on both sides (see page 32). The cushion cover will then be ready to use and will be washable when required.

Traditional Indian Napkins

Our love for printed fabrics has turned into a bit of an obsession – we just can't resist when we see a beautiful print! There's something so captivating about block-printed designs, with their bold colours, intricate patterns and rich cultural roots. Knowing that each piece is handcrafted by skilled artisans using traditional techniques makes it feel even more special.

This napkin design is our nod to the traditional Indian patterns we fell in love with, inspired by the fabrics we couldn't help but pick up during our trips to Jaipur. We like to print a full set of napkins; many people choose either a set of four, six or eight. Try printing half in one colourway then swap the colours around for the other half to offer a variation.

YOU WILL NEED

- Four white cotton napkins
- Printing blocks – we used Indian Leaf Border and Indian Flower Design (small)
- Two fabric paint shades – we used Midnight Blue and Indian Aqua
- Thin paintbrush
- Basic printing equipment (see page 18)

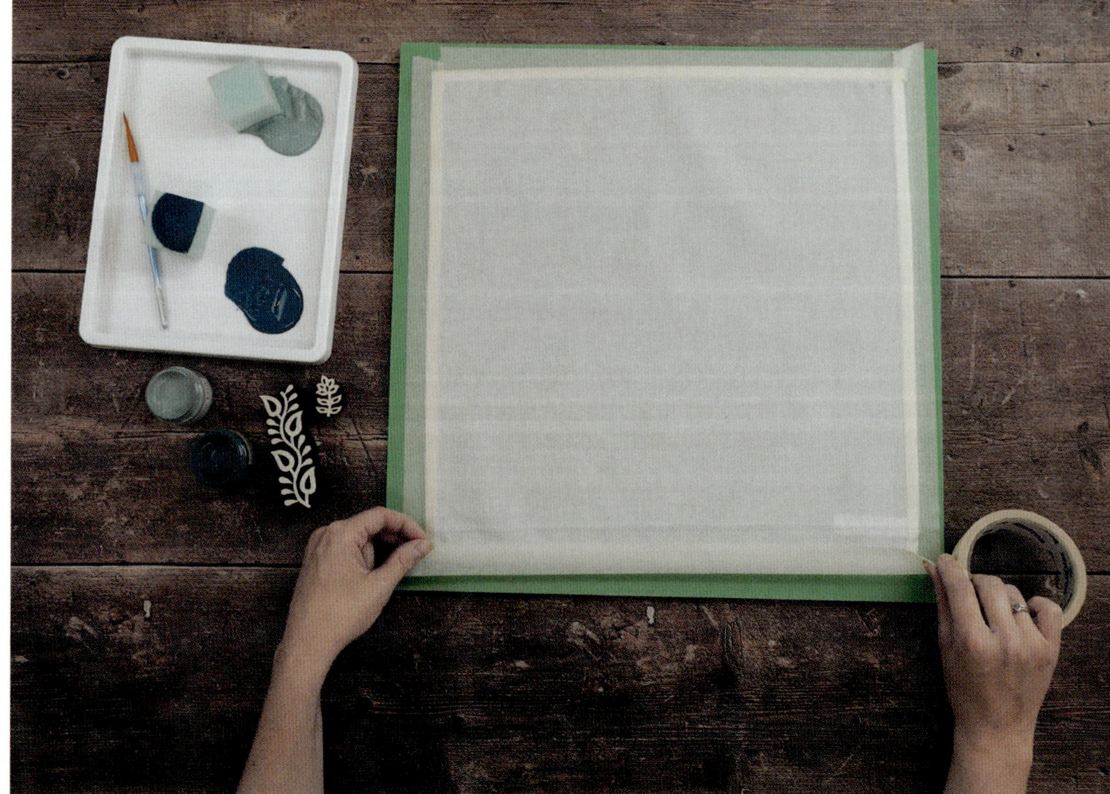

1 Lay one napkin on your foam mat. Apply masking tape to all four edges of the napkin and over the hemmed edges of the fabric. This will hold the napkin down while printing and keep the edges of the napkin paint-free, which will give you a more professional finish.

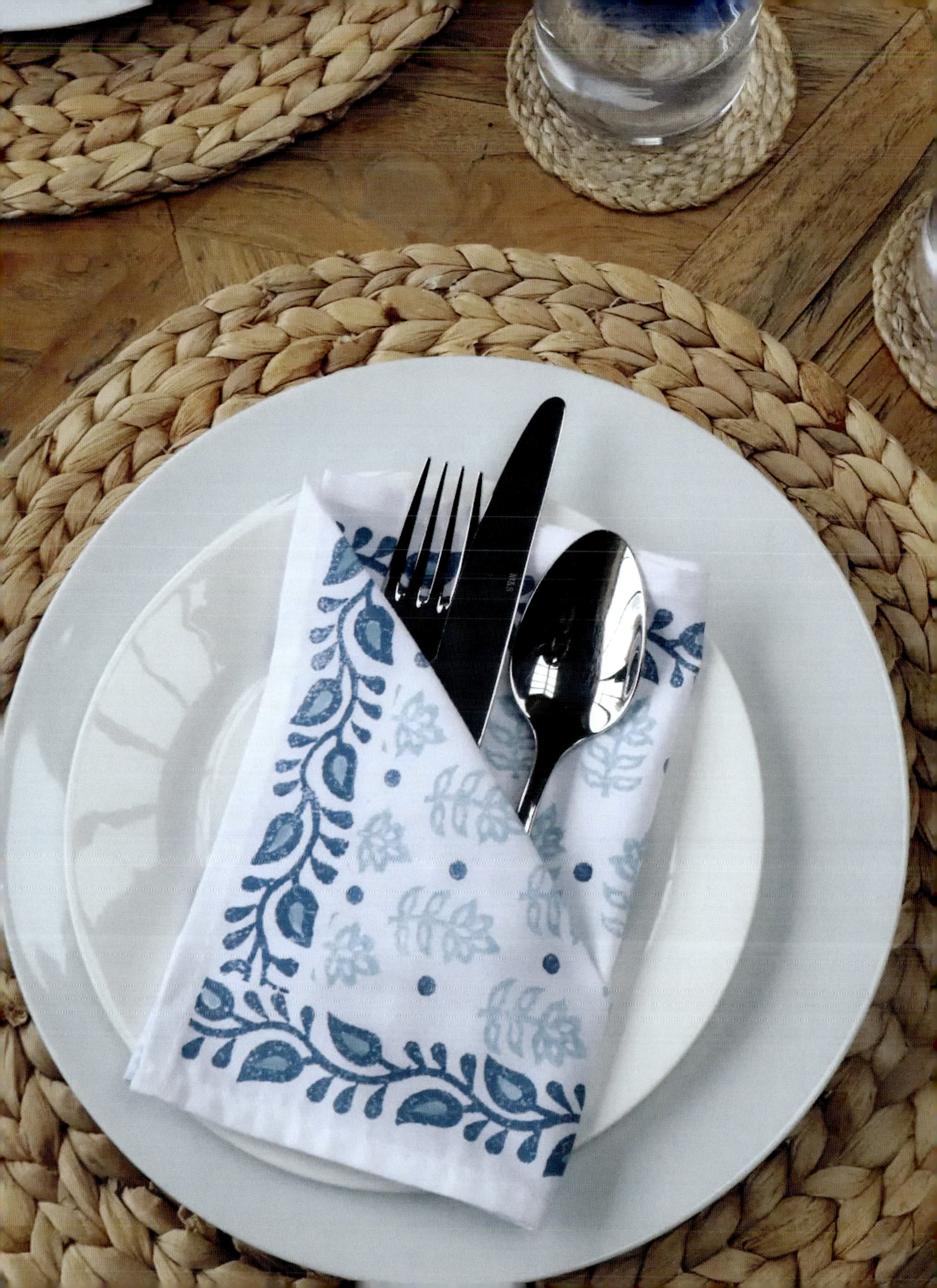

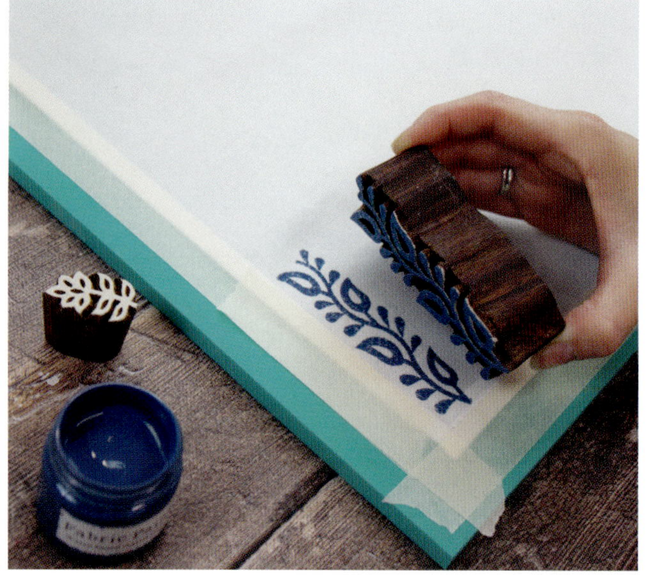

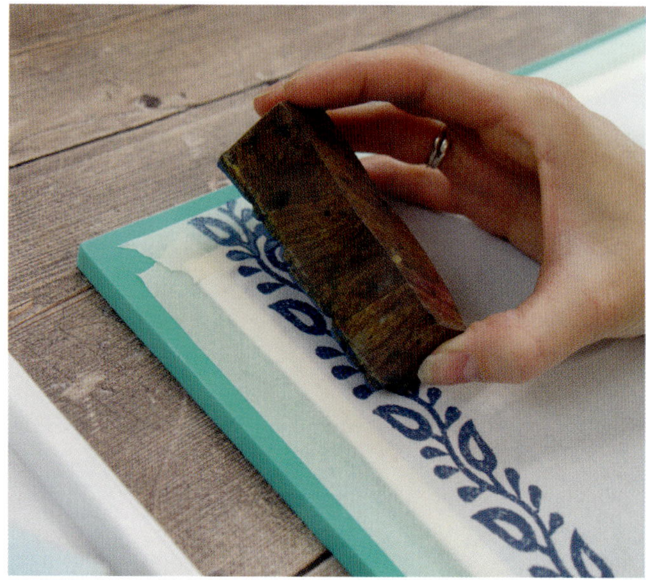

2 With this napkin design, we print the border first, and then fill in the remaining middle space. Start by printing your Indian Leaf Border print block in Midnight Blue in the bottom-left corner.

3 Continue to print the first edge of your napkin, making sure each design is touching for a continuous border print (see printing with borders, page 47). You will likely find that you aren't able to fit an exact number of whole border prints along the edge of the napkin, so your final print will overlap off the edge of the fabric and onto your masking tape, which will catch the extra paint.

4 Continue printing clockwise around all four sides of the napkin.

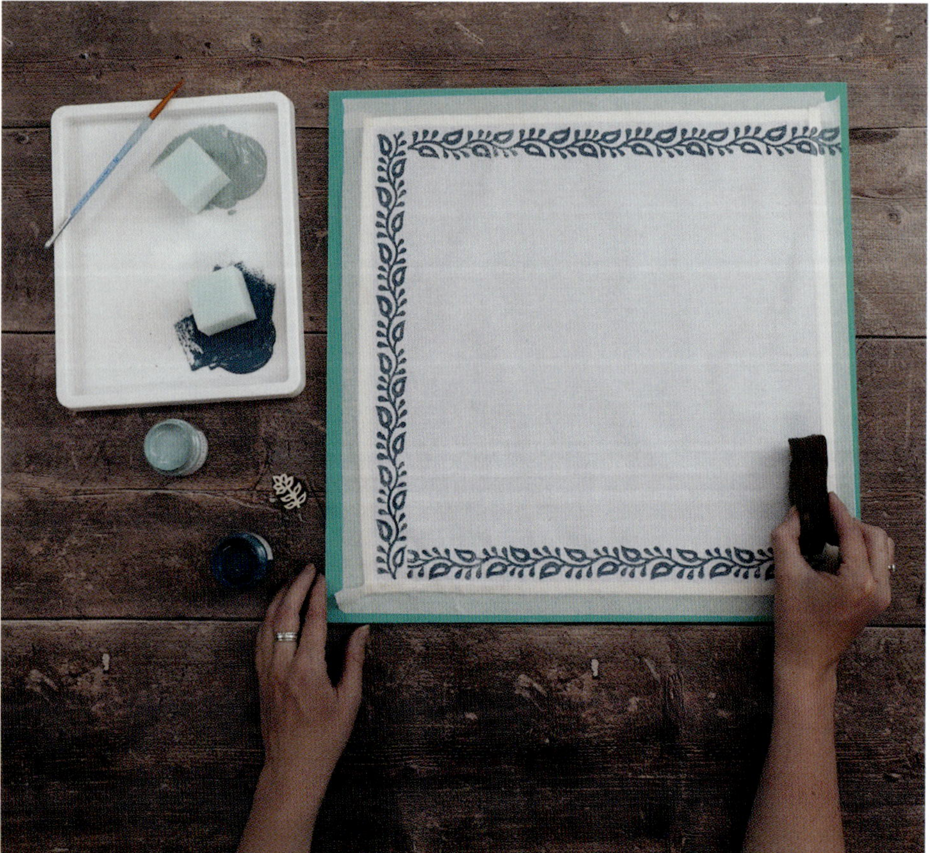

Printing Tip

When using a border or repeat design, practise with the printing block to learn how the design matches up when printed repeatedly. Remember, each block prints differently.

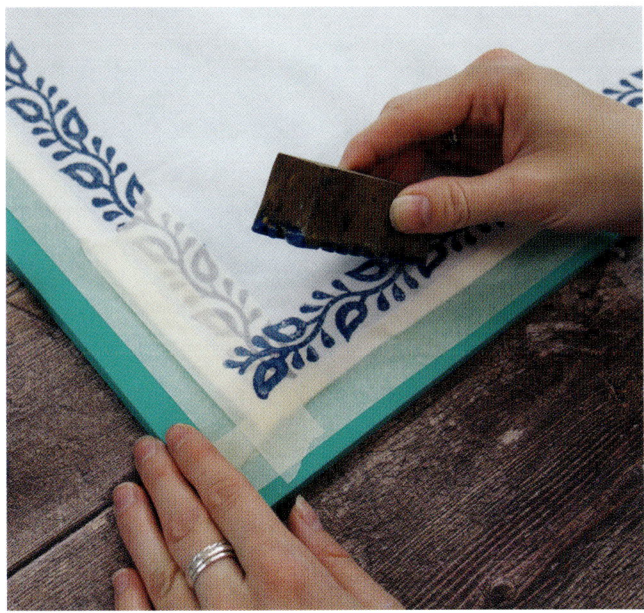

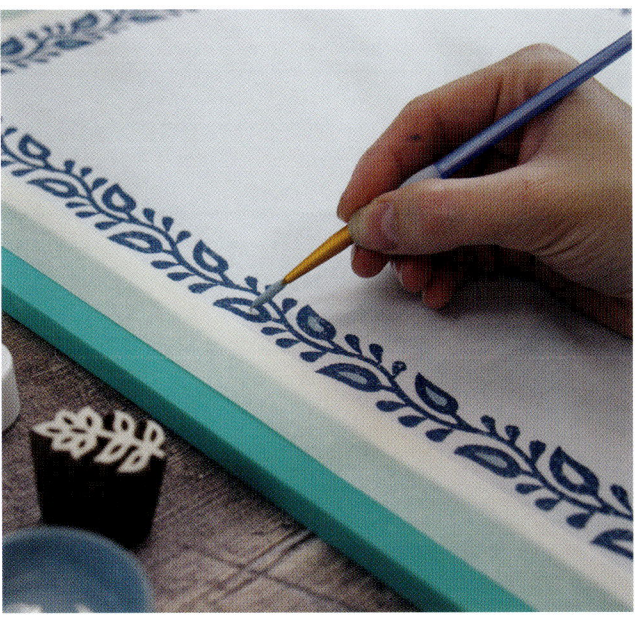

5 At the point where your final print meets the first, place a piece of masking tape over the first print (ensure it is dry before doing this to avoid smudging). This will stop the paint overlapping on this final corner, leaving you with a neat finish.

6 Use a thin paintbrush to add extra colour and detail to the border design. We infilled the leaf design on our Indian Leaf Border block with Indian Aqua paint.

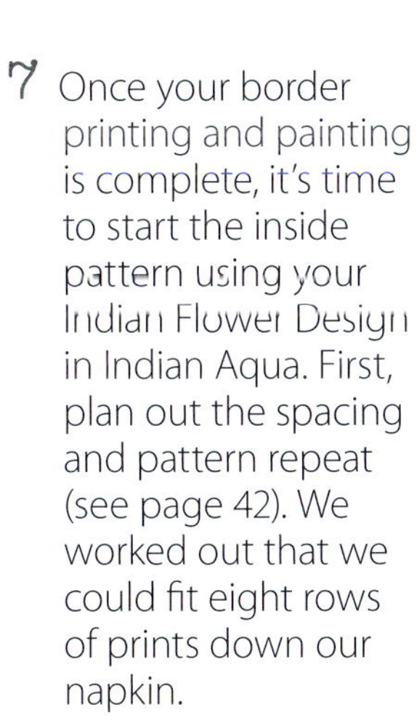

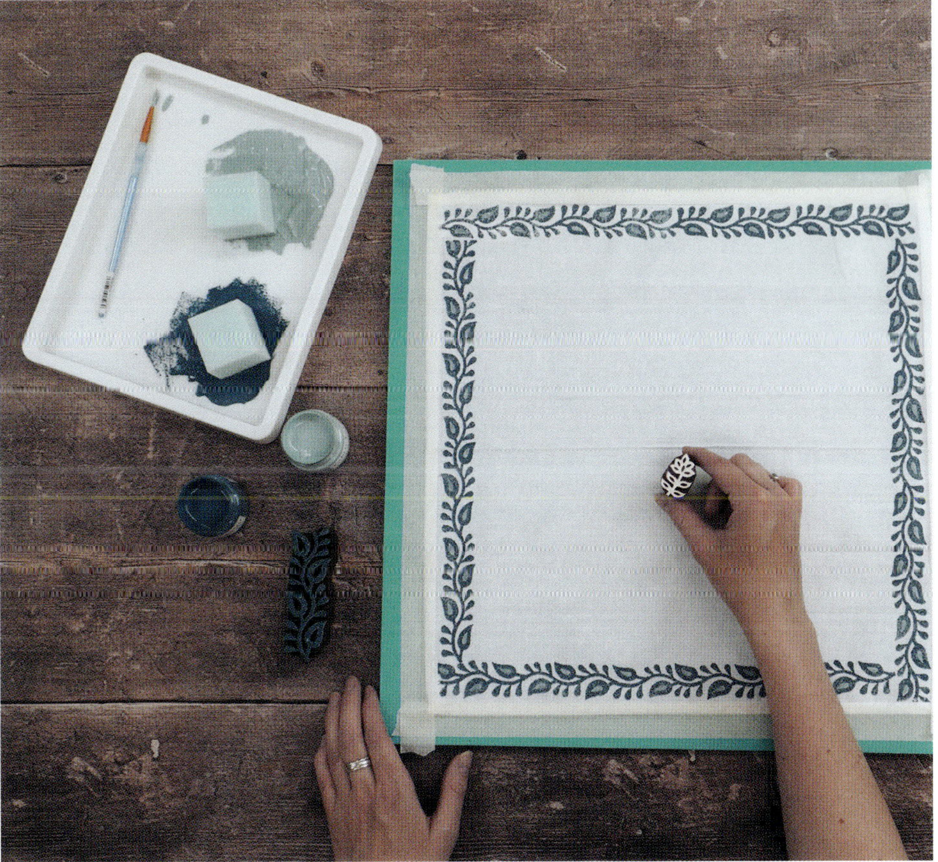

7 Once your border printing and painting is complete, it's time to start the inside pattern using your Indian Flower Design in Indian Aqua. First, plan out the spacing and pattern repeat (see page 42). We worked out that we could fit eight rows of prints down our napkin.

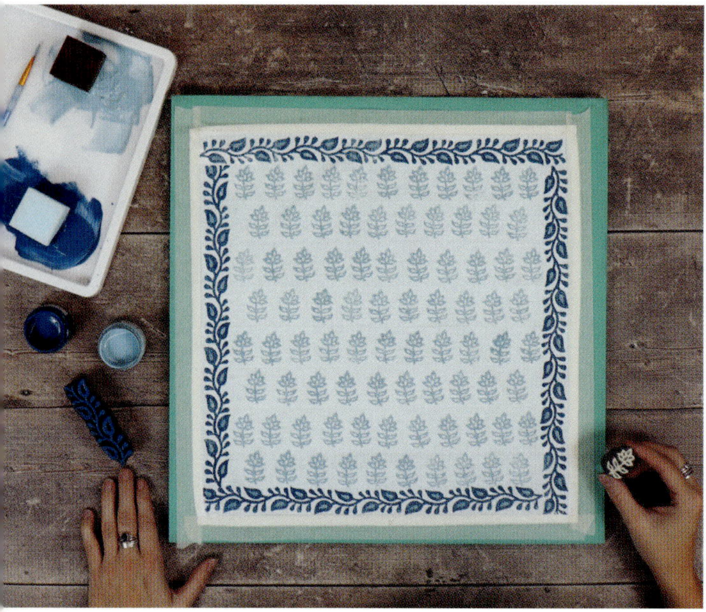

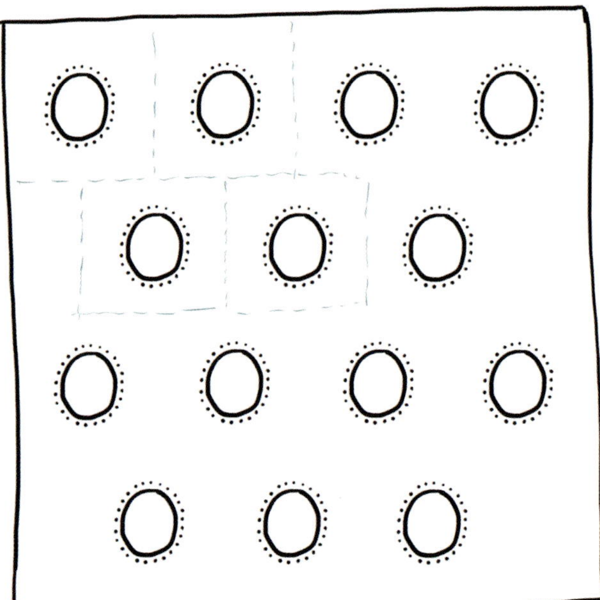

8 Use the fold and iron technique (see page 36) to create lines to follow when printing. We used a brick repeat pattern (see page 43).

9 Remember, with a brick repeat you have one less print on every second row.

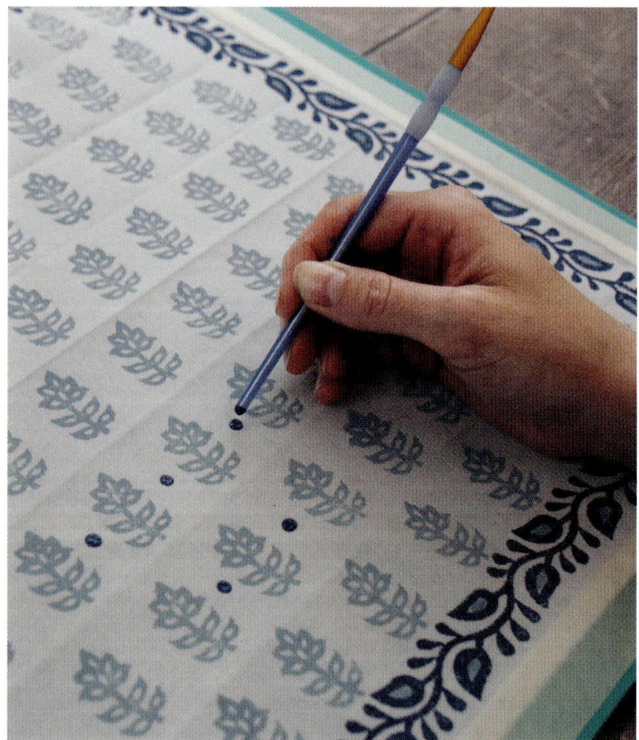

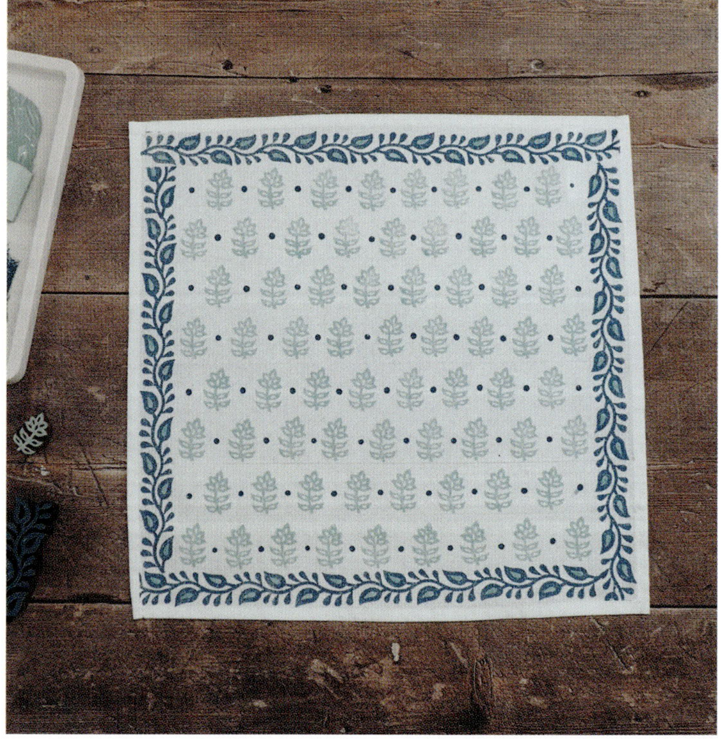

10 Use the end of your paintbrush to add a dot of darker-coloured paint between each print. This will fill in any white space and bring the entire design together.

11 Once the paint is dry, lift the napkin off your printing mat. Heat set your fabric paint to make it washable (see page 32).

Pigment Printing in India

Pigment printing is another technique we explore in India. Like the vibrant paints used in the UK, the paint is made by mixing pigment with a binder. The liquid is poured into wooden trays covered with wire mesh and fabric. To apply the paint, the printing block is tapped onto the fabric mesh in the tray, which coats the block with paint, preparing it for printing onto fabric. The paint is thinner, and the application method is much faster than using a sponge, which is crucial when printing large amounts of detailed fabric as quickly as possible.

With each trip, we expand our knowledge further. On our 2024 visit, our aim was to experiment printing with two-, three- and even four-colour printing blocks. This is a form of printing we'd like to replicate more in our own workshops, so it was the perfect time to learn a new technique.

There were thousands of printing blocks to choose from, so it can be a treasure hunt to find the multiple blocks that make up one design.

When working with a multi-block design, you print each block one at a time and on top of each other. Each layer will gradually fill the gaps in the previous print. The master block printers guided us on how to properly line up the layers, but much of our learning came from making mistakes and then understanding how to correct them.

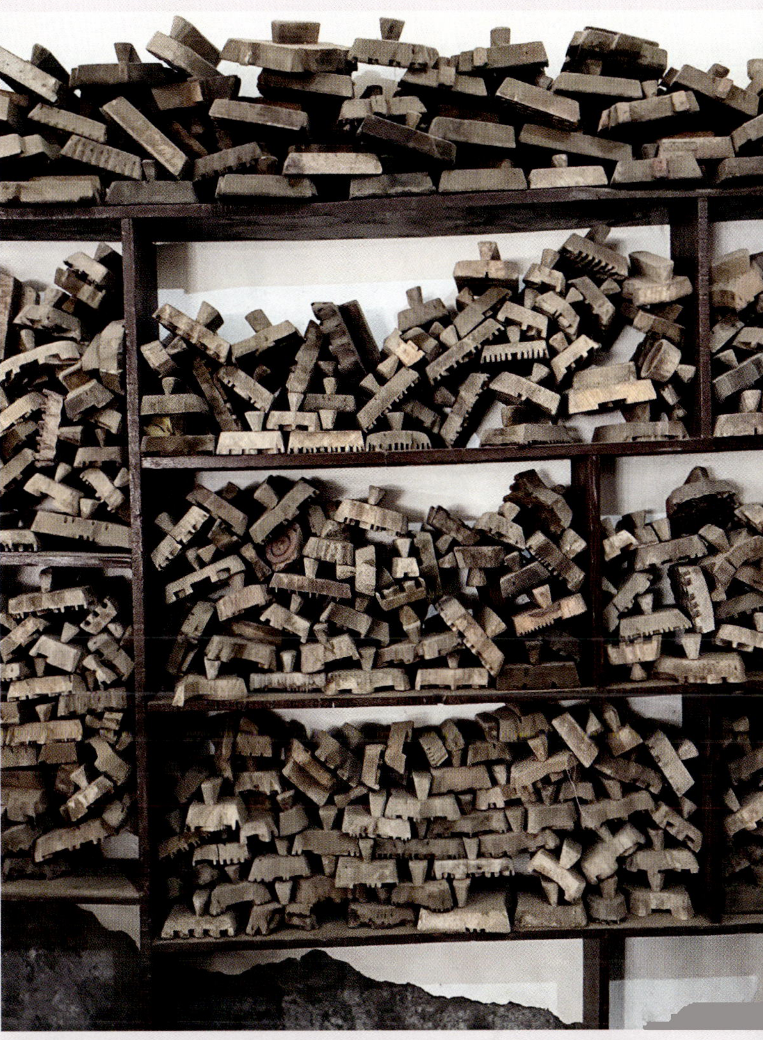

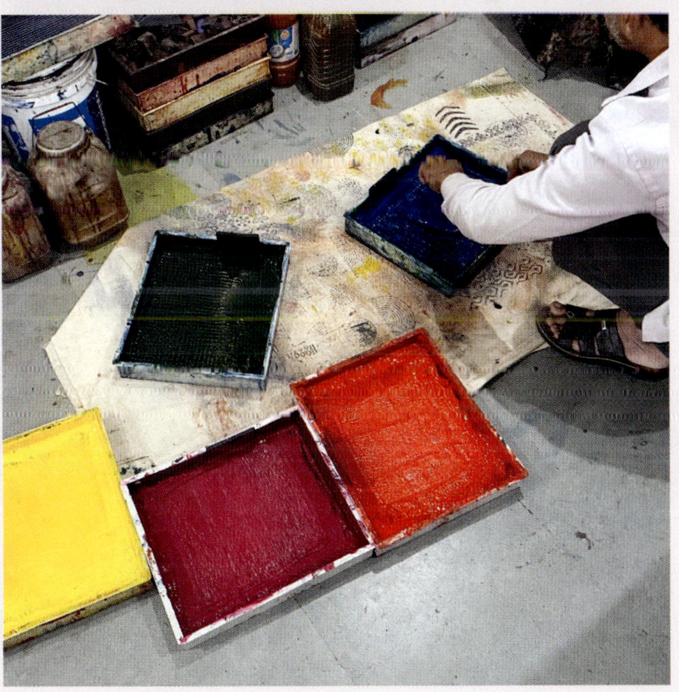

Above right: Printing block shelves in Bagru.

Right: Pigment paint trays in Bagru.

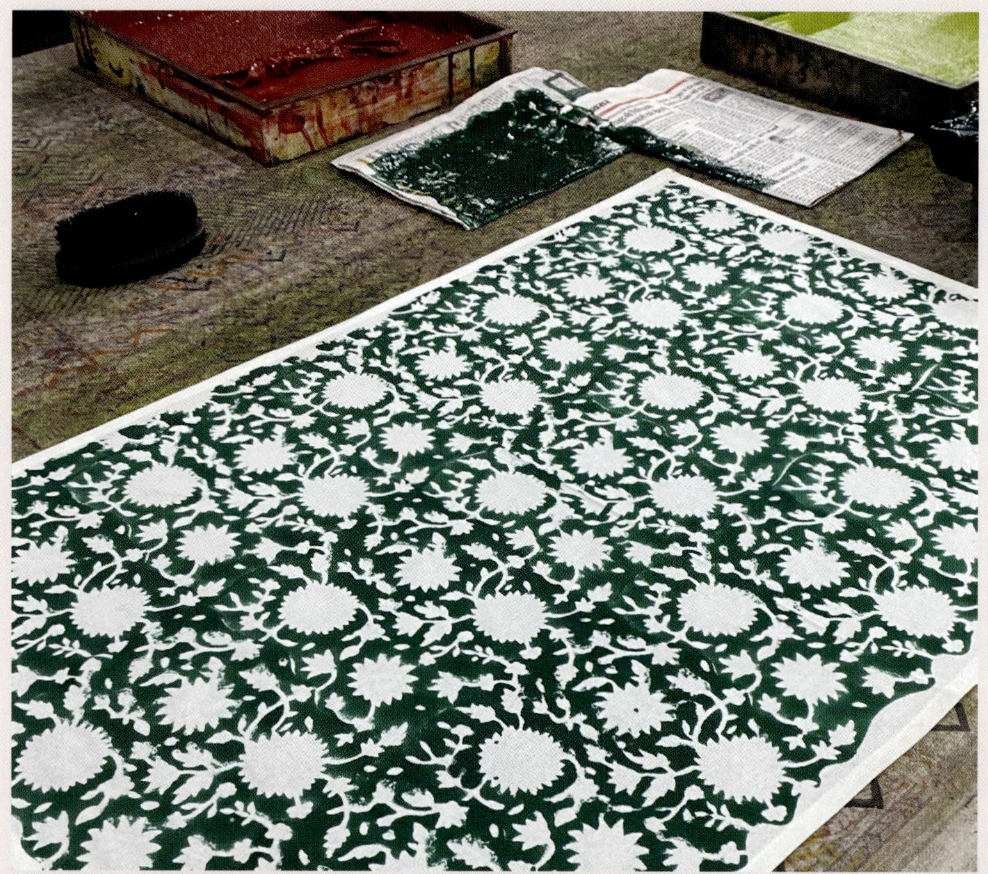

Anna experimented with a two-colour block-print design which she printed in blue and green. She started with the base print and, once this was dry, she could print over the top and add the more detailed layer.

Left: Anna's base layer in her first colour.

Below left: Anna's detailed layer in her second colour.

Below: Anna with her finished printed fabric.

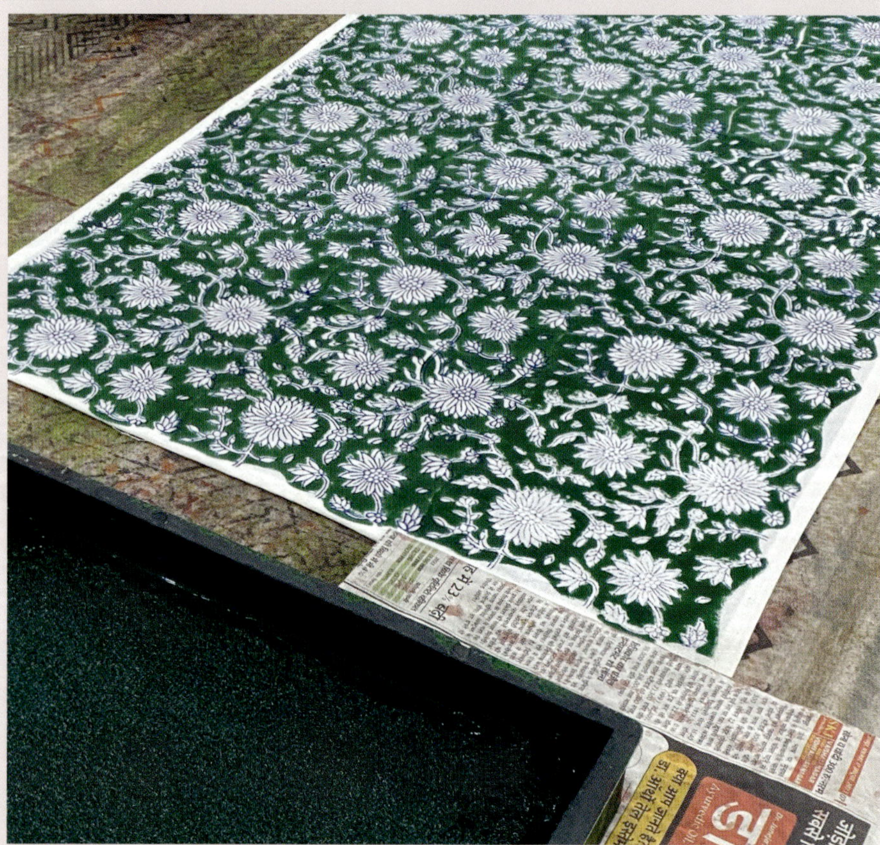

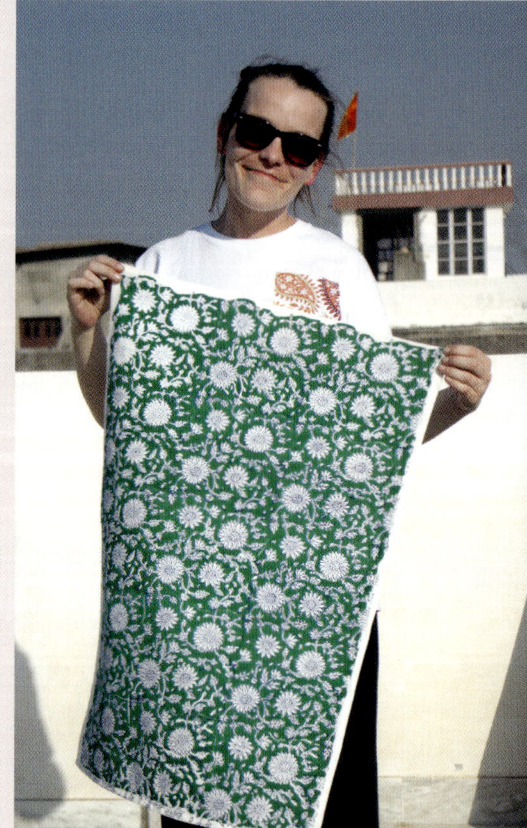

Tess printed with a three-colour paisley design. As the different layers get added, you can see the design become more intricate. The multiple layers and colours bring the design to life, making it more eye-catching and detailed.

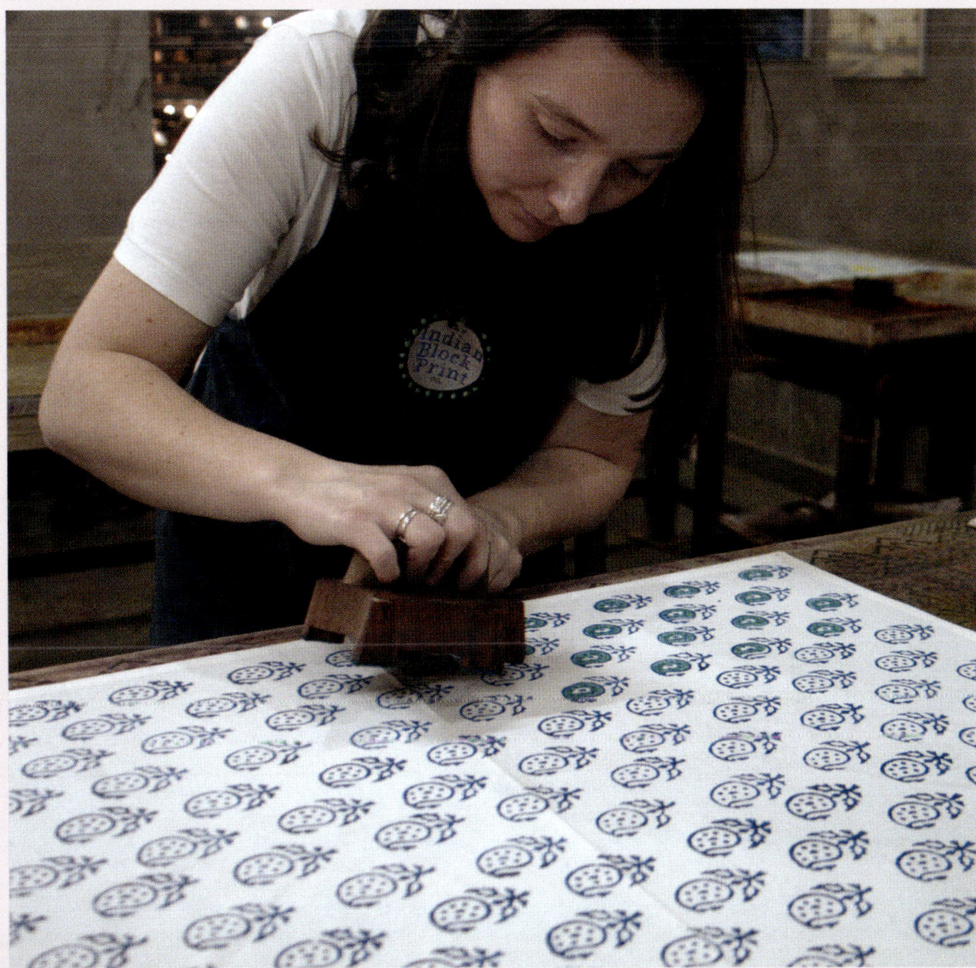

Below: Tess applies her second colour.

Below right: Tess with her final three-colour design.

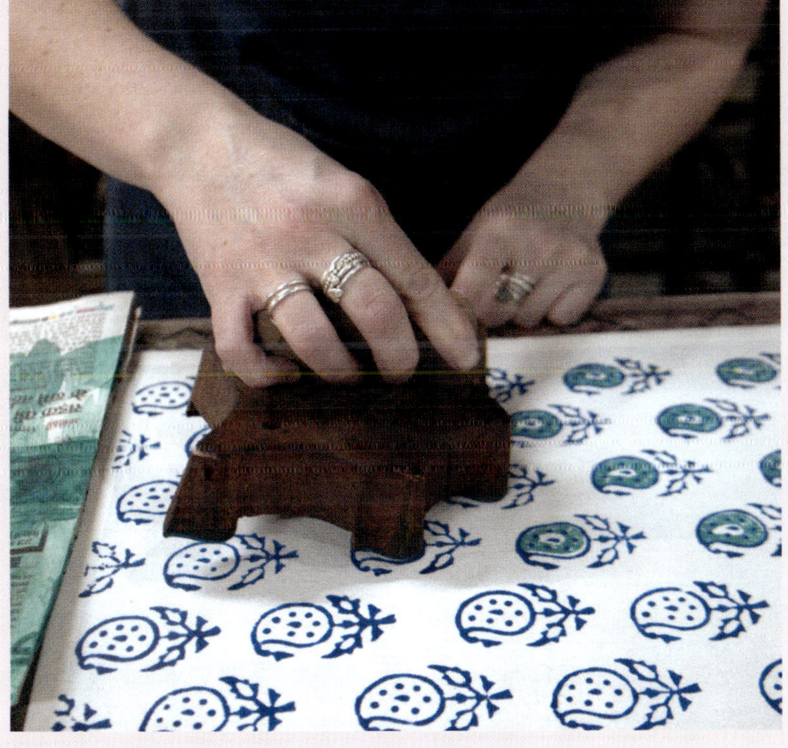

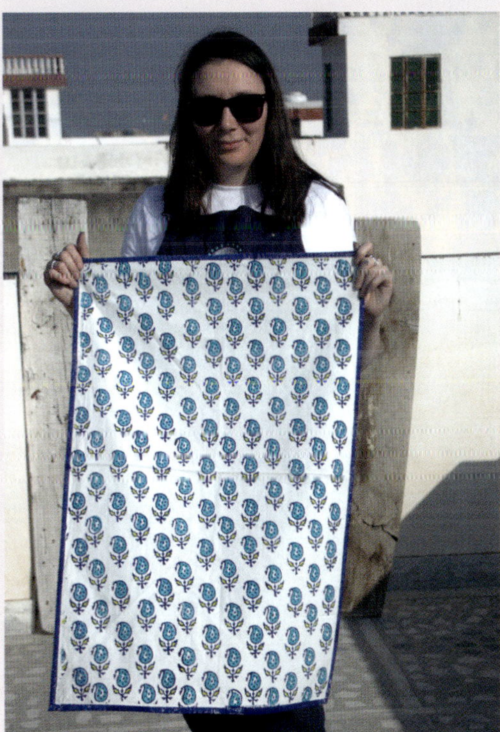

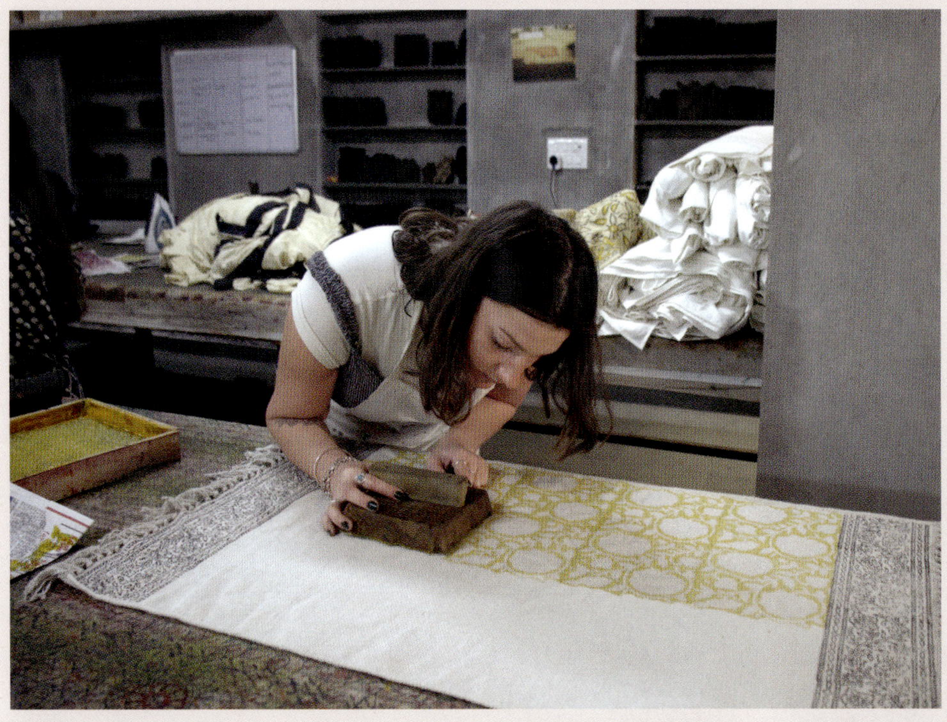

Annabel was extremely adventurous and printed a beautiful handwoven rug in a four-colour design.

Left: Annabel prints the borders and a yellow base layer.

Below left: She inserts the main pattern into the yellow base layer.

Below: Annabel with her finished four-colour rug.

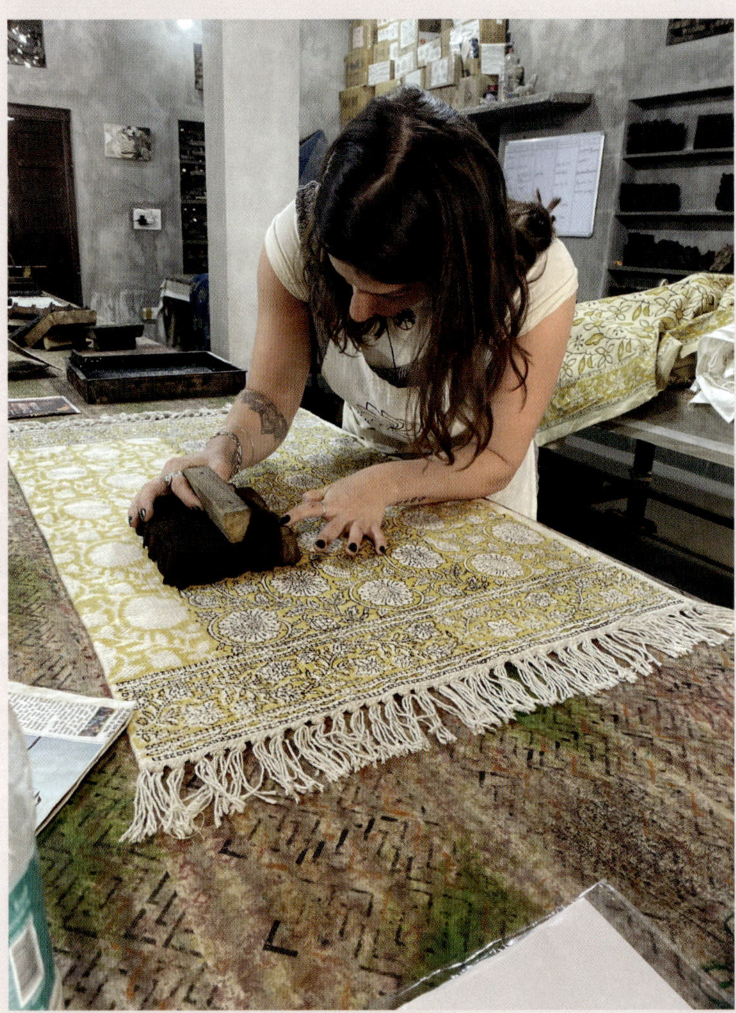

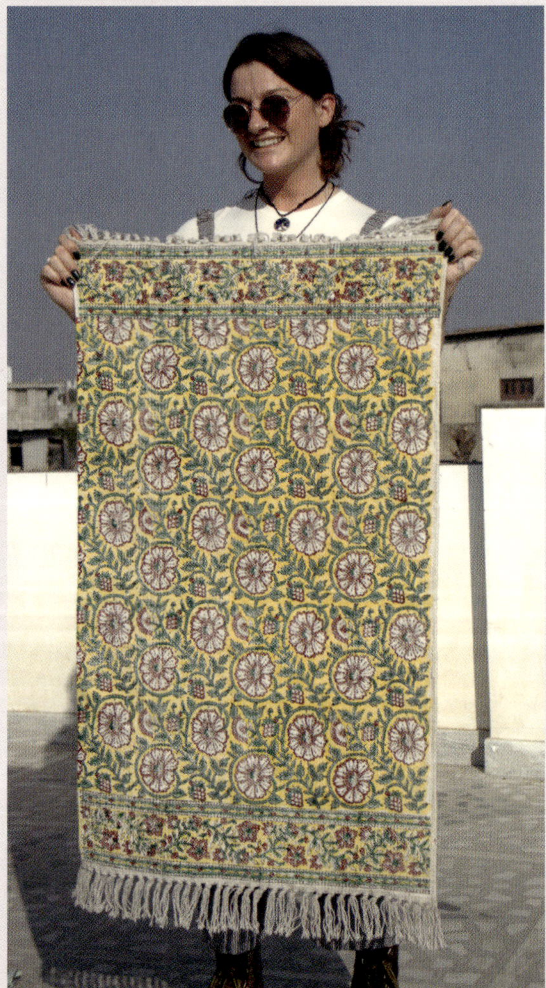

Using multi-layered printing blocks allows you to create stunning designs with intricate details. They do require precise printing and it's hard to get the prints lined up perfectly each time, but the little imperfections are what makes them handmade, which adds charm to the finished pieces.

Right: Tess, Maggie, Anna and Annabel in Bagru.

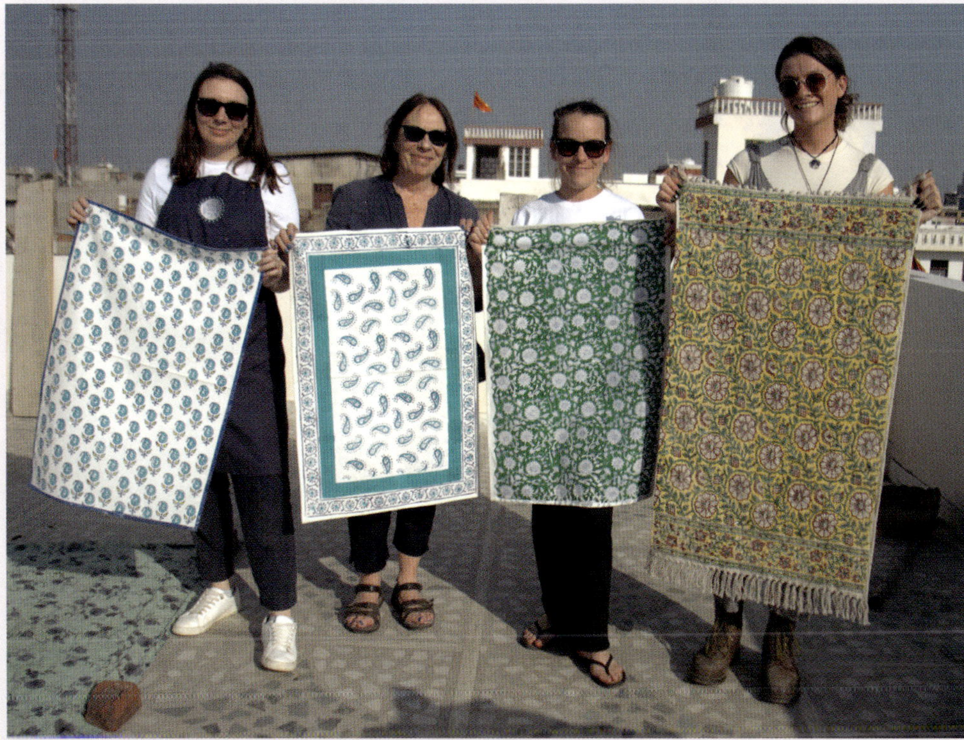

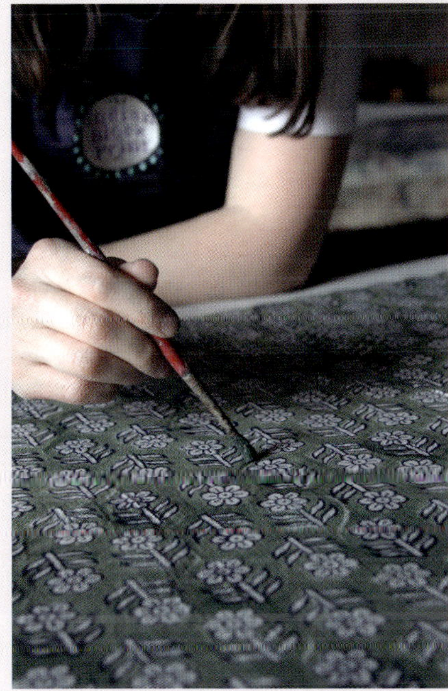

Touching up a hand-block printed design

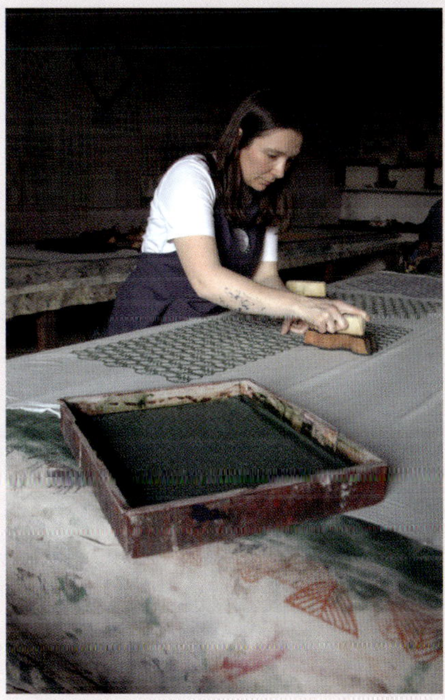

Tess printing at Studio Bagru, a workshop studio in Bagru.

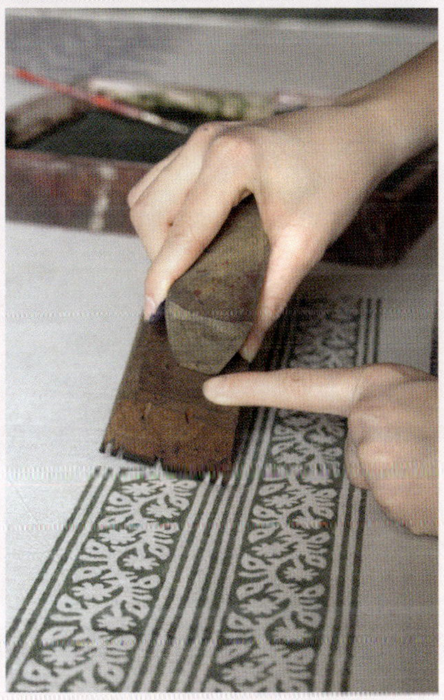

Printing with borders.

By focusing on the experience and learning rather than the result, we can explore and try new things, practise techniques and appreciate the art of printing in its simplest form. It's a great chance for us to go back to basics and enjoy the playful, learning side of printing. There's a special joy in just being part of the process without worrying about making something perfect.

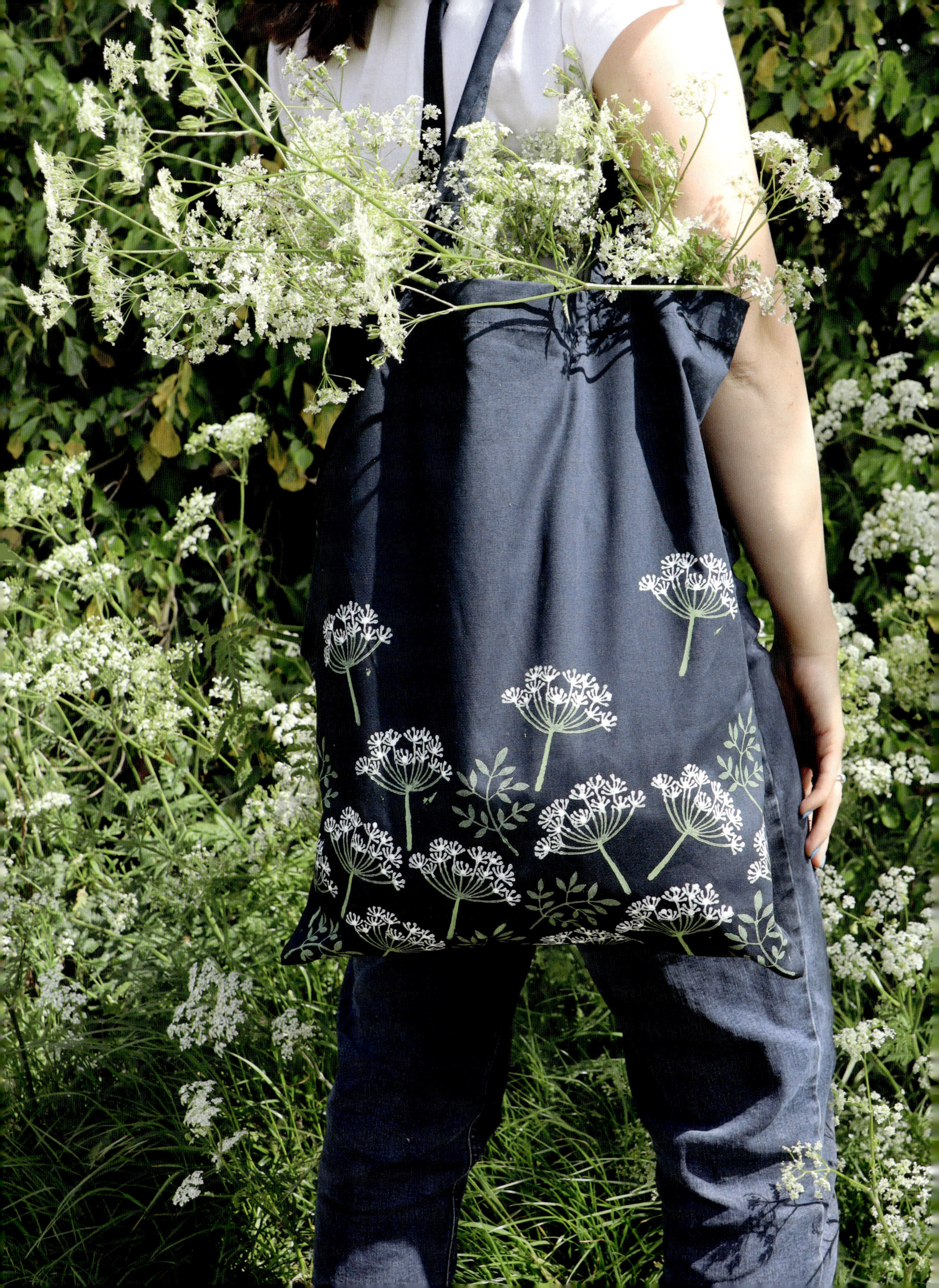

Cow Parsley Tote Bag

I n Oxfordshire's countryside cow parsley adds a touch of beauty to the green fields and hedgerows, transforming the landscape. As spring arrives, its delicate white flowers pop up and sway gently in the breeze, making the scenery even more charming for our countryside walks. It's a time of year we both look forward to as it brings with it fresh inspiration.

Our navy cow parsley tote bag has become a favourite for both of us, and a design that we have printed year after year. The bright white paint against the dark fabric really brings the print to life.

1 The Elegant Cow Parsley design uses two colours: light green for the stems and white for the flowers. Use a fabric or textile paint that is suitable for printing onto darker fabric. Practise the colour blend to ensure you're confident before getting started (see precise two-colour printing, page 24).

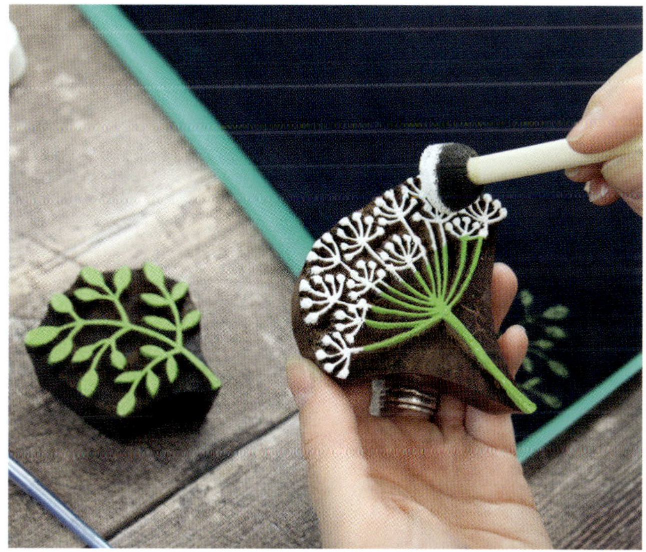

2 In the bottom-left corner of your bag print with your Leaf Bunch design using the light green fabric paint.

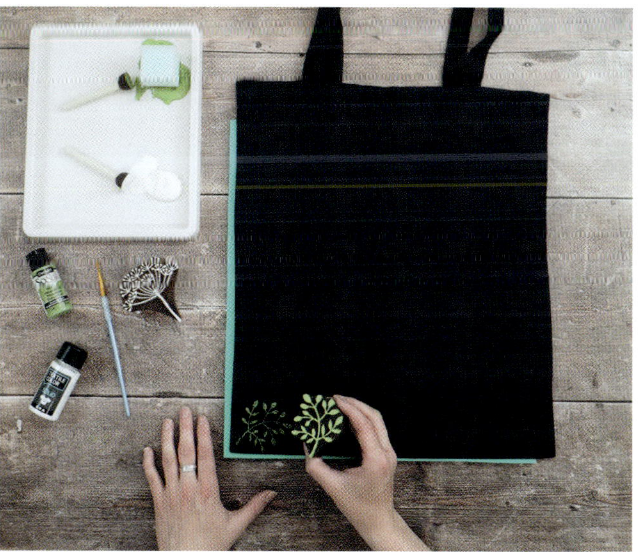

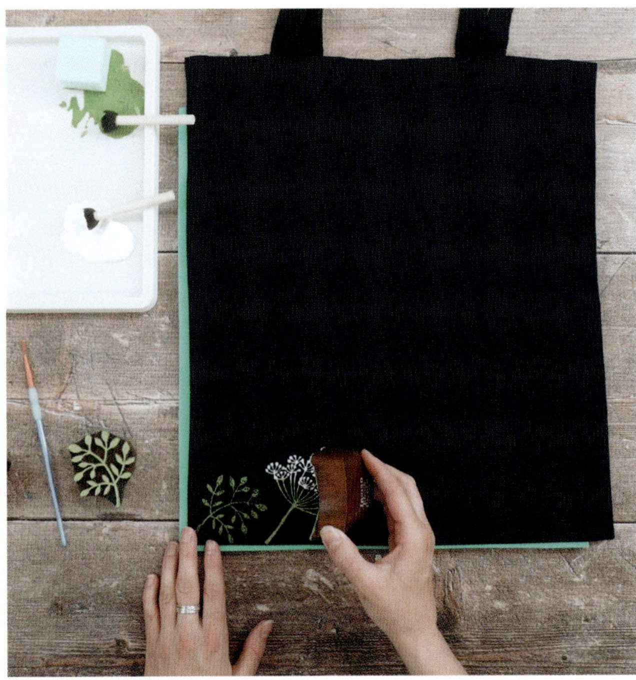

3 Take the Elegant Cow Parsley design, apply your two colours and print it right next to your initial print. Angle the printing block so it fits snugly next to your Leaf Bunch.

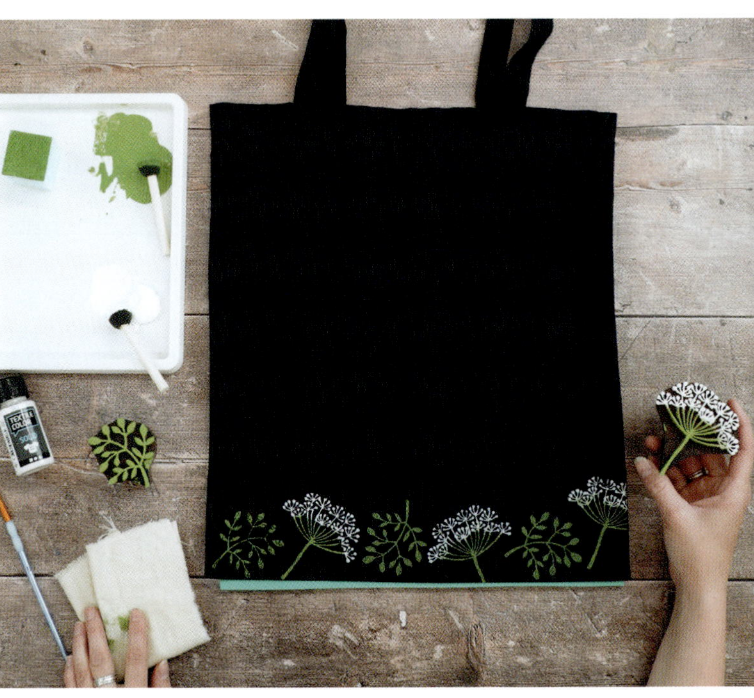

4 Continue to alternate between the two designs and keep changing the direction of each print to help the design feel natural and free-flowing. Don't squeeze the designs in; it's fine if half a print goes off the edge of your tote.

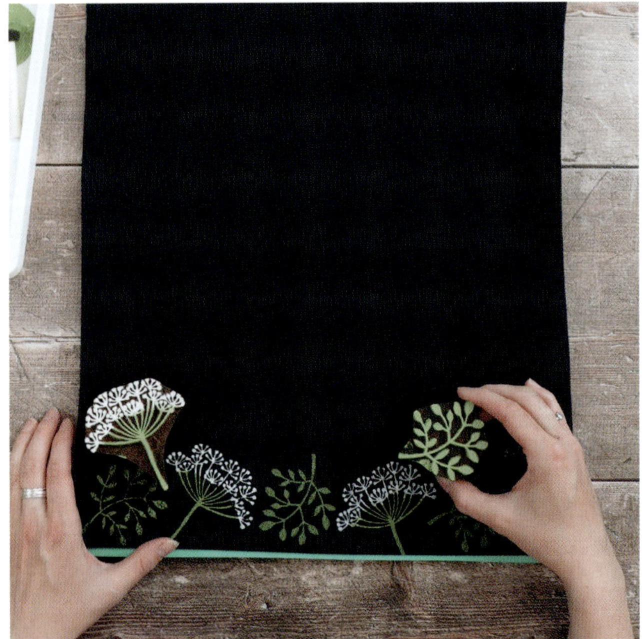

5 Once you've completed the first row, move up to print a second layer. Working in rows helps to ensure the design is well spaced.

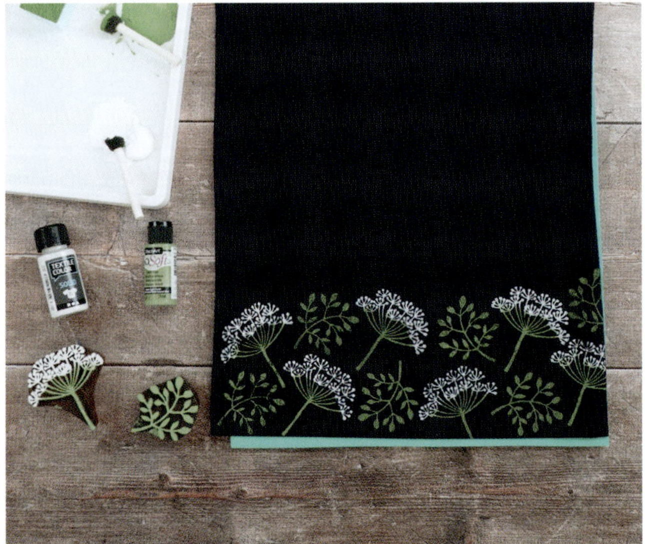

6 Slot the prints into gaps, thinking about placement before putting your blocks down, and keep changing the direction of the design. Continue until you have printed two rows to fill the bottom third of the bag. Printing just this section gives a thicker, meadow feel to the design.

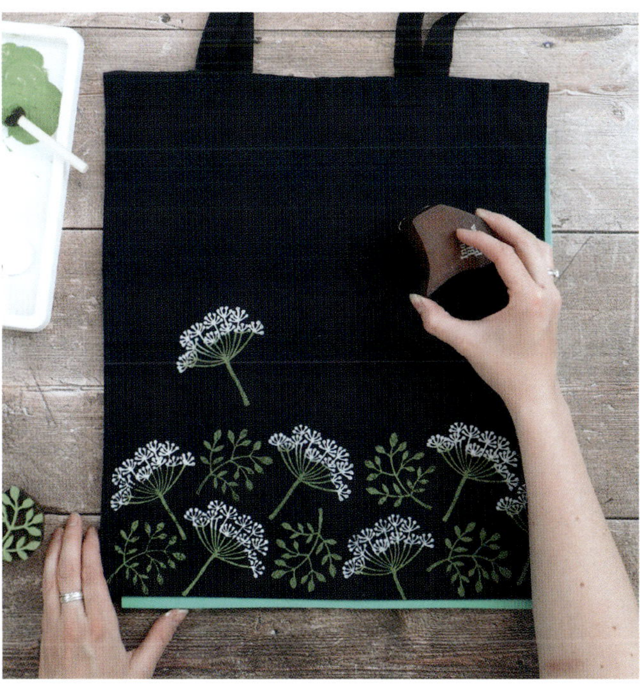

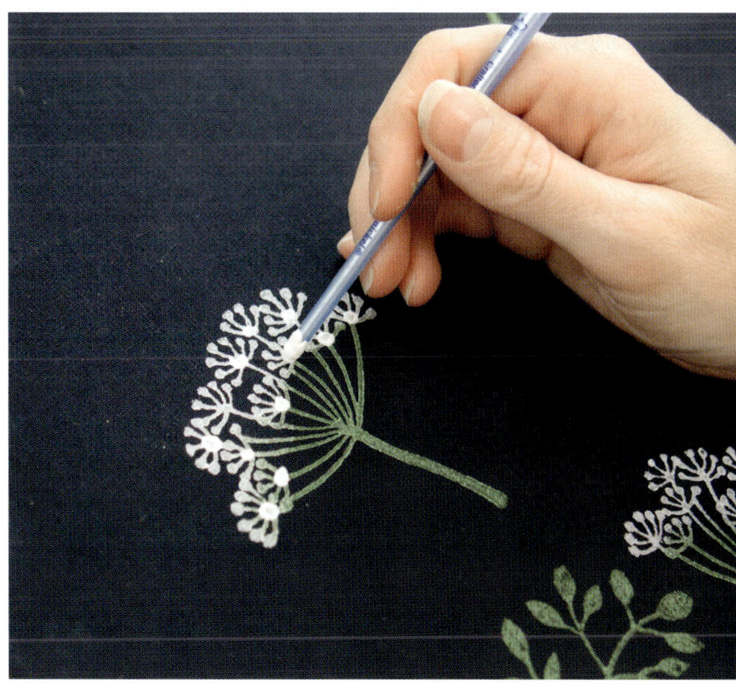

7 Scatter several Elegant Cow Parsley prints in the empty space in the top two-thirds of the bag to bring the design together.

8 To add the finishing touch, use the end of a paintbrush to add white dots to the top of the Elegant Cow Parsley prints. This enhances the blossom effect.

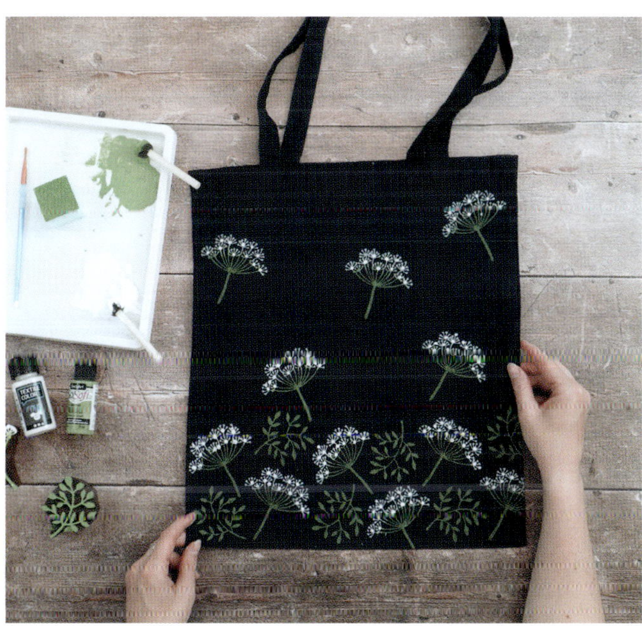

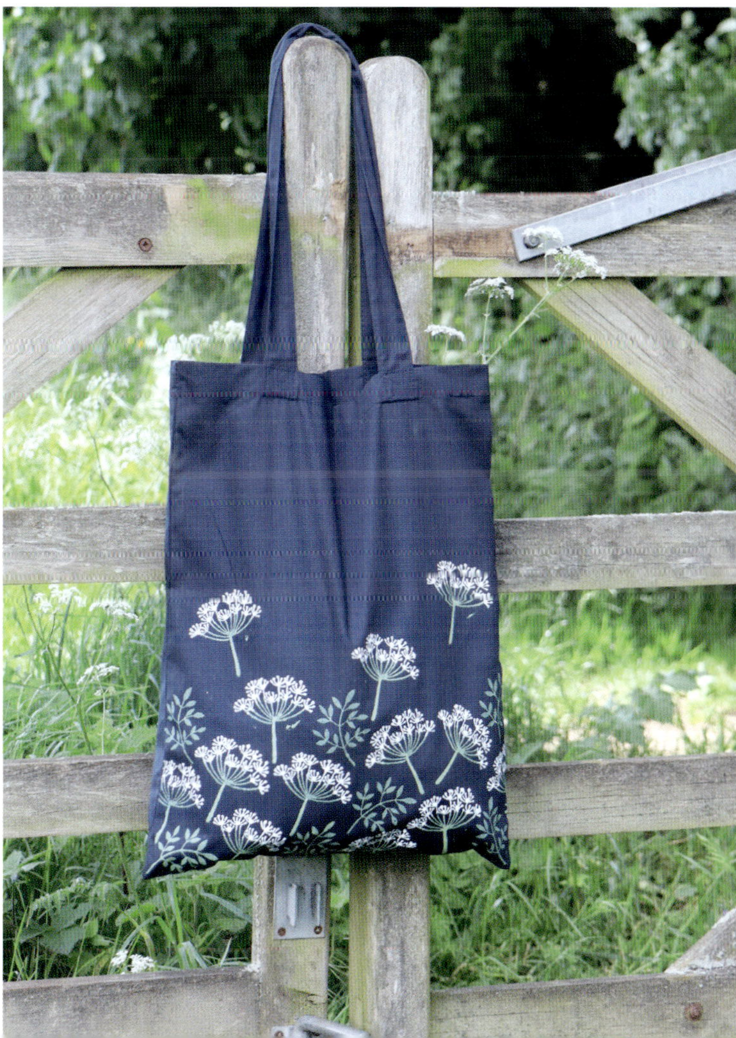

9 Dots of paint take longer to dry, so we suggest leaving your bag for 30 minutes. Once dry, turn the bag over and repeat Steps 2–9 on the opposite side.

Sensational Scarf

Hand-printing your own scarf is a wonderful project for any block printer to try. You have the freedom to choose your own designs, colours and patterns to work with, allowing you to create a scarf that matches your wardrobe and is uniquely yours. A scarf can also make a personalised gift, which will make a cherished present for someone special.

The great thing about a scarf is you don't have to print all the fabric. We tend to stick with printing each end of the scarf and leaving the middle plain, which you can't see anyway once someone is wearing it. This scarf will work in a variety of colours. Choose three tones that work together; start with your darkest colour, and, as you work your way up the scarf, lighten the shade at each stage.

YOU WILL NEED

- White cotton scarf
- Printing blocks – we used Indian Circle Pattern Border, Scalloped Border (small) and Tall Indian Leaf
- Fabric paints – we used Lavender, Violet and White
- Basic printing equipment (see page 18)

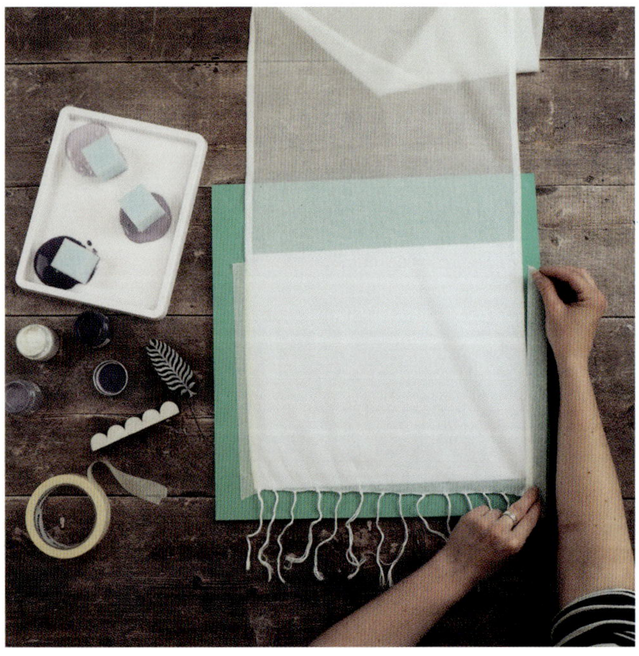

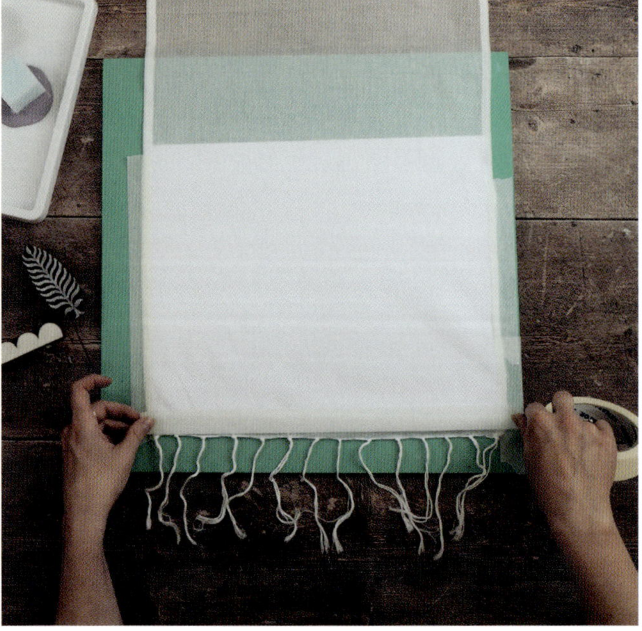

1 Iron the scarf to remove any creases. When printing a scarf, you want to ensure the fabric is flat and taut. To do this, use masking tape or pins to secure the scarf to the printing mat. Pop a piece of paper under your scarf – if the fabric is thin, this will catch any paint from transferring through to your mat. Add masking tape to the edge of the scarf to cover 2–3 mm each side.

2 Add a straight line of masking tape to the bottom of your scarf. Our fringed edge causes the scarf to taper inwards at the bottom, so we start our first row of prints 1.5 cm up from the bottom of the fabric.

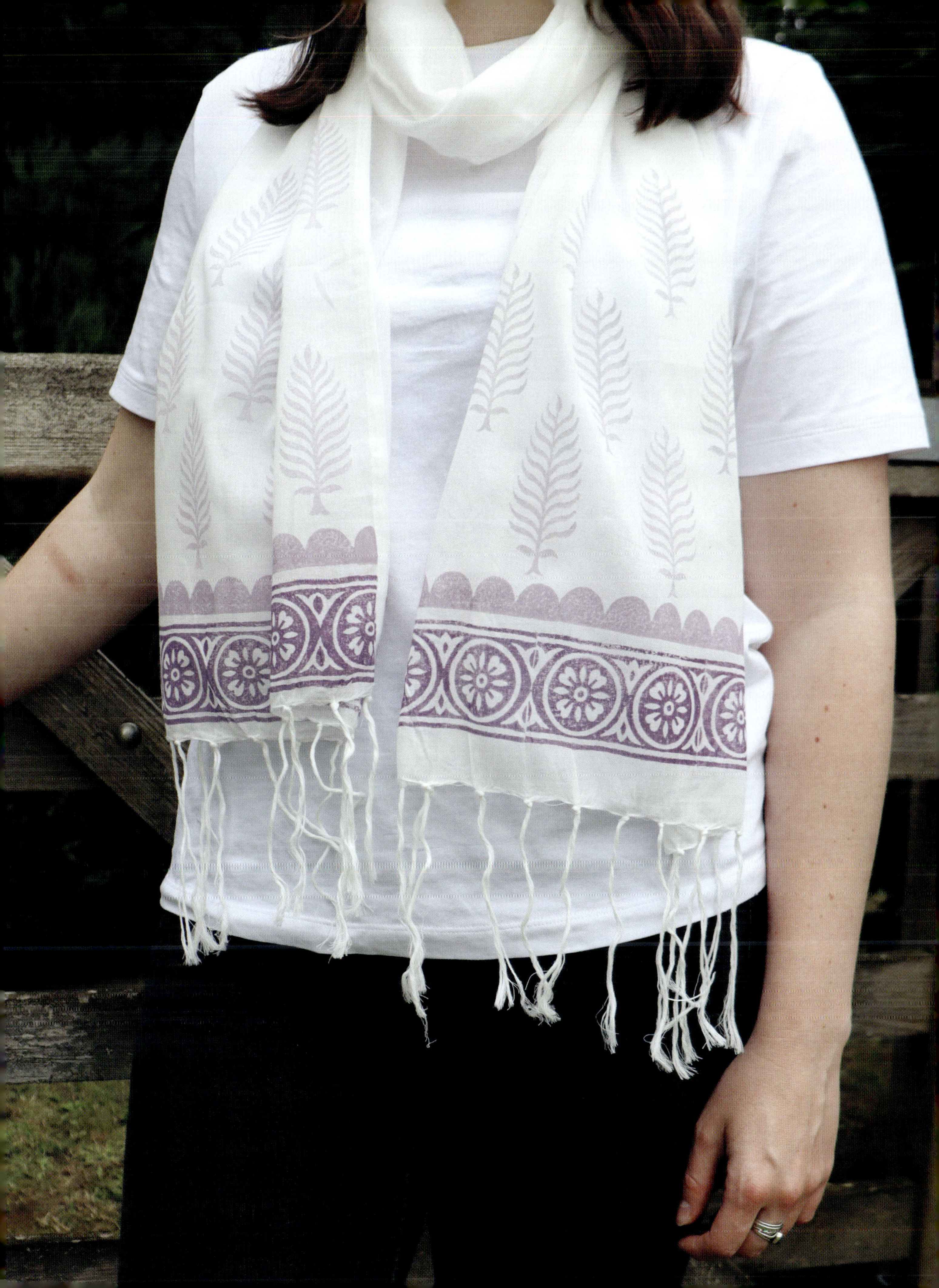

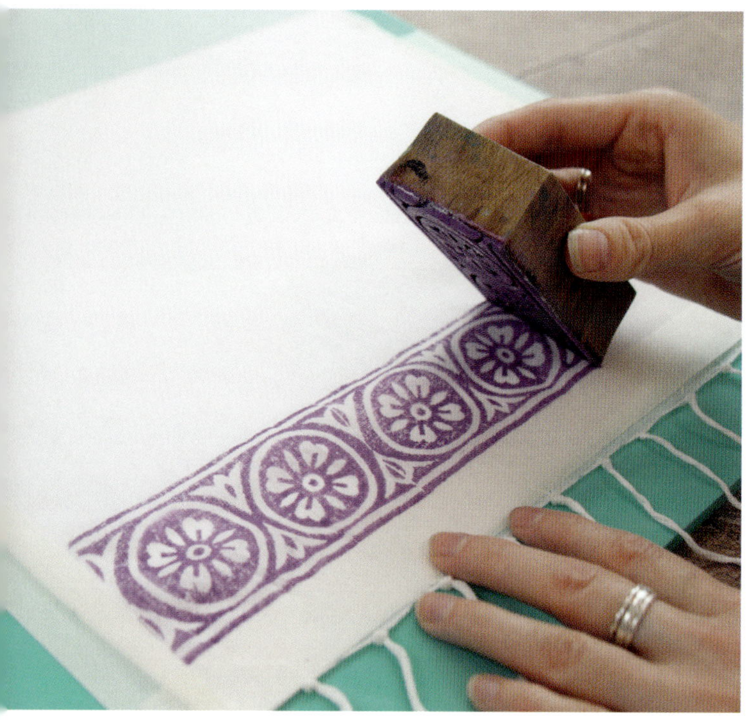

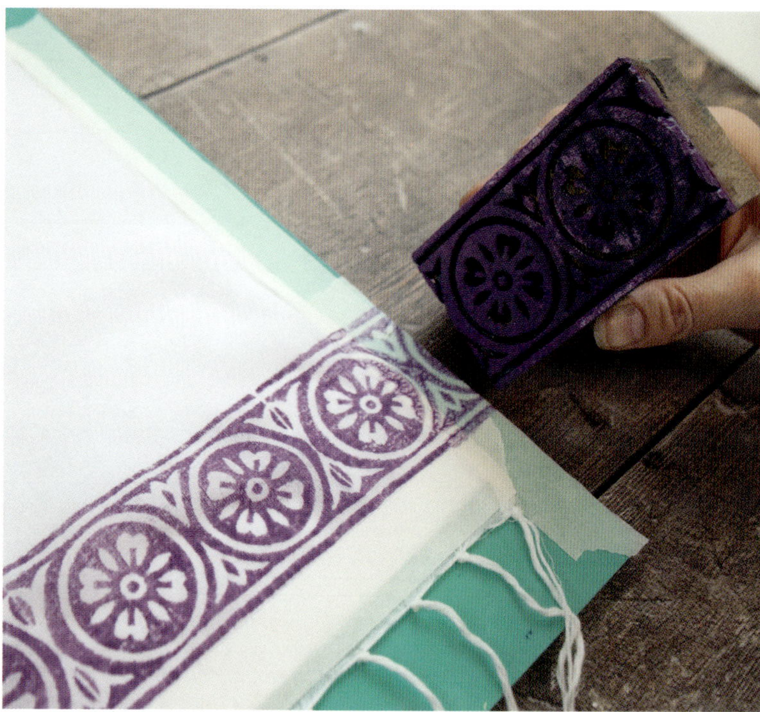

3 We started our scarf design with our Indian Circle Pattern Border block in Lavender, beginning on the left-hand side and working across the scarf (see printing with borders, page 47). Apply masking tape as a straight line to follow and ensure each print touches to create a continuous design.

4 If your border print doesn't fit across the width of your scarf an exact number of times, you can do a partial print. Ensure the masking tape is positioned over the hemmed edge and then print over the tape and onto your mat. When you lift your scarf up, once the printing is finished, you'll be left with a neat edge and a partial print that fits perfectly onto the fabric.

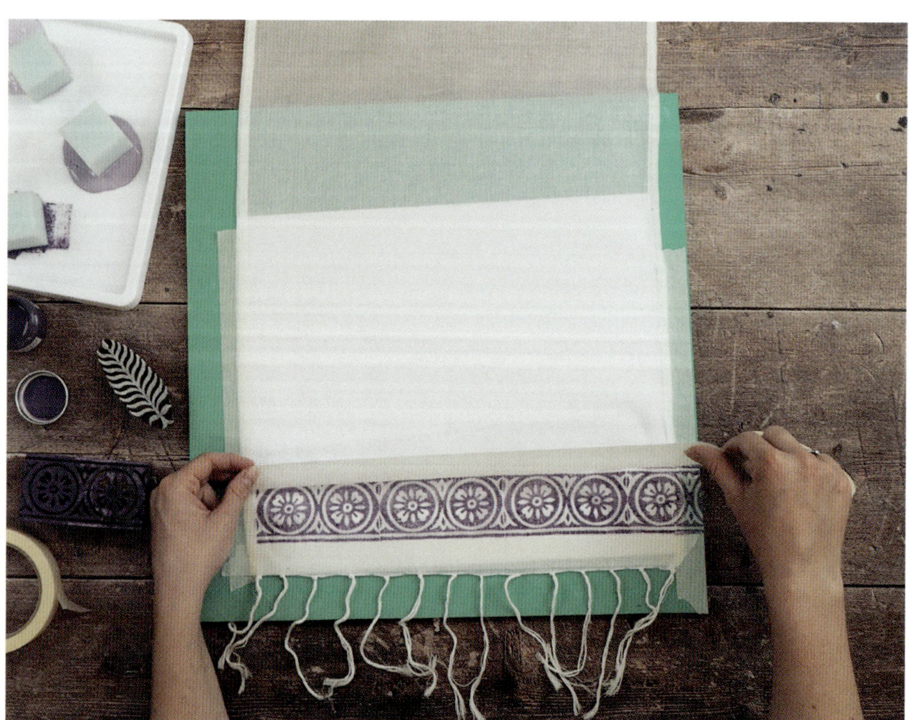

5 After completing the first border, move on to the next. Lay down a new piece of masking tape as a straight line to follow for your second border design.

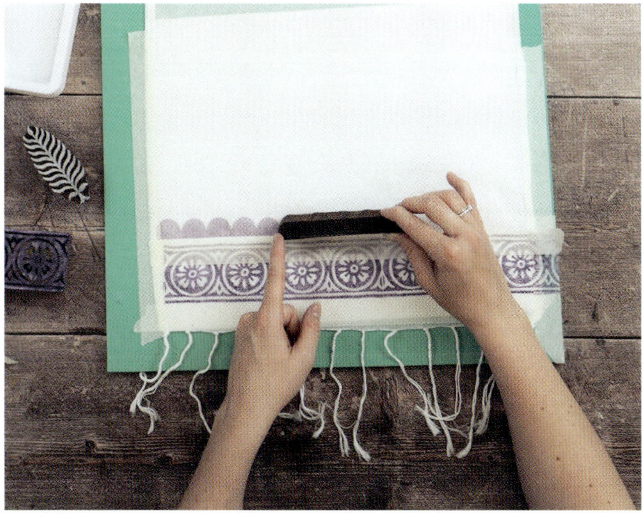

6 Print the next border in the same way you printed the first. Here we printed our Scalloped Border block using our lighter purple colour, Violet.

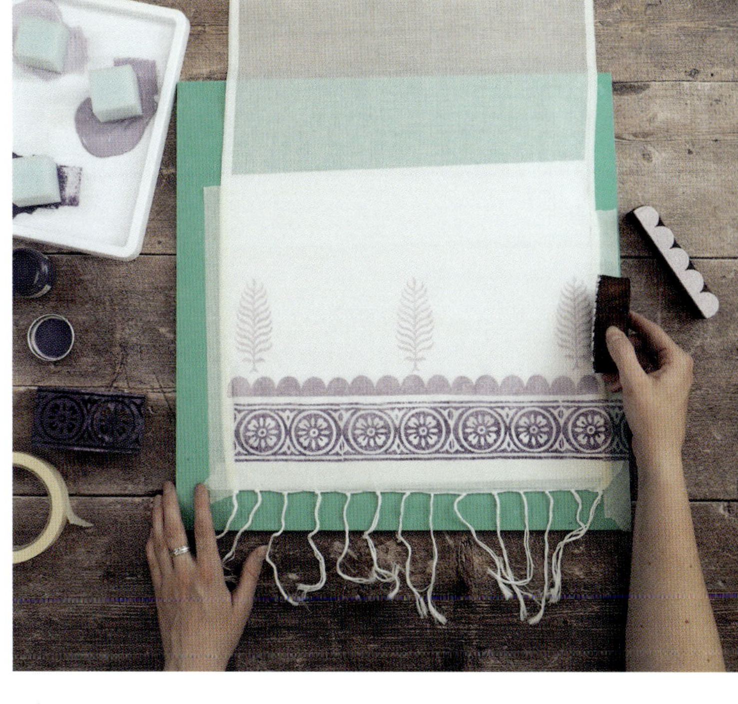

7 Once you've completed your two border prints, it's time to work on the pattern for the rest of the fabric. We're using a Tall Indian Leaf design and we've mixed White with our Violet paint to create a third, lighter shade to print with. We're going to print in a half-drop repeat pattern (see page 43). To help with spacing, first print your two outer prints and the centre design, then fill in the remaining gaps either side of the centre print.

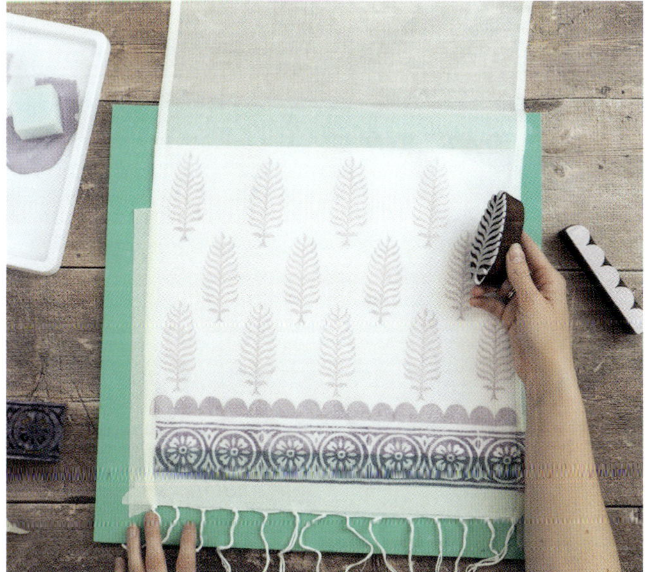

8 With a half drop repeat pattern, your next row will have one less print, the row above that will swap back to the original number of prints, and so on. Follow this pattern as you work your way up the scarf. For this design, we only print one-third of the scarf.

9 Once you reach this point, remove the tape holding the scarf onto your mat and repeat all the steps on the opposite end. Let the fabric dry before removing the scarf from your printing mat.

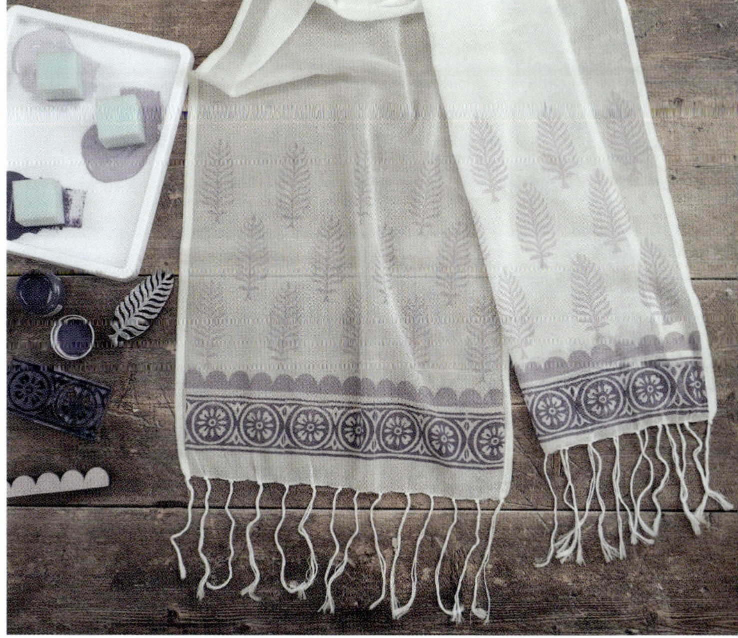

Natural Dye Printing in India

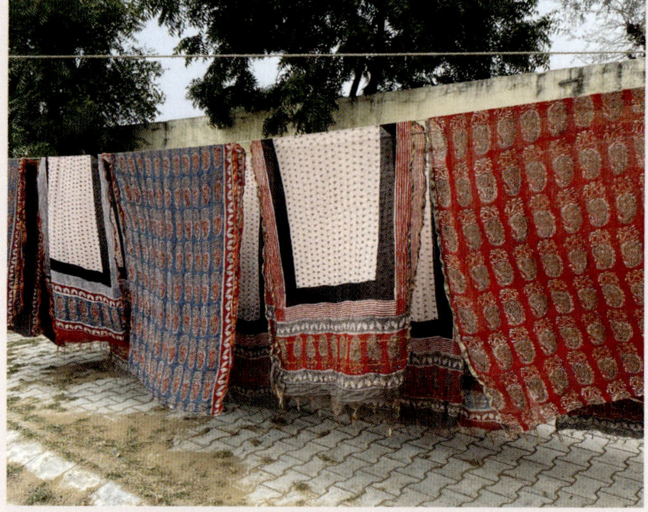

Above: Drying fabric in the sun.

Natural dye printing is a popular medium in India, especially in regions known for their traditional textile crafts, such as Rajasthan. In Bagru you'll find lots of natural dyes being used, including indigo, madder and turmeric. These eco-friendly dyes are sourced from plants, minerals and other natural sources.

In India natural dyes are used in block printing for a variety of reasons – the main being tradition, sustainability and the unique qualities these dyes offer. They are also better for the environment. Unlike synthetic dyes, which can contain harmful chemicals and contribute to pollution of the land and water sources, natural dyes are eco-friendly, biodegradable and can act as an organic fertiliser when returned to the ground.

Natural dyes also produce earthy tones that give textiles a unique look. These colours often have a softer, more organic appearance compared to synthetic dyes, such as the pigment paints we looked at earlier that come in bright colours, making them a popular choice in the world of block printing.

The process of printing with natural dyes is labour intensive. One of the key elements when printing with a natural dye is that the fabric must be prepared in a certain way to ensure the natural dyes adhere to the fabric. This step is called mordanting. The fabric is scoured to remove any oils or dirt, and is then soaked and simmered in a mordant solution. By mordanting fabric, the natural dyes can penetrate the fibres, making for a stronger connection between the dye and the fabric.

The preparation of each natural dye for printing also takes a series of processes to extract the dye from the plant or material. It often involves drying, grinding and boiling. The dyes can appear a lighter colour when printed onto the fabric; the true final colour isn't revealed until later in the process.

The fabric is left to dry in the sun and then soaked and simmered in further mordant solution. This brings out the true tones of the natural dyes, enhancing the colours and brightness of the printed fabric.

It's enlightening to experience the diverse forms of printing in India, giving us an opportunity to understand and appreciate cultural traditions and ancient craft techniques.

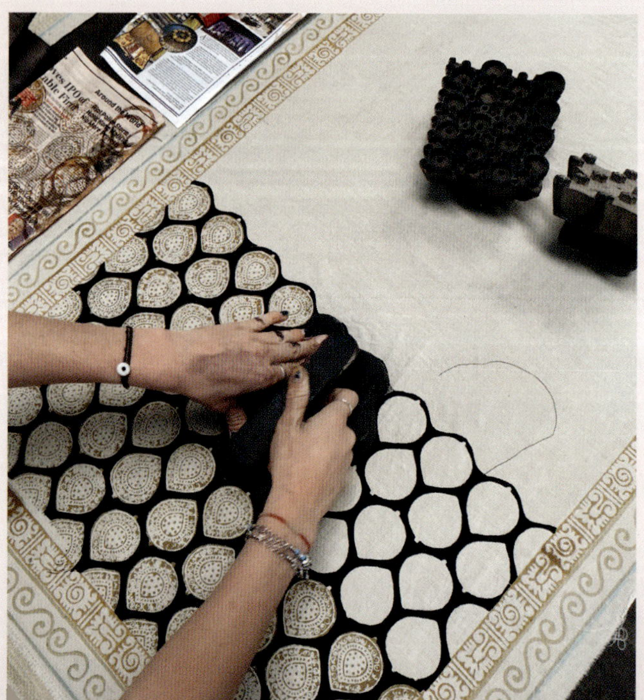

Left: Block printing with natural dyes, such as iron, tannins and turmeric.

Opposite: Soaking fabric in a mordant solution.

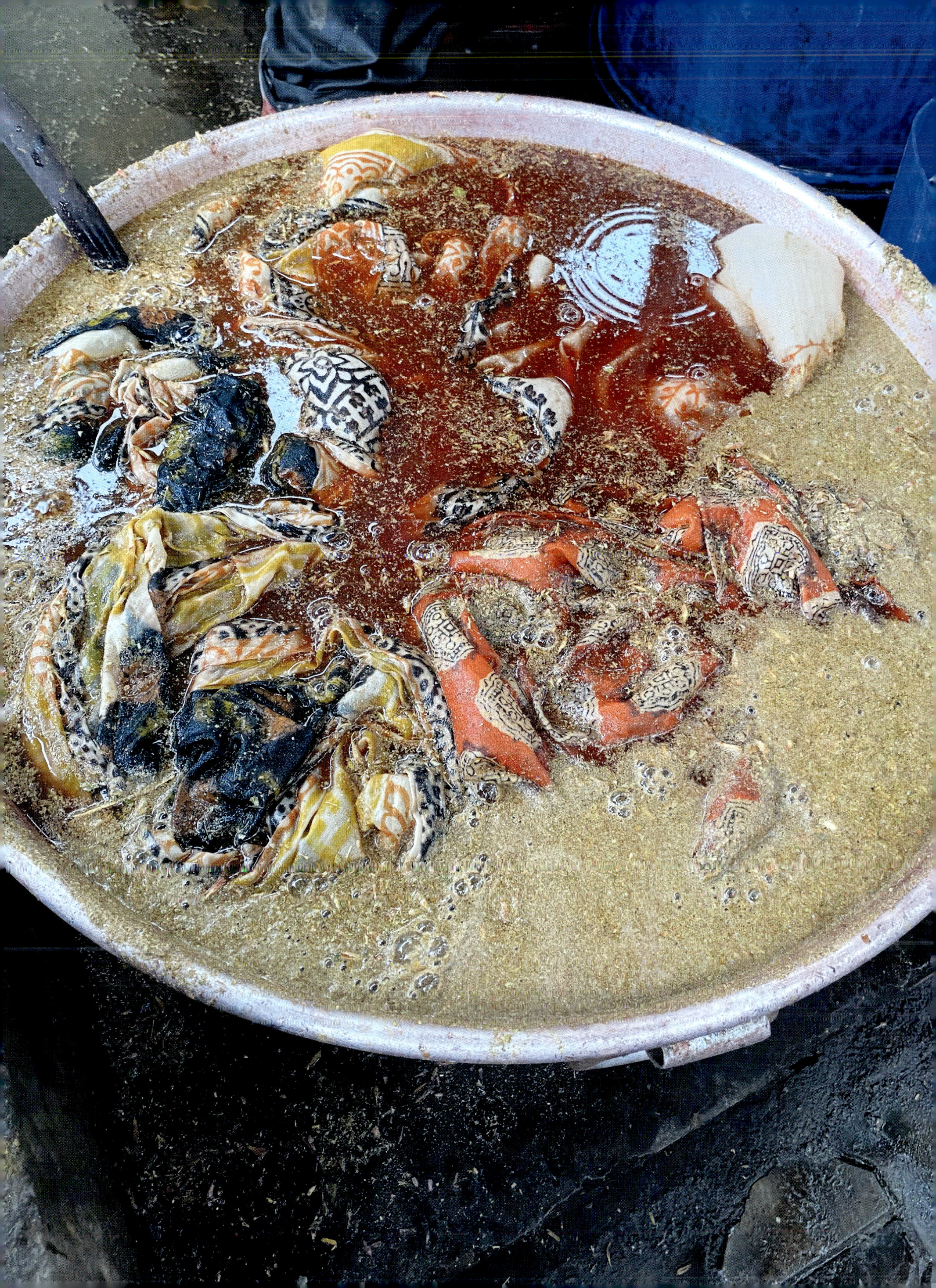

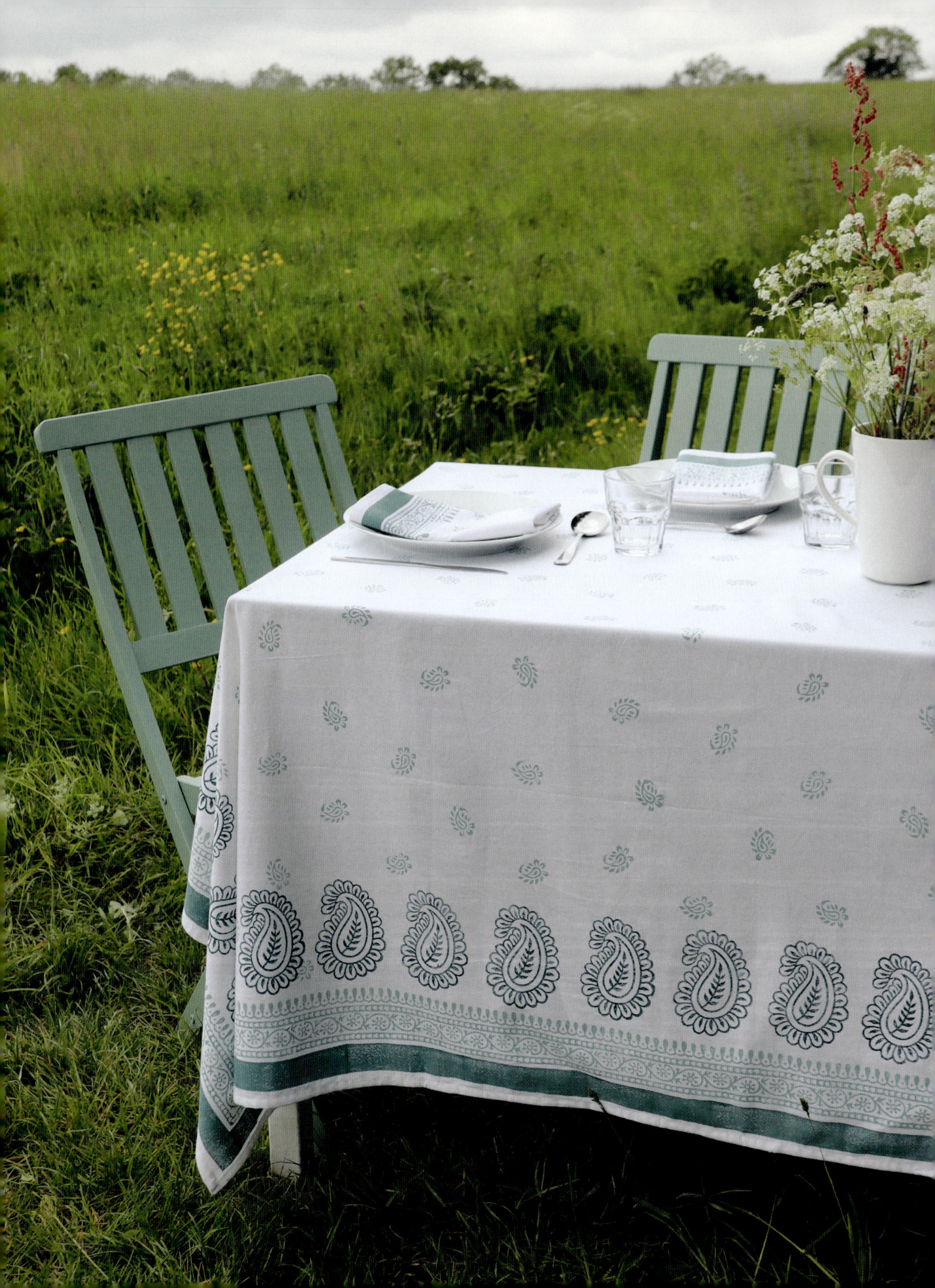

Brilliant Borders Tablecloth

Alfresco dining is one of our favourite things to do in the warmer months. Sitting in the garden enjoying the warmer weather until the sun goes down gives you that wonderful feeling of being on holiday. Hand-block printed tablecloths come in such a wonderful array of styles but can often be expensive. Printing your own allows you to choose your favourite colours and blocks to create a one-of-a-kind design. Our intricate, patterned tablecloth uses an antique printing block that we picked up in Jaipur. You can print on a plain cotton tablecloth or recycle an old one, and matching napkins will complete the set.

YOU WILL NEED

- Cotton tablecloth (square or rectangular)
- Printing blocks – we used Solid Straight Line, Large Indian Paisley, Mini Paisley and an antique border design (could substitute for our Decorative Border)
- Fabric paints – we used Aquamarine, White, Teal and Black
- Sheets of A4 paper
- Thin paintbrush
- Basic printing equipment (see page 18)

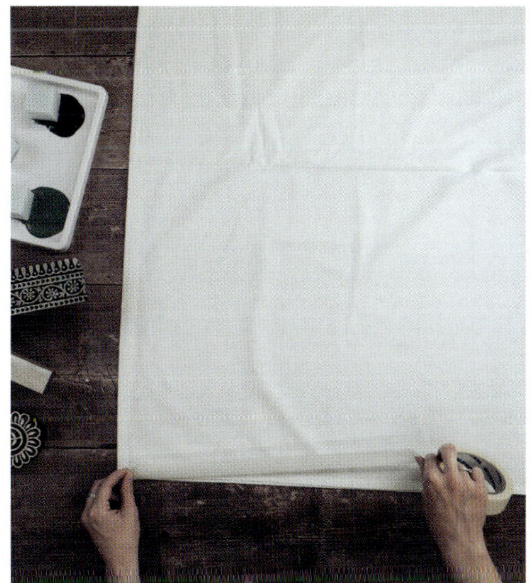

1 Wash and iron your tablecloth in preparation for printing. You need a large, clear area for printing bigger items, such as a dining or garden table. Spread out your tablecloth and apply masking tape around the hemmed edge to give you a straight line to follow when printing the border design.

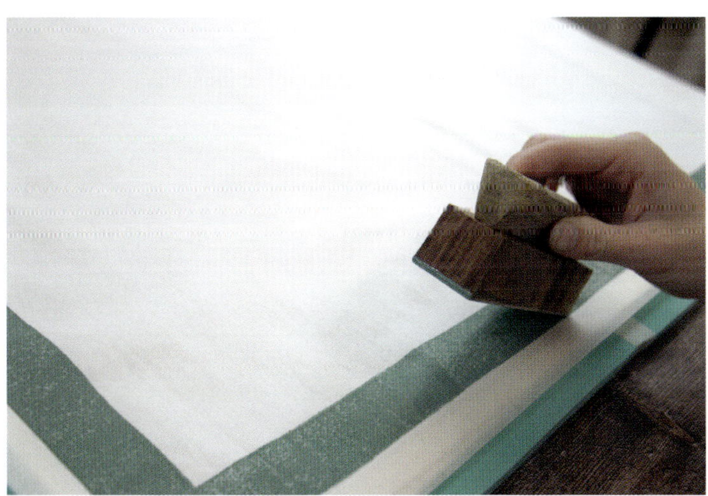

2 A solid straight line gives a great base for the design to work up from. When printing with a solid border, we like to double print the design by printing it twice – one on top of the other – to strengthen the print and darken the colour. To do so, starting from a corner, print your first border design around all four sides of your tablecloth until you reach back to where you started, then print again all the way around, overlapping the prints. You can only do this with a design like a solid straight line as it's easy to line up. We're printing our base border design in our second-darkest colour, Aquamarine.

3 Once you've double printed your solid line border, you can move on to your next design. We're using an antique handled block, which we bought in Jaipur.

Reset your straight line to follow by adding a new piece of masking tape – this will most likely go over your previous border print. We leave a 3–5-mm gap between each border design. To create a lighter colour, we mixed White with our Aquamarine paint. Start your first print half a print away from the corner.

4 Once you reach the corner of your fabric with your intricate border design, you can try an advanced printing technique, which we learnt in India, called a mitred corner. This is where you use a piece of paper to block off half your corner print. Start by folding the straight edge of an A4 piece of paper to create a 45-degree angle.

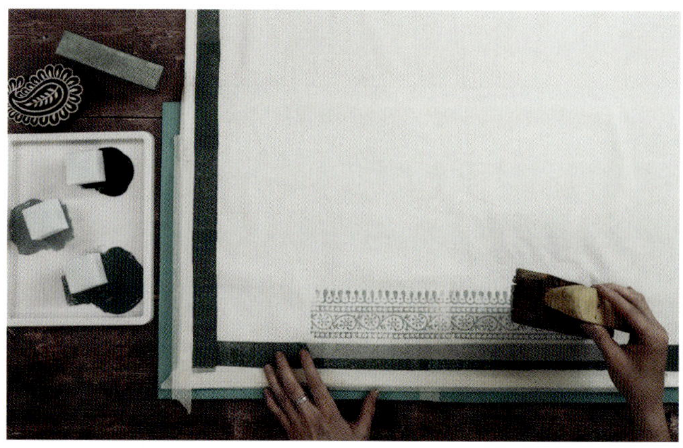

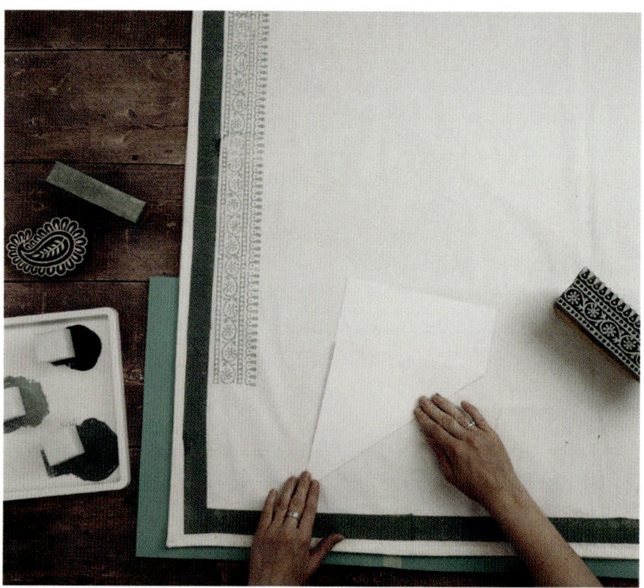

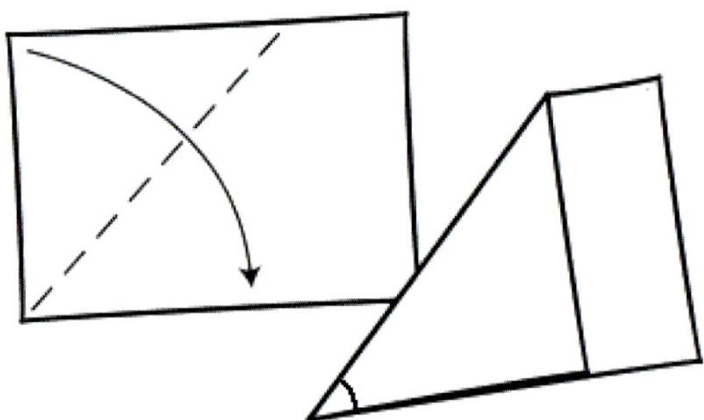

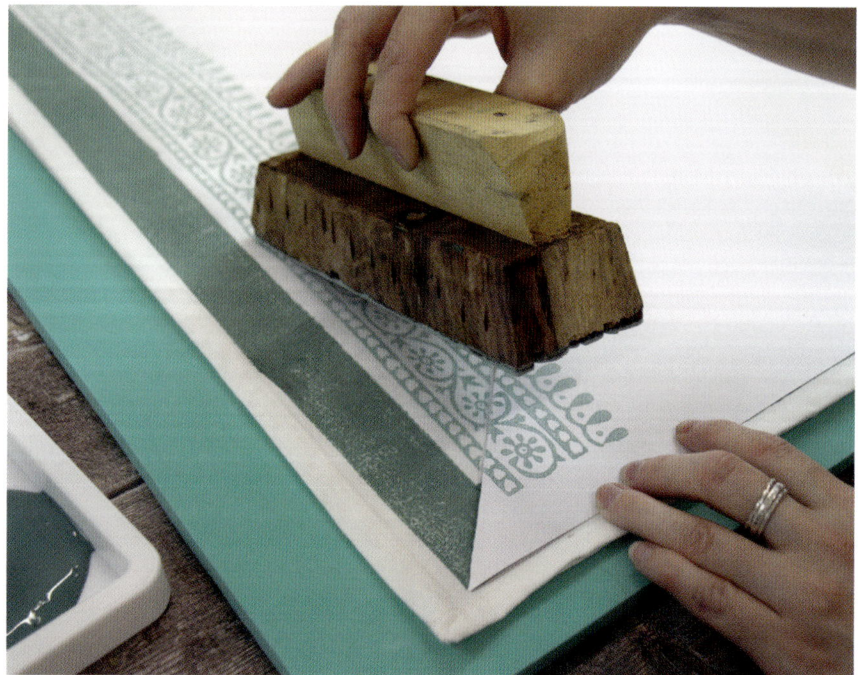

5 Position the folded paper along the straight edge of the corner you are printing onto. This will cover the fabric on the other side of the corner and cut the print off. Put your printing block down onto the fabric and over the paper, wiggling it as you normally would.

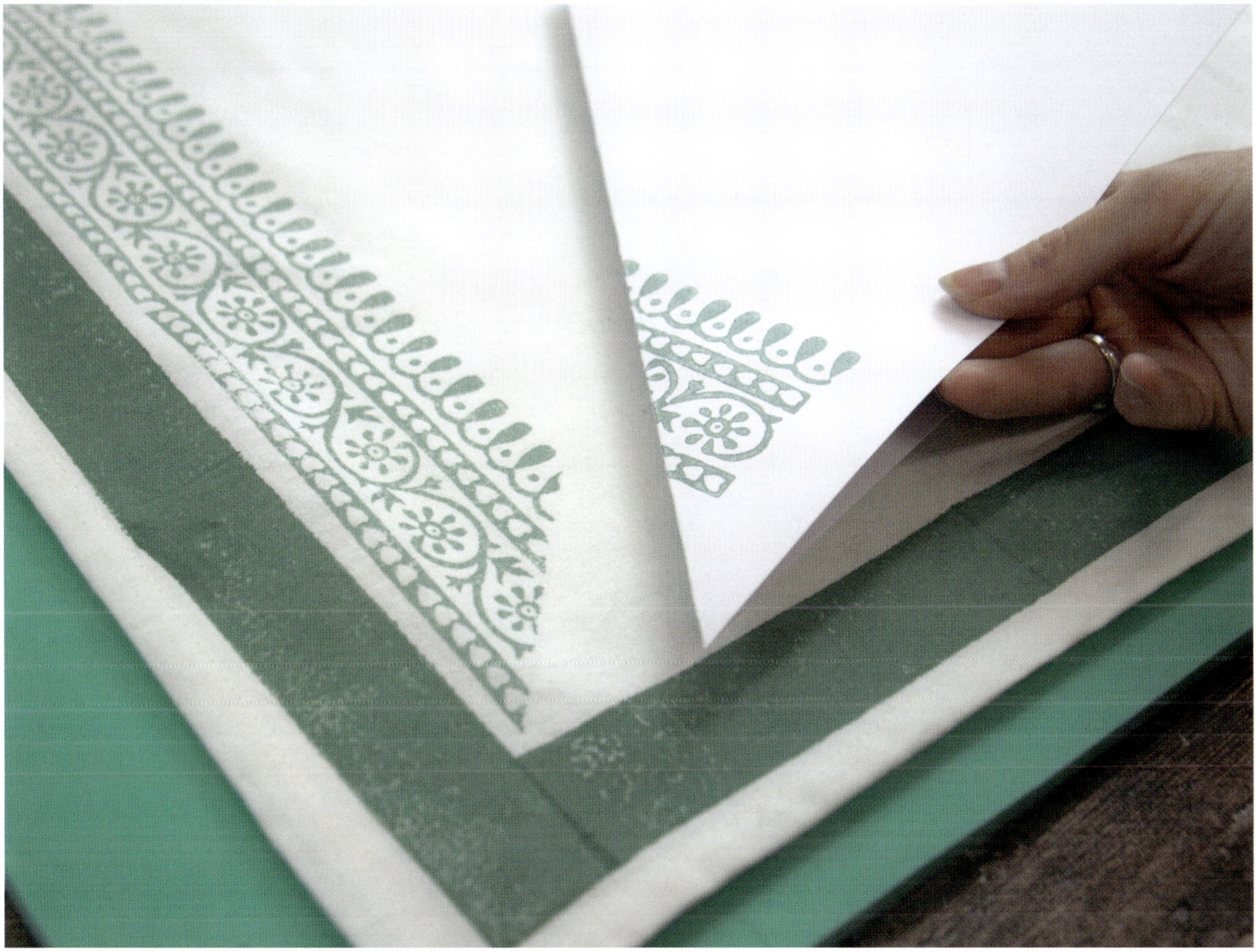

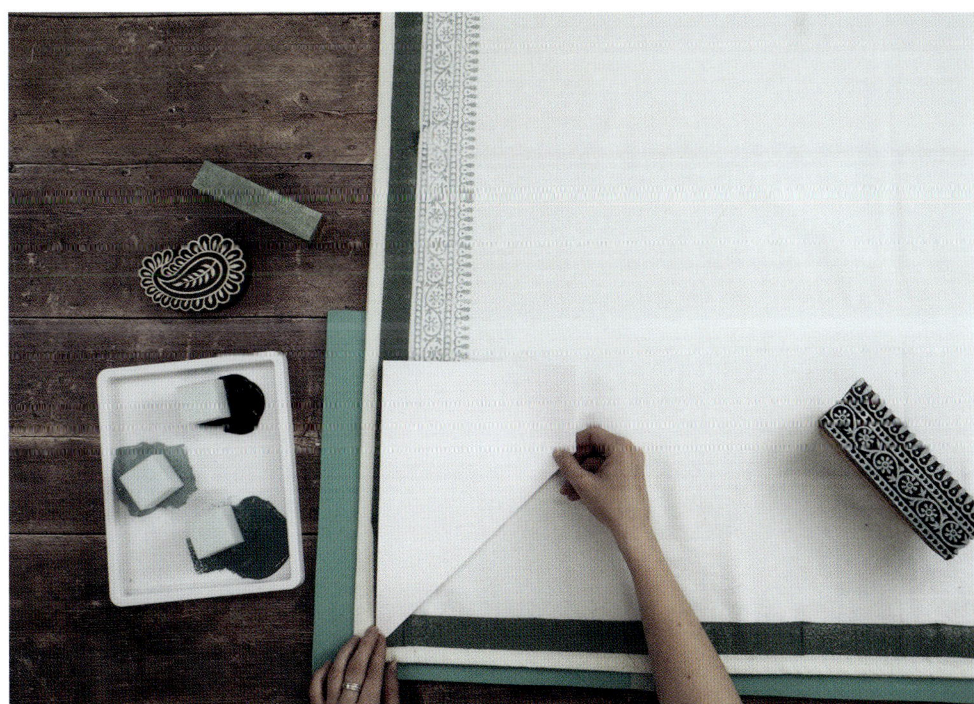

6 Lift the printing block up to reveal your partial corner print, and allow to dry.

7 Position a clean piece of folded paper on the side of the fabric you have just printed, lining the paper up along the edge of the fabric.

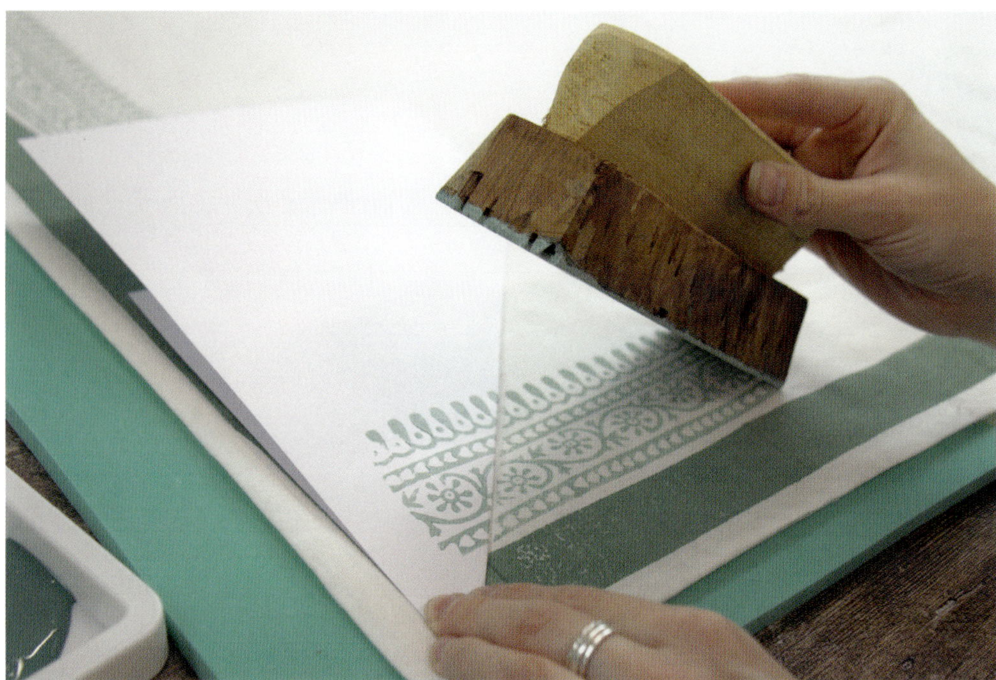

8 Print your border design onto the fabric. It's important your print also overlaps onto the paper – without this, the mitred corner will not work correctly.

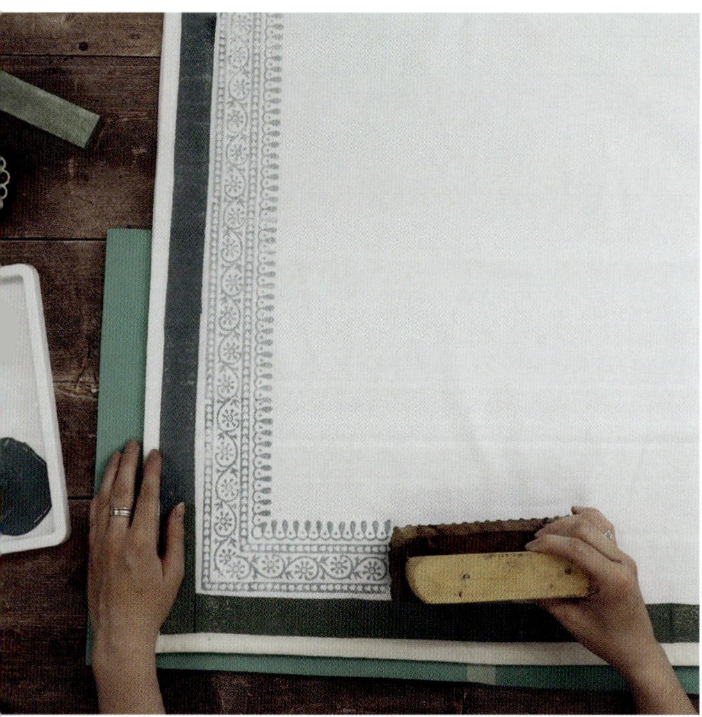

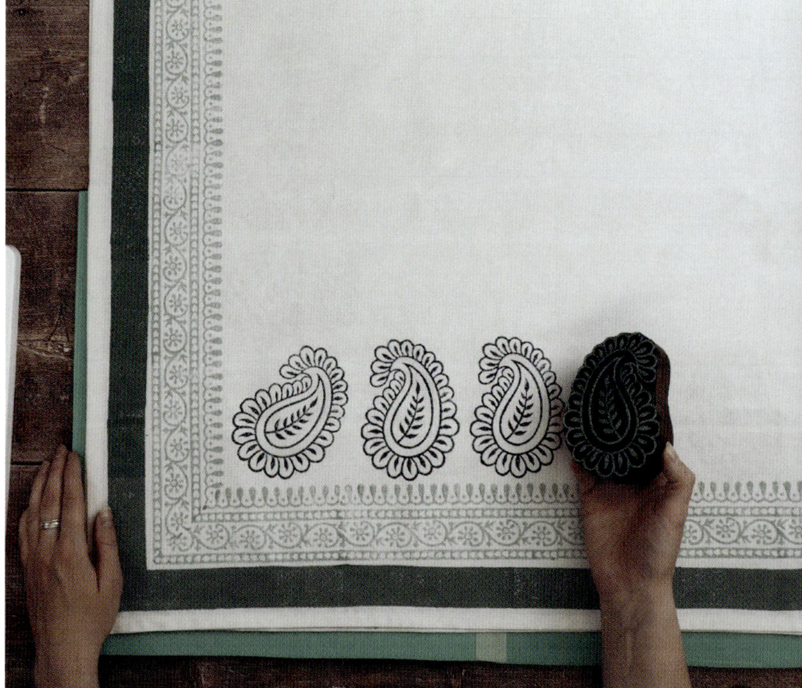

9 Lift your printing block and remove the paper to reveal your corner print. It's difficult to get an intricate print to match perfectly on both sides, so touch up the print with a thin paintbrush, if required. Leave to dry.

10 Move on to printing the final row of designs to complete the border pattern – we used Large Indian Paisley. We added a drop of Black to a Teal colour to darken the tone. You can print these around the fabric by eye or lay another line of masking tape to follow. Evenly space out each print around the tablecloth, and at each corner print a Large Indian Paisley design at a 45-degree angle.

11 In order not to detract from the detailed border and to bring the design together, we added a light, random mini paisley design around the middle of the tablecloth in the same lightened Aquamarine paint that we used for the intricate border design. Continue until all the fabric is printed.

12 Print a set of matching napkins in the same colourway, which you can use alongside your tablecloth in the summer.

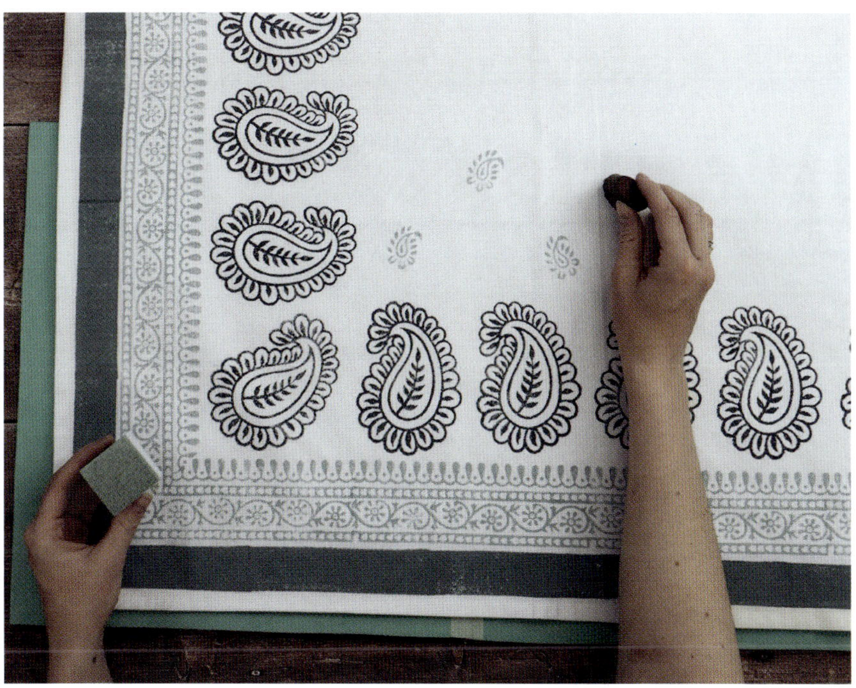

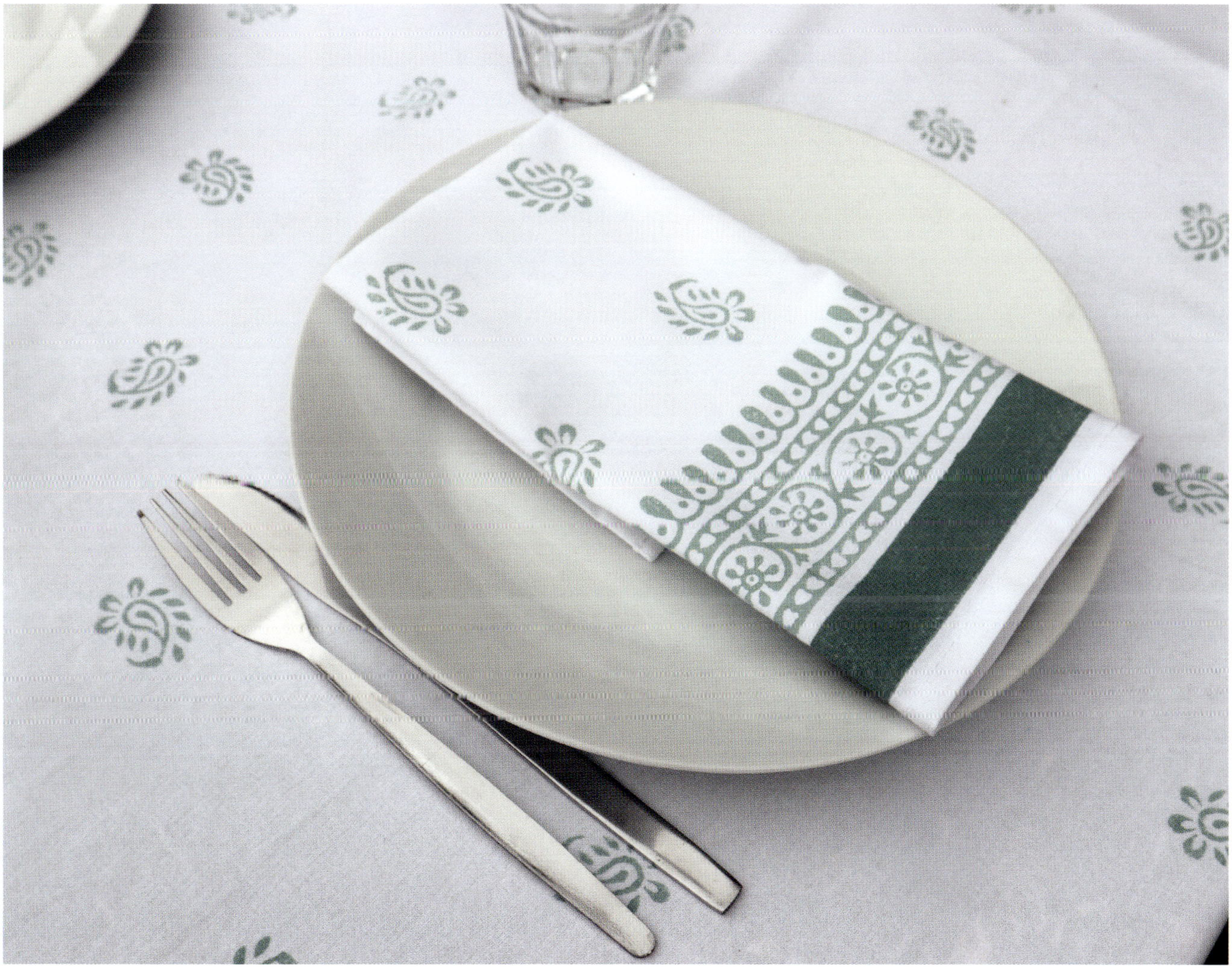

Pretty Paisley Pillowcases

One of our favourite DIY projects that brings colour, pattern and a unique style to any home is hand-printed bedding. While it may seem like a challenging task, even a few simple prints can create something truly stunning. Here, we will start by printing a border design around the outside of the pillowcase and then filling in the middle space with a gorgeous paisley pattern. Throughout this project, we'll guide you through the process of hand-printing on cotton pillowcases, helping you add a personal touch to your bedroom.

YOU WILL NEED

- Set of cotton pillowcases
- Sheet of A3 paper or card
- Printing blocks – we used Thin Solid Line Border, Large Paisley and Set of 3 Paisley Patterns
- Fabric paints – we used Midnight Blue and Navy
- Basic printing equipment (see page 18)

1 Wash and iron the pillowcase to remove any creases. Insert a piece of A3 paper or card inside the pillowcase to stop paint transferring through to the other side.

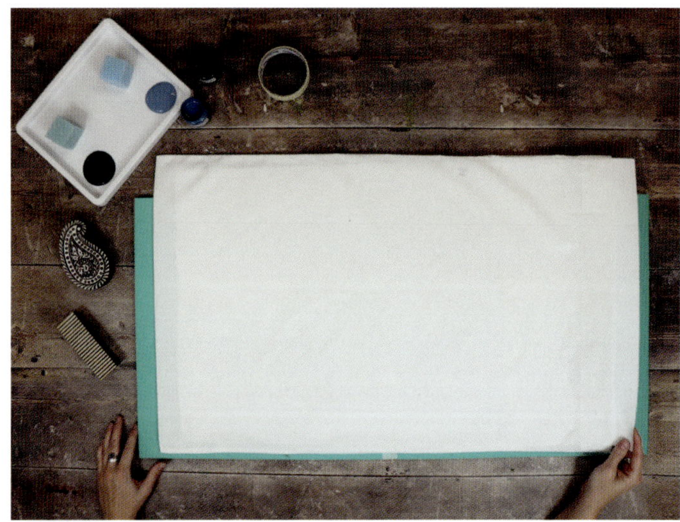

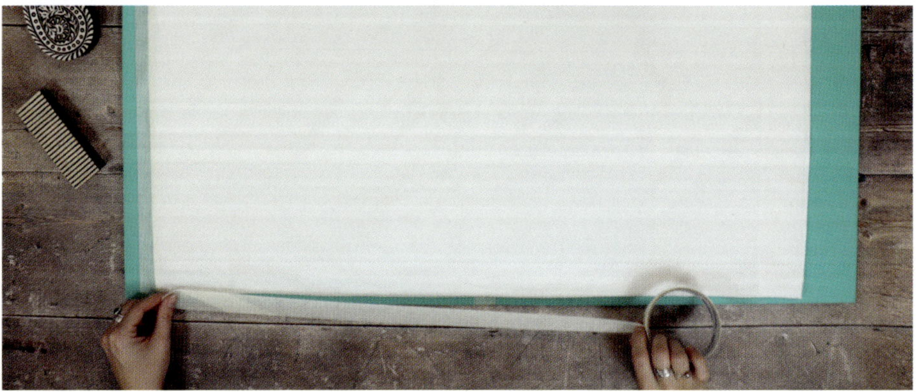

Printing Tip

To help with spacing, always start with the border design around the outside of your piece of fabric, then work your way inwards.

2 Apply masking tape to the edges of the fabric. This will hold the pillowcase down and onto your printing mat and act as a straight edge to follow when printing the border design.

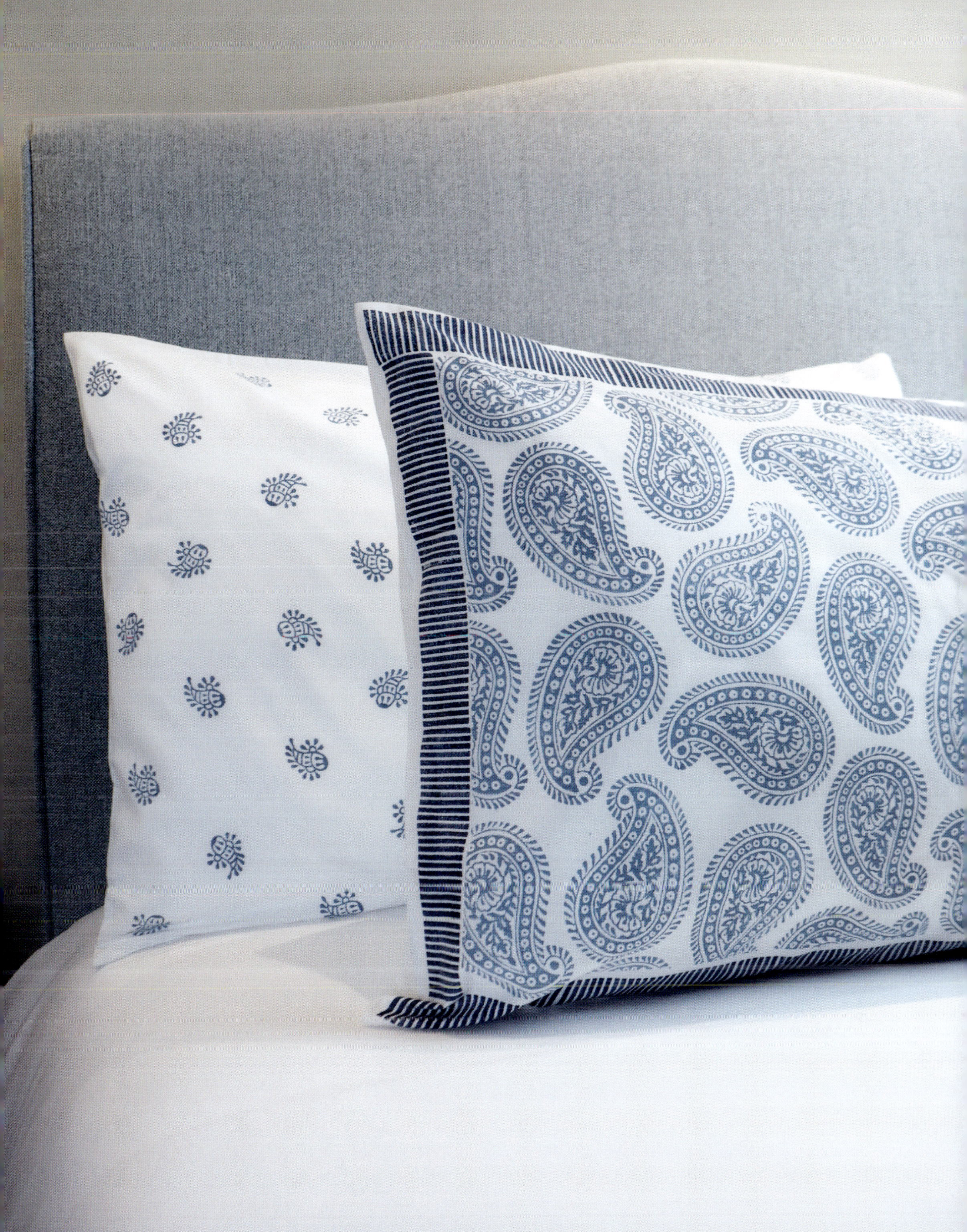

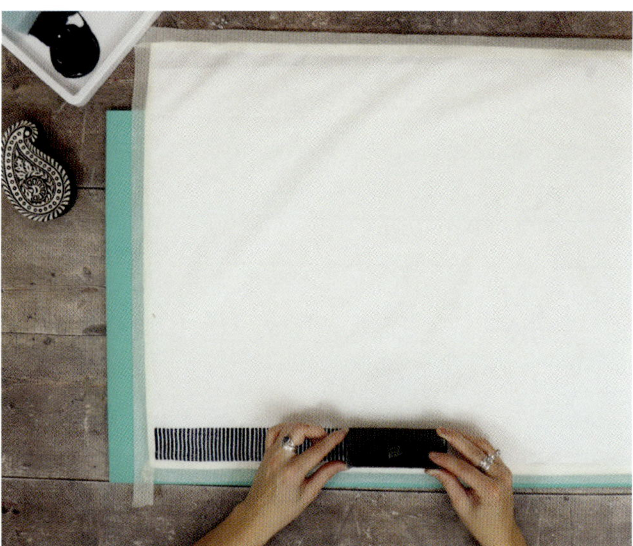

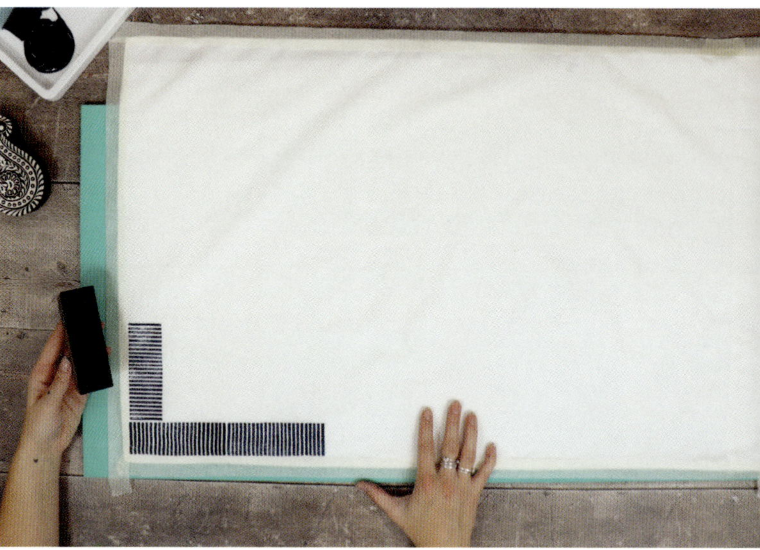

3 Using your border printing block and Midnight Blue fabric paint, start printing around the edge of the pillowcase, following your masking tape line.

4 We are using a simple cornering technique: print each corner print at a right-angle, then continue onto the next side with your border print.

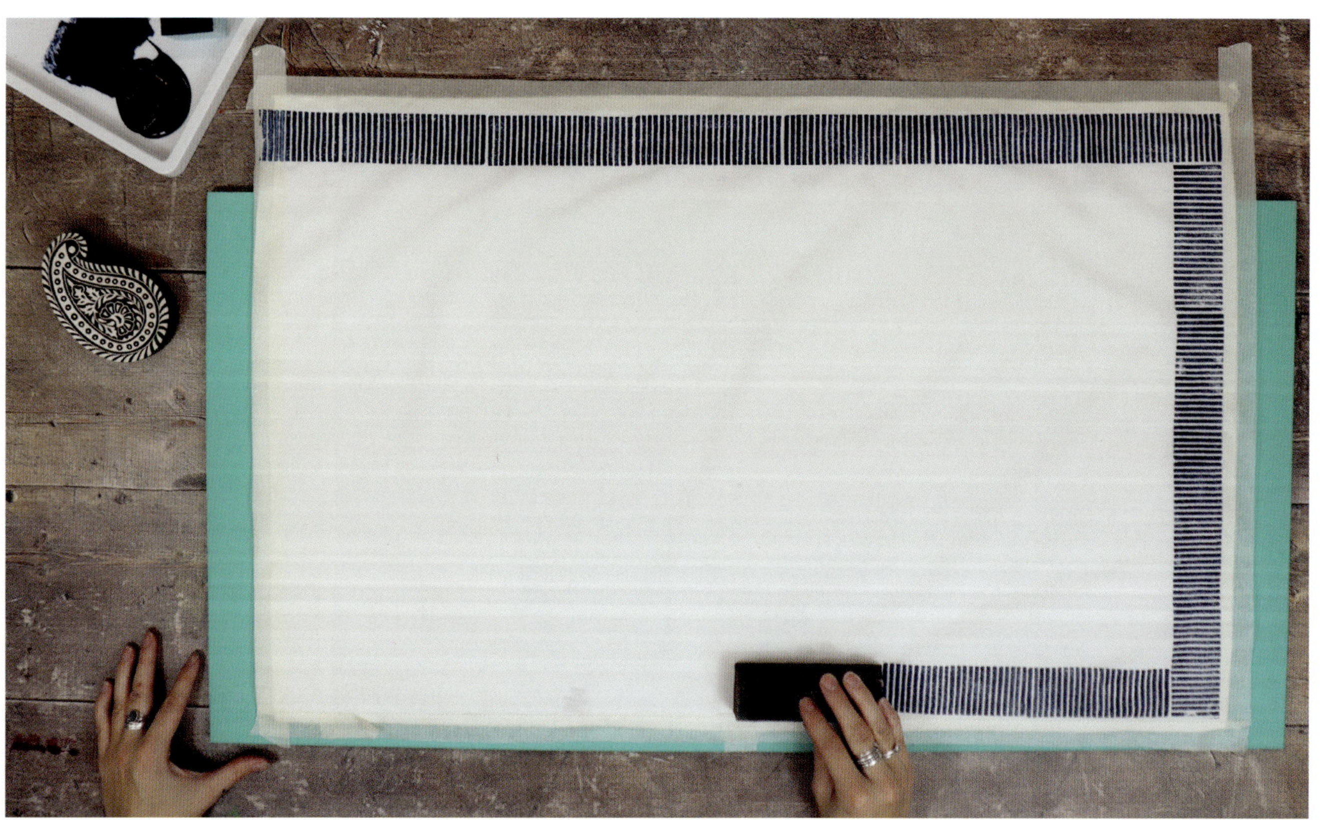

5 Continue to print the Thin Solid Line Border design, turning the pillowcase as you work your way around, so you are always printing the edge closest to you. Reaching across the fabric to the other side can cause smudging.

6 Once you have completed the border design, let this dry before starting on the middle section. Once dry, cover the border design and edge of the pillowcase using thick masking tape, as the middle prints may overlap.

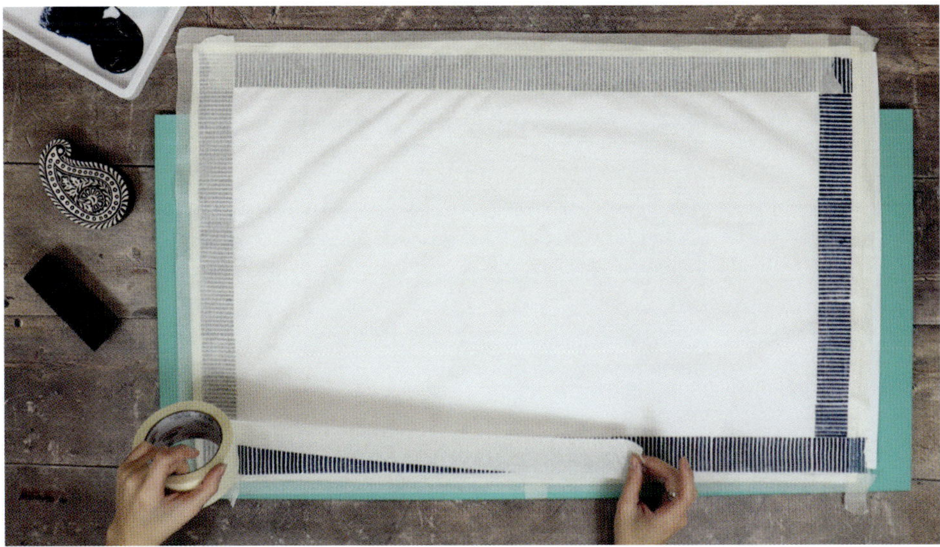

7 We are using a Large Paisley design, which we will print in one colour: Navy. Start from one corner and use a random printing technique (see page 40). Ensure the prints around the edge of the middle space overlap onto the masking tape – this will help with the end result.

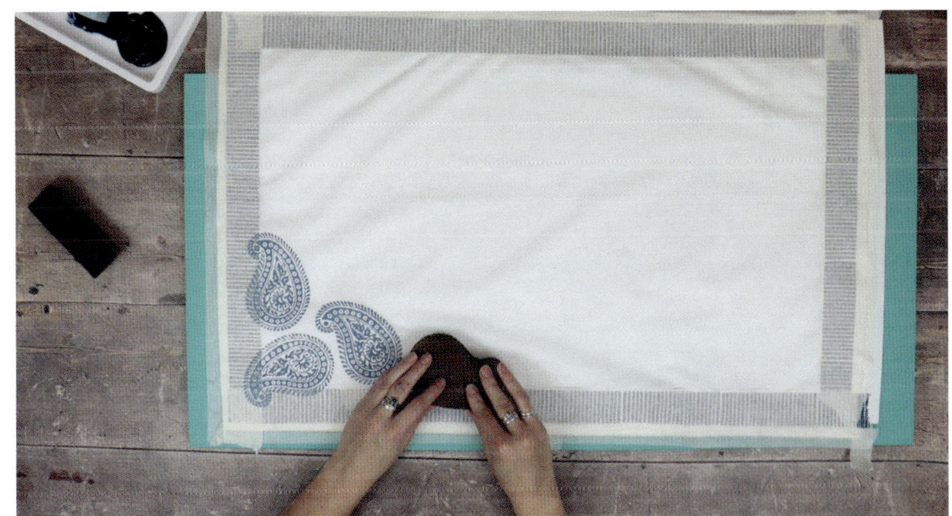

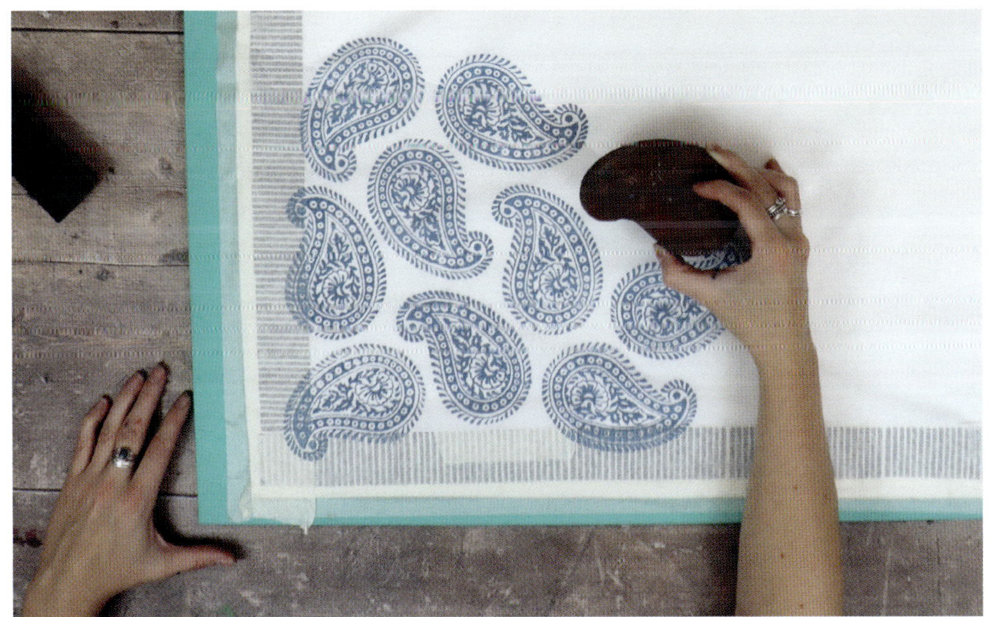

8 With a random pattern like this, make the prints one at a time, ensuring you are turning the design and printing at a different angle every time to create the free-flowing, random effect. It helps to fan out across the fabric, trying to ensure each print fits next to the last.

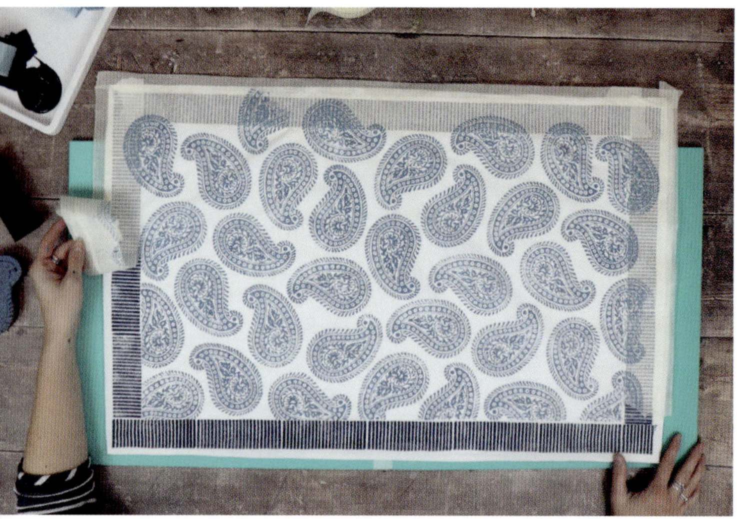

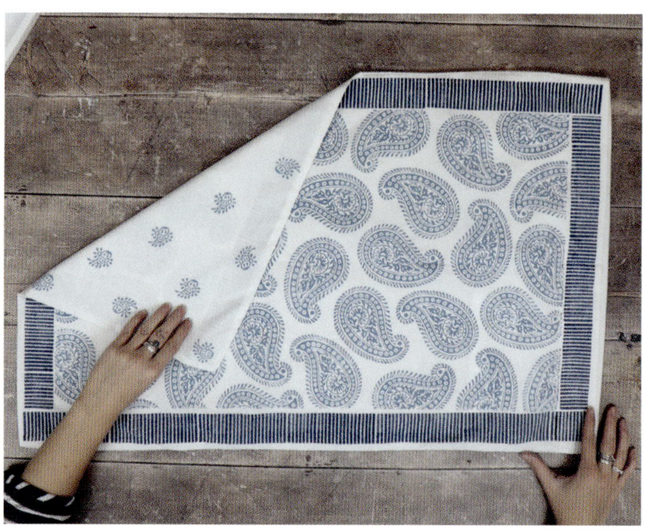

9 Once the entire space is printed, allow the paint to dry before removing the tape. The half prints around the edge of the pillowcase give the finished item a professional feel.

10 You can leave the reverse of the pillowcase plain or add a 'lighter' design, randomly printing a small paisley print (using a block from the Set of 3 Paisley Patterns) in the same colour.

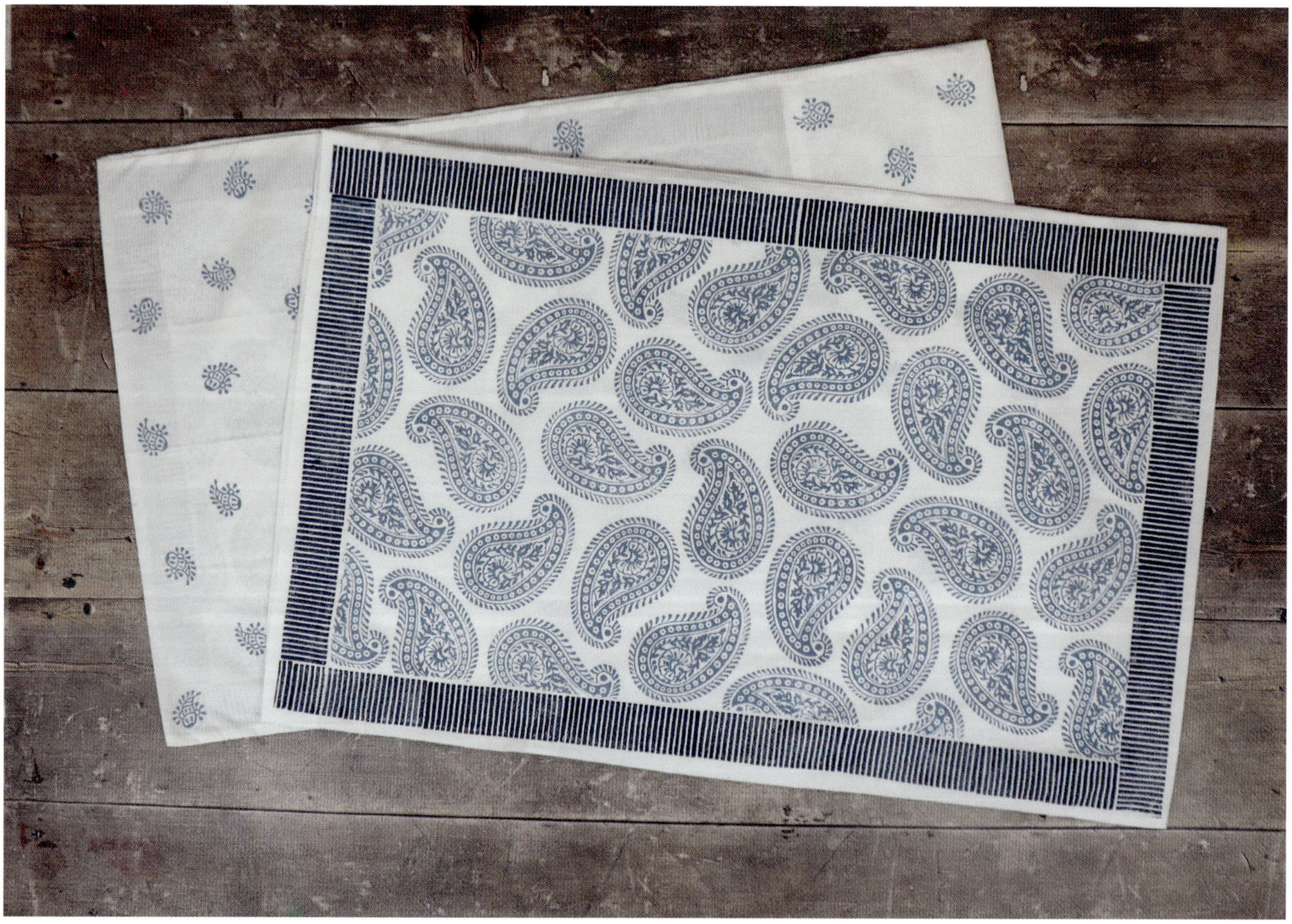

11 Repeat the steps to print a matching pillowcase.

Female Block Carvers

It's rare to find female carvers in India, so you can imagine how thrilled we were to meet Kamine on our latest visit. As a female-founded team, we place great importance on encouraging, collaborating with and supporting women to train as block carvers in an industry greatly dominated by men. We learnt on our trip that Kamine is not the only female block carver who lives in her village, and that there are other women training in wood-block carving.

Upon researching, we found there are efforts to support women in various traditionally male-dominated crafts in India. NGOs and craft organisations are working to provide training and create more inclusive work environments. These supportive initiatives aim to break down the gender barriers, increase awareness and empower women to enter fields traditionally dominated by men – all crucial steps towards enabling more females to enter the block carving industry.

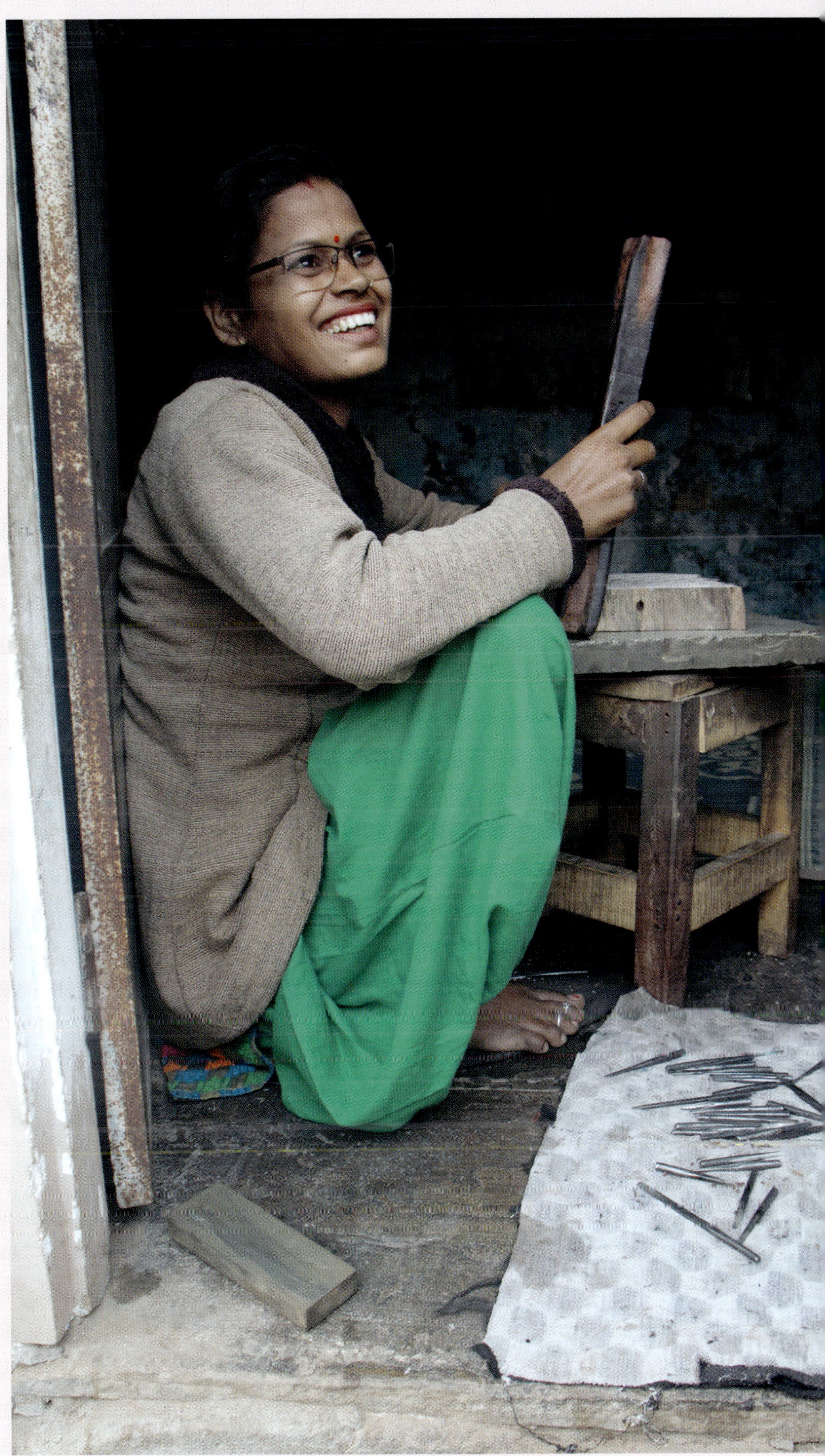

Right: Kamine, a female wood-block carver.

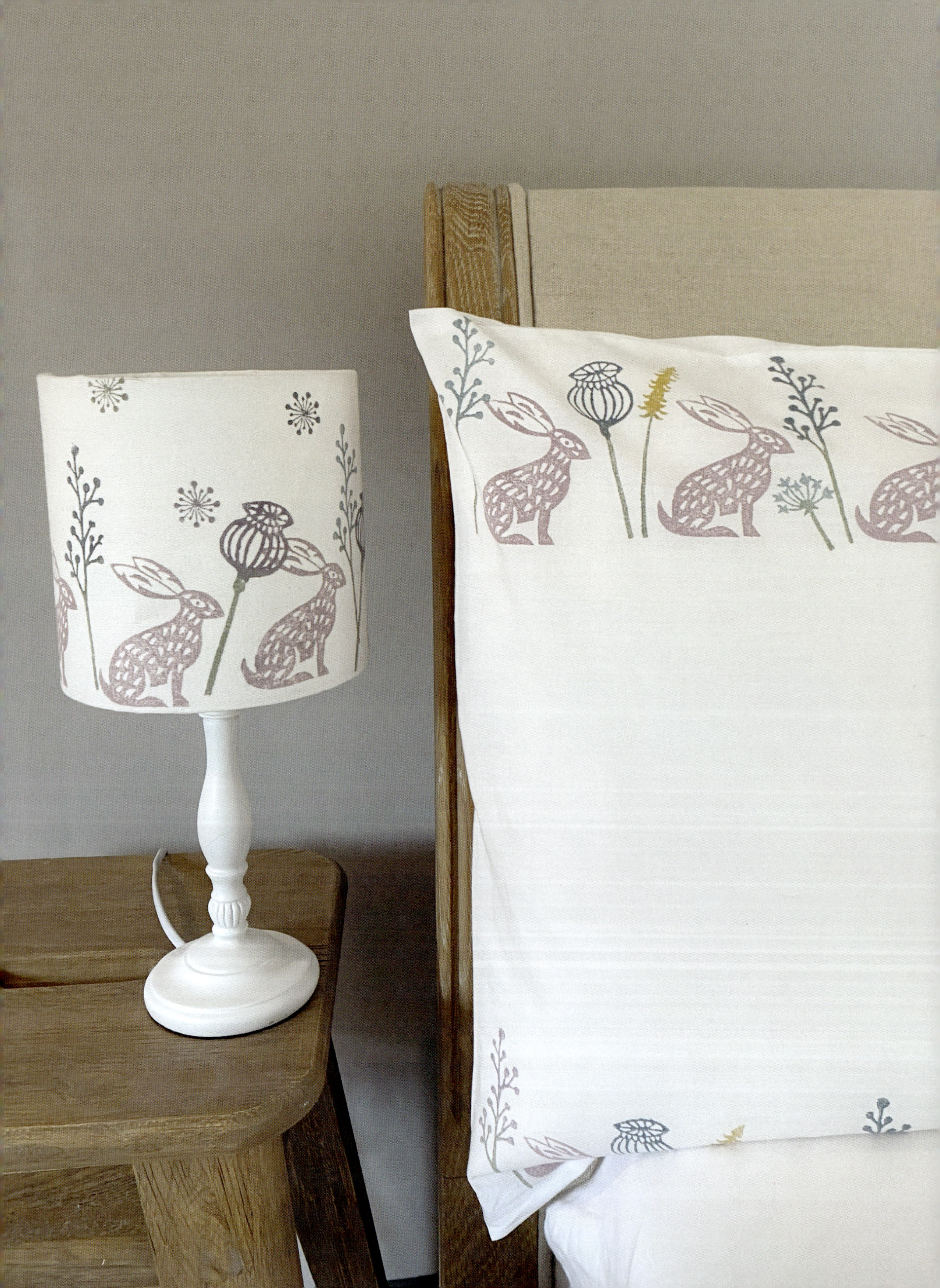

Meadow Scene Lampshade

Learn how to transform a piece of printed fabric into a functional lampshade, using your favourite colours and prints to create your own personalised design. Once you know how achievable lampshades are to make, you will question whether to ever buy one again! In addition to your printing materials, you will need a 'flat-packed' lampshade-making kit – these are available in a variety of shapes and sizes.

1 When printing a fabric design for a lampshade, it's especially important to practise the design. Cut out a piece of fabric the same height as your lampshade panel so you can test how the design will fit within the available space.

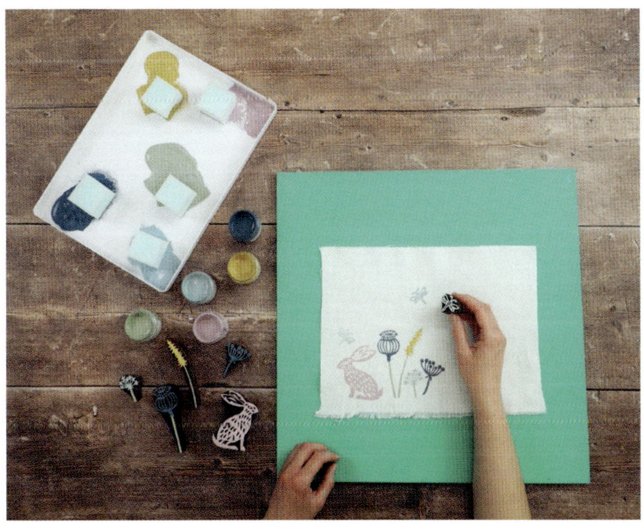

2 It can be difficult to line the fabric panel up straight on the lampshade panel once printed, so it's best to attach the fabric to the lampshade panel first and then print. To attach the fabric, lay your lampshade panel grid side up and place your fabric over the top.

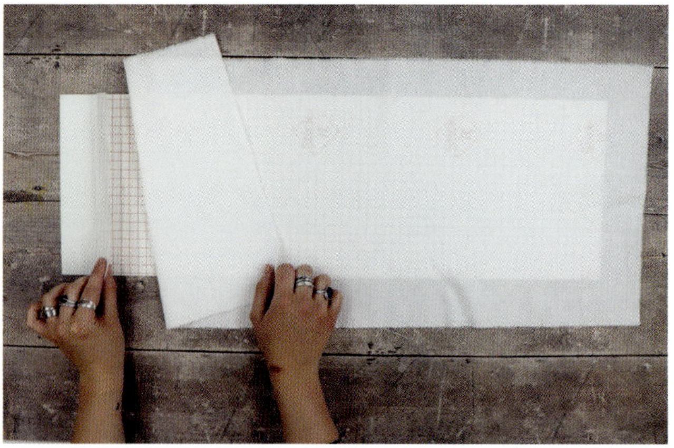

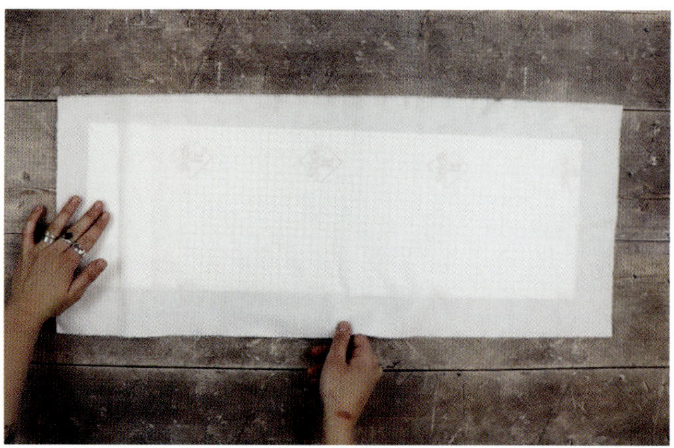

3 Peel back the gridded paper to reveal the sticky panel by about 5 cm.

4 Attach your fabric to the panel.

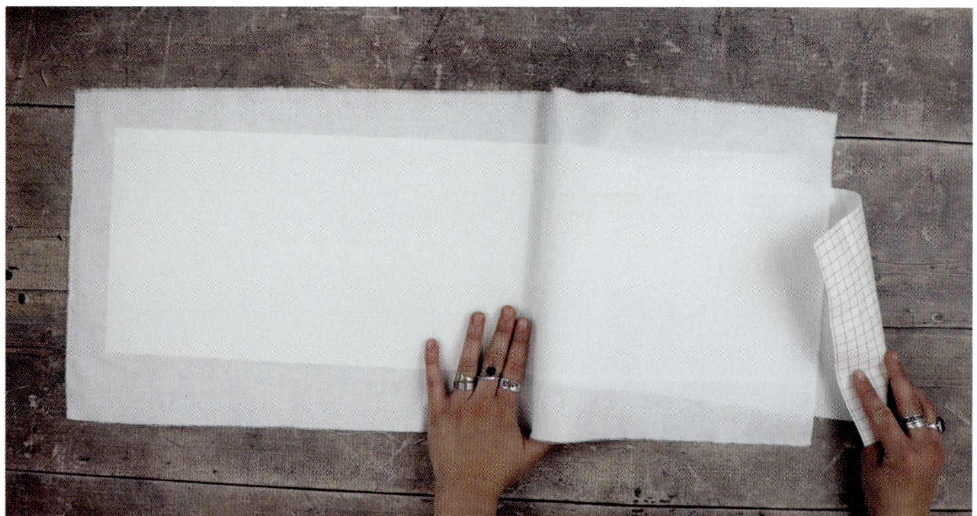

5 Continue slowly peeling back the paper and smoothing your fabric onto the sticky panel until the entire panel is smoothed with your fabric.

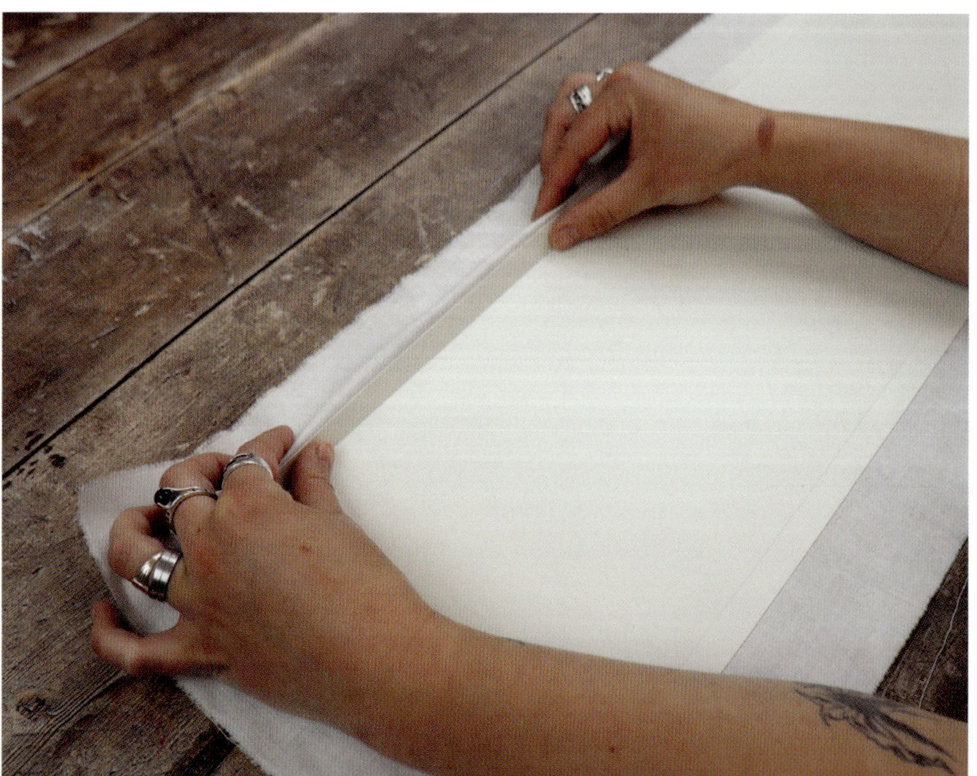

6 You'll see a 2-cm strip of plastic at the top and bottom of the panel. Bend these back to create crease lines – your print area will be between these two lines.

7 Now your fabric is attached, and your printing area is visible, it's time to add your design to the panel, using your Summer Meadow and Sitting Hare blocks and Indian Yellow, Indian Aqua, Khaki, Midnight Blue and Violet fabric paints. The panel will create a harder printing surface, so ensure you give your printing blocks an extra wiggle to get good contact between the blocks and the fabric for a strong print.

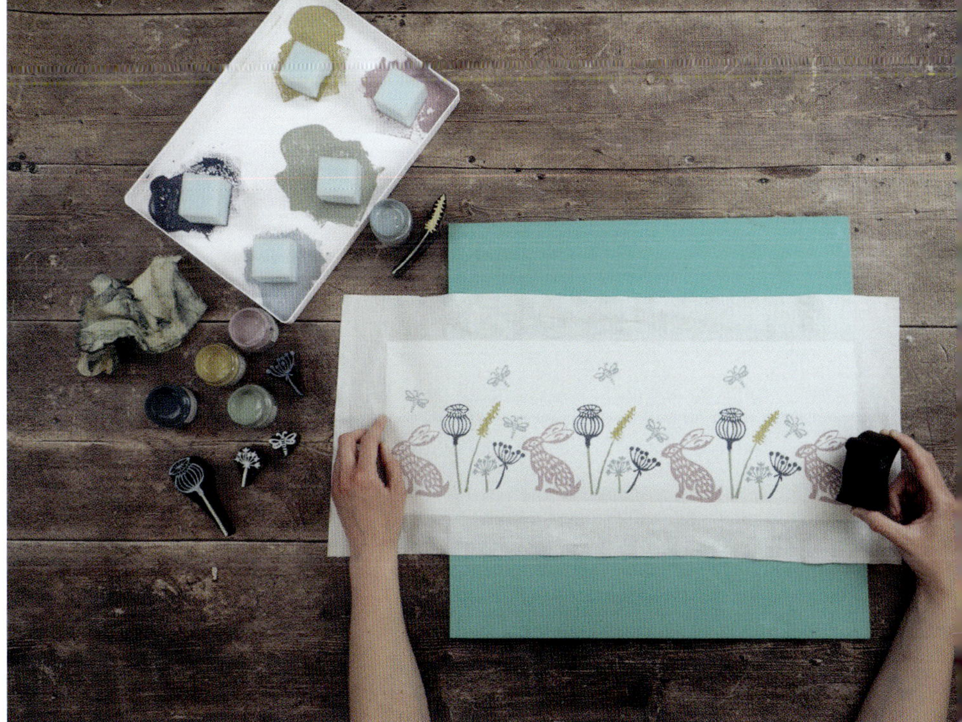

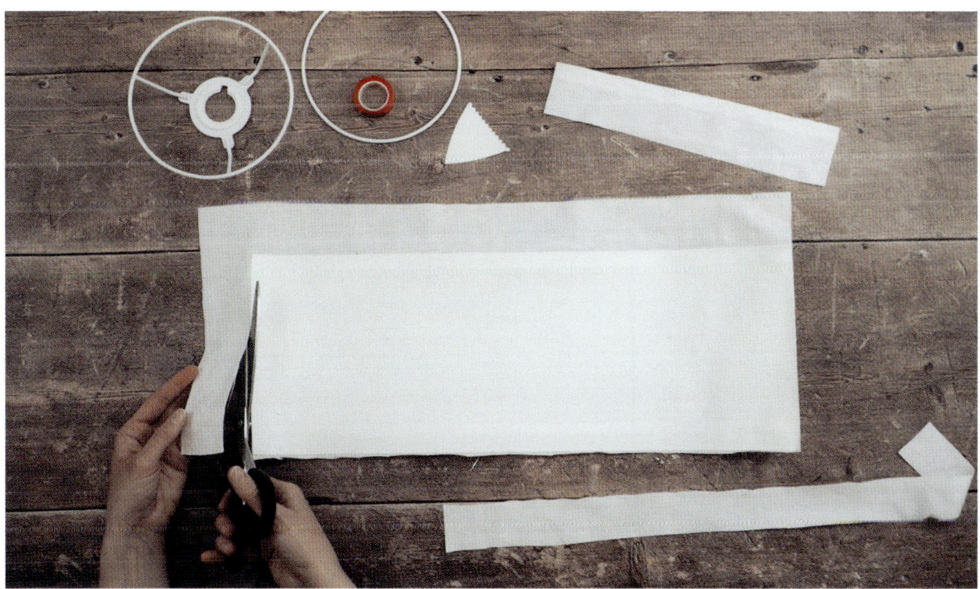

8 Once the printing is dry, flip the panel over so the print side is facing down. Using a pair of sharp fabric scissors, cut around all four sides of the panel, removing the excess fabric.

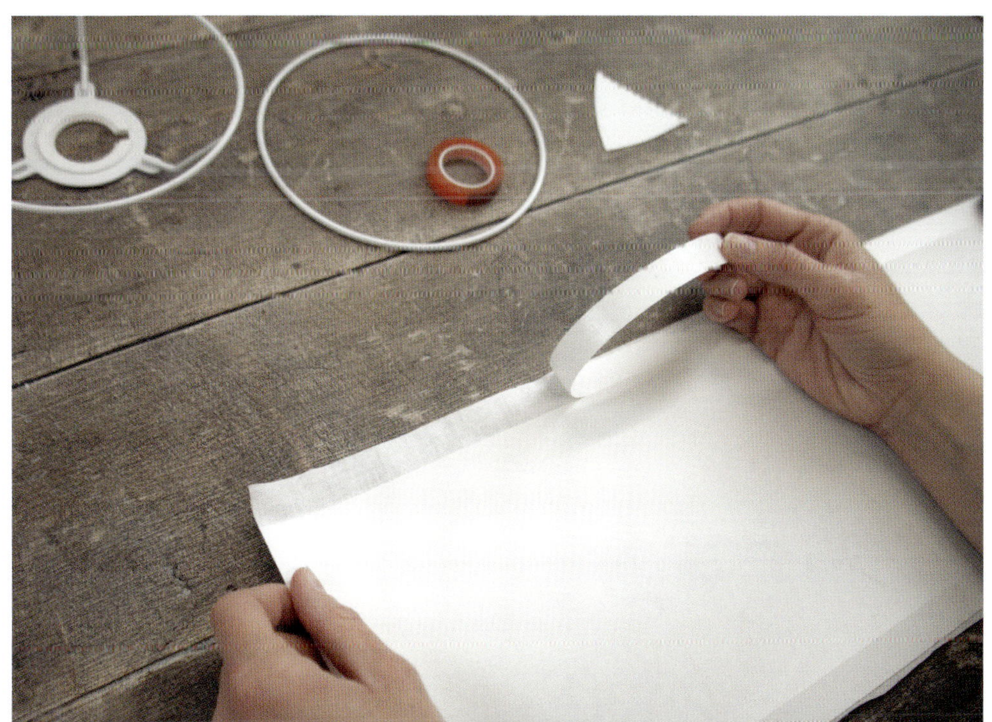

9 Snap back and forth the piece of excess on the top and bottom of the long side of the panel. Once this has clicked and broken away from the main panel, you can then pull and remove it, leaving just the fabric behind underneath.

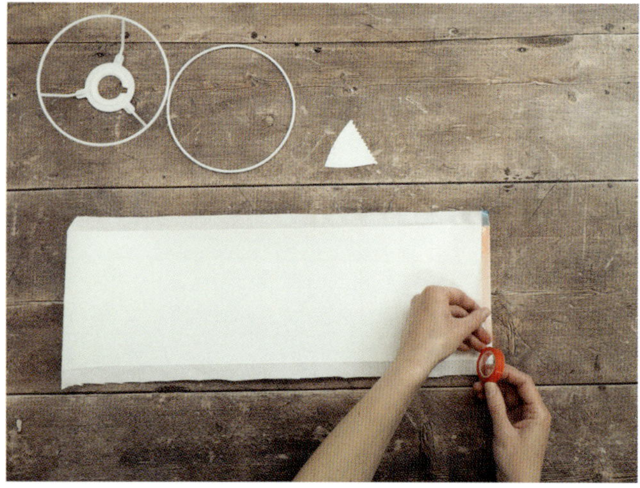

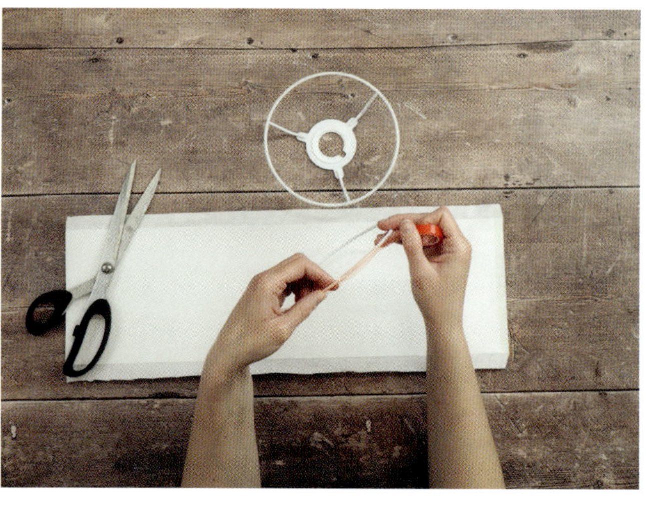

10 Apply a piece of double-sided tape to the right-hand side of the panel, as close to the edge as you can. This tape will hold the two ends of the lampshade panel together once rolled.

11 You can also apply double-sided tape to both lampshade rings. Remove the red upper layer to reveal the sticky tape.

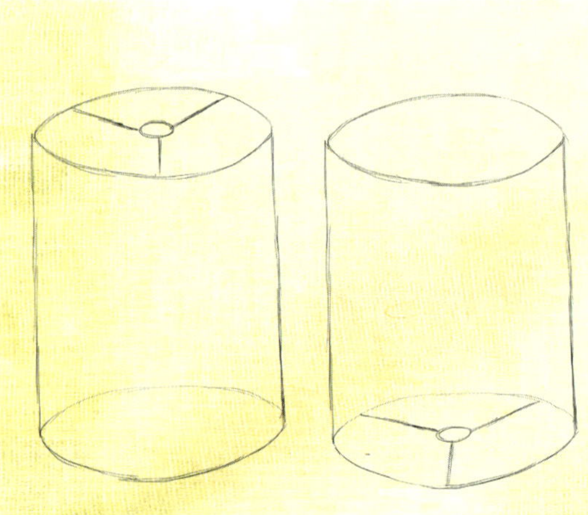

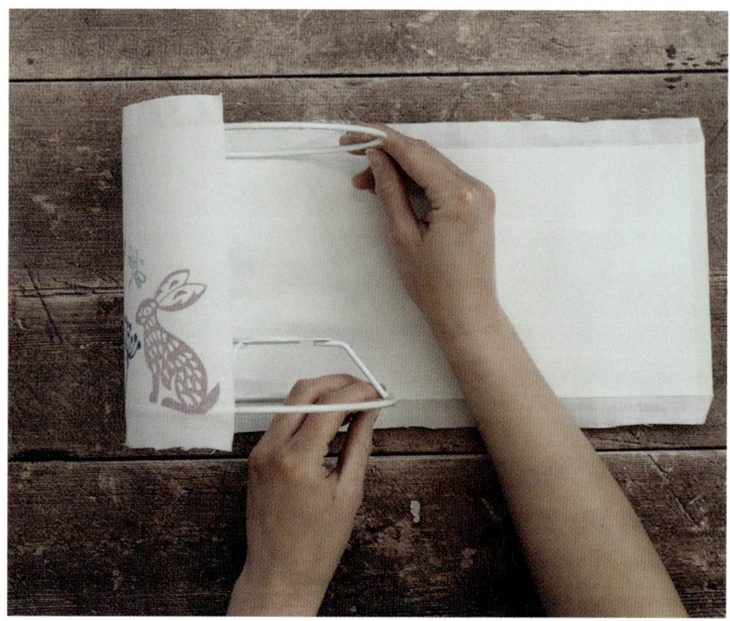

Printing Tip

The positioning of the rings is important, as it varies depending on where you plan to use your lampshade. For a ceiling shade, the ring with the bulb attachment will be at the top. For a lampshade, the ring with the bulb attachment will be at the bottom. Read the instructions carefully to ensure you get this part correct before moving on.

12 Check the design on the fabric is the correct way up, then position your rings correctly (see Printing Tip). Lower both rings onto the panel at one end, keeping them at the very edge of the panel but not touching the fabric. Slowly start to roll the rings along the panel, keeping them level with each other and on the edge. The panel will stick to the tape on each ring as you move along the panel length. If you go off course, you can reverse and then continue forward.

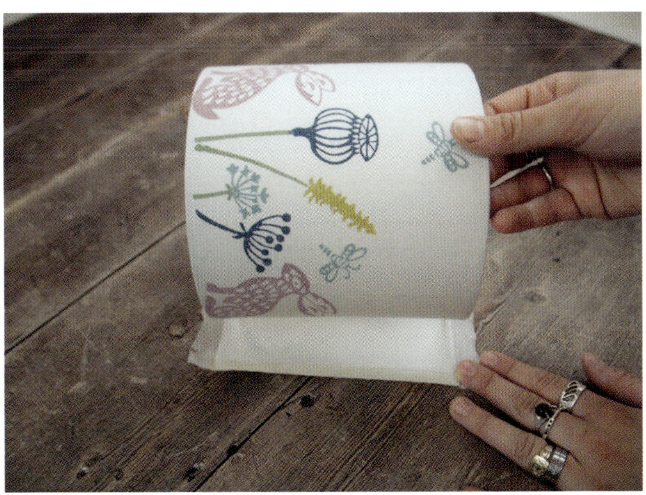

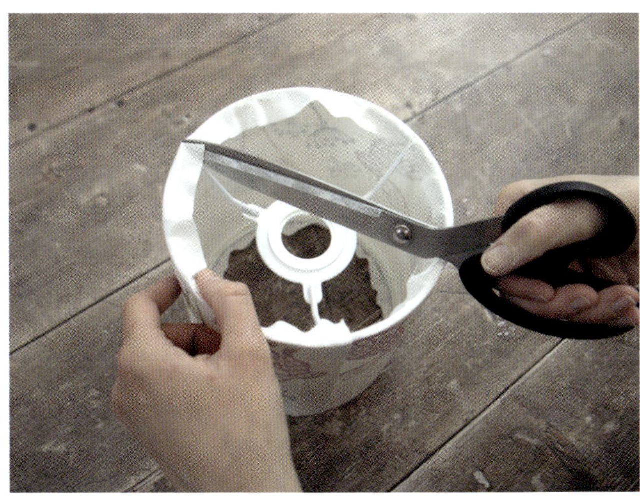

13 Once you reach the opposite end, ensure you have removed the red layer from your sticky tape, and then roll over the tape to join both ends of the shade to each other.

14 Use your scissors to make snips in the fabric so the material easily folds around the poles on the bulb ring.

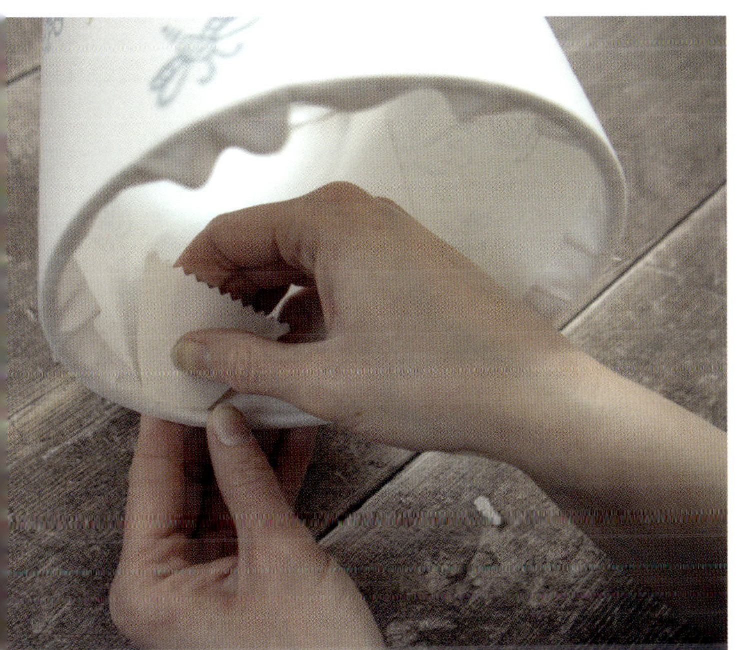

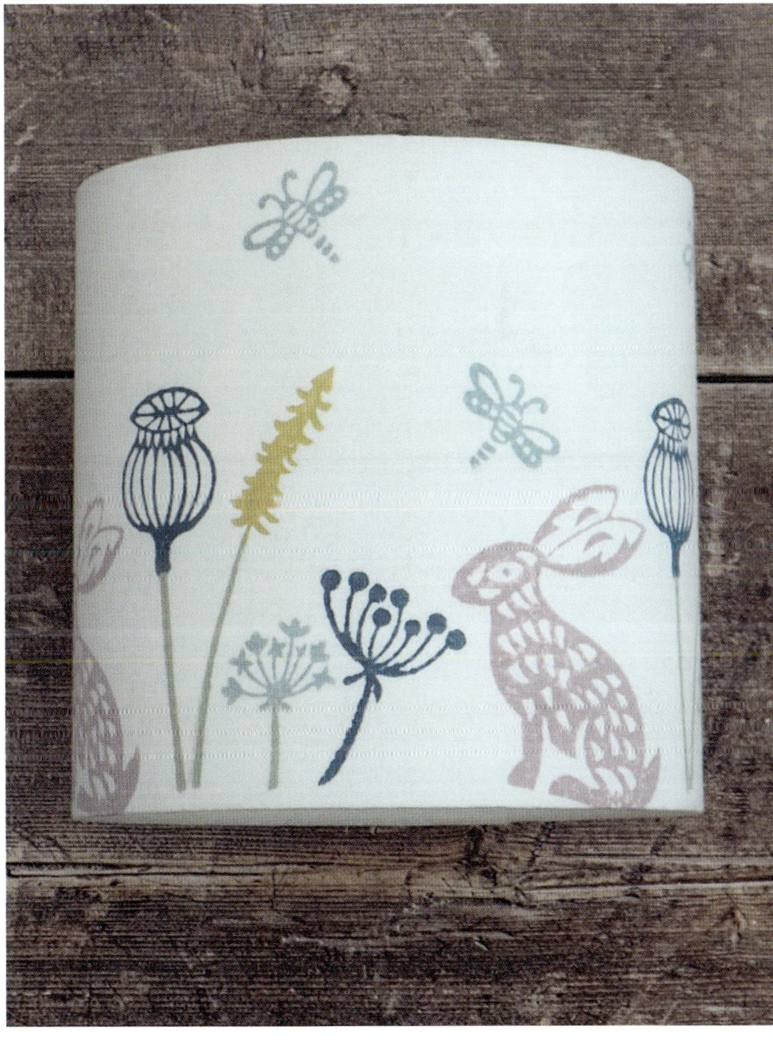

15 Using the fabric tucking tool in your lampshade kit, tuck the excess fabric around the ring. Continue until the excess fabric around the top and bottom of your lampshade is tucked in neatly.

16 Cut away any loose threads using scissors, and your lampshade is complete.

Lovely Linen Cushions

Combining both block printing and sewing makes for an excellent creative project. Having even basic sewing skills means you are able to stitch your own fabric creations, giving you much more flexibility in what you can create with your block-printed fabric. Printing a length of flat fabric can be easier than printing a pre-made fabric item as you are not limited by the boundaries of that item. Printing your own fabric allows you to fully customise your creation – you can pick the designs, colours and pattern that you use. Combining this with sewing also gives you the opportunity to make one-of-a-kind items, such as a beautiful hand-printed cushion.

YOU WILL NEED

- Piece of linen fabric: 34-cm wide and at least 125-cm long
- Fabric scissors
- Ruler
- Pencil
- Printing blocks – we used 3-Part Indian Flower
- Fabric paints – we used Midnight Blue, Indian Aqua and Khaki
- Sewing machine
- Sewing pins
- Cushion insert: 32 x 52 cm
- Basic printing equipment (see page 18)

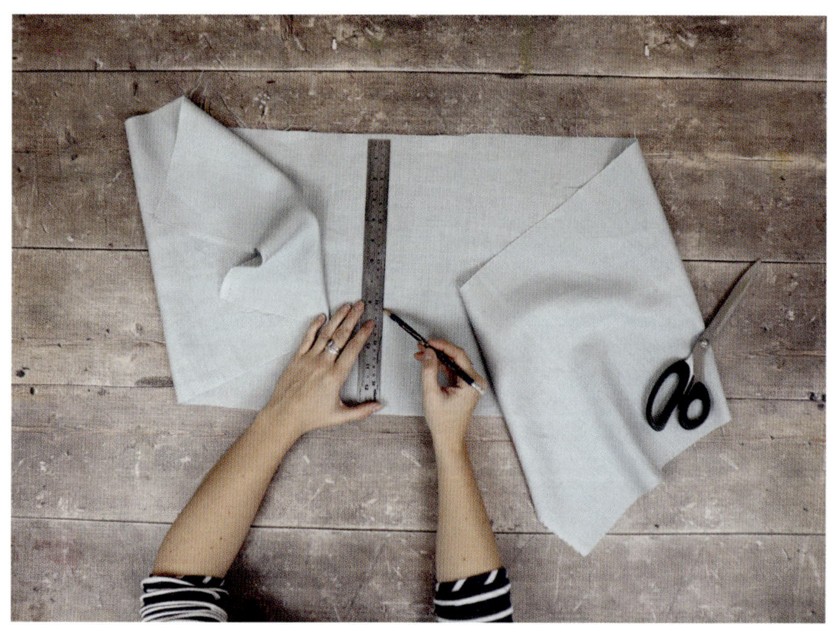

1 Begin by cutting your fabric to the required sizes, measuring and marking with a ruler and pencil and trimming using fabric scissors. You'll need three pieces: one for the front and two for the back, in the following sizes:

Piece 1 (front): 54 x 34 cm

Piece 2 (back): 39 x 34 cm

Piece 3 (back): 31 x 34 cm

These measurements include a 1-cm seam allowance on each side to provide space for sewing.

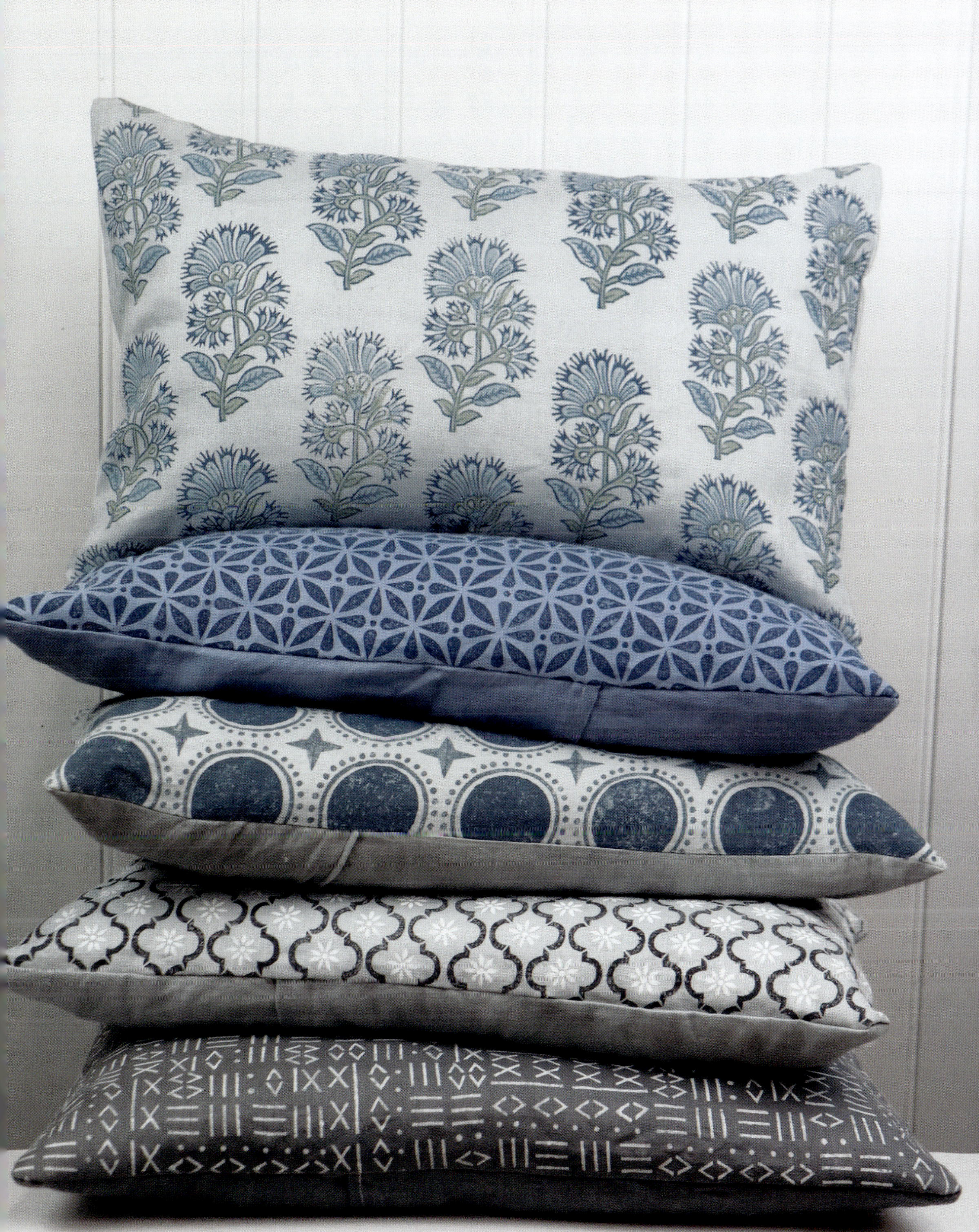

Printing Tip

Before printing, we suggest practising the spacing for the pattern on a piece of scrap linen fabric, cut to the same dimensions as your cushion. We've chosen to print our 3-Part Indian Flower design using a half-drop repeat (see page 43), as this layout provides balanced coverage across the fabric.

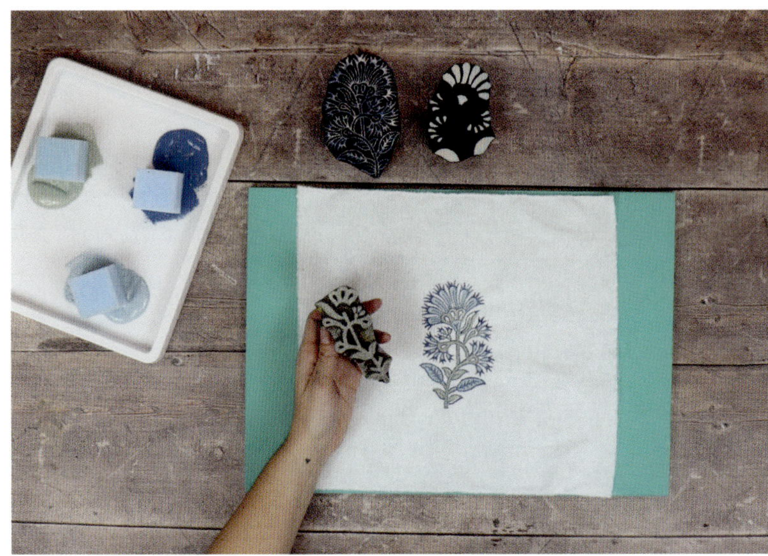

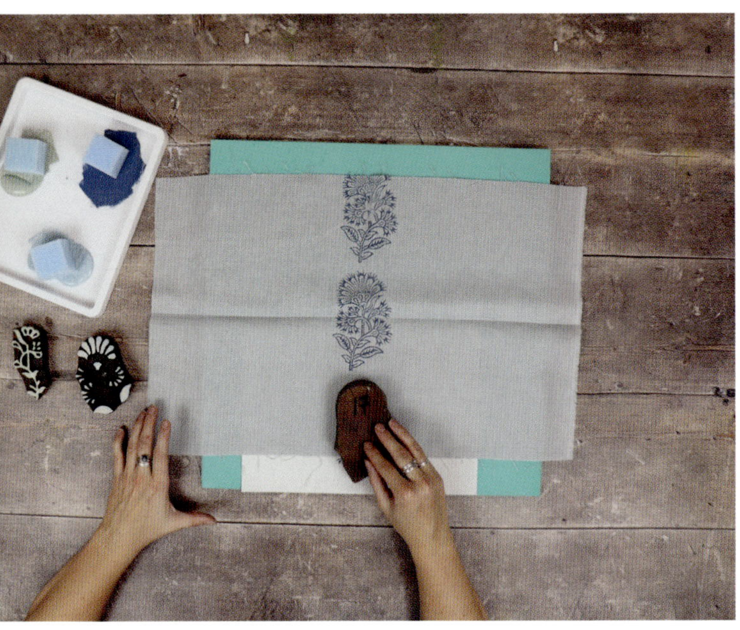

2 For our design, we're using a 3-Part Indian Flower printing block, which is an advanced block print made of three separate pieces. Each part needs to be printed in a different colour and layered over the top of each other (see precise two-colour printing, page 24). You'll need to practise fitting the pieces together on scrap fabric or paper and experiment with the colour combination to ensure the pattern can be clearly seen.

3 We will be printing only on the front panel (Piece 1). To ensure even spacing, first fold the fabric in half, then fold it again and press it with an iron to create crease lines that mark the centre. Begin by printing your first (outer) block in the middle of the fabric along the crease using Midnight Blue. Next, add two more prints directly above and below the centre, staying along the same crease line. It's fine if some prints extend off the fabric onto the printing mat, as this contributes to the overall pattern design.

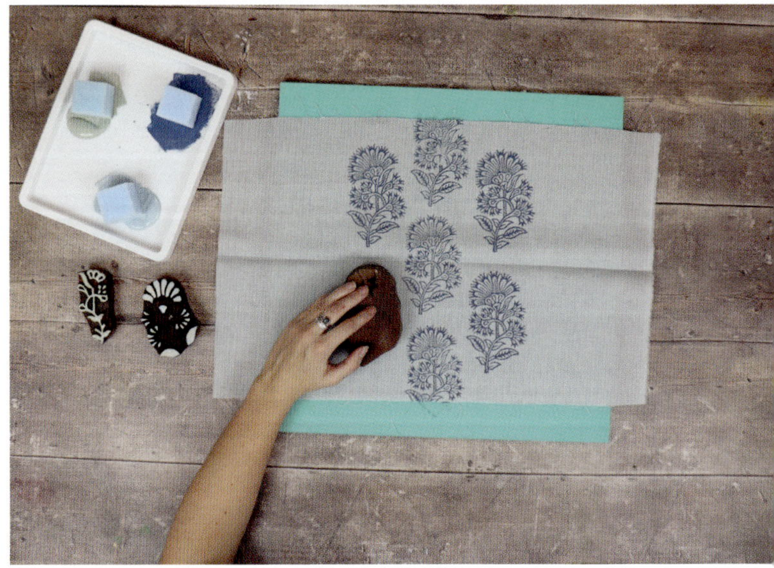

4 To create the half-drop repeat pattern, place the next prints slightly lower than the central row, aligning them to fill the gaps between the previous prints on either side.

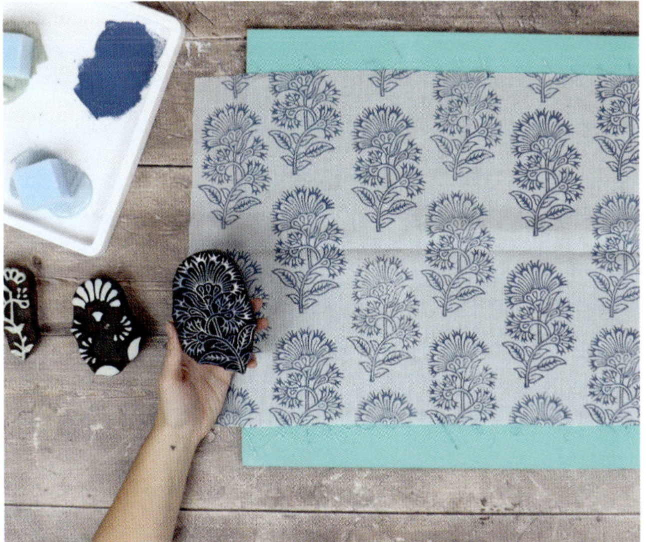

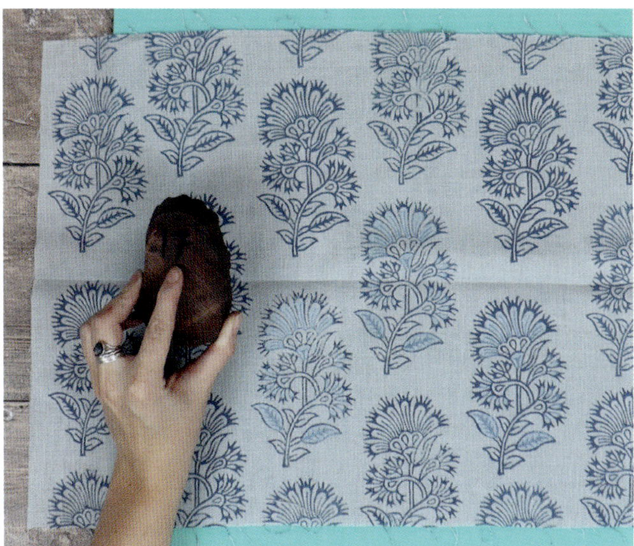

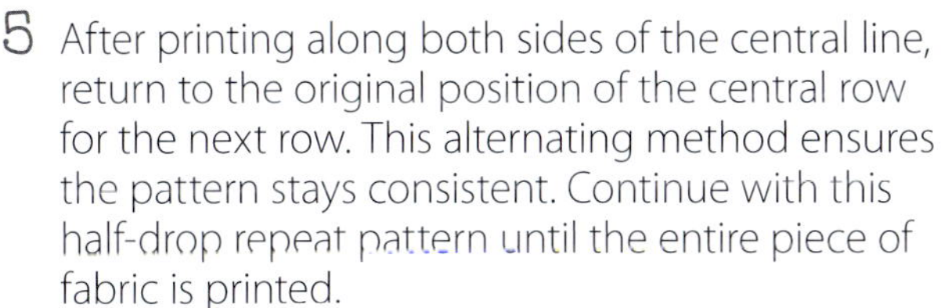

5 After printing along both sides of the central line, return to the original position of the central row for the next row. This alternating method ensures the pattern stays consistent. Continue with this half-drop repeat pattern until the entire piece of fabric is printed.

6 Once the first layer of prints is dry, repeat the printing process using the next part of the three-part design, in your lighter colour. We used Indian Aqua. Carefully line each print up in the correct position.

7 Repeat the process again with the final part of the block design in your third colour – we used Khaki – completing the printed design. Leave to dry.

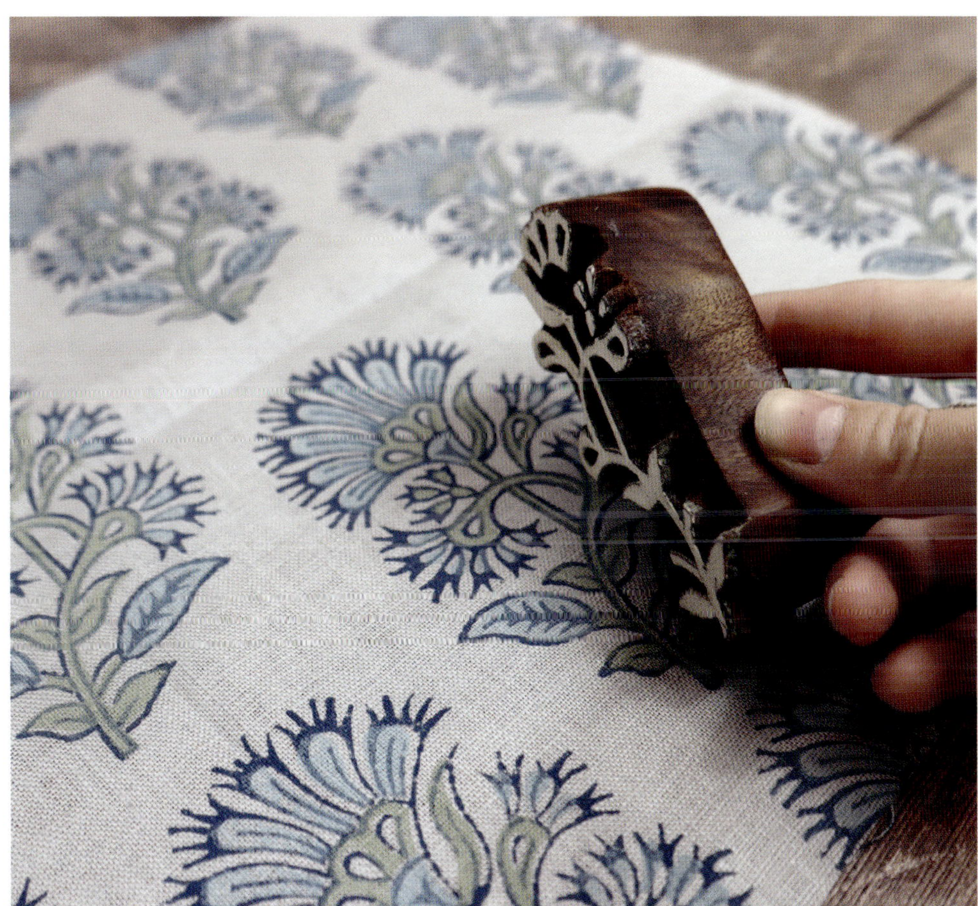

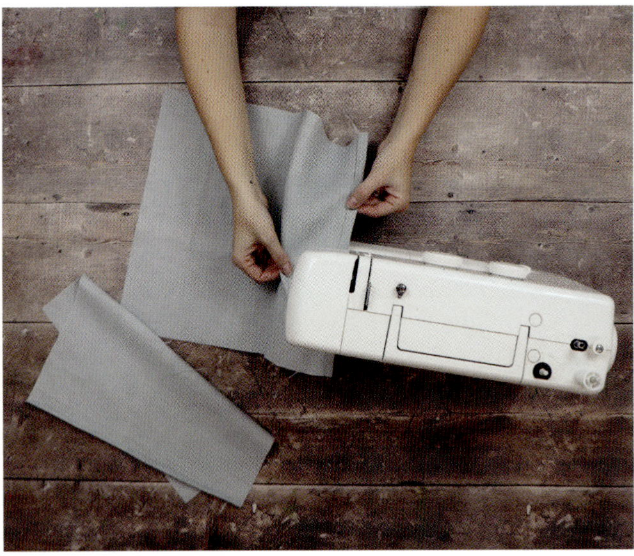

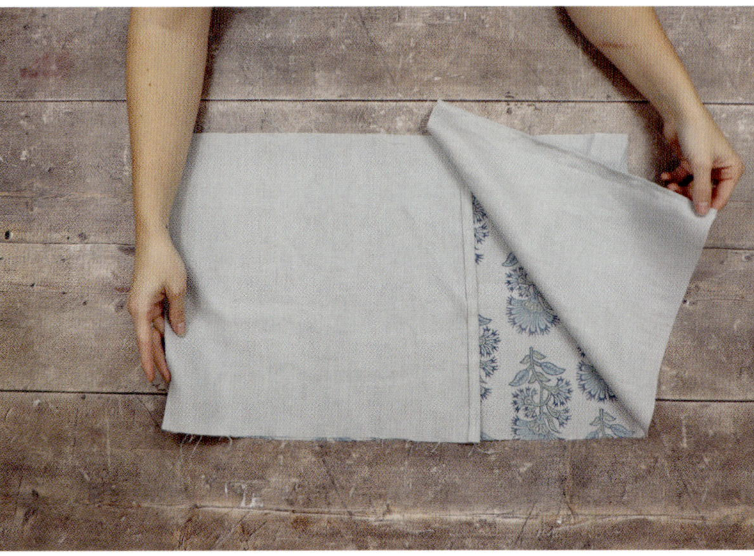

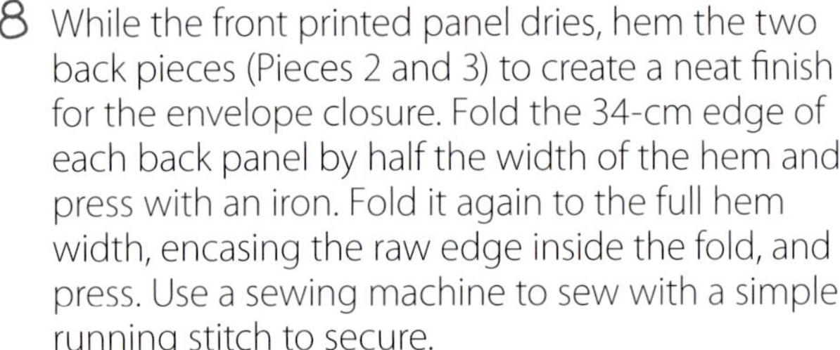

8 While the front printed panel dries, hem the two back pieces (Pieces 2 and 3) to create a neat finish for the envelope closure. Fold the 34-cm edge of each back panel by half the width of the hem and press with an iron. Fold it again to the full hem width, encasing the raw edge inside the fold, and press. Use a sewing machine to sew with a simple running stitch to secure.

9 Once the front panel is dry, place the three pieces of fabric together for sewing. Start by laying the printed front panel face up. Next, place the larger back panel (Piece 2) on top, with the hemmed edge facing inwards towards the printed side. Then, place the smaller back panel (Piece 3) on top of the larger one, again with the hemmed edge facing inward. The two back panels should overlap, creating the envelope opening.

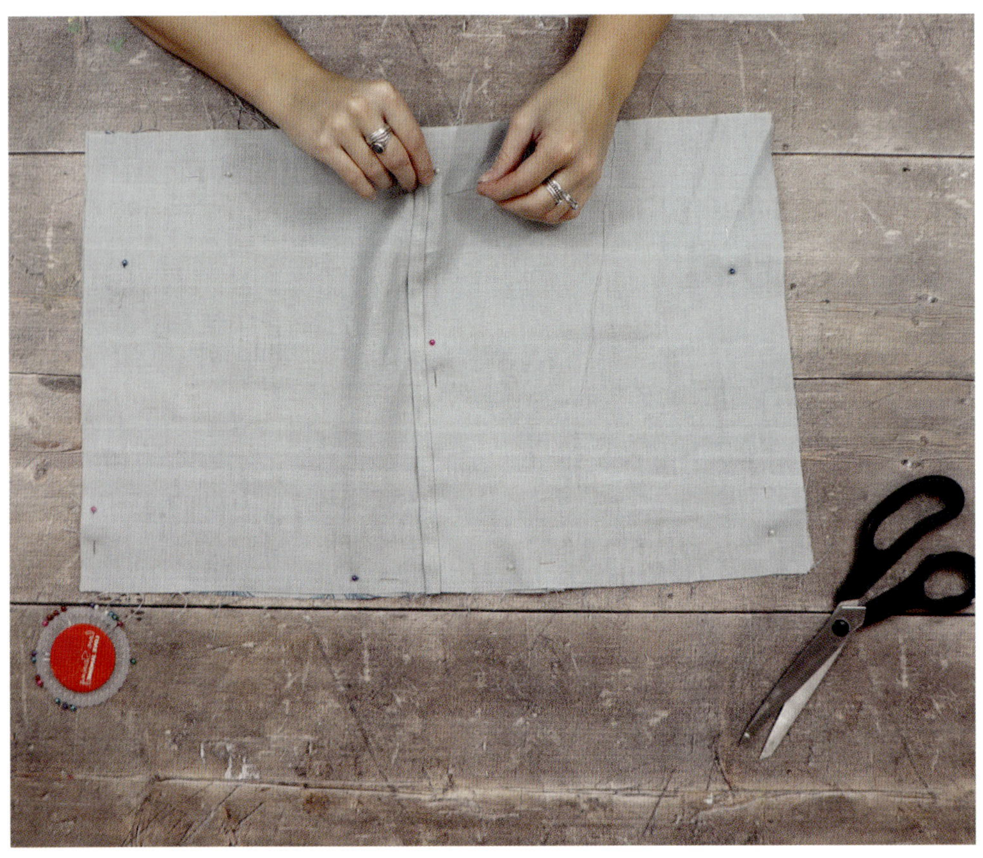

10 Pin all the layers together, ready for sewing.

11 Either using a sewing machine or by hand, sew around all four edges of the fabric, joining the front and back panels together. Sew through all layers neatly to ensure a sturdy, secure finish.

12 Turn the cushion cover the right side out, pushing each corner out as you do so. Iron again to smooth out your sewn seams. Insert the cushion pad to finish your hand-printed cushion, and display with pride.

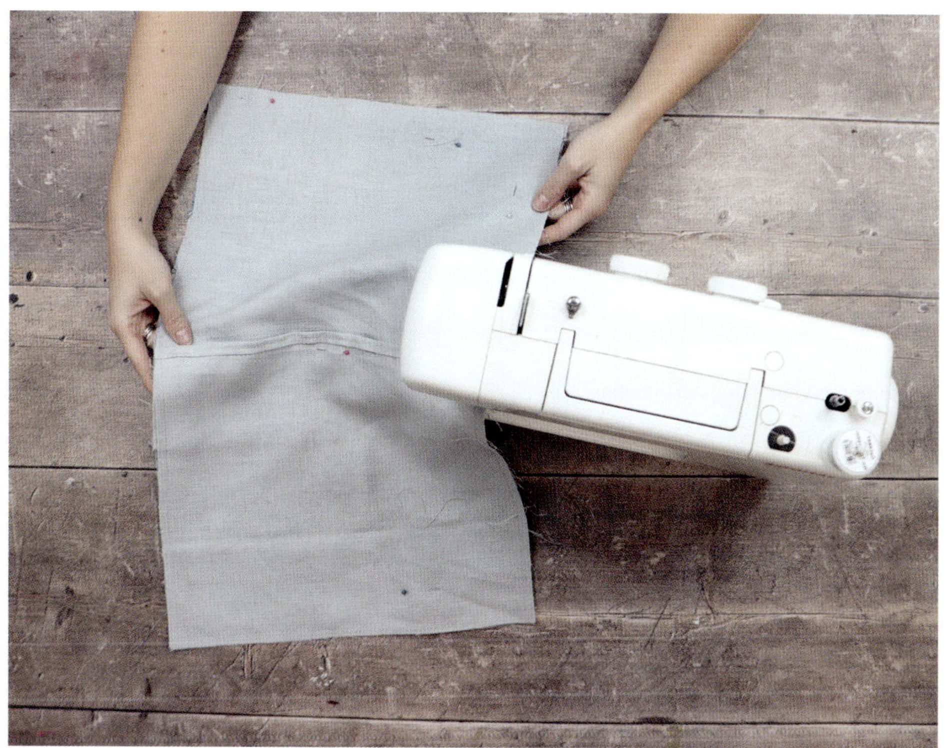

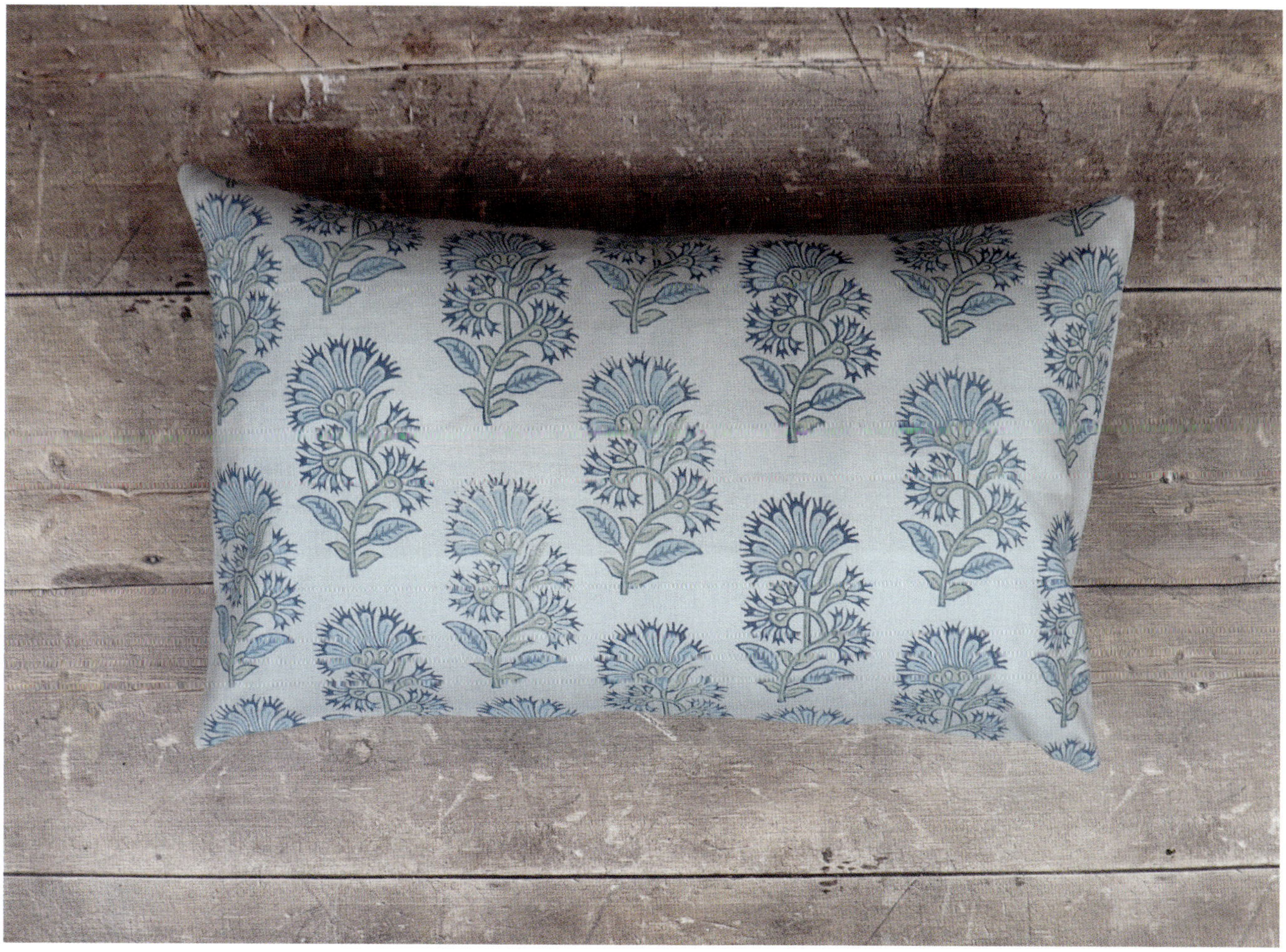

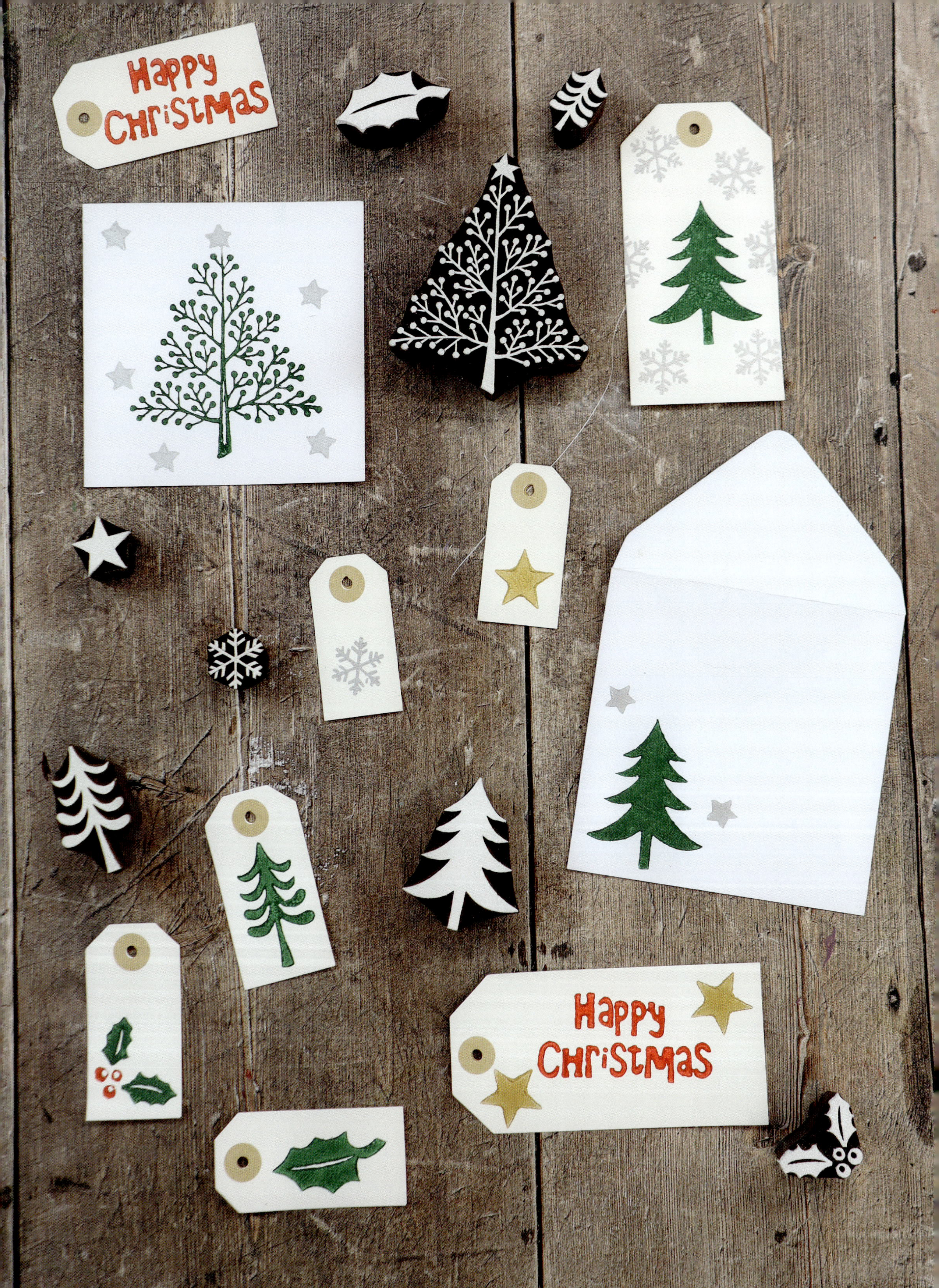

Happy Christmas
Happy Christmas

Crafty Cards and Tags

There's always an occasion to make something truly personal, whether you're creating a birthday card for a special friend, sending Christmas cheer or welcoming a new neighbour into their home. While it might seem like printing on paper would be easier than on fabric, it's the opposite. That's why we recommend beginners start with fabric, before moving on to paper and stationery once they feel confident. The challenge with paper lies in its sometimes-slippery surface, which can cause the paint to slide, making achieving consistent prints more difficult. However, we've got a few helpful tips to ensure you get perfect prints every time.

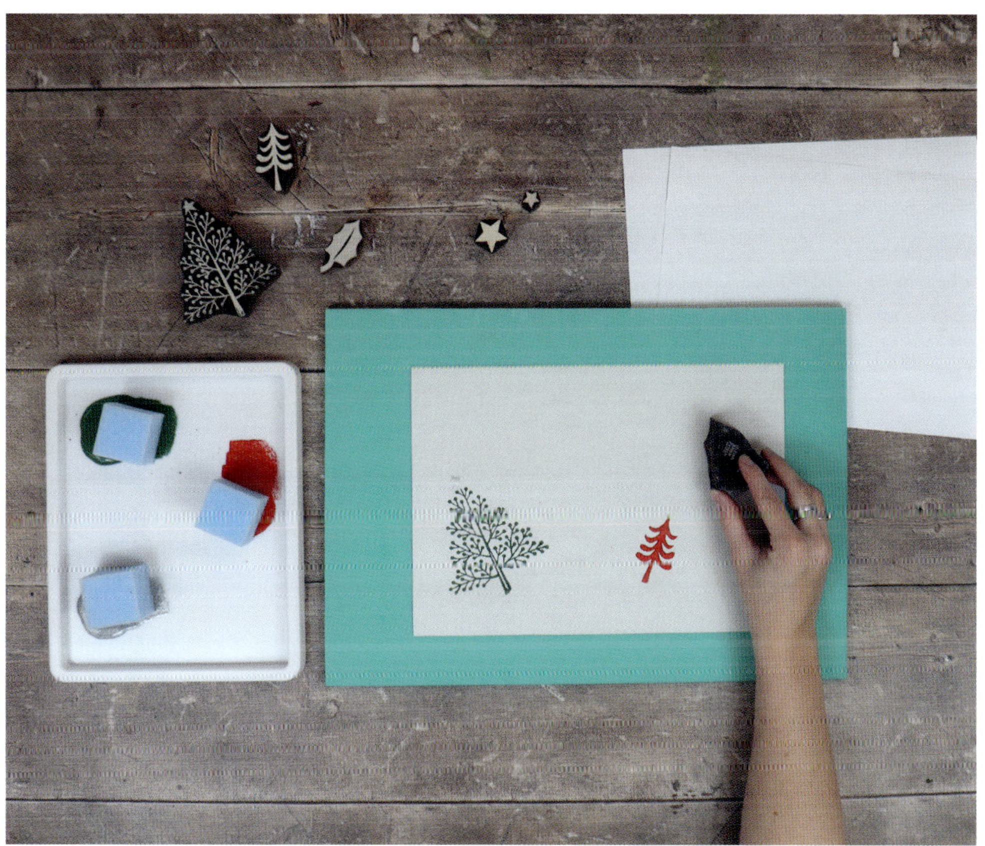

1   You can find great-quality stationery blanks, which aren't very expensive. We like to practise on plain scrap paper first to ensure we are getting good results before moving on. This will help you get used to printing onto a new material.

Printing Tip

Stationery blank items can have a shiny side and a rough side. Always print on the rough side.

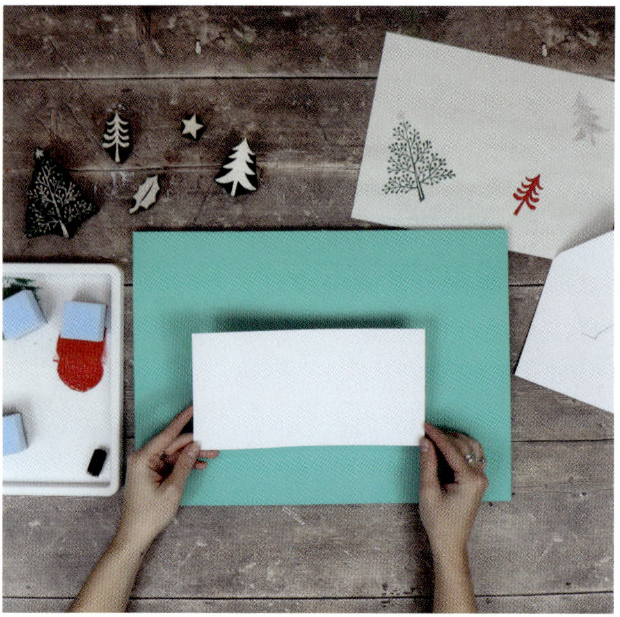

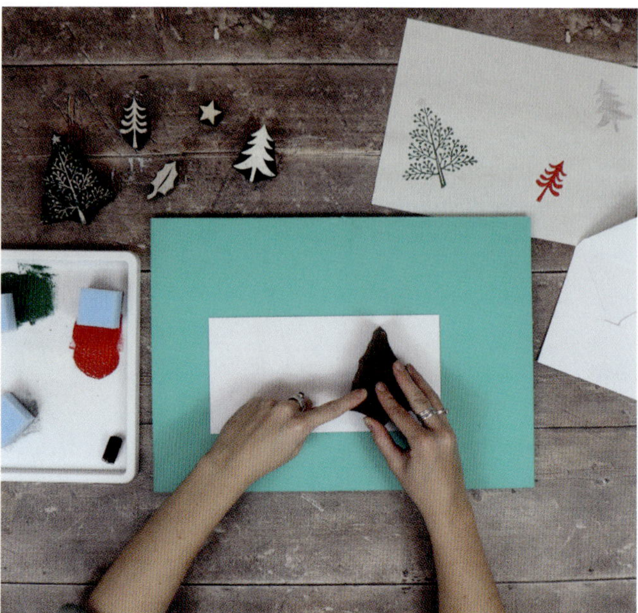

2   Lay your blank card open and flat onto your printing mat. It's important to print the card open, not folded over as this will give you a double-hard surface to print onto.

3   When putting your printing block down and onto the card, do this slowly. Apply pressure to the printing block with your right hand, as you would when printing onto fabric, while keeping your left hand in place as extra support to avoid slipping. Wiggle the printing block up and down to ensure you are getting good contact between the block and the card. As paper and card can be a harder surface than fabric, we always say, 'Once you think you've wiggled enough, wiggle again.' This will ensure you get a successful print. Be careful not to twist the printing block as this will cause smudging.

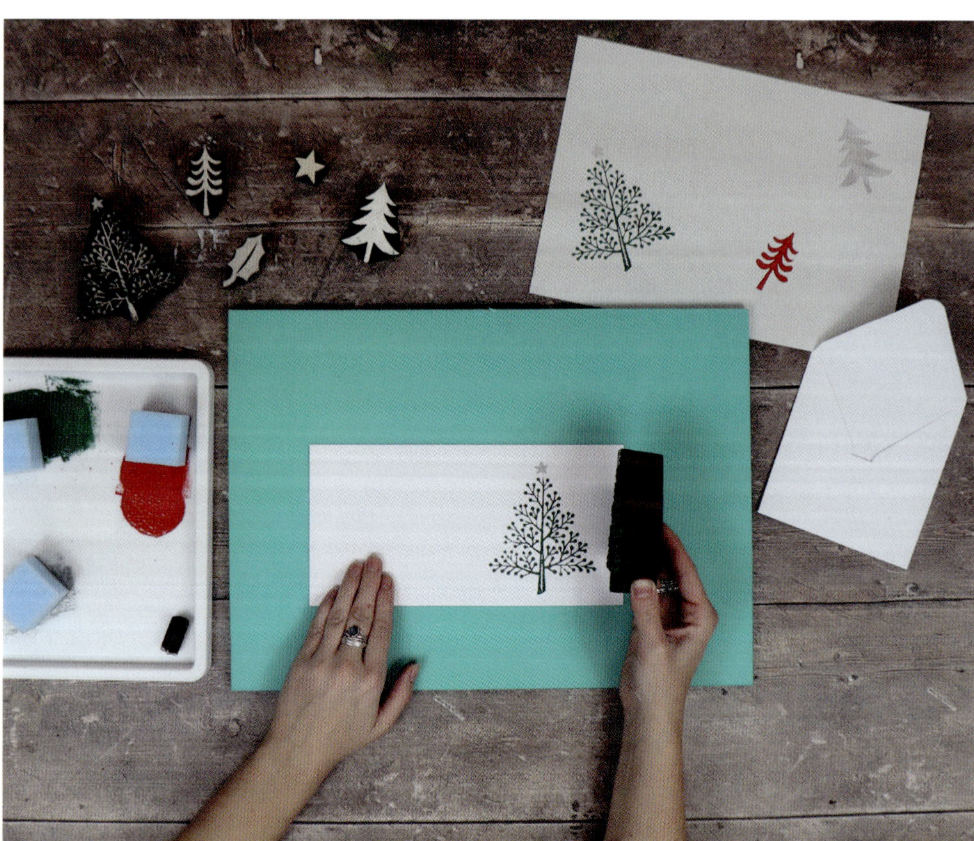

4   Pull the printing block straight up and off the card, using your left hand to hold the card flat on the table.

5 Add all the printed designs and let the card dry before folding. You may want to add a print to the envelope for an extra-special touch.

6 Follow the same steps above for printing onto gift tags. Use smaller designs that fit on the tags, and add string to them once dry.

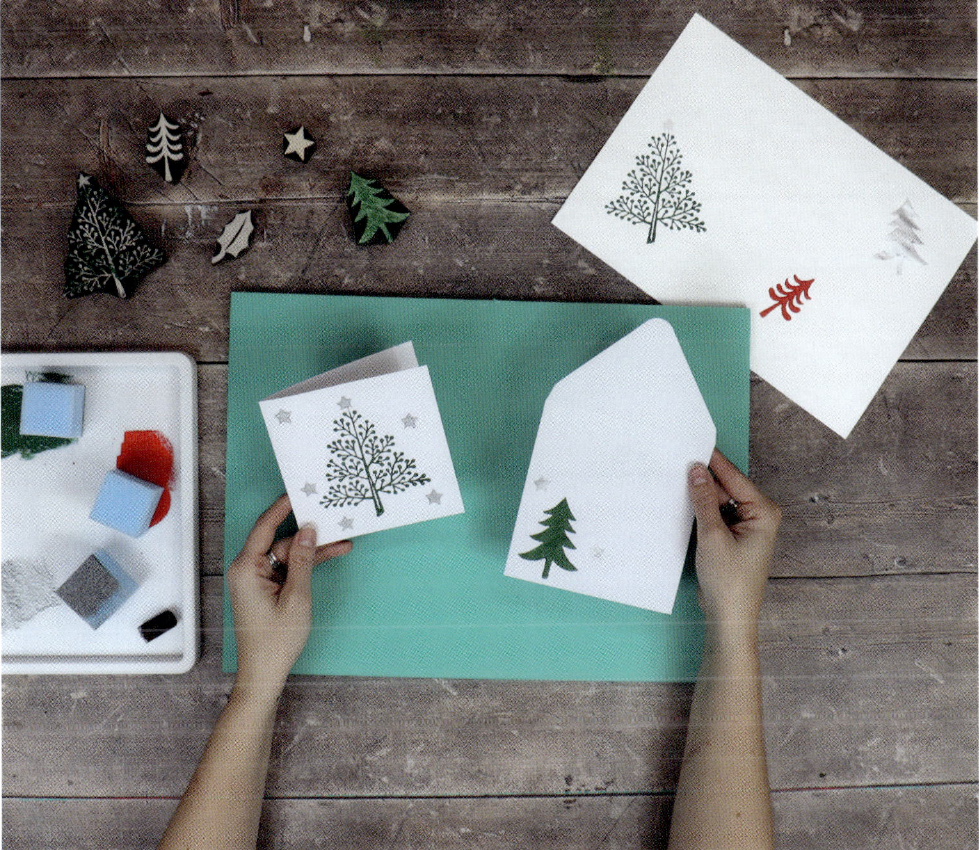

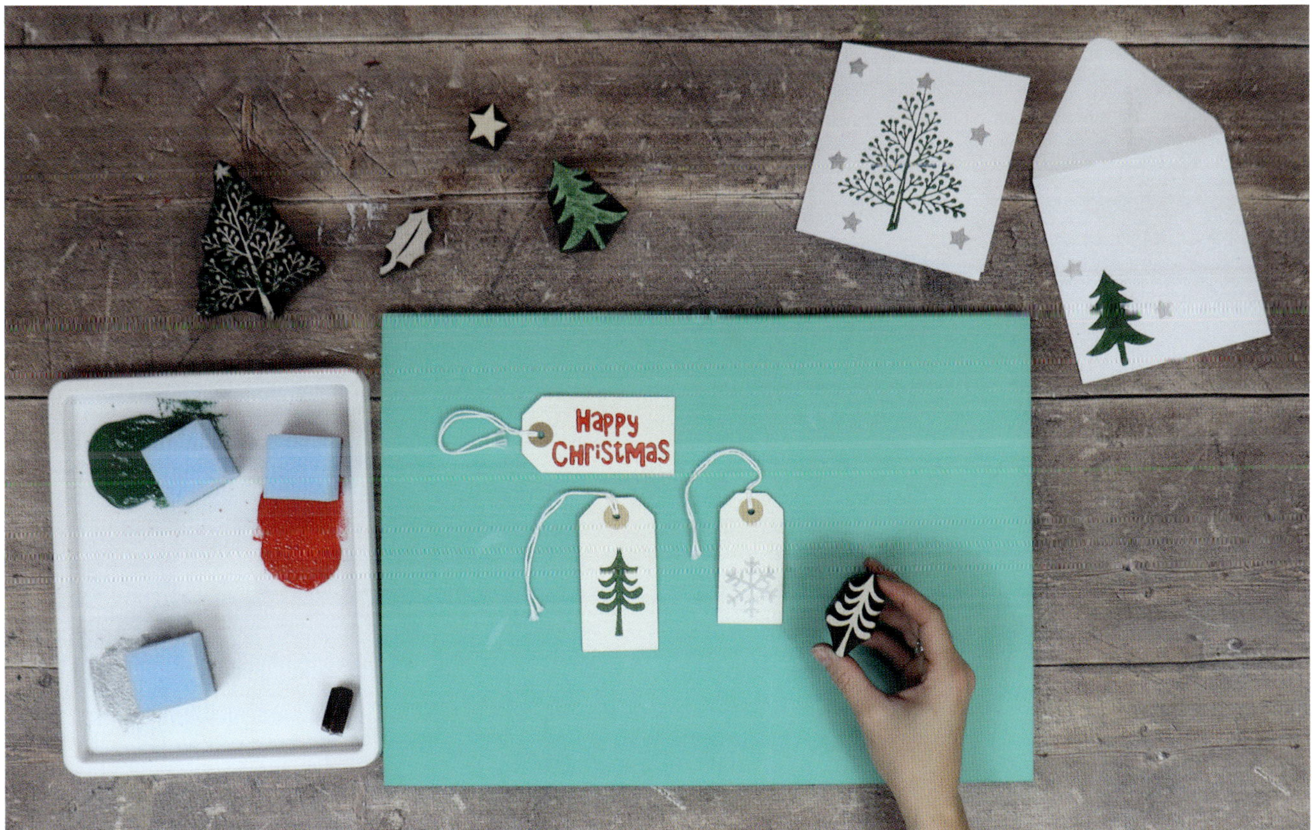

Christmas Gift Wrap

For truly unique Christmas gifts that look spectacular under the tree, hand-printing your own wrapping paper is a wonderful way to make use of your printing blocks. Brown paper can have a shiny side and a rough side – always make sure you print with the rough side facing up. Start by measuring how much paper you need to wrap the gift. It's easier and more efficient to print the correct size piece of paper, otherwise you may find you waste time printing off-cuts. A simple one-colour print in a single festive colour is fun and easy to print and can give a chic minimalist effect that is sure to impress.

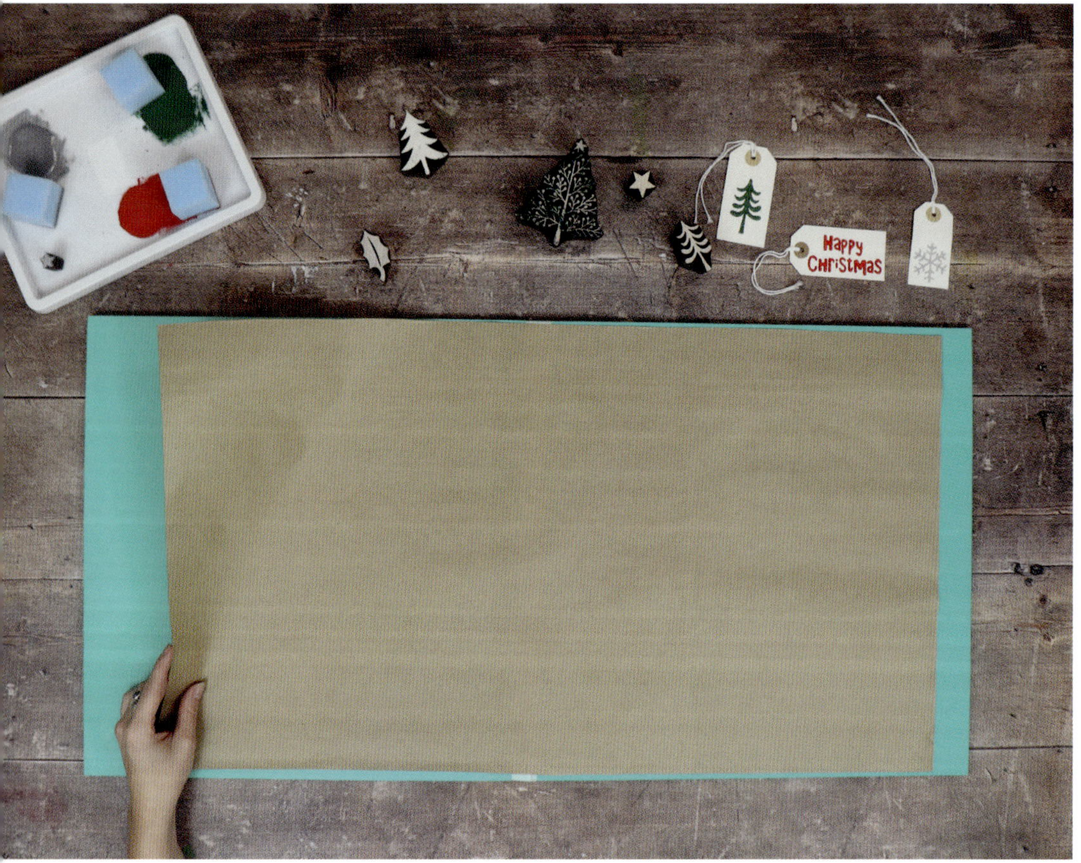

1 Lay your brown kraft paper out onto your printing mat. Use drawing pins in each corner to hold the paper flat. You won't see the small holes made by the pins once you have wrapped the item.

Printing Tip

The size of the item you are wrapping determines the number of prints you should make. If you're wrapping a small item, use a small design block and print the pattern more frequently across the paper. For larger items and bigger sheets of paper, use a larger design with less-frequent printing.

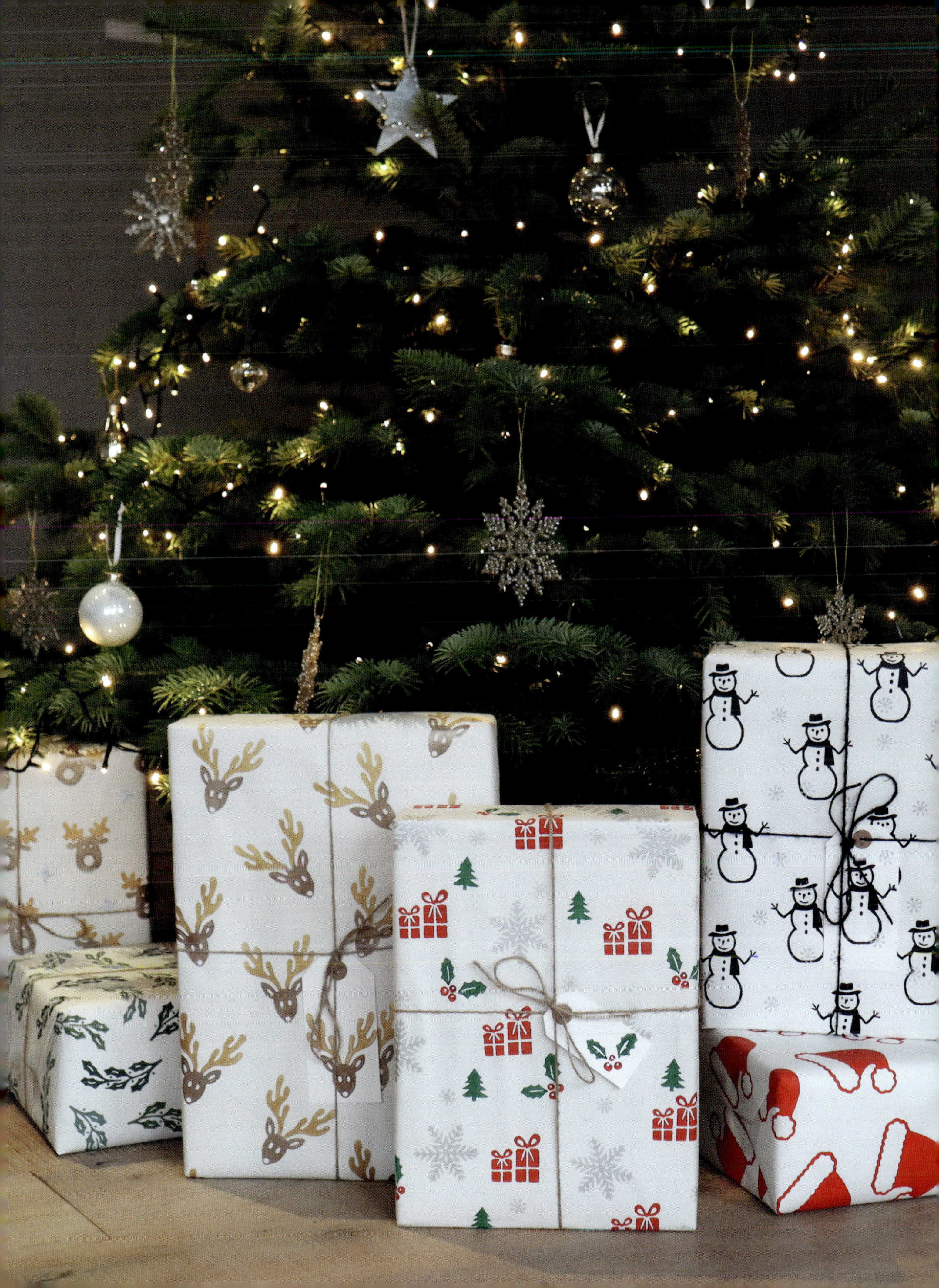

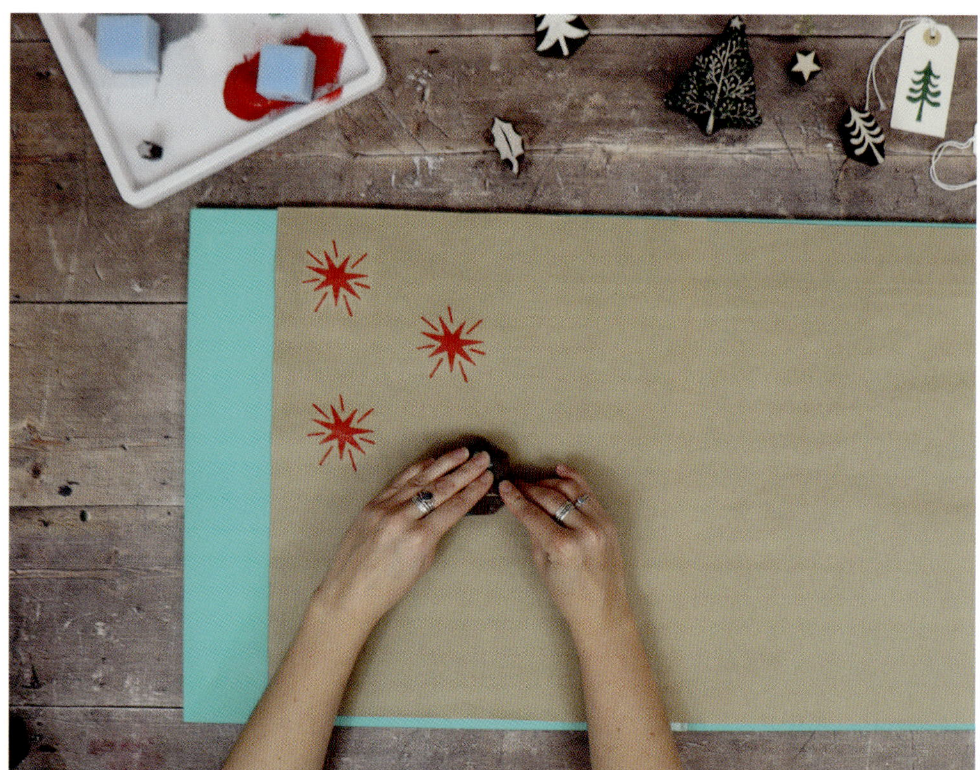

2 Following the same printing technique as we used on the cards and tags (see page 117), hold the Christmas Starburst printing block in your right hand, and support it with your left to avoid any slipping. Ensure you are applying the correct pressure to avoid the printing block from puncturing through the paper.

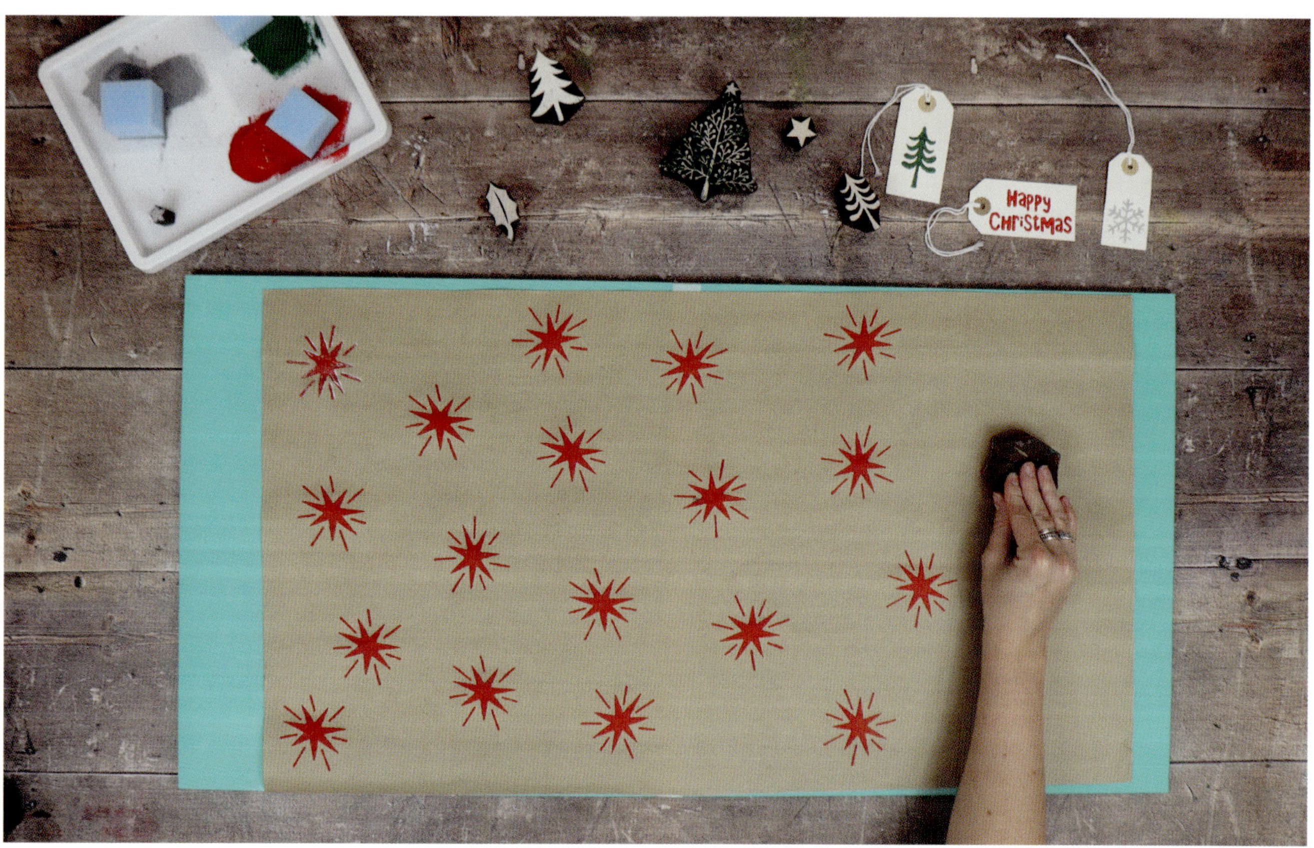

3 Start from one end and work your way across the paper until the entire sheet is printed in your chosen design. Once finished, leave the paper to dry before use.

4 Use your printed paper to wrap your item.

5 Pair your gift with string or twine and a printed gift tag (see page 117) to complete the look.

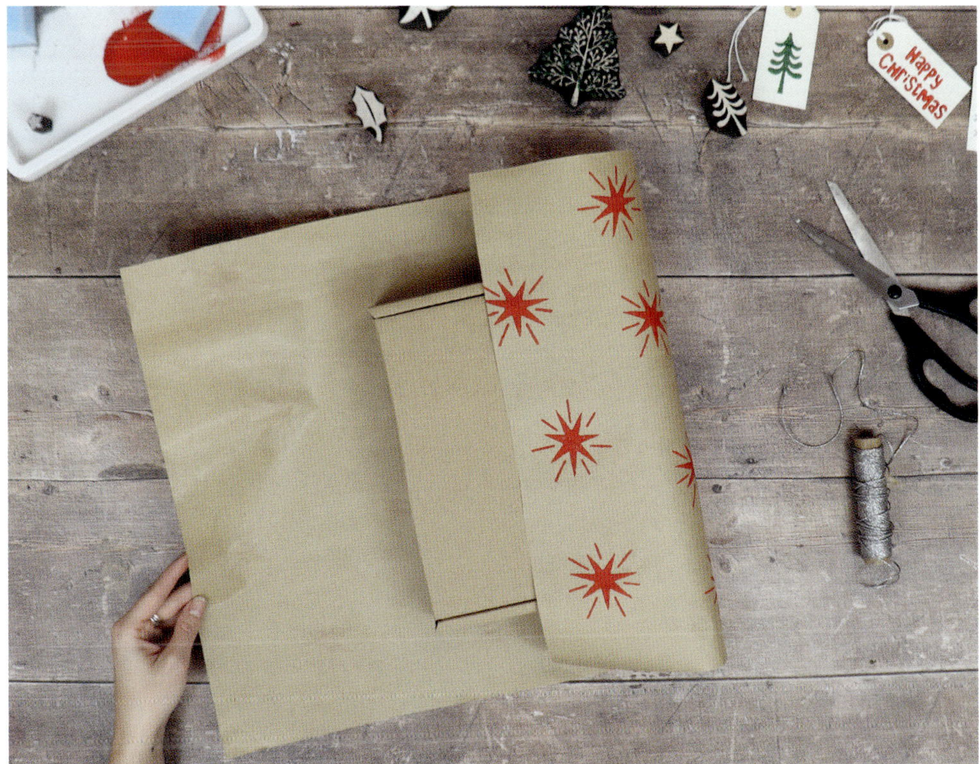

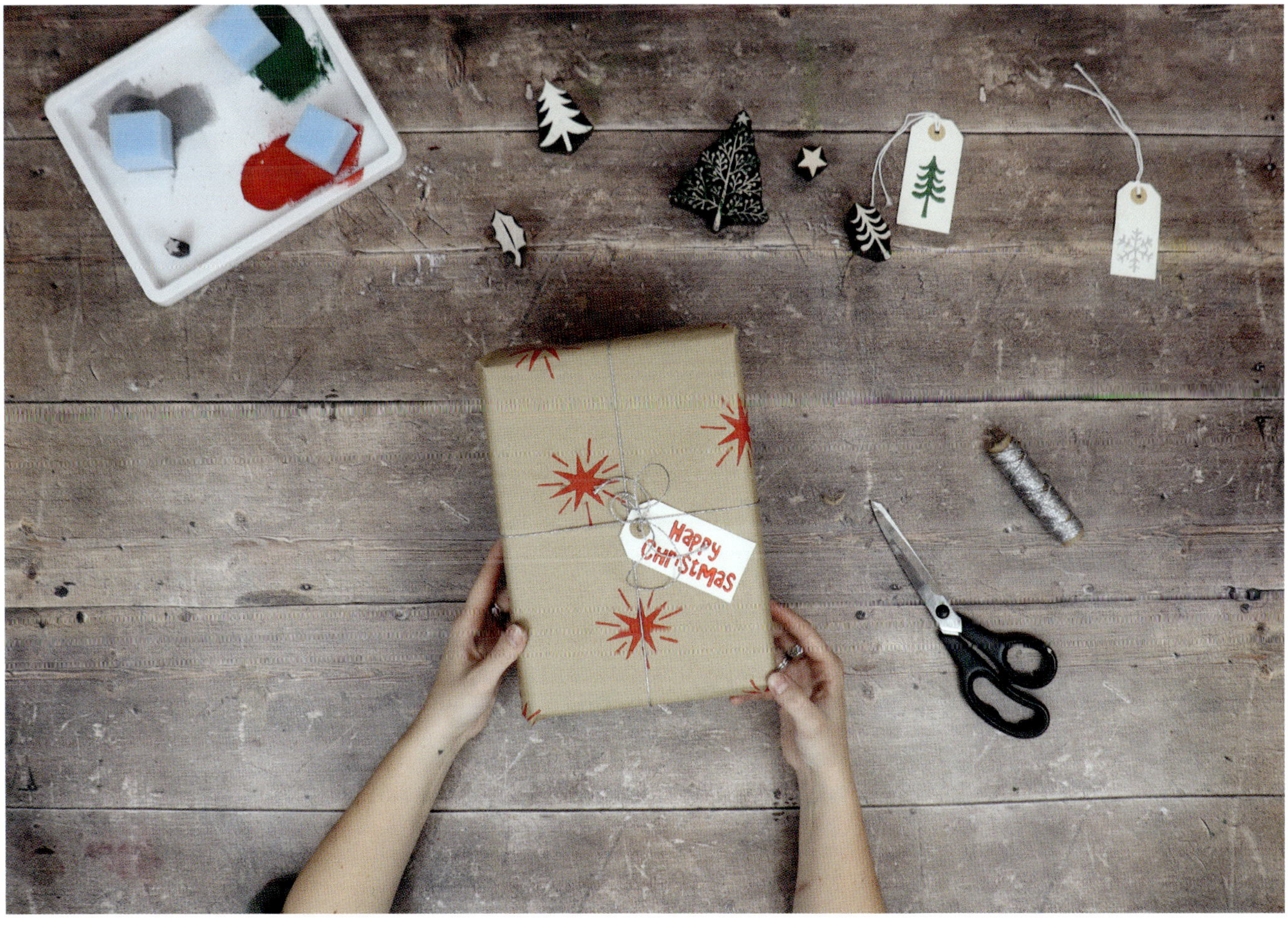

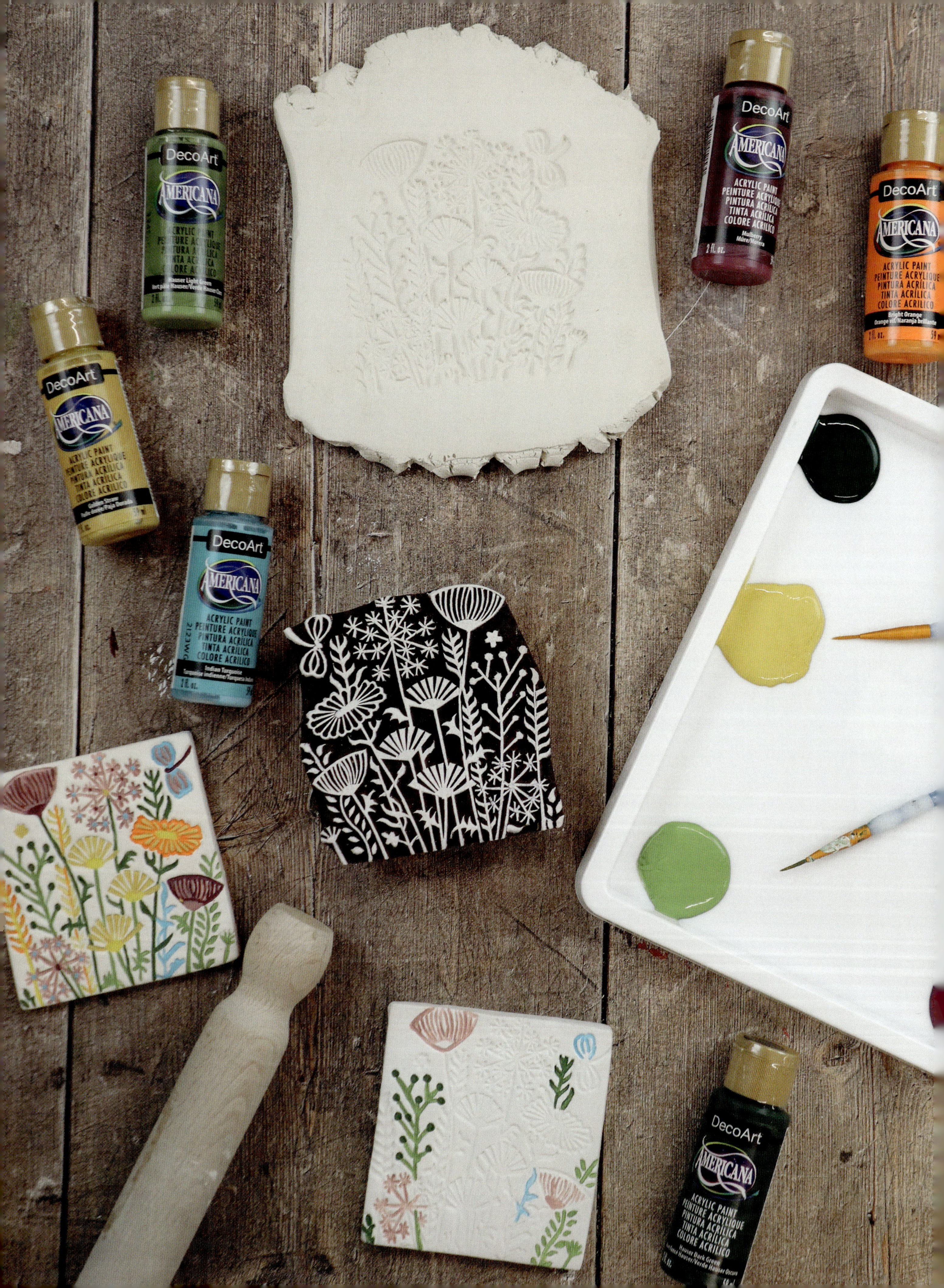

Colourful Clay Tiles

Block printing into clay introduces a whole new dimension to your artistic repertoire, offering endless creative possibilities for crafting functional, decorative and sculptural pieces. It was one of Maggie's first uses of wooden printing blocks in her pottery café, which has now been running for 23 years. The use of blocks has been a popular way to indent patterns into wet clay, which can then be painted. Here we are using air-drying clay, but if you have access to a kiln you can use earthenware or stoneware clay. This step-by-step project will show you how to print, cut and paint your own handmade tiles, which can be used as a decorative item, a unique coaster or to create a beautiful tiled splashback in a kitchen or bathroom.

YOU WILL NEED

- Talcum powder or flour for dusting
- Knife
- Packet of white air-drying clay
- Rolling pin
- Levelling sticks or straws
- Square printing block – we used Meadow
- Cookie cutter – we used a 10-cm square cutter
- Water bowl and sponge
- Wooden chopping board
- Acrylic paints – we used Hauser Light Green, Hauser Dark Green, Indian Turquoise, Bright Orange, Golden Straw and Mulberry
- Thin paintbrushes
- Spray varnish or PVA glue

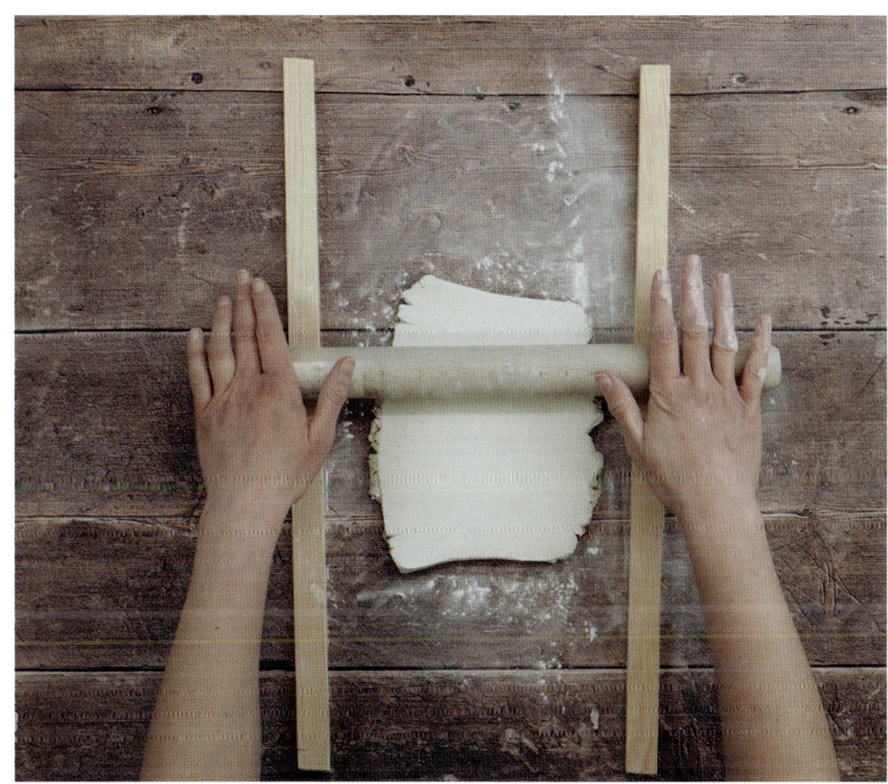

1 Sprinkle your work surface with talcum powder or flour to avoid any clay sticking. Cut a chunk of clay to work with, using your rolling pin to roll it into a workable shape. Use levelling sticks or straws to avoid rolling the clay too thinly, which will cause it to crack; you want your clay to be around 1-cm thick for a tile.

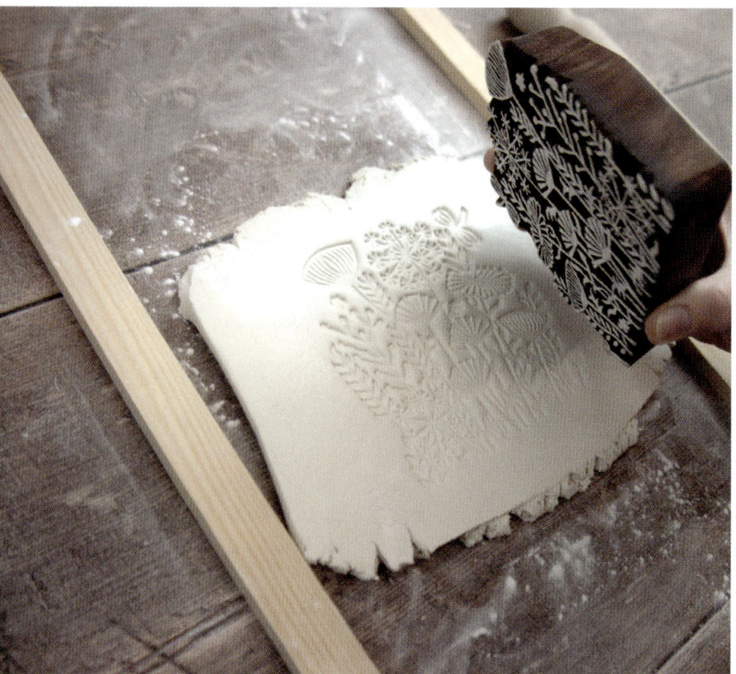

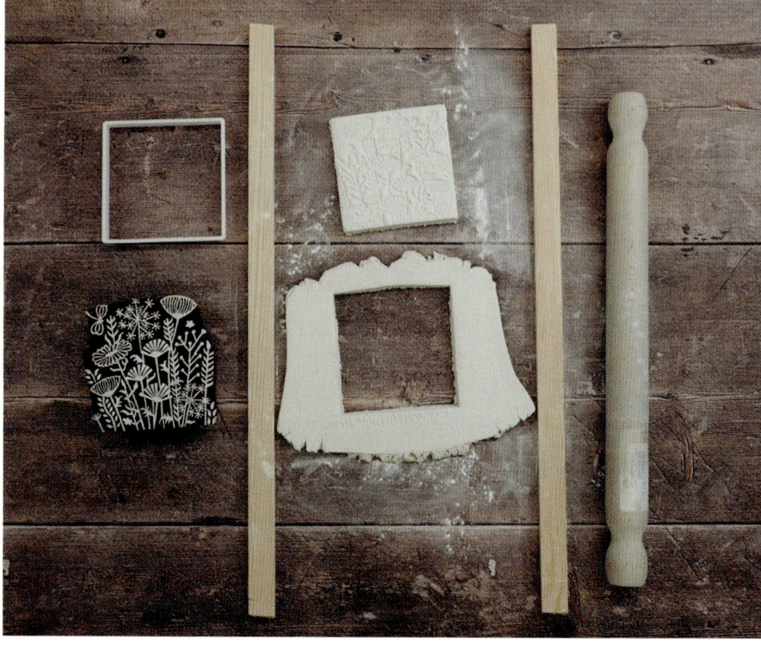

2 Once your clay is the correct thickness, sprinkle a small amount of talcum powder or flour over your square printing block. This will stop it sticking to the clay. Press your Meadow printing block evenly into the clay, being careful not to press too hard so the printing block doesn't break through to the other side – even pressure applied all over is best (this can take a few practices to get right).

3 Once your clay is imprinted, use your cookie cutter to cut out the square for your tile.

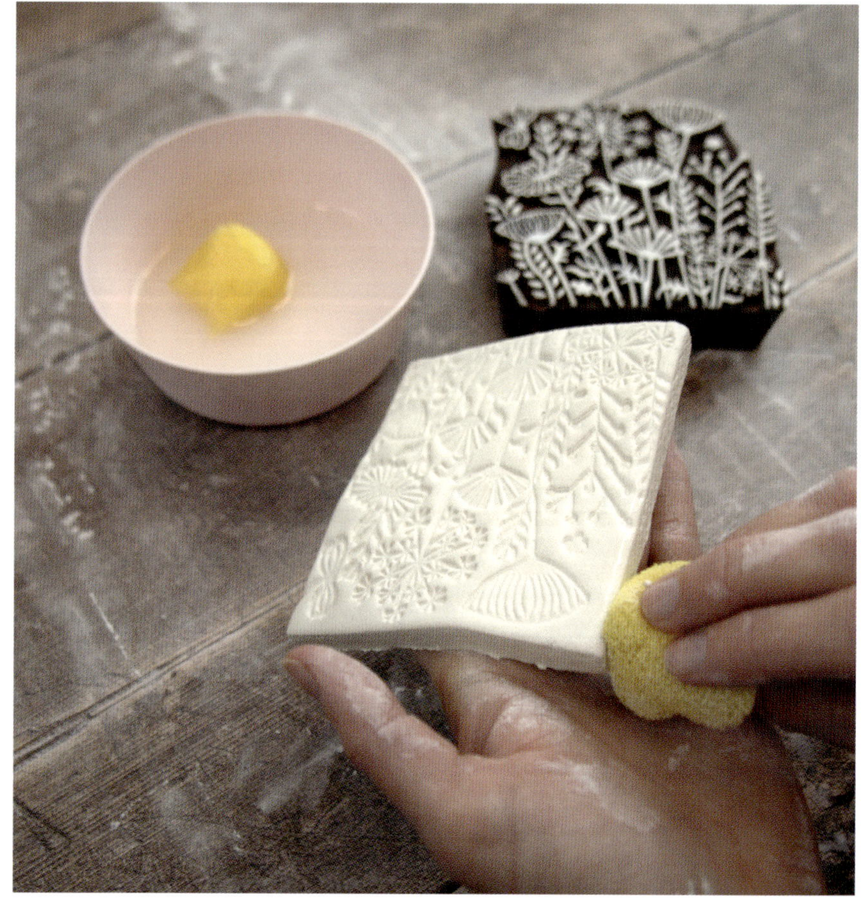

Printing Tip

Place a flat board, such as a plastic chopping board, over the top of your tile as it dries to keep it flat.

4 Use a wet sponge to smooth the edges of your tile, and leave to dry fully. This can take around 24–48 hours.

5 Once your tile is dry, begin painting with the acrylic paint, which works well on air-drying clay. You may need to apply several coats for a strong colour.

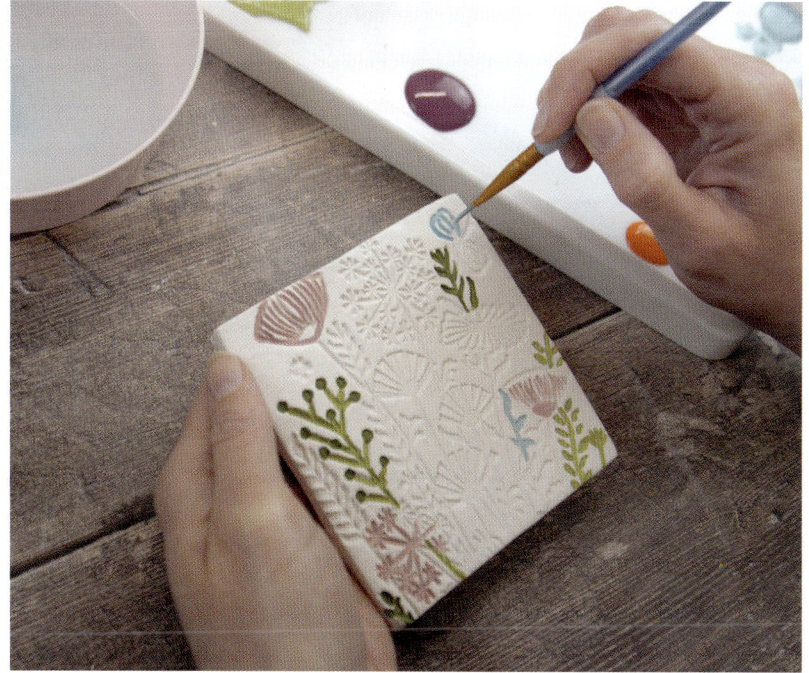

6 Once your tile is painted and dry, seal it with a spray varnish or a layer of PVA glue to protect it, prolong its durability and create a nice finishing effect.

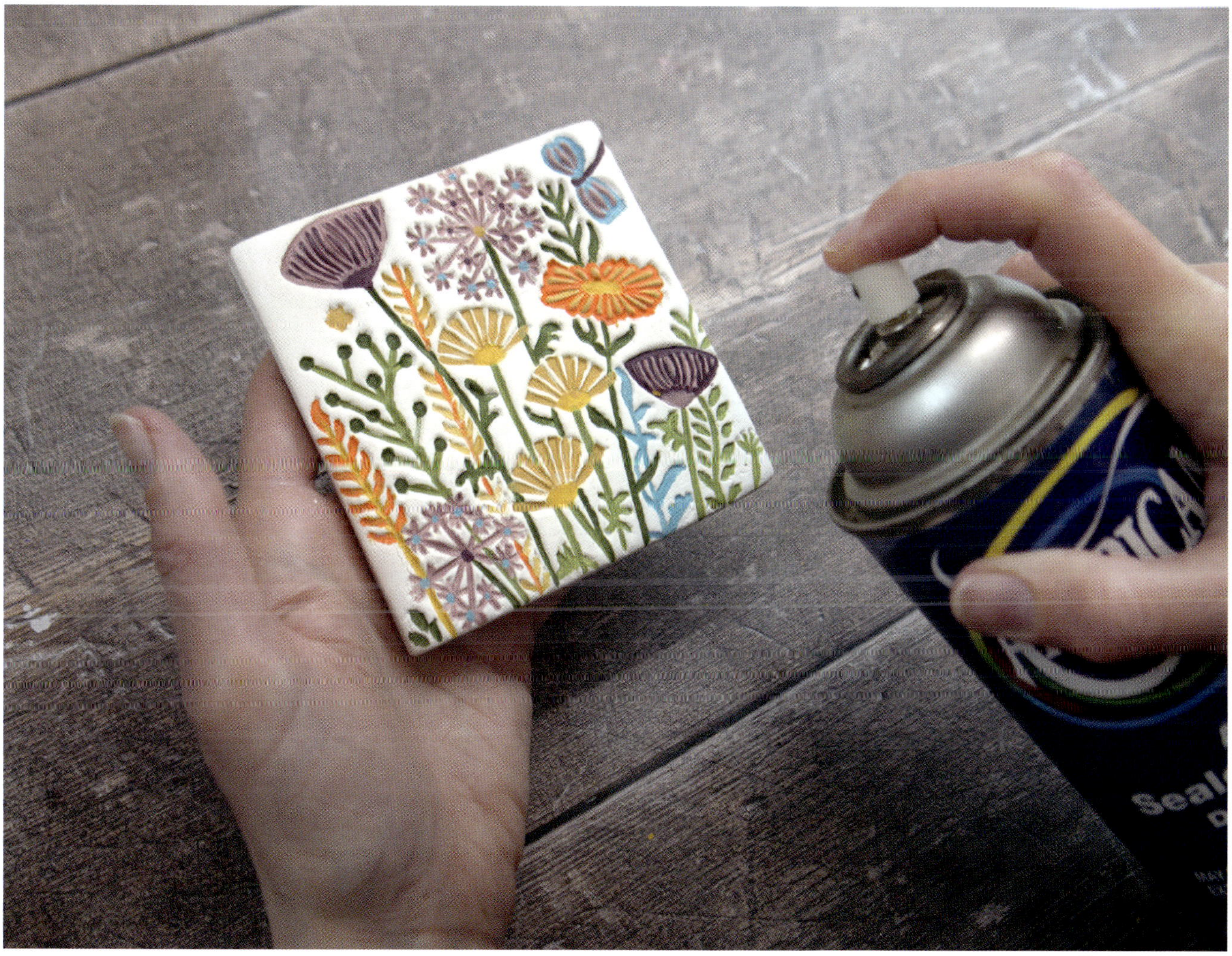

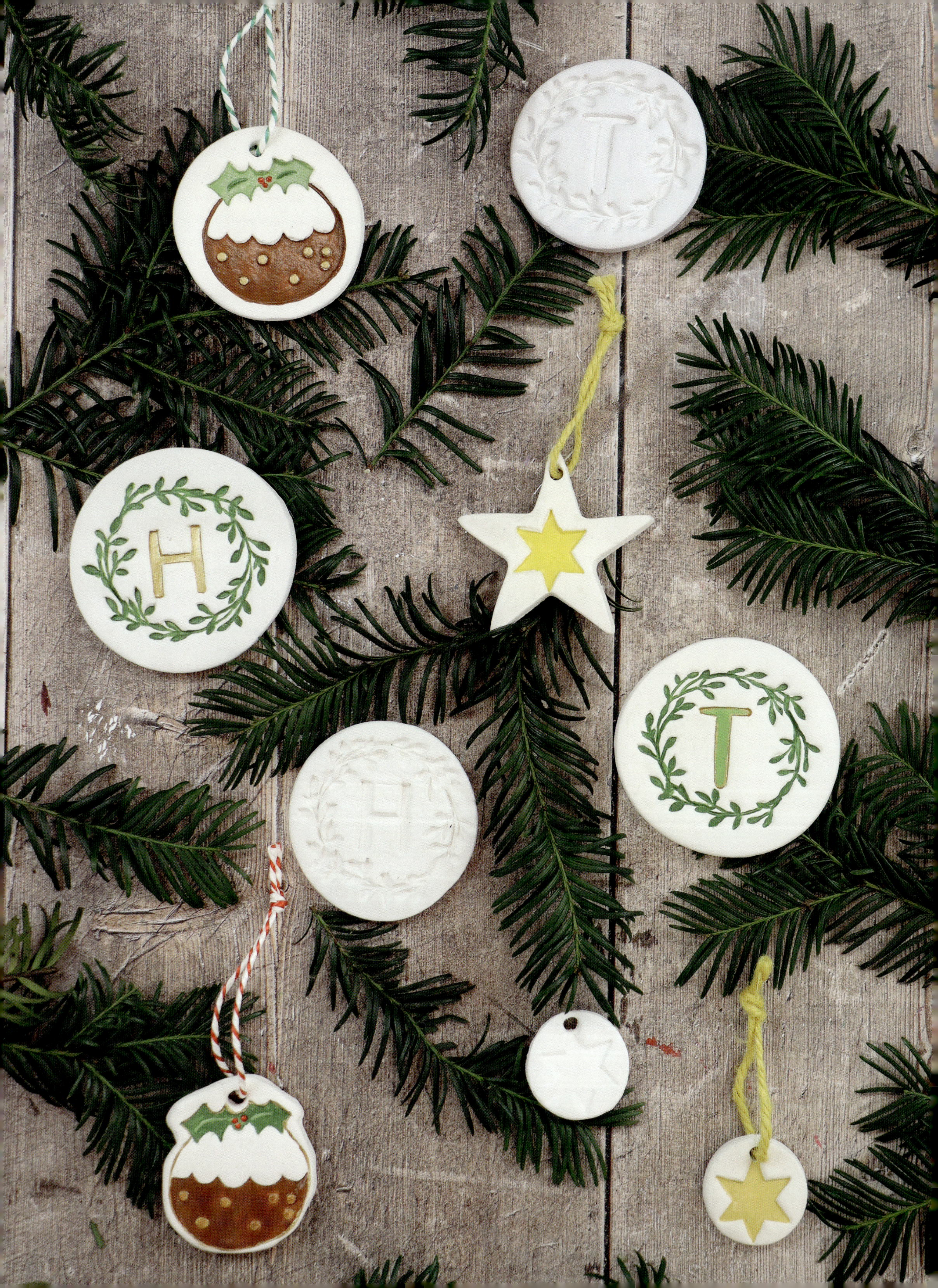

Clay Christmas Decorations

Another enjoyable and creative project to try with clay is to make Christmas tree decorations. These are so versatile, as the clay can be cut to any shape or size and feature any print design. By adding a hole at the top, they can be tied with ribbon or string to make the perfect ornaments to adorn your Christmas tree, hang in your home or give as thoughtful, handcrafted gifts.

1 Sprinkle your work surface with talcum powder or flour to avoid any clay sticking. Cut a chunk of clay to work with and use your rolling pin to roll it into a workable shape. Use levelling sticks or straws to avoid rolling the clay too thinly, which will cause it to crack; you want your clay to be around 5 mm thick for decorations.

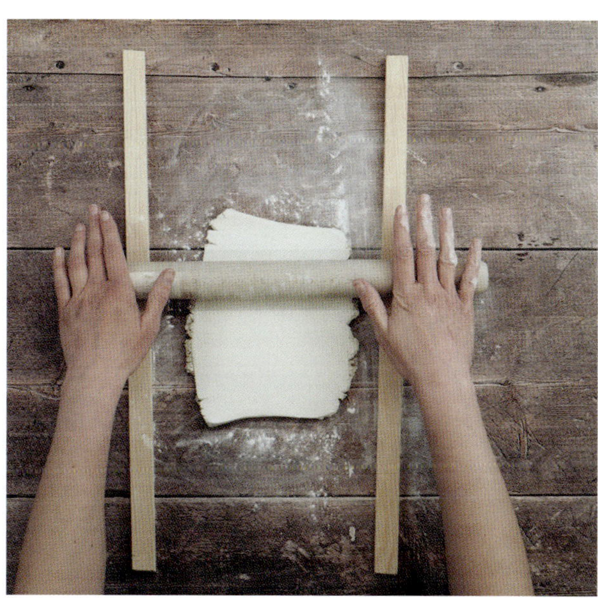

2 Once your clay is the correct thickness, sprinkle a small amount of talcum powder or flour over your Small Nordic Tree printing block to stop it sticking to the clay. Press your block evenly into the clay, being careful not to press too hard so it doesn't break through to the other side – even pressure applied all over is best.

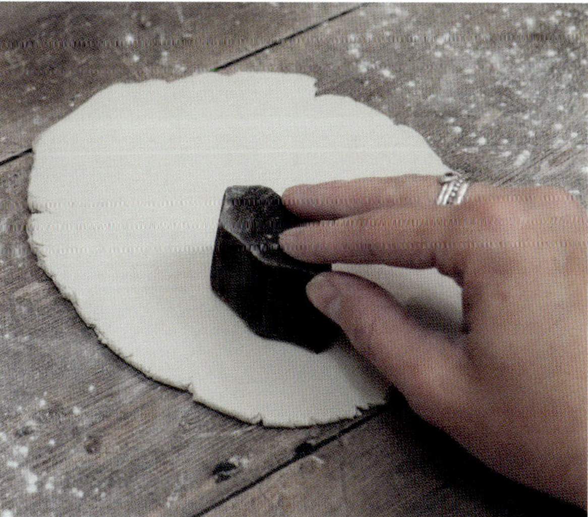

- Talcum powder or flour for dusting
- Knife
- Packet of white air-drying clay
- Rolling pin
- Levelling sticks or straws
- Printing blocks in various sizes – we used Small Nordic Tree here but also recommend Small Wreath, Small 6-Point Star and Christmas Pudding
- Cookie cutters in various shapes – we used a 7.5-cm circular cutter here
- Water bowl and sponge
- Acrylic paints – we used Chocolate Brown, Hauser Light Green, Hauser Dark Green and Gold
- Thin paintbrushes
- Spray varnish or PVA glue
- Paper or plastic straw
- Basic printing equipment (see page 18)

3 Take your chosen cutter and position it over the imprint in the clay. Press down to cut the shape out of your clay and peel away any excess around it.

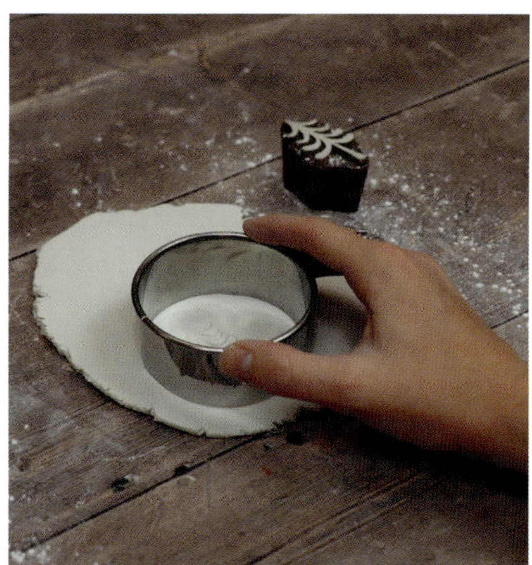
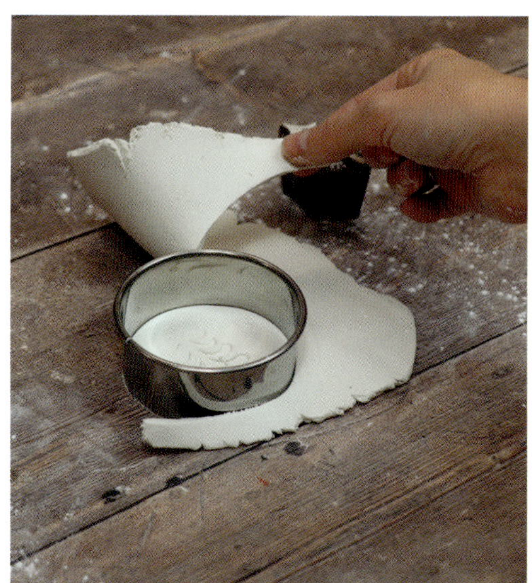

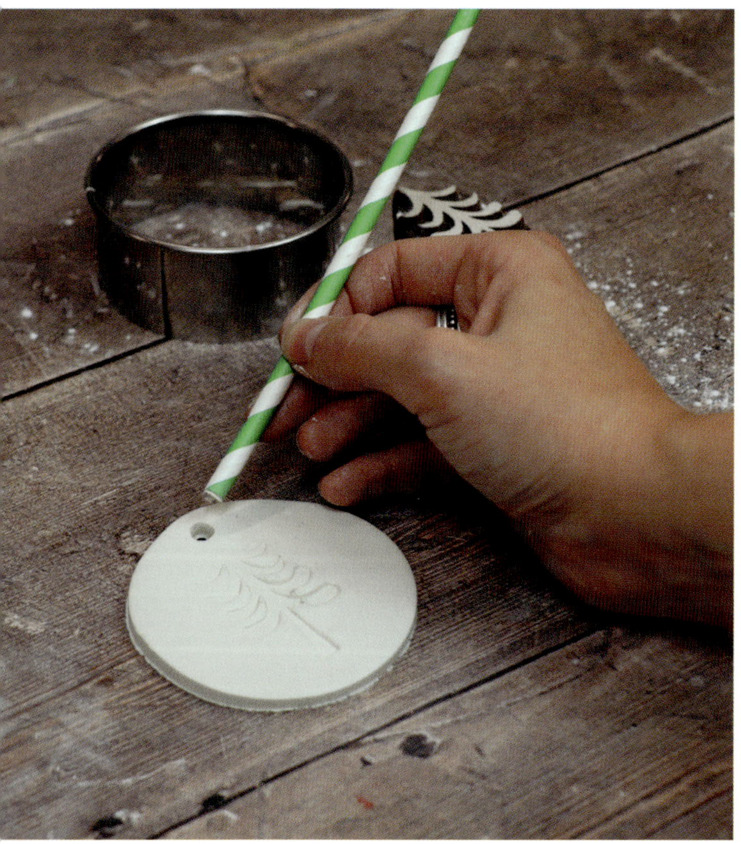
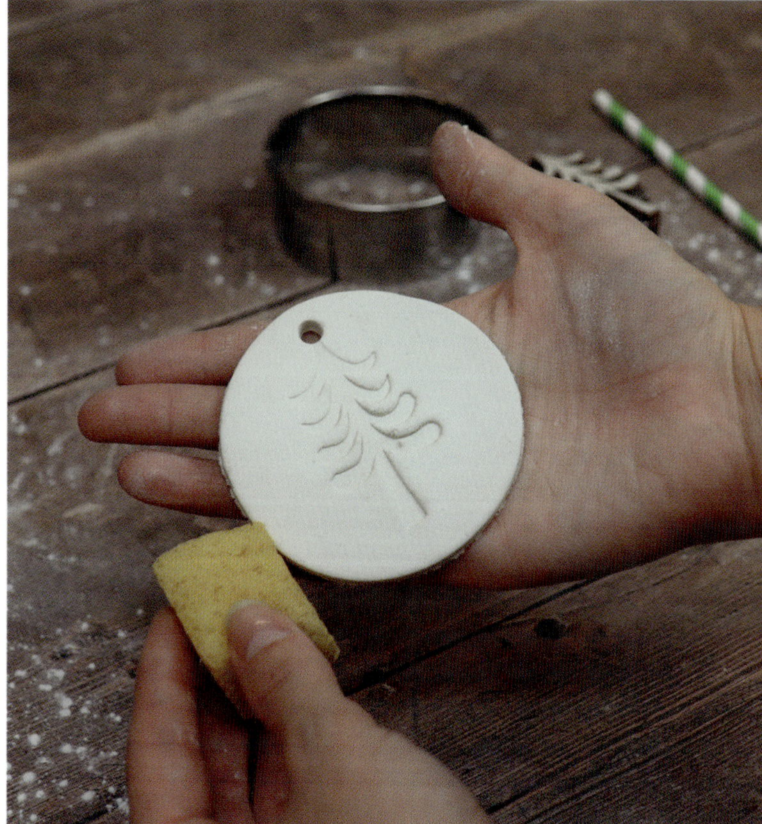

4 Use the end of a straw to create a hole in the top of your clay decoration, which will later be used for hanging. Press the straw into the clay and push all the way through until you feel it hitting your work surface. Pull the straw out and you will be left with a clean hole.

5 Gently pick up your clay decoration and, using a small damp sponge, smooth the edges before leaving it flat to fully dry for 24–48 hours.

6 Paint your designs with the acrylic paint, applying several coats for a strong colour. Once dry, seal your decorations with a spray varnish or layer of PVA glue to protect them, prolong their durability and create a nice finishing effect. Tie string or ribbon through the hole.

Right: A selection of decorations we made using the Small Wreath, Small 6-Point Star, Christmas Pudding and Individual Alphabet Letters (H & T) printing blocks.

Below: Clay decorations aren't just for Christmas! You can find our Colourful Clay Tiles on page 125.

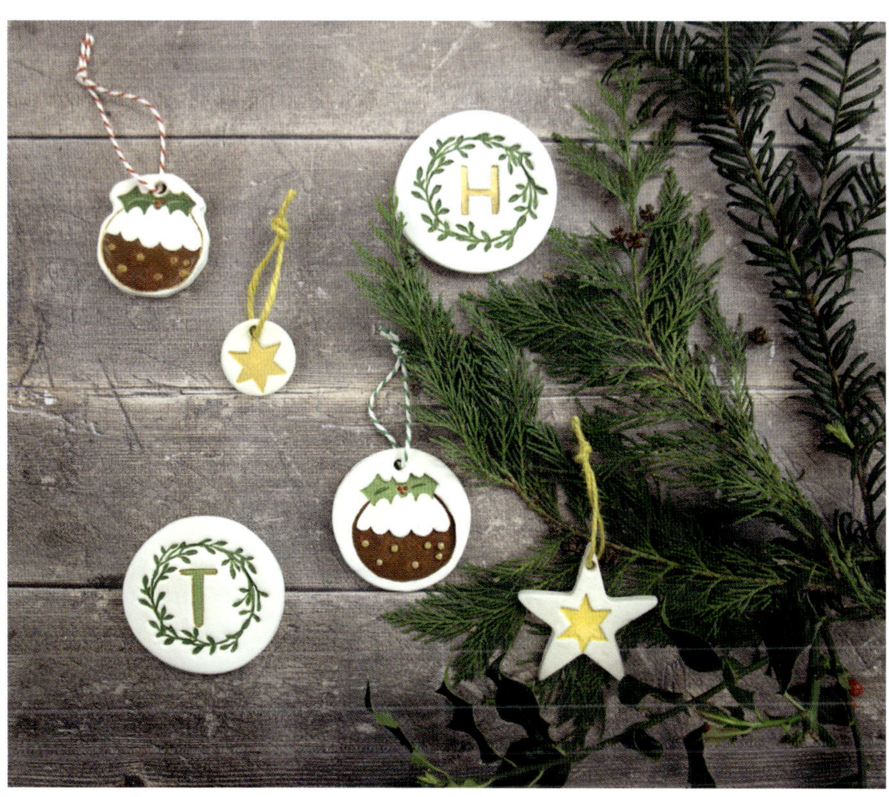

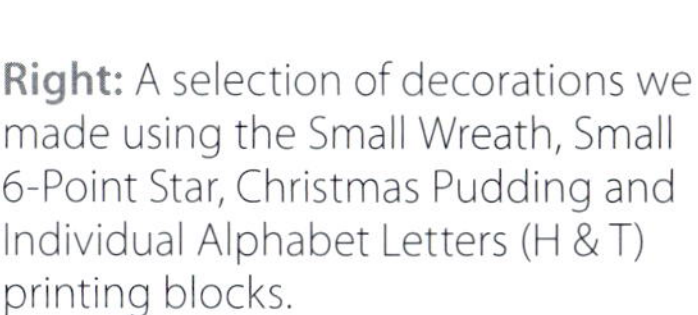

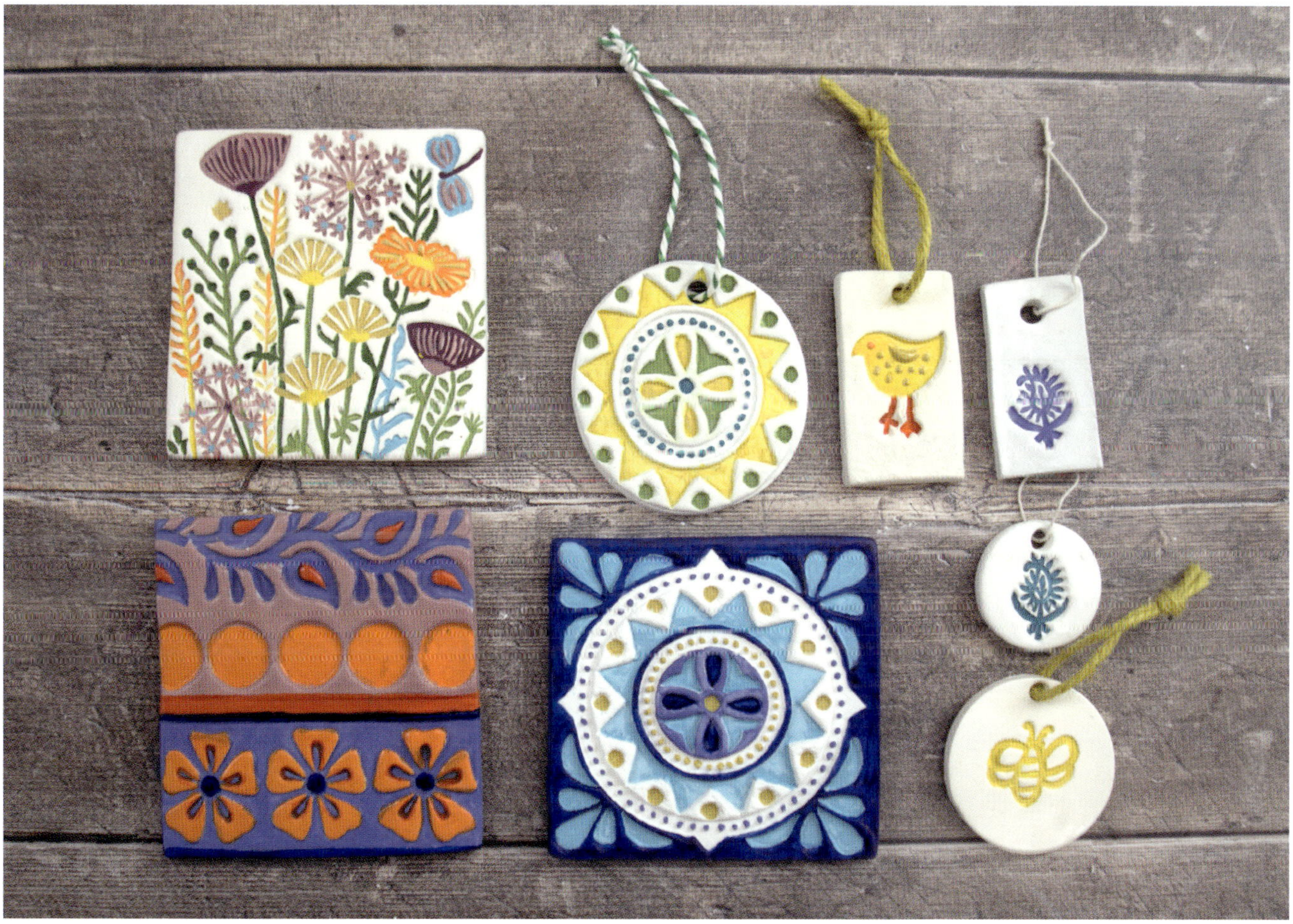

What Block Printing Means to Me

Amanda

Having battled both depression and eating disorders for many years, and as someone who struggles to quieten their internal monologue enough to 'practise mindfulness', block printing provides a perfect escape. When I'm printing, I am absorbed by the activity, my mind occupied with block choice, colour selection, positioning… and then lulled into calmness by the flow, applying the paint, positioning the block, applying pressure, lifting the block, repeating the process.

Completing a printed item, from a card to a curtain, creates immense satisfaction, when my usual working environment is full of activities that do not lead to a finite end result and can thus often be unsatisfying; the sense of achievement produces a positive boost! Then there are the workshops; not only great for learning new skills and challenging yourself, but a meeting of like-minded people, with fun, uplifting conversation and, over the years, the building of whole new friendship groups.

If you're thinking of trying it, I'd highly recommend to just do it! Find a block design that you love and start small – one print on a card, a couple of prints on the corner of a napkin… Don't listen to the voices that say you 'aren't a creative person' and give yourself permission to 'play'. Even if you only have 30 minutes, make it special – put on some music, make your favourite drink, tell people you can't be interrupted; do it for yourself!

Kate

I work with sixth-form students in a special needs school. Some students have physical disabilities such as cerebral palsy and have poor fine motor skills yet, with support, the accessibility of block printing as a craft means they can still contribute to very successful enterprise projects. It has had a huge impact on their well-being. Every year, the students make and sell several hundred block-printed Christmas cards and gift tags. Later in the year, they print textiles to sell and raise funds for local charities.

Over the years, I have witnessed their progression and independence develop during that time, which gives me immense satisfaction. I am so proud of all they have achieved, thanks to block printing.

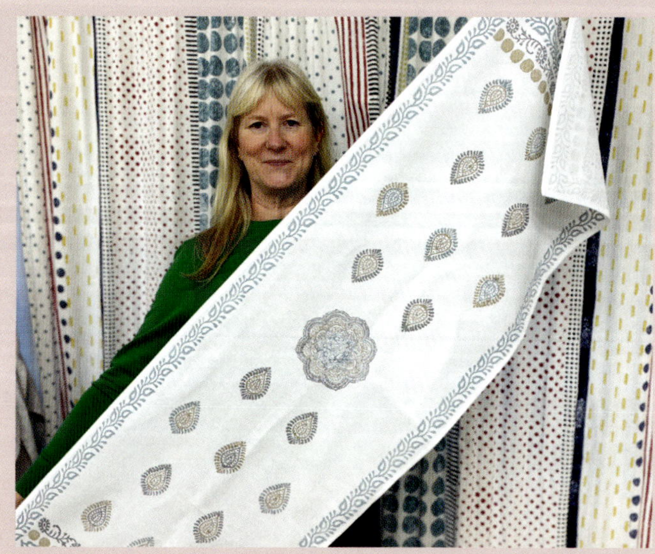

Above: Kate with her finished printed table runner in our Oxfordshire studio.

Right: Christine with her completed hand-printed lampshade.

Below: Jo with her printed paisley towel.

Below right: Kyla and Polly with their printed workshop creations.

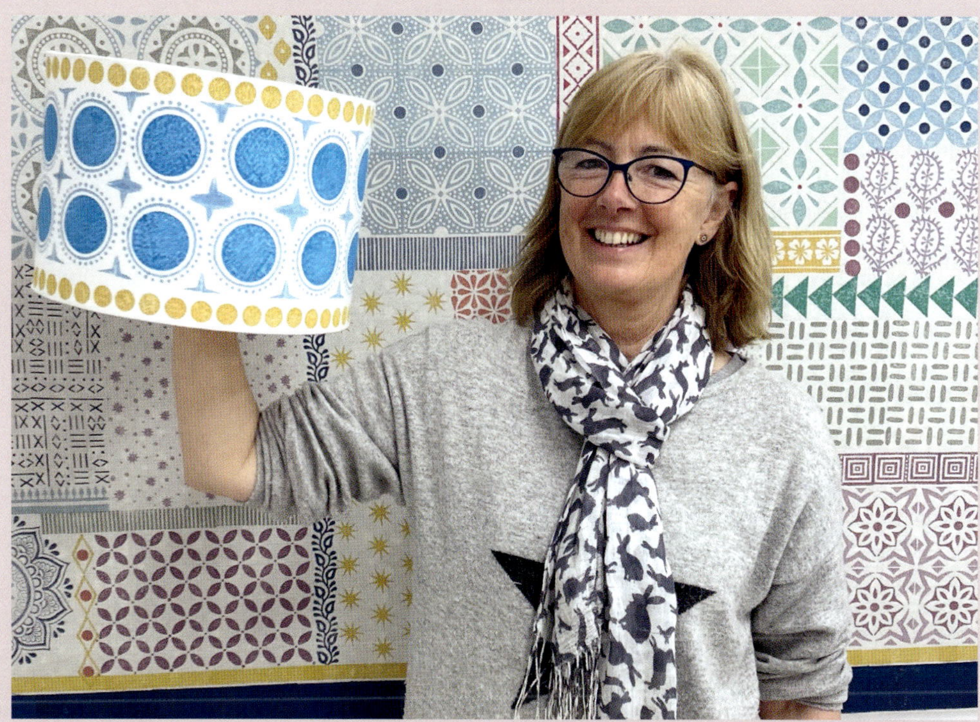

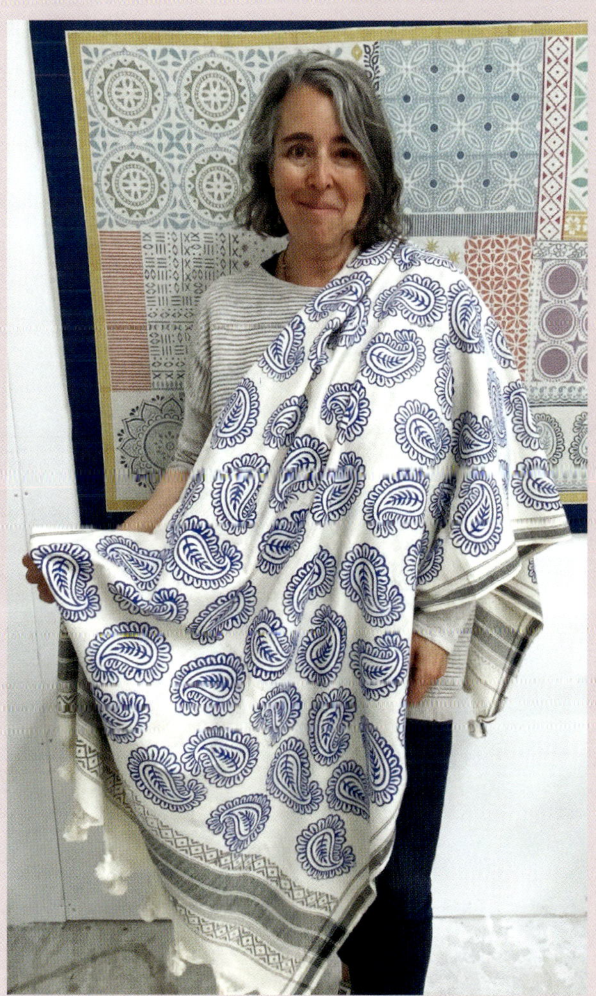

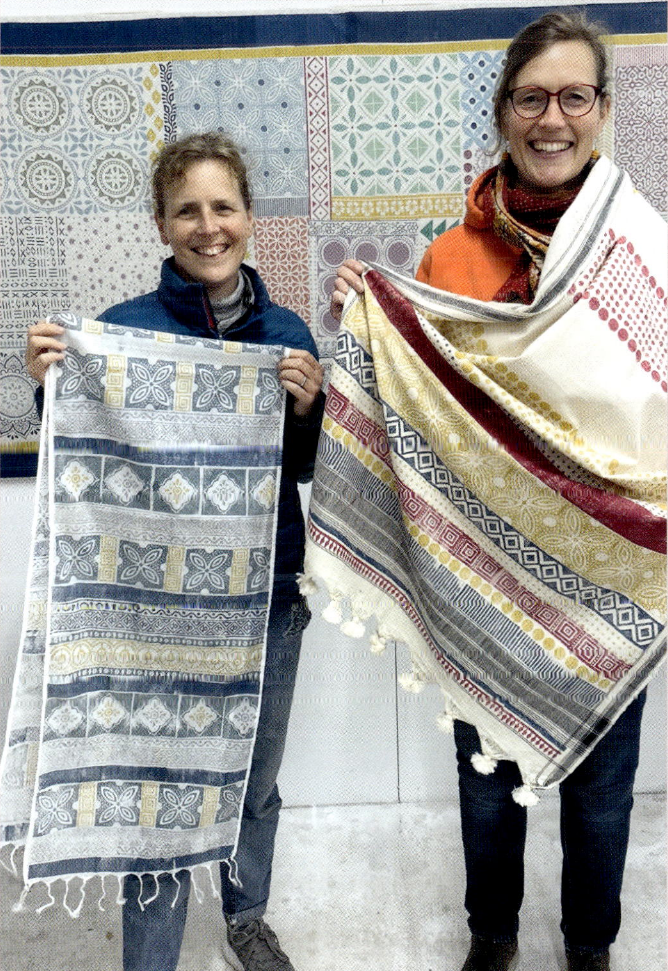

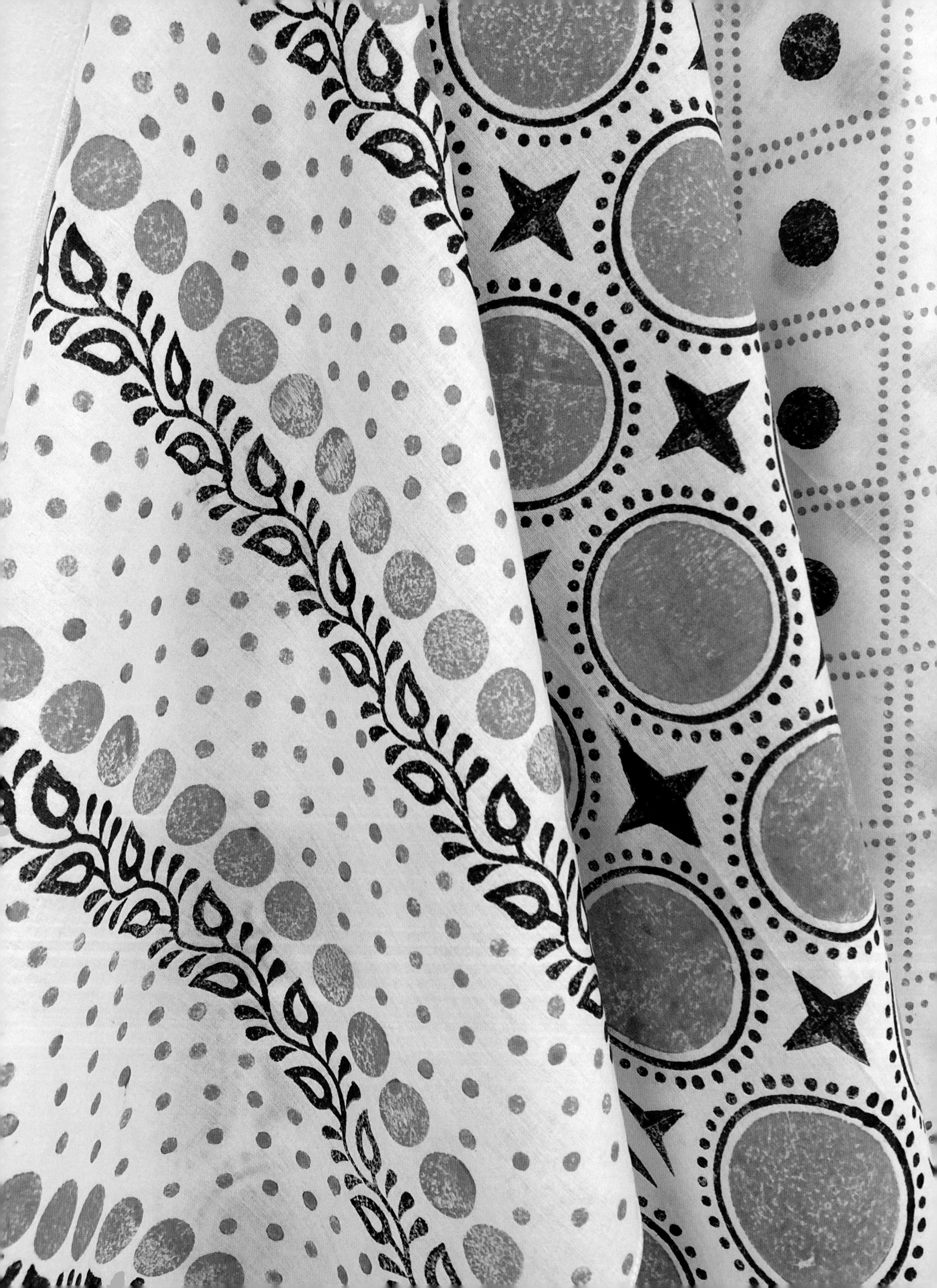

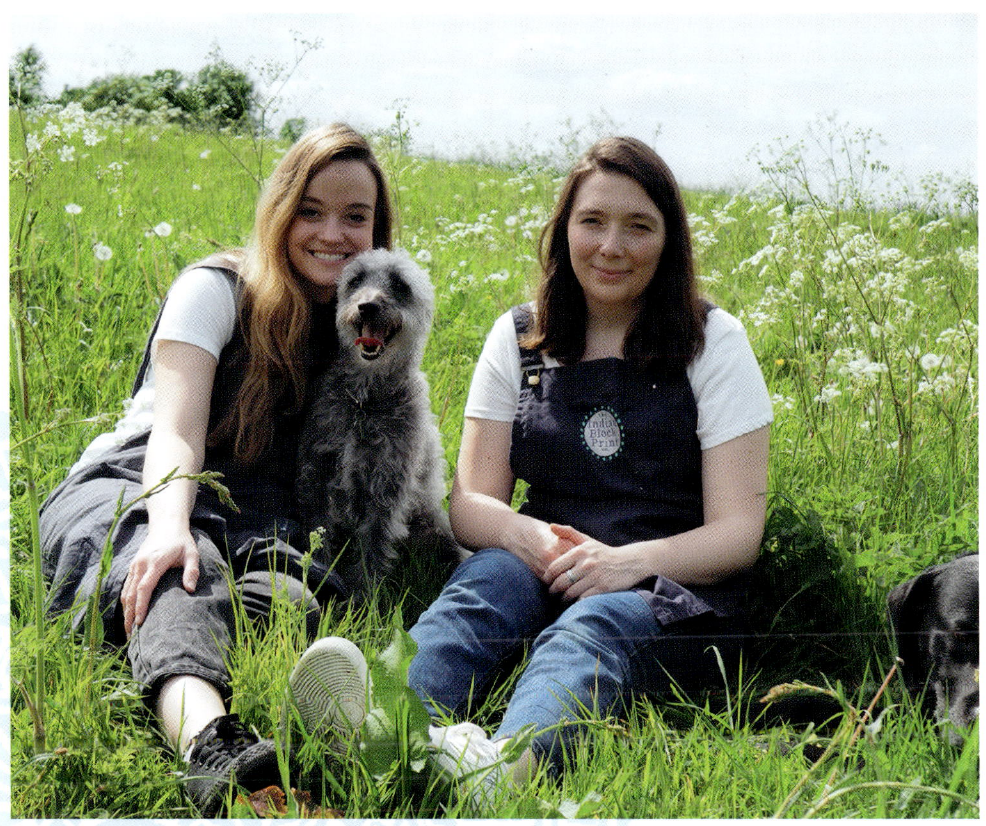

A Big Thanks to...

We hope the readers of this book have found the inspiration and guidance they need to start and continue with their own journey into the art of Indian block printing. Our aim was to connect the reader with the talented artisans of India, and to understand the centuries-old traditional art form which has evolved into a beautiful and contemporary craft that we can enjoy in our everyday lives.

We wanted to thank all the workshop guests we have met over the years, who have taught us so much about teaching and learning, and have made us better block printers.

A huge thanks to all our colleagues at the Indian Block Print Co., past and present, who have been as much a part of the creation of this project book as we have, and who have all helped make a dream become a reality.

A final thanks to the incredibly talented artisans we work with in India, who generously share their craft with us, without whom we wouldn't be able to do what we do.

Inspirational Gallery

Explore our gallery of inspiration, featuring photos from India, creations by others, and design ideas to spark your creativity. We hope it continues to inspire your journey into the art of Indian block printing.

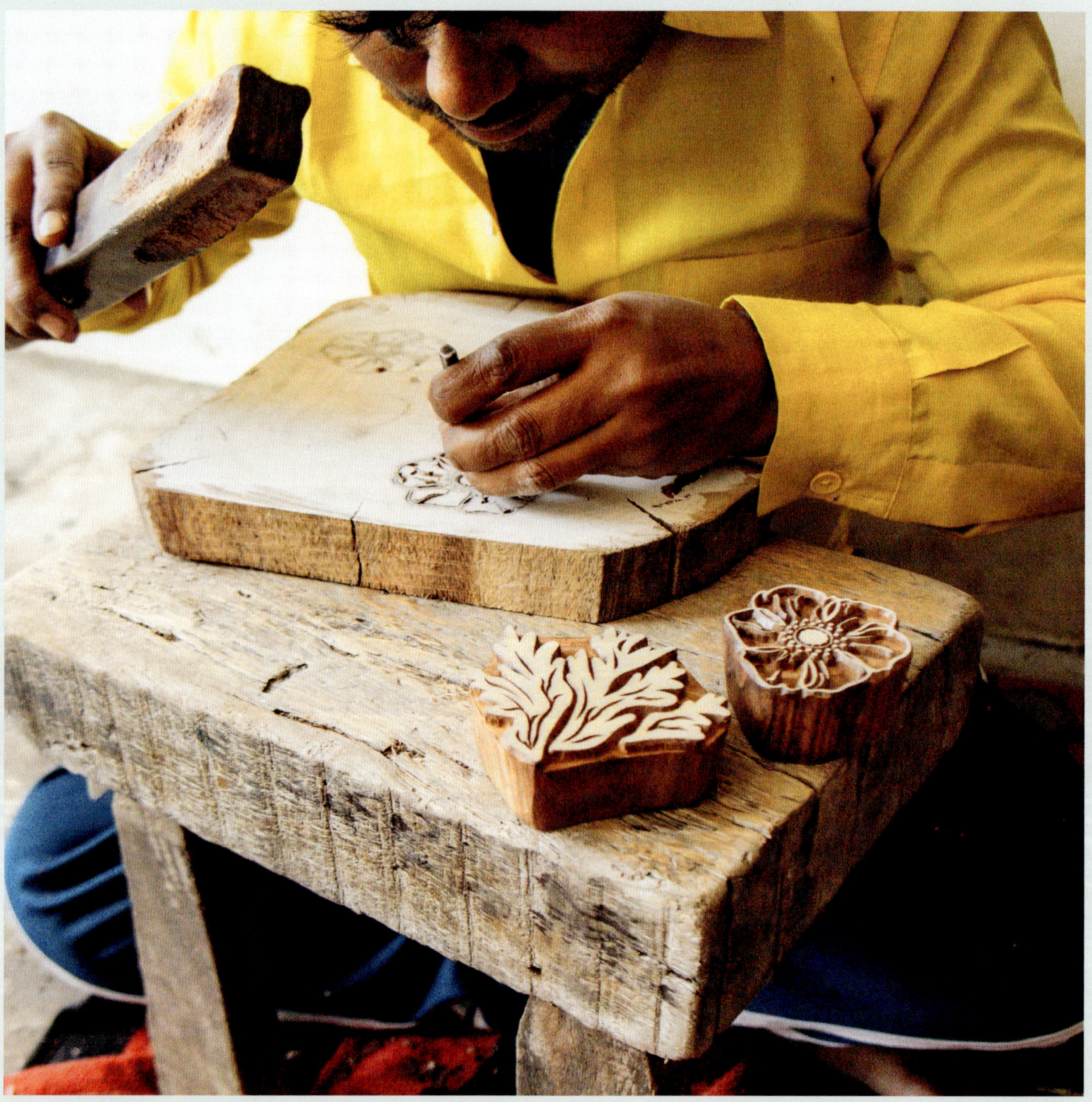

Above: The skill of the craftspeople in India is unsurpassed

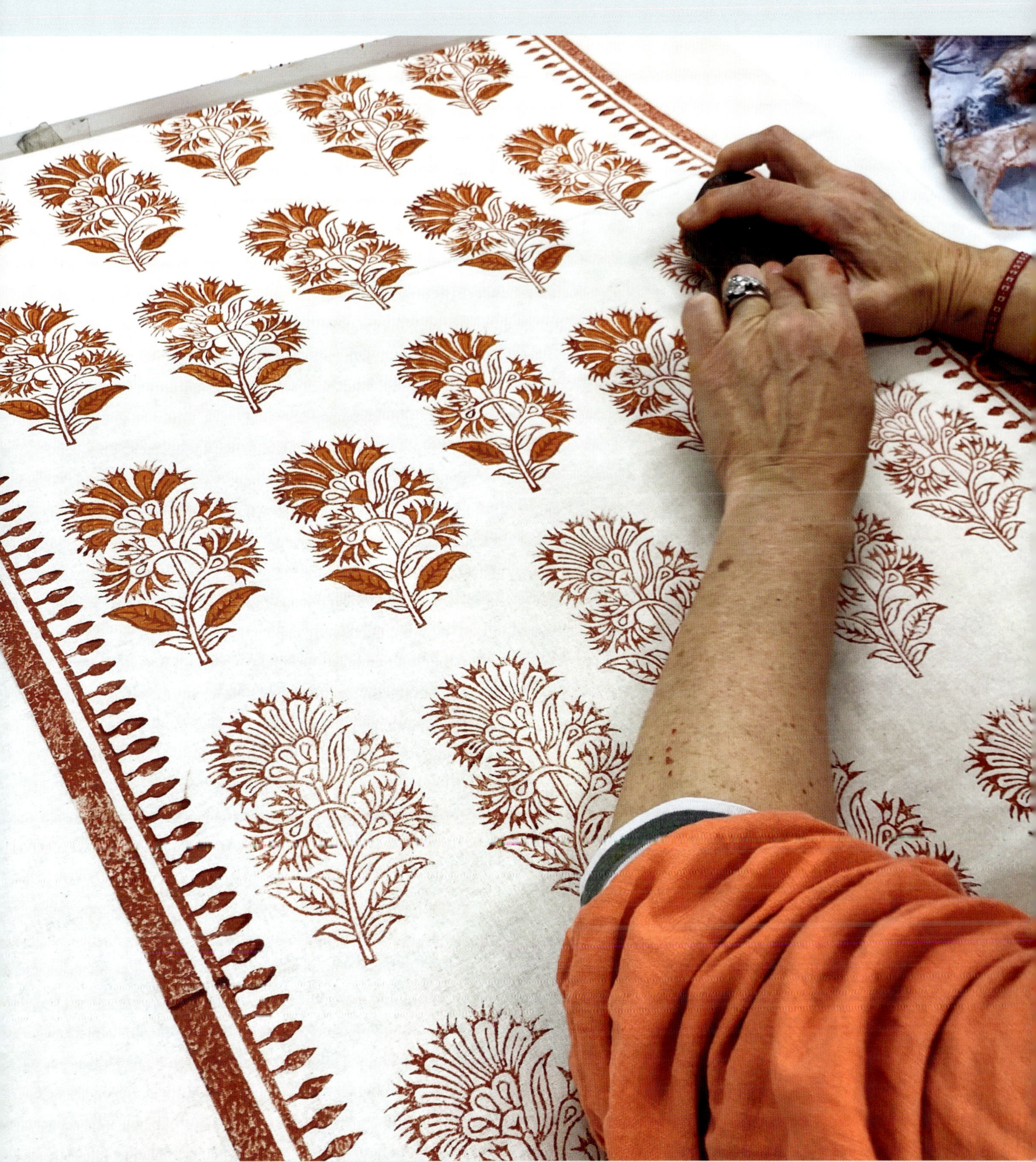

Above: A workshop guest printing a detailed, multi-layer flower design.

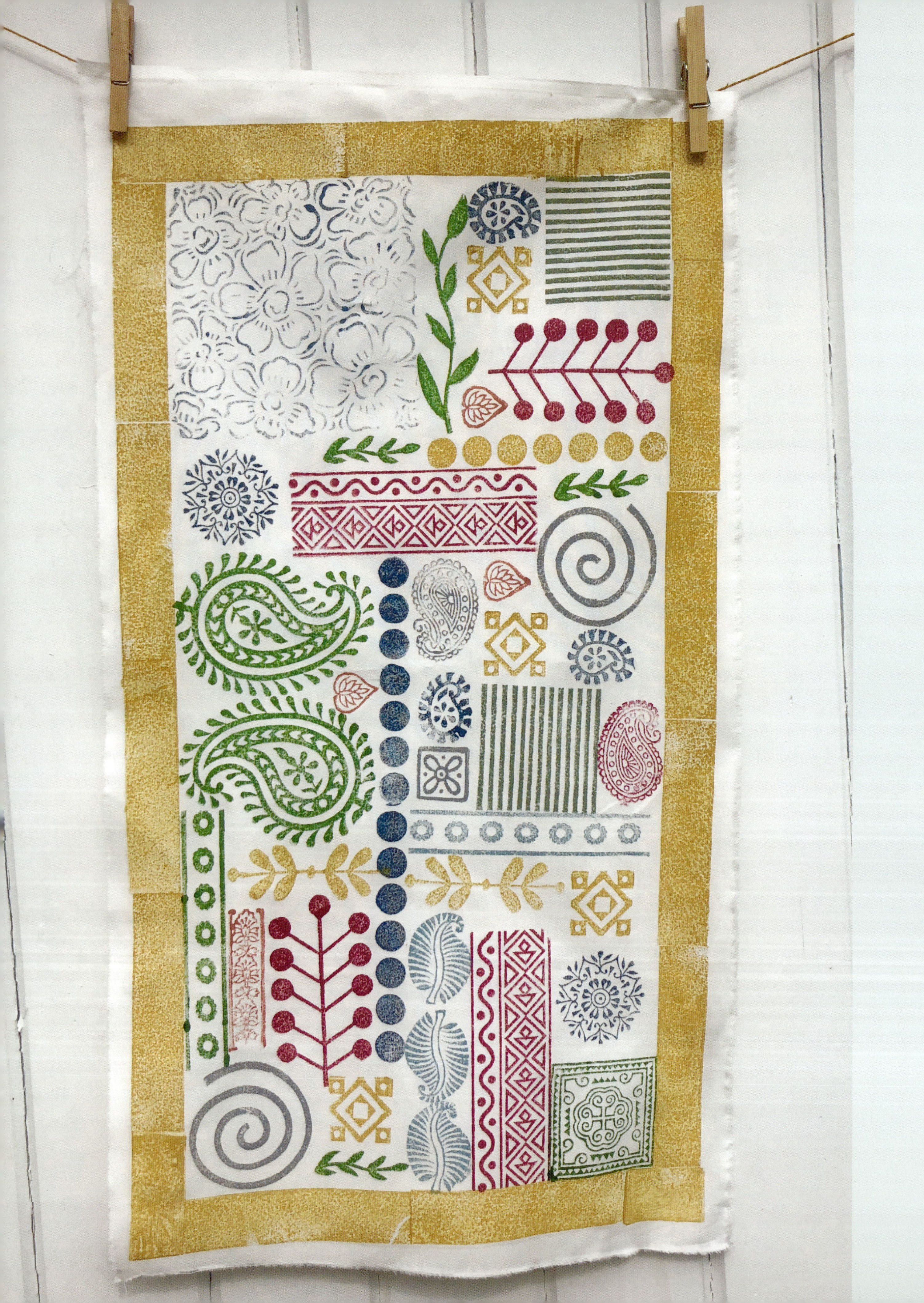

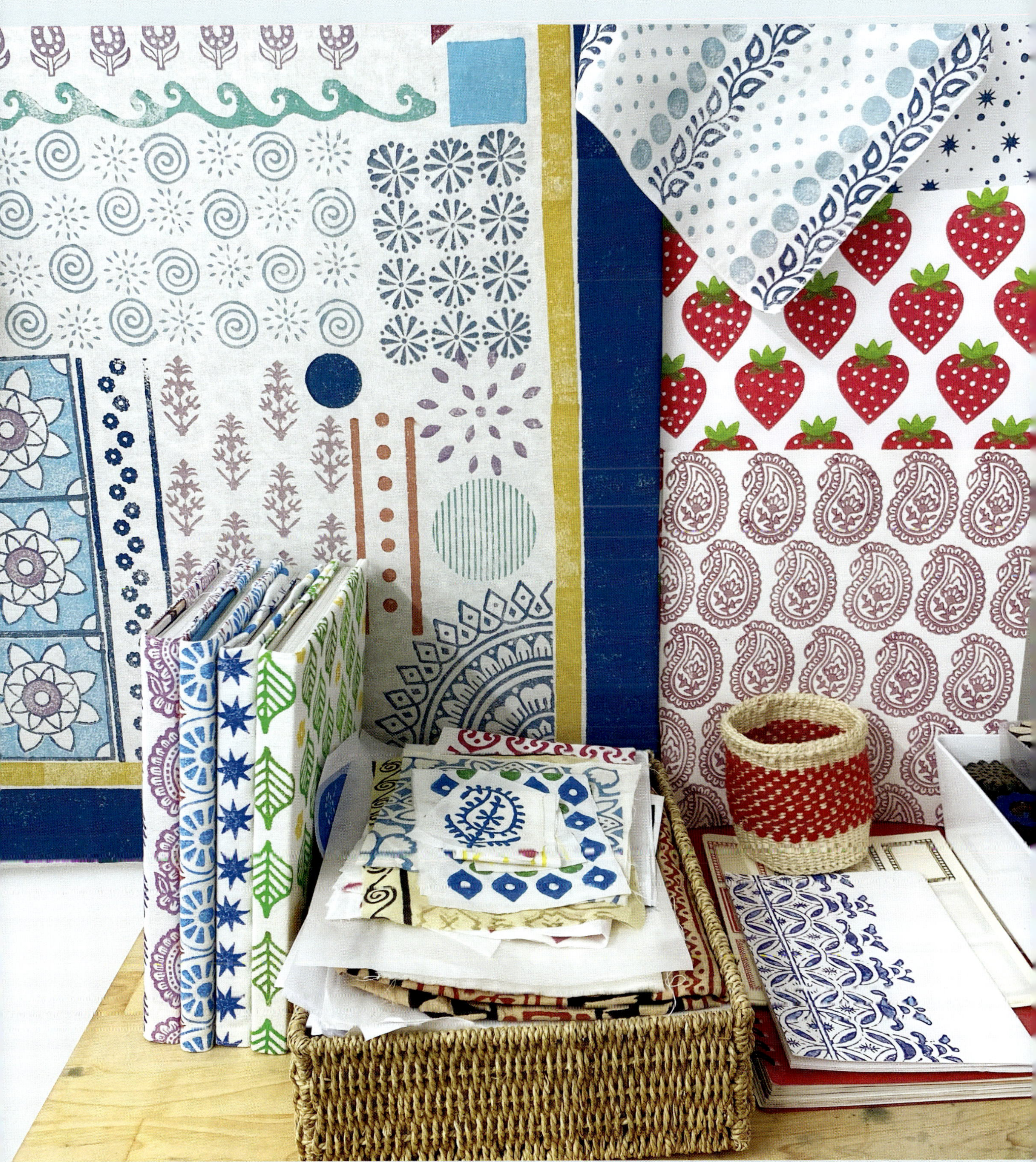

Opposite: Patchwork wall hanging created by a workshop guest. **Above**: A corner of our Oxfordshire studio.

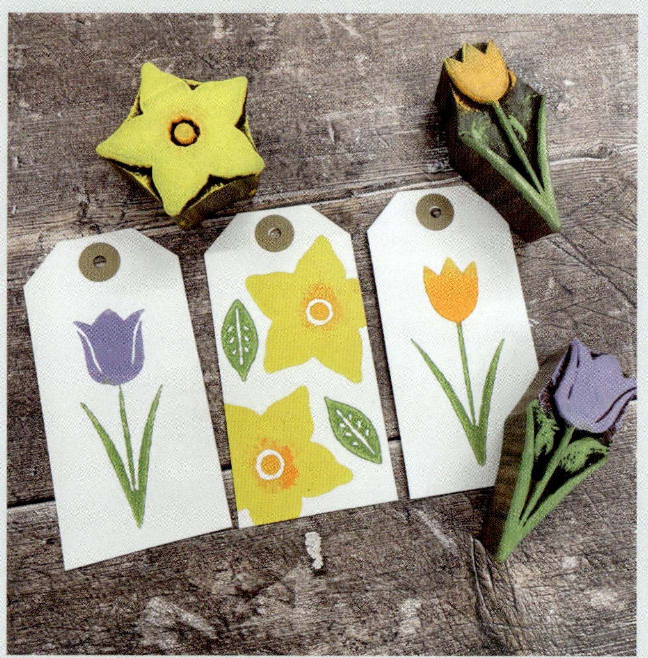

Above: Spring gift tags.

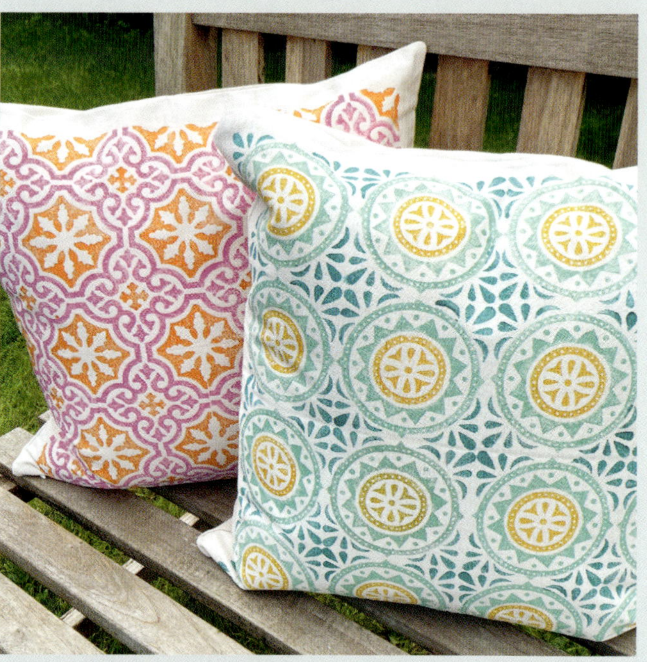

Above: Printed garden cushions. **Below:** On the printing table.

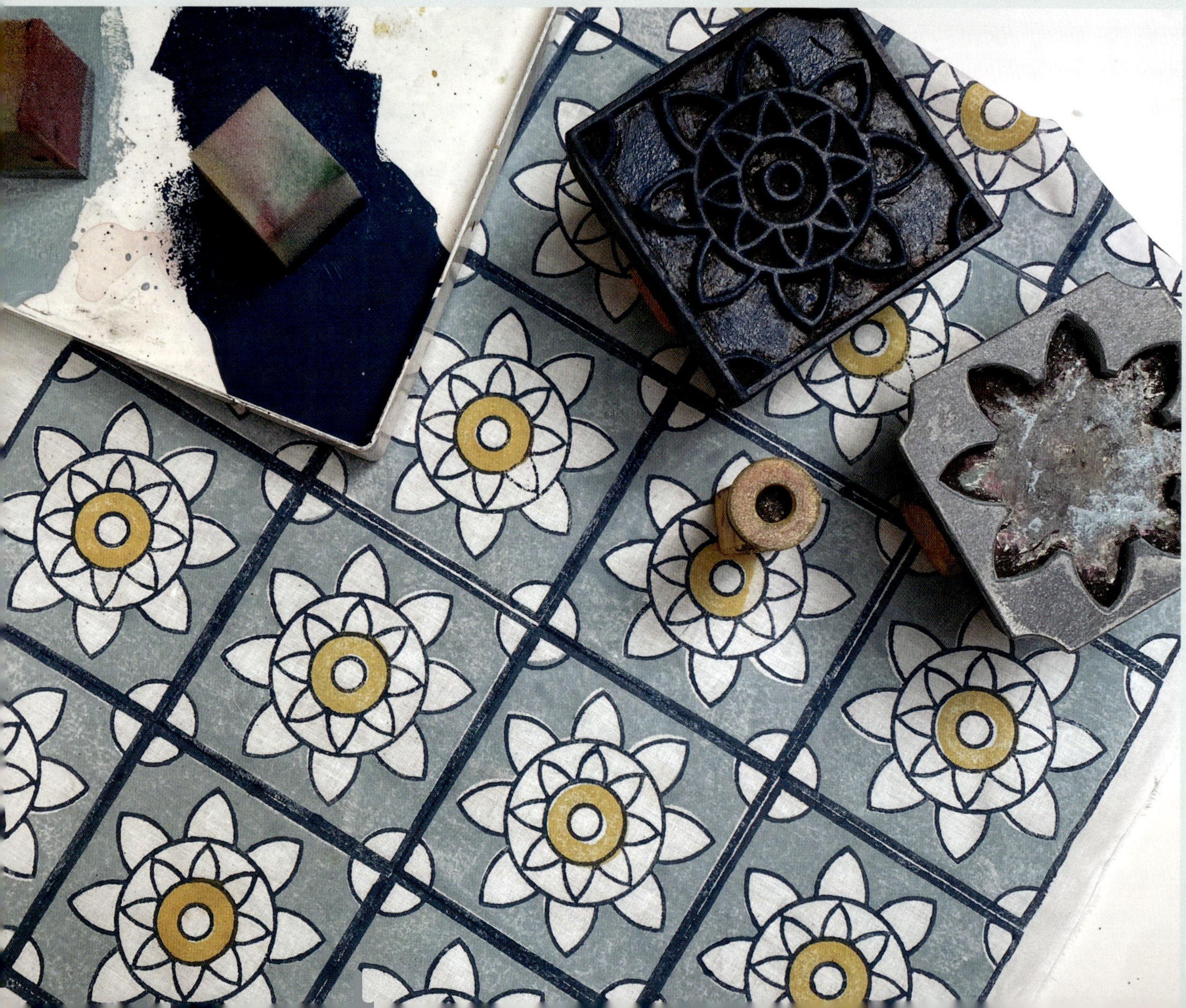

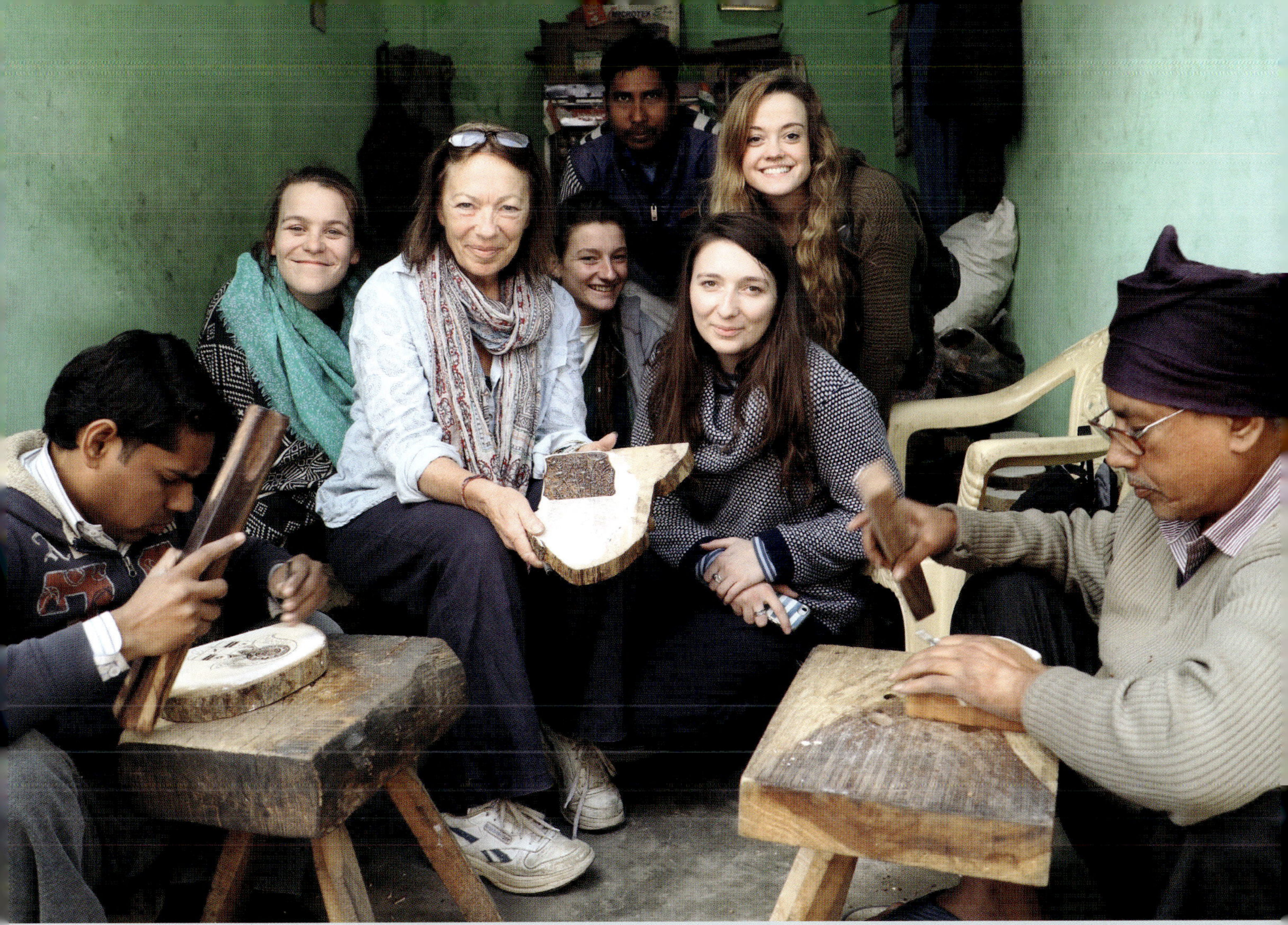

Above: Maggie,
Tess, Holly, Anna
and Annabel with
block carver Malik
in his workshop in
Uttar Pradesh, 2018.

Right: Tess block
printing in Bagru.

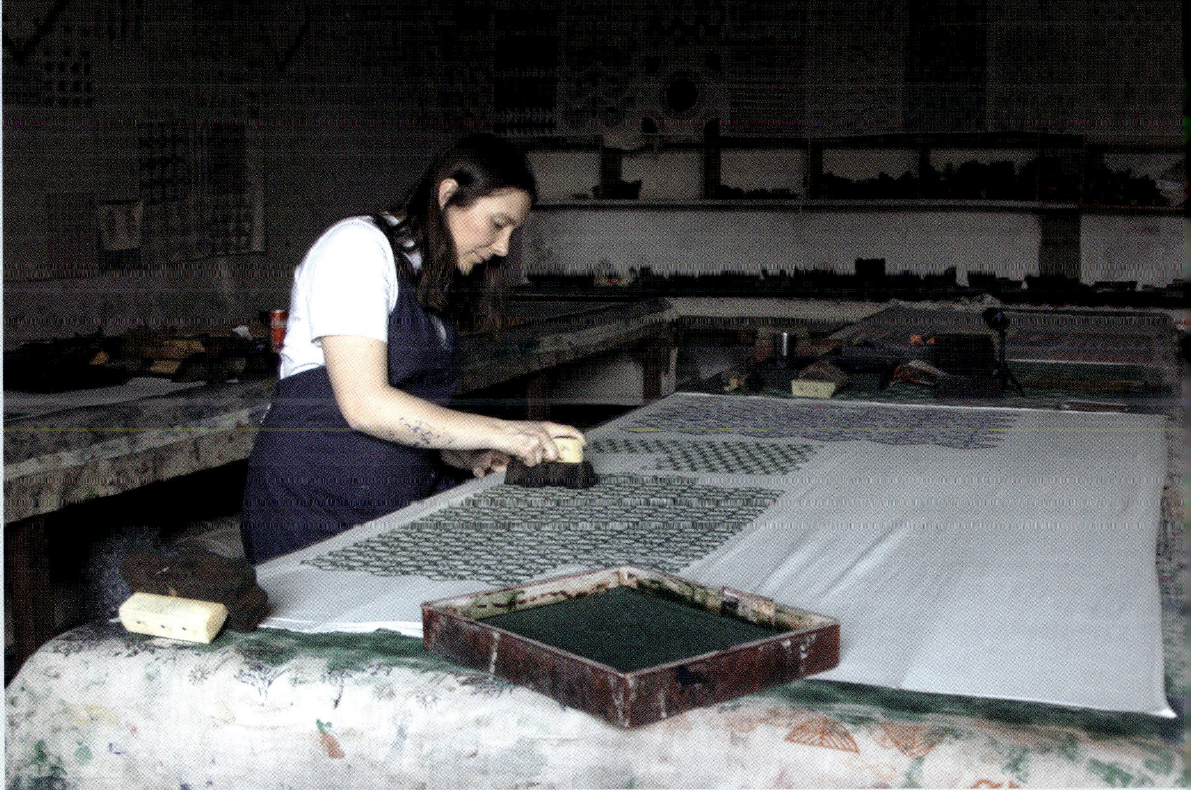

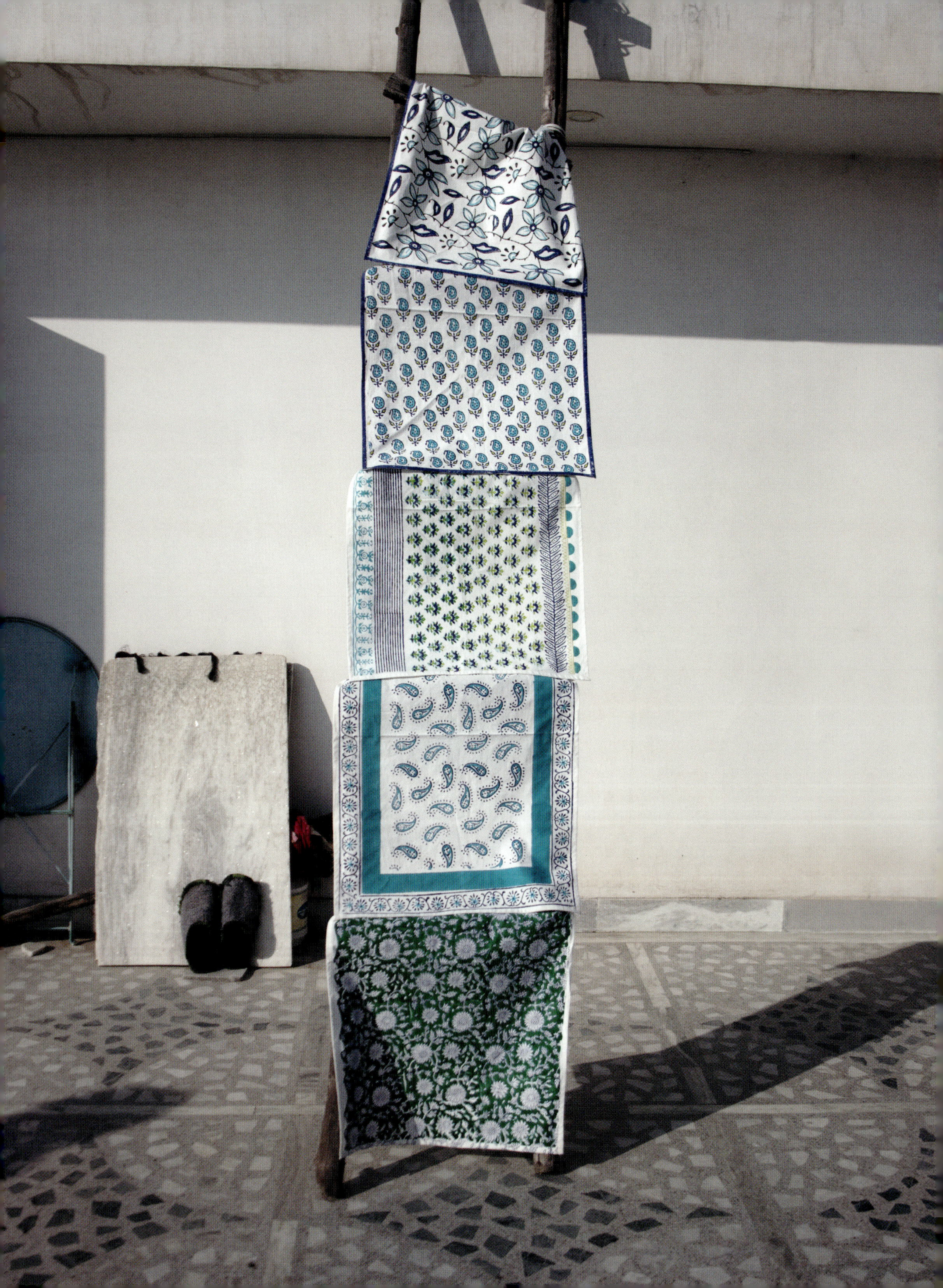

Resources

A wonderful aspect of the creative craft industry is the variety of free tutorials and inspiration available online. You can find plenty of ideas on YouTube, Pinterest and other social media. Often, a project starts with something that sparks your creativity.

We believe it's important to set aside time for creativity due to the many mindful benefits it can have, and we take pride in knowing that we may help and inspire someone's creative journey.

We have put together a series of step-by-step projects and instructional videos which you can find on our YouTube channel: www.youtube.com/@theindianblockprintco

If you're experimenting with different repeating patterns and placements at home, you can download our printable repeating pattern line guides from our website at: theindianblockprintco.com/products/ repeating-pattern-line-guides

Pinterest can also be a useful platform to help find inspiration and ideas, and to store images in one place. Useful keywords to search for would be: Indian Block Printing / Hand Block Printing / Fabric Printing / Wooden Block Prints

Suppliers

Block printing with Indian wooden blocks is still relatively niche in the crafting world, so there are only a select few suppliers offering these unique printing blocks.

Printing Blocks

We recommend purchasing high-quality wooden printing blocks to ensure excellent print quality and long-lasting durability. Printing blocks made of mango wood would not be advisable – look for teak or sheesham.

The Indian Block Print Co.
www.theindianblockprintco.com

Etsy
www.etsy.com

Textile Traders
www.textiletraders.co.uk

Blank fabrics and materials to print onto

We would suggest pre-washing any materials you purchase before printing to remove any stiffeners that may have been applied to the fabric, this will also get any shrinkage that may occur out of the way before printing.

Hobbycraft
www.hobbycraft.co.uk

The Indian Block Print Co.
www.theindianblockprintco.co.uk
Pre-washed cotton

Online Fabrics
www.online-fabrics.co.uk
Fabric by the metre – cotton, linen, calico

Ikea
www.ikea.com/gb/en
Calico and linen

Dunelm
www.dunelm.com

Opposite: Fabric printed at Studio Bagru in India, drying in the sun.

Paints for printing

You'll need a fabric/textile paint for printing onto material, and an acrylic paint for printing onto paper and card. You can purchase a 'fabric medium' which can be added to acrylic paint making them suitable for printing onto fabric. We suggest using onto water-based paint products.

Hobbycraft
www.hobbycraft.co.uk

The Indian Block Print Co.
www.theindianblockprintco.co.uk

George Weil
www.georgeweil.com

General printing supplies

Most of the equipment you will need can be found around the home; as you progress you may want to purchase more specialist equipment.

The Indian Block Print Co.
www.theindianblockprintco.com

Hobby Craft
www.hobbycraft.co.uk

George Weil
www.georgeweil.com

Hand Printed UK
www.handprinted.co.uk

International suppliers

USA

Artistic Artifacts
www.artisticartifacts.com
Printing blocks, paints and fabric

Artist Craftsman
artistcraftsman.com
Fabric paints, craft equipment

Decoart
shop.decoart.com
Acrylic and fabric paint

Australia

Basera
www.basera.com.au
Printing blocks

Kraft Kolour
www. kraftkolour.net.au
Fabric paint, acrylic paint, printing supplies

Credits

Step-by-step project photography by Emily Drewe

Illustrations, book research and development by Amy Malloy

India photography by Anna Hastings, Annabel Hucker and Maggie Sheehan

East façade of Hawa Mahal (p.13) by Chainwit., via Wikimedia Commons

Itten colour circle (p.50) by Stephen Hoskins and Michael Craine